PRISONS AND JAILS — A DETERRENT TO CRIME?

INFORMATION PLUS®
WYLIE, TEXAS 75098-7006
© 1995, 1997, 1999
ALL RIGHTS RESERVED

EDITORS:
ABBEY M. BEGUN, B.A.
NANCY R. JACOBS, M.A.
JACQUELYN F. QUIRAM, B.A.

CHAPTER I

HISTORY OF CORRECTIONS — REVENGE OR REHABILITATION?

A terrible stinking dark and dismal place situated underground into which no daylight can come. It was paved with stone; the prisoners had no beds and lay on the pavement whereby they endured great misery and hardship. — Inmate at Newgate Jail (1724)

The philosophy of punishment for crimes, like ideas of raising children, has changed over the centuries. Society's practices in most countries have evolved from avenging one's family either by killing the accused or a member of his family (blood feuds) to written codes setting down punishments. Jails and prisons have changed from holding places for prisoners waiting to be deported, maimed, whipped, or executed to being the actual punishment. The philosophies behind putting people in jails and prisons have ranged from revenge to rehabilitation to keeping criminals off the streets.

ANCIENT TIMES

Many ancient cultures allowed the victim or his family to deliver justice. The offender often fled to his family for protection. As a result, blood feuds developed in which the victim's family sought revenge against the offender's family. Sometimes the offender's family responded by striking back. Retaliation could continue until the families got tired of killing or stealing from each other or until one or both families were destroyed or financially ruined.

As societies organized into tribes and villages, local communities increasingly began to assume the responsibility for punishing crimes against the community. Punishments could be brutal, such as being boiled in oil or eaten by wild beasts. With the development of writing, societies usually listed the crimes and punishments. The Code of Hammurabi in Babylon (circa 1750 B.C.E. — Be-

fore the Common Era) is generally considered the first such set of laws. The laws of Moses in the Bible also recorded offenses against the community and their punishments. Nonetheless, personal revenge was still practiced. Indeed, the Bible reports 10 cities in which an accused murderer would be safe from the victim's family. The Justinian Code (Emperor Justinian of the Byzantine or Eastern Roman Empire, 529-565 C.E.) organized many of the early codes.

As empires developed, the owners of large tracts of land, and later the rulers, wanted a more orderly legal system than blood feuds, and so they established courts. These courts most often sentenced the offender to slavery in the victim's family for several years as restitution for the offense. Other punishments included laboring on public works projects, banishment, or death. The rise of organized religions often brought about more severe punishments since crimes became sins not only against the community, but also against God's will.

MEDIEVAL TIMES

As in ancient times, the medieval period of Europe had very harsh punishments. Torture and death were common forms of punishment. Sometimes torture and the death penalty were combined in such terrible instruments as the rack or the Iron Maiden. The rack stretched its victims until their bodies were pulled apart. The Iron Maiden was a box where a person was placed. When the door was closed, spikes entered the victim from both back and front. Public execution by burning, beheading, and hanging was common.

Confinement

Those arrested were usually imprisoned until they confessed to the crime and their physical punishment took place. The medieval church sometimes used long-term incarceration to replace executions. Some wealthy landowners built private prisons to enhance their own power, imprisoning those who disputed the landowners' pursuit of power or their whims. With the Assize of Clarendon (1166 C.E.), many crimes were classified as offenses against the "king's peace" and were punished by the state and not by the church, the lord, or the victim's extended family. At this time, the first prisons designed solely for incarceration were constructed.

Prisons

The only comfort a prisoner could get in the cold, damp, filthy, rat- and roach-infested prisons of medieval Europe was what he/she could buy. The keeper charged for blankets, mattresses, food, and even the manacles (chains). The prisoner had to pay for the privilege of being booked and released. Wealthy prisoners could pay for plush quarters, but most people suffered in terrible conditions, often dying from malnutrition, disease, or being victimized by other prisoners.

THE RISE OF NATIONS

In Europe, in the 1500s, while most jails still housed people waiting for trial or punishment, workhouses and debtors' prisons developed as sources of cheap labor or as places to house insane or minor offenders. Those found guilty of serious crimes could be transported instead of executed. England transported many prisoners to colonial Georgia and later to Australia, while France sent many to South America. Although less severe than the death penalty, many prisoners did not survive the harsh conditions of life in the early colonies.

COLONIAL AND EARLY POST-REVOLUTIONARY PERIODS

Just as in Europe, physical punishment was common in colonial America. Americans used stocks, pillories, branding, flogging, and maiming, such as cutting off an ear or slitting the nostrils, to punish offenders. The death penalty was used frequently. The Massachusetts Bay Colony listed 13 crimes that warranted execution. In early New York State, 20 percent of the offenses, including pickpocketing, horse stealing, and robbery, were capital crimes (warranting the death penalty).

Jails were used to hold prisoners awaiting trial or sentencing or as debtors' prison, but not as the punishment itself. Puritan beliefs that man was naturally depraved made it easier for the colonies and the first states to enforce harsh punishments. In addition, since Puritans believed that man had no control over his fate (predestination), most early Americans felt there was no need for rehabilitation.

Pennsylvania

The Quakers, led by William Penn, made colonial Pennsylvania an exception to the harsh punishments often practiced in the other colonies. The early criminal code of colonial Pennsylvania abolished executions for all crimes except homicide, replaced physical punishments with imprisonment at hard labor, and did not charge the prisoners for their food and housing. (For a return to this policy, see Chapter III.)

Ideas of the Enlightenment

The philosophy of the Enlightenment (the Age of Reason) emphasized the importance of the individual. After the French Revolution (1789), which was based on the ideas of the Enlightenment, western European countries abolished torture as a form of punishment and emphasized that the punishment should fit the individual's crime(s). Rather than inflicting pain as the main element of correction, the idea of changing the individual became the goal.

In England, John Howard (1726-1790) wrote about the horrible treatment of prisoners in *The State of the Prisons in England and Wales* (1777). He thought prisoners should not be harassed by keepers who extorted from them nor should they have to suffer malnutrition and disease. He advocated segregating prisoners by age, sex, and crimes; paying the staff; hiring medical officials and chaplains; and supplying prisoners with adequate food and clothing.

Howard called the facilities "penitentiaries" (from the word "penitent," meaning to be ashamed or sorry about doing something bad) because he based his ideas on the Quaker's philosophy of people's repenting, reflecting on their sins, and changing their ways. Public concern led the British Parliament to pass the Penitentiary Act of 1779, which called for the first secure and sanitary penitentiary. The law eliminated charging fees. Prisoners would live in solitary confinement at night and work together silently during the day. Nonetheless, although Parliament passed the law, it did not actually go into effect until the opening of Pentonville Penitentiary in North London in 1842.

THE REFORM MOVEMENT

The ideas of individual freedom and the concept that man could change society for the better using his reason permeated American society in the early 1800s. Reformers worked for abolition of slavery, for women's rights, and for the prohibition of liquor, as well as changes in corrections.

Pennsylvania System

In 1787, in Pennsylvania, a group campaigning for the more humane treatment of prisoners established the Philadelphia Society for Alleviating the Miseries of Public Prisons. Led by Dr. Benjamin Rush, this organization, which included many Quakers, campaigned for imprisonment of criminals rather than physical and capital punishment. The Quakers thought solitary confinement could reform criminals. In such cells, the offenders could think over their wrongful ways, repent,

and reform. In 1790, Pennsylvania established the Walnut Street Jail in Philadelphia for "hardened and atrocious offenders."

The association continued pressuring the legislature for more prisons, and finally, in 1829, the state built the Western Penitentiary outside of Pittsburgh and the Eastern Penitentiary near Philadelphia. The individual twelve-by-eight-by-ten cells with individual exercise yards isolated inmates from everyone so they could work, read their Bibles, and contemplate in order to be rehabilitated. The only voice the inmates heard was the chaplain on Sunday.

The reformers thought solitary confinement not only allowed the offenders to repent but was also a punishing experience since human beings are social animals. In addition, the system would be economical since, under these conditions, prisoners would not take long to see the error of their ways, and fewer guards would be needed. Many prisoners found the total isolation very difficult to endure. The jails, however, quickly became overcrowded warehouses for prisoners.

Auburn System

The Auburn System (New York, 1819) used the Quaker idea of solitary confinement at night but used a system of congregating (putting together) the inmates in a common workroom during the day. The prisoners could not talk to or look at each other. Any violation of the rules was met with immediate and strict discipline. Each supervisor had the right to flog an inmate who violated the rules.

Reformers thought the system economical because a single guard could watch a group of prisoners at work. Also, the work of the inmates would help pay for their upkeep. In addition, the offenders would learn about the benefits of work, as well as have time to meditate and repent. Both the Pennsylvania and Auburn systems believed offenders should be isolated and have a disciplined routine. European countries tended to adopt the Pennsylvania system, while most American states chose the Auburn system of congregate work and swift and harsh discipline. While these methods made it easier to run a prison, they did little to rehabilitate prisoners.

After the Civil War (1861-1865), huge industrial prisons were built to house thousands of prisoners in the Northeast and Midwest and in California. The western states used their old territorial jails, while the South relied on leasing out prisoners for farm labor.

THE CINCINNATI DECLARATION

Unfortunately, many prison administrators were corrupt, and convicts were mistreated and used as cheap labor. Meanwhile, a growing number of prison reformers were beginning to believe that the prison system should be more committed to reform. In 1870, the newly established National Prison Association (which later became the American Correctional Association) met in Cincinnati, Ohio, and issued a Declaration of Principles. The philosophy of the Auburn system (fixed sentences, silence, isolation, harsh punishment, lockstep work) was considered degrading and destructive to the human spirit. The values in the Declaration of Principles included

- The penal system should be based on reformation, not suffering, and prisoners should be educated to be industrious free citizens, able to function in society, not orderly inmates controlled by the guards.

- Rewards should be provided for good conduct.

- Indeterminate sentencing (not a mandated exact sentence) should include the ability for prisoners to earn their freedom early through hard work and good behavior.

- Citizens should understand that society is responsible for the conditions that lead to crime.

- Prisoners should recognize that they can change their lives.

ELMIRA REFORMATORY

The superintendent of the Elmira Reformatory (New York), Zebulon Brockway, used some of these ideas when New York opened the reformatory in 1876 for offenders 16 to 30 years old. Brockway believed that rehabilitation could be achieved through education.

Inmates who did well in both academic and moral subjects earned early release by accumulating points. Misbehavior and doing poorly in the educational courses prolonged one's sentence. Brockway used this technique because the New York legislature had passed a law allowing indeterminate sentencing and the release of inmates on parole when they showed they had been reformed. Brockway recognized it was hard to distinguish between those inmates who had truly reformed and those who pretended in order to be paroled.

PROGRESSIVE REFORMS

By 1900, this correctional philosophy had spread through the nation. Nonetheless, by World War I (1914-1918), the idea of using educational and rehabilitative approaches was being replaced by the use of strict discipline. The way the facilities were built, the lack of trained personnel, and the attitudes of the guards made Brockway's ideas difficult to implement. Also, the introduction of a system of probation kept the offenders easiest to rehabilitate out of the reformatories.

Nevertheless, the reform movement still survived. The progressives of the early twentieth century believed that if prisons applied the ideas of behavioral science to the inmates, the prisoners could be rehabilitated. The progressives worked to change the social environment from which criminals came and to design ways to rehabilitate individual inmates. By the 1920s, reformers were strongly advocating indeterminate sentencing, parole, and treatment programs as a way to rehabilitate offenders. This more scientific approach to corrections, however, was not put into practice until decades later.

While many of the reforms had merit, most could not be properly implemented due to inadequate funding or the unwillingness of prison officials to act. Also, as each reform apparently failed to solve the problem of crime, many people became disillusioned. Most people do not want to return to the exploitation and cruelty of prisons of the nineteenth and early twentieth centuries. At the same time, however, they do not want to hear inmates complain about their overcrowded conditions or their lack of services because the offenders are there to be punished for their actions.

PRISONS AS WORK PLACES

Despite the efforts of reformers, most citizens preferred prisons to pay their own way, and prison administrators constructed factories within the prison walls or hired the inmates out for chain gangs. In rural areas, inmates worked on prison-owned farms. In the South, prisoners, predominantly Black, were leased out to local farmers. Prison superintendents justified the hard labor as teaching the offenders the value of work and self-discipline, but economic motives were behind the factories and farms. In fact, some penologists believe that the harshness of the prisons made these inmates more vindictive against society.

Due to the rise of unions in the North, the 1930s saw an end to large-scale prison industry. Unions complained about competing with the inmates' free labor, especially amidst the rising unemployment of the Great Depression. By 1940, the states had limited what inmates could produce. By 1970, the number of prison farms had decreased substantially because they were expensive to operate and the prisons found it cheaper to purchase food. Also, agricultural work no longer prepared inmates for employment on the outside. Since the 1970s, however, support for prison factories has grown as a way to train inmates for outside jobs, to keep them from being bored and idle, and to teach them skills. Penologists think that prisoners benefit from work but should not suffer the exploitation that characterized the factories of the 1920s.

REHABILITATION MODEL

Beginning in the 1930s, the rehabilitation model of corrections reached its high point in the 1950s. Qualified staff were expected to diagnose the cause of an offender's criminal behavior, prescribe a treatment to change the individual, and determine when the inmate had become cured. Group therapy, counseling, and behavior modification were all part of the approach. These techniques did not work with all inmates, most states did not budget enough money for their correctional institutions to achieve these goals, and there were too many prisoners for the prison staff to treat effectively.

COMMUNITY CORRECTIONS

Advocates of community corrections of the 1960s and 1970s thought that rehabilitation needed to be done within the community, not in the prisons. They favored probation, educational courses, and job training. Starting in the 1960s, the judicial system began recognizing the constitutional rights of prisoners to live in tolerable conditions.

In 1965, the President's (Lyndon Johnson) Commission on Law Enforcement and Administration of Justice, a panel of experts on crime and the justice system, recommended improvements to the correctional system and initiated the first standards for operating prison facilities. The president's task force asserted that the success of a corrections system depended on having "a sufficient number of qualified staff."

It also recommended alternative community-based approaches, educational and vocational programs, and different treatments for special offender categories. As a result, the American Correctional Association's Commission of Accreditation established standards by which it assesses correctional facilities for voluntary accreditation.

JUSTICE MODEL

As the amount of crime increased, however, more citizens argued against rehabilitation, indeterminate sentencing, probation, parole, and treatment programs. They wanted criminals behind bars for a determinate amount of time, generally the longer the better. They wanted offenders to pay their debts to society and be off the streets so they could not be committing other crimes. As a result, the federal government and a growing number of states introduced mandatory sentencing and "three strikes you're out" life terms for habitual criminals, as well as limiting the use of probation, parole, and good time.

The rising number of offenders on parole and in the prisons and jails has taxed the system. Facilities have become overcrowded, and states experiencing budget problems cannot build prisons and jails fast enough or supply enough treatment and educational programs.

Meanwhile, state and federal courts have put caps on how many prisoners the facilities can hold and have told states that certain basic services are required. With determinate sentencing often eliminating parole, prisons have turned to gain-time to prevent overcrowding and to keep control. Gain-time, or good time, allows the prison officials to deduct a specified number of days from an offender's sentence for every month served in which the inmate breaks no rules.

REHABILITATION OR PUNISHMENT? PUBLIC OPINION

In 1996, nearly half (48.4 percent) of the respondents surveyed by the Survey Research Program (College of Criminal Justice, Sam Houston State University) thought that the most important goal of prison should be rehabilitation, while only 14.6 percent saw punishment as the most important goal of prison. One-third (33.1 percent) thought that crime prevention/deterrence was prisons' most

important goal. (See Table 1.1.) Republicans were more likely than Democrats to see prison as a tool for crime prevention/deterrence, while Democrats were more likely to consider it for rehabilitation.

TABLE 1.1

Attitudes toward the most important goal of prison

By demographic characteristics, United States, 1996

Question: "Once people who commit crimes are in prison, which of the following do you think should be the most important goal of prison?"

	Rehabilitation	Punishment	Crime prevention/ deterrence
National	48.4%	14.6%	33.1%
Sex			
Male	48.6	16.8	30.5
Female	48.2	12.5	35.5
Race, ethnicity			
White	47.7	16.1	31.9
Black	56.4	11.8	30.9
Hispanic	42.3	7.7	42.3
Age			
18 to 24 years	50.7	17.6	29.6
25 to 39 years	47.5	14.3	33.5
40 to 59 years	49.1	13.6	33.2
60 years and older	46.3	16.5	33.5
Education			
College graduate	54.9	11.5	28.5
Some college	50.9	14.5	32.4
High school graduate	40.4	17.1	38.3
Less than high school graduate	47.6	15.3	31.5
Income			
Over $60,000	53.3	15.7	26.2
$30,000 to $60,000	49.3	11.7	36.0
$15,000 to $29,999	47.7	15.4	34.4
Less than $15,000	47.1	18.6	30.0
Community			
Urban	54.2	8.9	31.5
Suburban	46.7	13.9	34.1
Small city	46.1	17.8	33.9
Rural/small town	48.0	16.1	32.8
Region			
Northeast	52.0	17.1	27.4
Midwest	49.6	14.3	34.6
South	44.2	14.7	35.7
West	51.0	13.3	30.9
Politics			
Republican	43.3	14.9	39.0
Democrat	53.8	13.5	30.0
Independent/other	47.5	17.0	31.5

Note: The "other," "don't know," and "refused" categories have been omitted; therefore percents may not sum to 100.

Table constructed by SOURCEBOOK staff from data provided by the Survey Research Program, College of Criminal Justice, Sam Houston State University.

Source: Kathleen Maguire and Ann L. Pastore, eds., _Sourcebook of Criminal Justice Statistics 1997_, Bureau of Justice Statistics, Washington, DC, 1998

CHAPTER II

EXPENDITURES

The money spent building and running prisons to house nonviolent offenders offers a new twist on the aphorism "spend it now or spend it later." We are spending unnecessary billions now, to no lasting effect, and will have to spend massive amounts later to address not only the social and economic causes of crime, but to correct the damages caused by unnecessary incarceration and its side effects of blighted lives, broken families, and disrupted careers. — Michael Tonry, Professor of Law, University of Minnesota

Although state governments spend a greater proportion of funds on education and welfare, the amount they are spending on corrections is increasing. There are several factors that influence the growing expenditures. More people are being sent to prison and are staying longer because of mandatory sentencing and longer sentences. Numerous prison and jail systems are under court order to alleviate overcrowding and to provide adequate health care. Additional buildings are being built and beds added to accommodate the rising number of prisoners. (See Chapter VI.)

Moreover, additional funds must be found to pay for growing health care needs as more prisoners are infected with AIDS and tuberculosis and as prisoners sentenced to mandatory life imprisonment without parole begin to age. In New York state, for example, half of the prison health budget goes to care for inmates with AIDS.

TOTAL JUSTICE EXPENDITURES

According to the most recent edition of *Justice Expenditure and Employment Extracts* (Bureau of Justice Statistics, 1997), the United States spent about

FIGURE 2.1

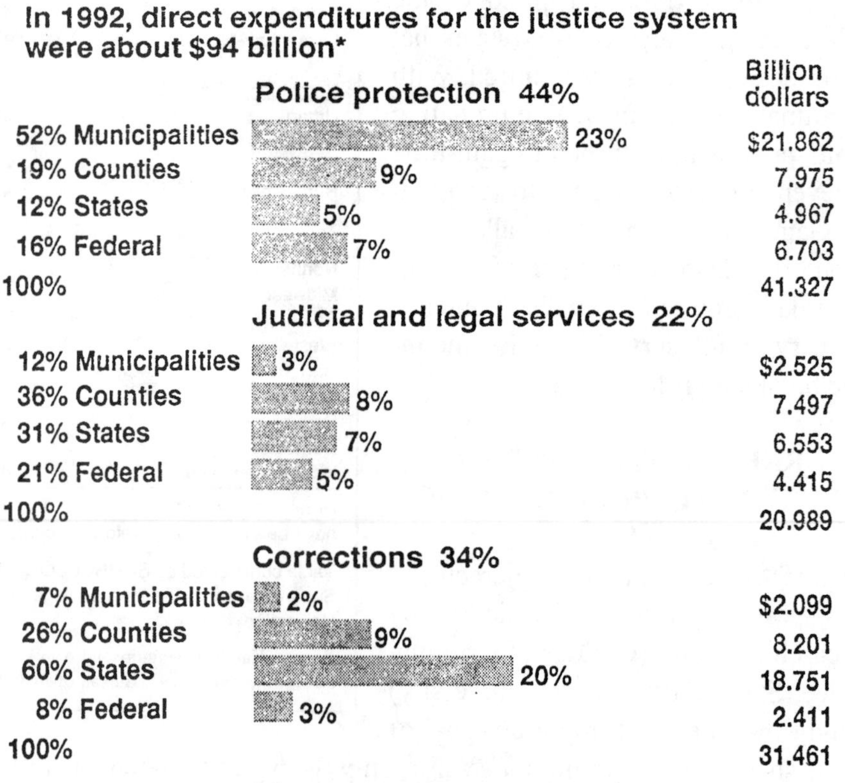

In 1992, direct expenditures for the justice system were about $94 billion*

Police protection 44%

		Billion dollars
52% Municipalities	23%	$21.862
19% Counties	9%	7.975
12% States	5%	4.967
16% Federal	7%	6.703
100%		41.327

Judicial and legal services 22%

12% Municipalities	3%	$2.525
36% Counties	8%	7.497
31% States	7%	6.553
21% Federal	5%	4.415
100%		20.989

Corrections 34%

7% Municipalities	2%	$2.099
26% Counties	9%	8.201
60% States	20%	18.751
8% Federal	3%	2.411
100%		31.461

*Detail may not add to 100% because of rounding.

Source: Sue A. Lindren, *Justice Expenditures and Employment Extracts, 1992*, Bureau of Justice Statistics, Washington, DC, 1997

8

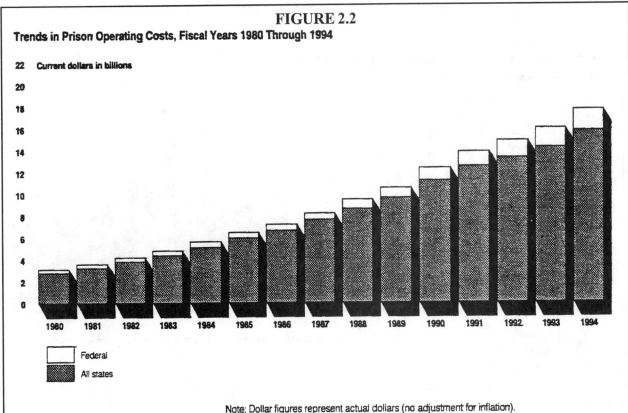

FIGURE 2.2

Trends in Prison Operating Costs, Fiscal Years 1980 Through 1994

Note: Dollar figures represent actual dollars (no adjustment for inflation).

Source: *Federal and State Prisons: Inmate Populations, Costs, and Projection Models*, U.S. General Accounting Office, Washington, DC, 1996

$94 billion on the entire justice system in 1992 (latest figures available). Corrections spending accounted for one-third of the total expenditures, police protection for 44 percent, and judicial and legal services for 22 percent. The states were responsible for most of the corrections spending. (See Figure 2.1.)

GROWING OPERATING COSTS

Prison operating costs (routine expenses such as salaries, health care, food, and maintenance) grew steadily from 1980 to 1994, reflecting in part the growth in prison populations. Total U.S. prison operating costs grew from about $3.1 billion in 1980 to about $17.7 billion in current dollars in 1994, an increase of 224 percent based on constant or inflation-adjusted dollars. The cumulative operating costs over the period totaled $137.7 billion. (Figure

TABLE 2.1

Federal and State Prison Operating Costs in Current Dollars, Fiscal Years 1980 Through 1994

	Costs in thousands of current dollars		
Fiscal year	Federal	State	Total*
1980	$319,274	$2,787,369	$3,106,643
1981	346,517	3,229,234	3,575,751
1982	368,000	3,794,178	4,162,178
1983	435,000	4,346,273	4,781,273
1984	529,245	5,066,666	5,595,911
1985	500,941	5,934,160	6,435,101
1986	555,097	6,619,534	7,174,631
1987	580,120	7,601,594	8,181,714
1988	878,502	8,586,498	9,465,000
1989	900,334	9,611,020	10,511,354
1990	1,148,678	11,194,236	12,342,914
1991	1,318,741	12,514,171	13,832,912
1992	1,585,498	13,290,202	14,875,700
1993	1,767,019	14,239,710	16,006,729
1994	1,918,067	15,776,174	17,694,241
Total*	**$13,151,033**	**$124,591,019**	**$137,742,052**

Note 1: Dollar figures represent actual dollars (no adjustment for inflation).

Note 2: According to BOP, the federal cost data presented are actual obligations, adjusted for equipment and other capital item costs.

*Details may not add to total due to rounding.
BOP and U.S. Bureau of the Census.

Source: *Federal and State Prisons: Inmate Populations, Costs, and Projection Models*, U.S. General Accounting Office, Washington, DC, 1996

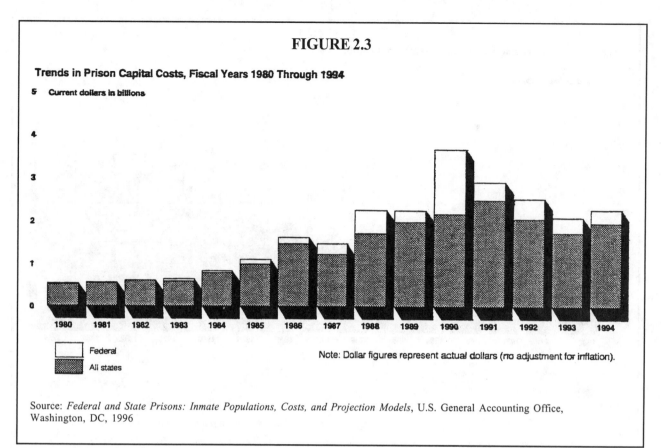

FIGURE 2.3

Trends in Prison Capital Costs, Fiscal Years 1980 Through 1994

5   Current dollars in billions

☐ Federal

▨ All states

Note: Dollar figures represent actual dollars (no adjustment for inflation).

Source: *Federal and State Prisons: Inmate Populations, Costs, and Projection Models*, U.S. General Accounting Office, Washington, DC, 1996

2.2 and Table 2.1 present costs in current dollars.)

Of this total, federal prison operating costs grew from about $319 million in 1980 to about $1.9 billion in 1994, an increase of about 242 percent based on constant dollars. State prison operating costs rose from about $2.8 billion in 1980 to $15.8 billion in 1994, a similar increase of 222 percent based on constant dollars. (Figure 2.2 and Table 2.1 present costs in current dollars.) In California, operating costs expanded from about $320 million in 1980 to $2.6 billion in 1994, an increase of 357 percent in constant dollars. In Texas, operating costs soared from about $105 million in 1980 to $1.2 billion in 1994, an increase of 529 percent based on constant dollars.

Operating Budgets

The Criminal Justice Institute, in *The Corrections Yearbook — 1998* (Camille

TABLE 2.2

Federal and State Prison Capital Costs in Current Dollars, Fiscal Years 1980 Through 1994

Fiscal year	Costs in thousands of current dollars		
	Federal	State	Total[a]
1980	$21,766	$515,854	$537,620
1981	20,807	541,939	562,746
1982	6,500	604,715	612,215
1983	54,000	589,325	643,325
1984	42,072	792,963	835,035
1985	111,787	992,071	1,103,858
1986	145,382	1,473,544	1,618,926
1987	249,279	1,226,049	1,475,328
1988	544,392	1,715,463	2,259,855
1989	266,994	1,984,518	2,251,512
1990	1,505,953	2,175,823	3,681,776
1991	419,262	2,497,997	2,917,259
1992	475,733	2,057,383	2,533,116
1993	366,144	1,726,171	2,092,315
1994	311,687	1,965,763	2,277,450
Total[a]	**$4,541,758**	**$20,859,578**	**$25,401,336**

Note 1: Dollar figures represent actual dollars (no adjustment for inflation).

Note 2: According to BOP, the federal cost data presented are actual obligations, adjusted for equipment and other capital item costs.

[a]Details may not add to total due to rounding.

Source: *Federal and State Prisons: Inmate Populations, Costs, and Projection Models*, U.S. General Accounting Office, Washington, DC, 1996

Graham Camp and George M. Camp, Middletown, Connecticut, 1998), reported that fiscal year (FY) 1998 operating budgets totaled $28.3 billion in all adult agencies. The average operating budget was 93 percent of an agency's total budget. The 1998 FY operating budget for California's adult correctional agencies was $3.8 billion, and for Texas it was $2 billion. The FY 1998 federal operating budget for adult correctional agencies was $2.8 billion.

GROWING CAPITAL COSTS

Capital costs include major equipment and building expenditures. In the case of prisons, capital costs are mainly the costs of building new facilities. Total U.S. prison capital costs grew from about $538 million in 1980 to about $2.3 billion in current dollars in 1994, an increase of 141 percent in constant dollars. Federal prison capital costs spiraled from about $22 million in 1980 to about $312 million in 1994, an increase of about 715 percent in constant dollars. State prison capital costs rose from about $516 million in 1980 to about $2 billion in 1994, an increase of about 116 percent in constant dollars. Cumulative capital costs totaled $25.4 billion from 1980 through 1994. (Figure 2.3 and Table 2.2 present costs in current dollars.)

In California, capital costs skyrocketed from $16 million in 1980 to $413 million in 1994, an increase of 1,327 percent in constant dollars. In Texas, capital costs soared from $20 million in 1980 to about $577 million in 1994, an increase of 1,531 percent based on constant dollars.

In 1997, according to the Criminal Justice Institute (*The Corrections Yearbook — 1998*), 15 jurisdictions (14 states and the federal government) opened 31 correctional facilities. Of the 13 jurisdictions that reported costs, the average construction cost per bed was $48,601.

PROJECTED COSTS

The Federal Bureau of Prisons (BOP) estimates that its operating costs could grow to about $4.7 billion by 2006. The BOP also projected that its capital costs for new federal prisons scheduled to begin operations between 1996 and 2006 could total more than $4 billion. (See Table 2.3.) According to Justice officials, these cost increases were projected on the basis of historically high rates of prison population increases. Since the rate of increase in prison populations from 1994 to 1995 was below average, compared to the preceding five years, the BOP cost projections may be overestimated.

The National Council on Crime and Delinquency, located in San Francisco, California, a private organization engaged in research, training, and advocacy programs to reduce crime and delinquency, estimated that state prison population increases from 1995 to 2000 could result in total additional capital and operating costs of $32.5 billion to $37 billion for this period. About $10.6 billion to $15.1 billion could be needed to construct additional state prisons, and another $1.9 billion would be needed by the end of the decade to operate these prisons.

TABLE 2.3

Projected Federal Prison Operating and Capital Costs, Fiscal Years 1996 Through 2006

Fiscal year	Costs in thousands of current dollars		
	Operating	Capital	Total
1996	$2,440,394	$445,903	$2,886,297
1997	2,843,292	506,552	3,349,844
1998	3,054,347	553,493	3,607,840
1999	3,365,142	424,136	3,789,278
2000	3,604,601	341,741	3,946,342
2001	3,805,956	303,576	4,110,532
2002	3,958,572	287,608	4,246,180
2003	4,163,304	282,823	4,446,127
2004	4,343,282	283,718	4,627,000
2005	4,528,328	287,555	4,815,883
2006	4,721,072	293,005	5,014,077

Note: According to BOP, projections of operating and capital budgets are based on estimated obligations—as presented in the Office of Management and Budget's fiscal year 1998 budget for the federal government—adjusted for equipment and other capital item costs.

Source: *Federal and State Prisons: Inmate Populations, Costs, and Projection Models*, U.S. General Accounting Office, Washington, DC, 1996

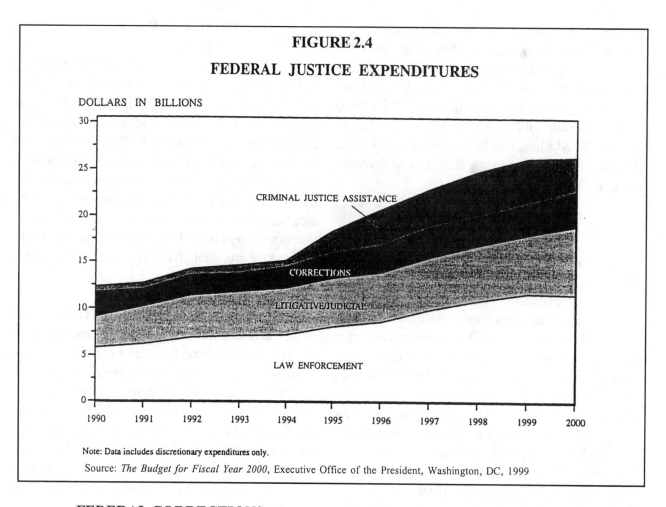

FIGURE 2.4

FEDERAL JUSTICE EXPENDITURES

DOLLARS IN BILLIONS

CRIMINAL JUSTICE ASSISTANCE

CORRECTIONS

LITIGATIVE/JUDICIAL

LAW ENFORCEMENT

Note: Data includes discretionary expenditures only.

Source: *The Budget for Fiscal Year 2000*, Executive Office of the President, Washington, DC, 1999

FEDERAL CORRECTIONS

As the number of inmates increases each year, so does the amount appropriated (authorized) by Congress and spent (expenditures) for corrections. (The amount Congress originally approves is not always the amount spent.) In 1997, Congress approved $2.7 billion. The appropriation for 1998 was $3 billion and for 1999, $3.8 billion. (See Figure 2.4 for federal justice expenditures.)

STATE CORRECTIONS

In 1997, according to the National Association of State Budget Officers (*1997 State Expenditure Report*, Washington, DC, 1998), state governments spent an estimated 3.8 percent of their funds on corrections (Figure 2.5). The $29.7 billion spent on corrections in 1997 was an increase of 51.5 percent over the 1993 spending of $19.6 billion. An estimated $1.3 billion was spent on capital construction, mostly building prison facilities. Figure 2.6 shows that shares of state spending have shifted since 1987. Only Medicaid and

corrections represented a larger share of total state spending in 1997 than they did in 1987.

The Criminal Justice Institute (*The Corrections Yearbook —1998*) estimated that the states spent a daily average of $55.51 per adult inmate as of January 1, 1998, compared to $43.54 as of January 1, 1988. At $100.07 per inmate, Alaska had the highest daily expenses, and at $24.37 per inmate, Alabama had the lowest daily expenditures.

Budget Increases

Double-digit annual increases in state correctional spending were not unusual during the 1990s. State prison populations totaled 530,000 in 1990, doubled to 1,077,000 by the end of 1996, and reached 1,131,581 by the end of 1997. Furthermore, according to the National Conference of State Legislatures (NCSL), attempts to save money through privatization, imposing costs on inmates, and putting inmates to work have proved unsuccessful in controlling costs.

According to the NCSL, total state appropriations rose by an average 5.9 percent in fiscal year (FY) 1999. West Virginia had the largest rate of increase, up 24.4 percent from 1998, due to pay raises, benefits, a new correctional facility, and other expansions. Delaware's spending increased 21.5 percent from 1998, resulting from building and operating more prisons. Colorado's spending, up 17.7 percent over 1998, was due to an increase in its corrections budget. (See Table 2.4.)

On the other hand, fund appropriations for three states and the District of Columbia declined between FY 1998 and FY 1999. Washington, DC's expenditures dropped 38.1 percent because the federal government took over the corrections system. New Jersey dropped 6.6 percent, resulting from plans to reduce overtime pay because of improved security and plans to place less serious offenders in alternative programs. Tennessee reduced funding by 0.5 percent because of lower administrative expenses from consolidating several prison facilities during 1997 and 1998. Texas lowered funding by 0.4 percent due to lower administrative expenses (Table 2.4).

Probation and Parole

In 1998, according to the Criminal Justice Institute, the reporting states had a total probation and parole budget of about $3.4 billion, an increase of about 44.3 percent since 1992 (*The Corrections Year-book—1998*). In 1997, the cost per day for a probationer under regular supervision was $3.16. Intensive supervision (more frequent contact with an agent) averaged $11.35 per day, while electronic supervision averaged $11.16. The average daily cost for a regular supervision parolee was $4.63; for intensive supervision, $7.85; and for electronic supervision, $10.85. Some jurisdictions combined their probation and parole budgets, causing their average costs to fall between the costs for separate parole and probation agencies.

ANNUAL JAIL EXPENDITURES

Local jails spent an estimated $9.6 billion during the year ending June 30, 1993 (the latest year for which the BJS computed statistics for the whole country; Table 2.5). This estimated total (not adjusted for inflation) was more than triple the $2.7 billion spent a decade earlier in 1983. Gross salaries and wages, employer contributions to employee benefits, purchases of food, supplies, contractual services, and other op-

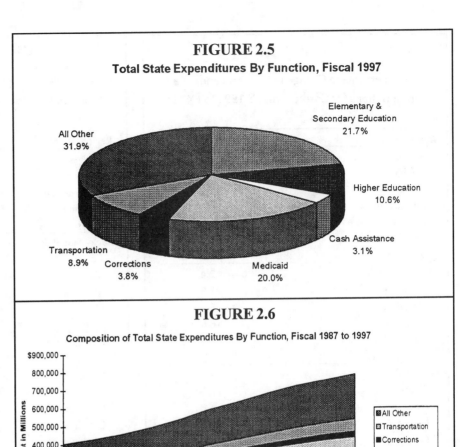

FIGURE 2.5
Total State Expenditures By Function, Fiscal 1997

Elementary & Secondary Education 21.7%
Higher Education 10.6%
Cash Assistance 3.1%
Medicaid 20.0%
Corrections 3.8%
Transportation 8.9%
All Other 31.9%

FIGURE 2.6
Composition of Total State Expenditures By Function, Fiscal 1987 to 1997

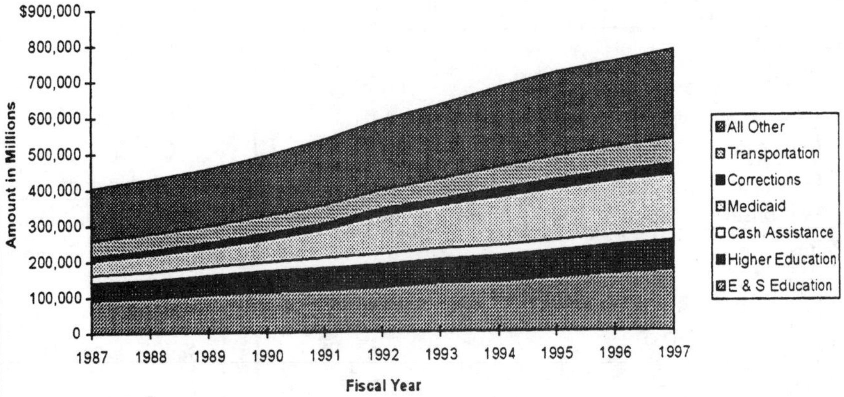

All Other
Transportation
Corrections
Medicaid
Cash Assistance
Higher Education
E & S Education

Source of both figures: *1997 State Expenditure Report*, National Association of State Budget Officers, Washington, DC, 1998

TABLE 2.4

Percentage Change in General Fund Appropriations for Corrections, FY 1998 to FY 1999

Region/State	General Fund
New England	**7.9%**
Connecticut	5.9
Maine	7.2
Massachusetts	9.9
New Hampshire	4.2
Rhode Island	4.2
Vermont	10.2
Middle Atlantic	**2.4**
Delaware	21.5
Maryland	5.8
New Jersey	-6.6
New York	4.0
Pennsylvania	5.9
Great Lakes	**6.2**
Illinois	11.6
Indiana	0.1
Michigan	1.3
Ohio	9.5
Wisconsin	8.5
Plains	**8.3**
Iowa	6.8
Kansas	4.9
Minnesota	4.7
Missouri	12.7
Nebraska	7.6
North Dakota	4.0
South Dakota	5.0
Southeast	**4.7**
Alabama	1.0
Arkansas	2.8
Florida	3.3
Georgia	6.8
Kentucky	7.5
Louisiana	3.3
Mississippi	3.7
North Carolina	1.7
South Carolina	1.5
Tennessee	-0.5
Virginia	11.5
West Virginia	24.4

(continued)

TABLE 2.4 (Continued)

Percentage Change in General Fund Appropriations for Corrections, FY 1998 to FY 1999 (continued)

Region/State	General Fund
Southwest	**3.1%**
Arizona	12.7
New Mexico	4.2
Oklahoma	10.0
Texas	-0.4
Rocky Mountain	**12.0**
Colorado	17.7
Idaho	1.8
Montana	12.6
Utah	7.3
Wyoming	4.2
Far West	**5.7**
Alaska	2.6
California	5.9
Hawaii	11.8
Nevada	4.0
Oregon	4.7
Washington	3.9
Other Jurisdictions	
District of Columbia	-38.1
Puerto Rico	—no response—
Total	**5.0%**

Source: NCSL, 1998.

Source: "State Budget Actions, 1998," copyrighted by the National Conference of State Legislatures, Denver, CO, 1998

erating costs accounted for 71 percent of expenditures. Construction costs, major repairs, equipment, improvements, land purchases, and other capital outlays accounted for the remaining 29 percent. In 1983, operating costs made up 79 percent of all expenditures, while capital outlays were 21 percent (Table 2.5).

Jail Budgets

The average budget for local jails in FY 1997 was $34 million, according to the Criminal Justice Institute, Inc. New York City had the largest agency budget — $786 million, followed by Los Angeles with $361 million, and Dade County (Miami), Florida, with $192 million. The average food budget was $2 million, and the average medical budget was $3.8 million.

Average Operating Costs Per Inmate

In 1997, the overall cost per jail prisoner per day was $54.53, up from $37.82 in 1985, but down from $55.41 in 1996, according to the Criminal Justice Institute, Inc. Costs per prisoner per day vary from location to location. Suffolk, New York, had the highest cost per prisoner per day at $118.00, followed by New York City at $111.00, and Norfolk, Massachusetts, at $102.10. McCraken, Kentucky, reported the lowest costs per prisoner per day at $22.02. Elkhart, Indiana, at $25.82 per prisoner per day, and Mobile, Alabama, with $27.50 per prisoner per day, also had low costs.

In 1996, because of an oversupply of jail beds in Texas, some states (Arkansas, Colorado, Hawaii, Massachusetts, Missouri, New Mexico, Oklahoma, Oregon, Utah, and Virginia) transferred inmates to Texas. Other states, such as Alaska and Idaho, were considering doing so. It was cheaper for these states to ship inmates to Texas than to house the prisoners themselves.

It would cost $52 per day per inmate in Oregon and $36 in Texas. To house a prisoner in Hawaii would be $28,000 annually, but to house the inmate in Texas would cost Hawaii $15,000. Commenting for *The Honolulu Advertiser*, the Hawaii House Speaker said that "it's cheaper to send 300 [prisoners] to Texas for $5 million than to build a new prison facility."

HIDDEN COSTS

In *Seeking Justice* (New York, 1997), The Edna McConnell Clark Foundation, an organization seeking a "more rational, humane, and effective criminal justice system," asserted that many costs of operating and constructing prisons are not revealed by looking at budgets. For example, servicing the debt on bonds sold to construct prisons raises the price of construction, an expense taxpayers are often unaware of. According to the foundation, the cost of building one maximum security bed in New York State is about $100,000. However, with interest on the debt, the price rises to about $300,000.

Some prison expenses are paid by other agencies, such as mental heath and education departments. These costs are not part of the corrections budgets but are part of the cost of corrections.

Rising health costs have also not been factored in. For example, a federal court ordered New York City to build 84 communicable disease cells at a cost of $450,000 per cell for inmates who had contracted tuberculosis. The growing number of inmates with AIDS and the projected increase in the number of elderly inmates, from 5,000 in 1994 to about 126,400 in 2020, will certainly increase the costs of running the prisons. The average cost for housing an elderly inmate is three times as much as for housing a younger prisoner.

The National Conference of State Legislatures estimated that, with its "no parole" provision, Virginia will double its prison population and need $2 billion or more during the next 10 years to cover building costs. Researchers from the RAND Corporation, a California think tank, concluded that "to support implementation of the law, total spending for higher education and other government services would have to fall by more than 40 percent over the next eight years." In addition, imprisonment reduces the number of taxpayers and wage earners for society and creates more families on public support.

TABLE 2.5

Local jail expenditures for annual period ending June 30, 1983, 1988, and 1993

Year	Expenditures (in $1,000's)		
	Total	Operating[a]	Capital[b]
1983	$2,711,357	$2,129,748	$581,609
1988	4,555,649	3,574,940	980,709
1993			
Reported[c]	$7,749,283	$5,523,296	$2,225,987
National estimate[d]	9,628,000	6,860,000	2,769,000

[a]Operating expenditures include total salaries, wages, contributions to employee benefits and other expenditures, such as purchase of food, supplies, and contractual services.
[b]Capital expenditures include construction costs (for new buildings, major repairs, and improvements), equipment, and purchase of land.
[c]Approximately 29% of all jails (housing 19% of all inmates) were unable to report

expenditures. Of the 2,342 facilities that reported complete data, 142 could only report expenditures as part of a larger jurisdictional or governmental unit budget. Expenditures for these facilities were based on the estimated percentages of the total budget applicable to each facility.
[d]National totals were estimated and rounded to the nearest million dollars.

Source: *Jail and Jail Inmates 1993-94*, Bureau of Justice Statistics, Washington, DC, 1995

COST CONTAINMENT

With the public fearing crime and favoring a tough-on-criminals approach, costs for corrections will likely increase. However, as taxpayers have not shown themselves willing to pay additional taxes, cuts will either have to be made elsewhere or less costly alternative ways to punish offenders will have to be found. Prisons are finding ways to cut costs by having more work programs, limiting inmate services, and charging prisoners for services. More and more jails and prisons are charging for medical care (see Chapters III and IV) and restricting activities, such as banning television and weight training rooms.

Some states are considering or have already signed into law bans on tennis and basketball courts. A Mississippi law allows the prisons to "hot-bunk," a system of rotating inmates through shifts of labor, sleep, and training. Some Florida county jails have removed all television sets. Although many of these restrictions were implemented to cut costs, most were designed to toughen life for the convicted and, hence, deter others from committing crimes.

Opponents argue that the restrictions will not deter anyone and will lead to strained conditions that could cause riots. However, many of the prisons where amenities were banned did not have the luxuries in the first place. For example, Mississippi banned individual air conditioners although no prisoner had one. In Louisiana, inmates could not participate in martial arts classes, even though none were offered. (See Chapter IV for a survey on wardens' views on the issue of prison amenities.)

Prisoners Pay a Share

Many states are looking to the prisoners to pay some of the costs. By 1995, more than 24 states had passed laws making inmates pay for some of their imprisonment. In Arizona, inmates pay a utility fee for televisions or any major electrical appliance. In Texas, deductions are made from inmates' wages from work outside of the prison. (See Chapters IV, V, and VI for more information on prison amenities and work.)

In 1998, Governor Jane Hull of Arizona signed a jail-food bill into law. Arizona expects to save its taxpayers up to $2.5 million per year under the new law that permits counties to charge jail inmates $1 per day to offset the cost of feeding them. Juveniles are exempt from the law unless they are being tried in adult court. Any prisoner who cannot afford the $1 per day fee will still be fed, but any money received from friends or relatives must go to pay for the inmate's meals before he or she is able to buy extras, such as snacks and toiletries, with it.

In Little Rock, Arkansas, prisoners who ruin their jail laundry are being billed for the damages, and in Cedar Rapids, Iowa, inmates who fail to pay their room and board will have their post-release earnings garnisheed. According to Linn County, Iowa, Sheriff Donald Zeller, "If they are violating the law, they should be the ones to pay for it." Sheriff Zeller regularly charges delinquent ex-inmates with court-ordered property liens. Other sheriffs have used post-release installment plans to collect what they can.

Opponents of the plans to make prisoners pay often cite the fact that billing inmates can burden already low-income families. Furthermore, it seems unfair that a prisoner later found innocent or eventually released should be charged. However, the idea has spread with support from legislators. Court challenges to the plans have failed, and jailhouse collections have saved taxpayers money.

CHAPTER III

JAILS

Jail managers will be dealing with more inmates, and more of them will be long-term state inmates staying on in our jails for years. We need to plan ahead. We need to be mindful of the security realities involved in holding longer-term inmates. And finally, we need to make sure that the inmates who become motivated to change their behavior will have access to the services needed to guide those changes in socially appropriate ways. — Richard A. Van Den Heuvel, "When Jails Become Prisons," *American Jails*, November/December, 1994

Although many people use the words "jails" and "prisons" interchangeably, they are different types of facilities. Jails are locally operated correctional facilities. Inmates sentenced to jail usually have received a sentence of a year or less. The purpose of jails is to

- Receive individuals pending arraignment (brought into court to hear the charges) and hold them until their trials, conviction, or sentencing.

- Readmit probation, parole, and bail-bond violators and absconders (those who run away or "skip bail").

- Temporarily detain juveniles pending transfer to juvenile authorities.

- Hold mentally ill persons pending their movement to appropriate health facilities.

- Hold individuals for the military, for protective custody, for contempt, and for the courts as witnesses.

- Release convicted inmates to the community upon completion of sentence.

- Transfer inmates to federal, state, or other authorities.

- Sometimes operate community-based programs with electronic monitoring or other types of supervision.

NUMBER OF JAIL INMATES

On June 30, 1998, the nation's jails held 592,462 inmates, more than twice the 256,615 persons incarcerated in 1985, 46 percent more than the 405,320 held in 1990, and 17 percent more than the 507,044 prisoners in 1995. (See Table 3.1.)

The jail inmate population rose from 163 per 100,000 U.S. residents on July 1, 1990 to 219 per 100,000 residents on July 1, 1998. (See Table 3.2.) The average daily jail population for the year ending June 30, 1998, was 593,808, an increase of 7 percent from 1997 and almost one and one-half times as many as in 1990 (Table 3.3).

REASONS FOR THE GROWING POPULATION

An Increasing Number of Arrests

Underlying this dramatic growth in the local jail population has been the rise in the number of arrests for all criminal infractions except traffic violations. Arrests grew from 12.5 million in 1986 to 15.3 million in 1997, a 22 percent increase. The most arrests were for drug abuse violations (1.6

TABLE 3.1

Number of persons held in State or Federal prisons or in local jails, 1985, 1990-98

Year	Total inmates in custody	Prisoners in custody Federal	Prisoners in custody State	Inmates held in local jails	Incarceration rate*
1985	744,208	35,781	451,812	256,615	313
1990	1,148,702	58,838	684,544	405,320	458
1991	1,219,014	63,930	728,605	426,479	481
1992	1,295,150	72,071	778,495	444,584	505
1993	1,369,185	80,815	828,566	459,804	528
1994	1,476,621	85,500	904,647	486,474	564
1995	1,585,586	89,538	989,004	507,044	600
1996	1,646,020	95,088	1,032,440	518,492	618
1997					
June 30	1,725,785	99,175	1,059,531	567,079	645
December 31	1,743,886	101,755	1,075,052	--	652
1998					
June 30	1,802,496	107,381	1,102,653	592,462	668
Percent change, 6/30/97 - 6/30/98	4.4%	8.3%	4.1%	4.5%	
Annual average increase,					
12/31/85 - 6/30/98	7.3%	9.2%	7.4%	6.9%	
12/31/90 - 6/30/98	6.2	8.3	6.6	5.2	

Note: Jail counts are for midyear (June 30). Counts for 1994-98 exclude persons who were supervised outside of a jail facility. State and Federal prisoner counts for 1985 and 1990-97 are for December 31.
--Not available.
*Total of persons in custody per 100,000 residents on July 1 of each reference year.

TABLE 3.2

Jail Incarceration Rate, 1990-1998

Year	Jail incarceration rate*
1998	219
1997	212
1996	196
1995	193
1994	188
1993	178
1992	174
1991	169
1990	163

*Number of jail inmates per 100,000 U.S. residents on July 1 of each year.

Source of both tables: Darrell K. Gilliard, *Prison and Jail Inmates at Midyear 1998*, Bureau of Justice Statistics, Washington, DC, 1999

---

million) and larceny-theft and driving under the influence (1.5 million arrests each.) (See Table 3.4.)

Drug Arrests

The largest growth among those arrested occurred among drug law violators. Between 1993 and 1997, total arrests increased 8.3 percent. However, while property crime arrests dropped 7 percent and violent crime arrests decreased 2 percent, drug abuse violation arrests were up 37.7 percent from 1993 and 48 percent from 1988.

Jail Inmates Held for State/Federal Authorities

The nation's jail population also grew as a result of the overcrowding at state and federal prisons. At the end of 1997, 31 jurisdictions reported a total of 33,736 state prisoners (3 percent of all state prisoners) held in local jails or other facilities due to crowding in state prisons. In 1997, Louisiana (36.9 percent) and West Virginia (24.4 percent) had the largest percentage of state prisoners housed in local jails. Five other jurisdictions — Colorado (14 percent), Arkansas (13.7 percent), Virginia (13.2 percent), New Mexico (11.9 percent), and New Jersey (10.1 percent) reported that at least 10 percent of their prison inmates were lodged in local jail facilities. (See Table 3.5.)

Sentences Remain the Same

The growth in the local jail population since 1983 has not been the result of longer sentences. The National Judicial Reporting Program found that between the late 1980s and the mid-1990s, the average maximum sentence among those entering jail remained constant at seven months (although a prisoner is unlikely to actually serve the maximum sentence). According to the Criminal Justice Institute (Camille Graham Camp and George M. Camp, *The Corrections Yearbook — 1998*, Middletown, Connecticut, 1998), the 1997 average length of stay of inmates in jail systems was 47.3 days — 93.9 days for sentenced inmates and 38.6 days for pretrial inmates.

TABLE 3.3

Average daily population and the number of men, women, and juveniles in local jails, midyear 1990-98

	1990	1991	1992	1993	1994	1995	1996	1997	1998
Average daily population[a]	408,075	422,609	441,889	466,155	479,757	509,828	515,432	556,586	593,808
Number of inmates, midyear[b]	405,320	426,479	444,584	459,804	486,474	507,044	518,492	567,079	592,462
Adults	403,019	424,129	441,780	455,500	479,800	499,300	510,400	557,974	584,372
Male	365,821	384,628	401,106	411,500	431,300	448,000	454,700	498,678	520,581
Female	37,198	39,501	40,674	44,100	48,500	51,300	55,700	59,296	63,791
Juveniles[c]	2,301	2,350	2,804	4,300	6,700	7,800	8,100	9,105	8,090
Held as adults[d]	--	--	--	3,300	5,100	5,900	5,700	7,007	6,542
Held as juveniles	2,301	2,350	2,804	1,000	1,600	1,800	2,400	2,098	1,548

Notes: Data are for June 30 in 1992-95 and 1998; for June 29, 1990; and for June 28 in 1991 and 1996.
Detailed data for 1993-96 were estimated and rounded to the nearest 100. Previously published numbers for 1994 and 1995 have been revised to include only inmates held in jail facilities.
--Not available.
[a]The average daily population is the sum of the number of inmates in a jail each day for a year, divided by the total number of days in the year.
[b]Inmate counts for 1990-93 include an unknown number of persons who were under jail supervision but not confined. Detailed counts for 1994-96 were estimated based on the number of inmates held in jail facilities.
[c]Juveniles are persons defined by State statute as being under a certain age, usually 18, and subject initially to juvenile court authority even if tried as adults in criminal court. In 1994 the definition was changed to include all persons under age 18.
[d]Includes juveniles who were tried or awaiting trial as adults.

Source: Darrell K. Gilliard, *Prison and Jail Inmates at Midyear 1998*, Bureau of Justice Statistics, Washington, DC, 1999

JAILS WITH CROWDED CONDITIONS

The National Institute of Justice conducts the *National Assessment Program* (NAP) survey periodically to determine the needs and problems of state and local criminal justice agencies. Surveys are mailed to police chiefs, sheriffs, jail administrators, prosecutors, public defenders, judges, court administrators, probation and parole directors, attorneys general, and commissioners of corrections. The questions are tailored towards the concerns of each group. Jail administrators were asked about crowding issues, jail alternatives, and classification. The 1994 survey is the most recent.

In the 1990 NAP survey, 52 percent of the jail administrators indicated that they were operating under crowded conditions (more than 110 percent

TABLE 3.4

Total Estimated Arrests,[1] United States, 1997

Total[2]	**15,284,300**	Embezzlement	17,400
		Stolen property; buying, receiving, possessing	155,300
Murder and nonnegligent manslaughter	18,290	Vandalism	318,400
Forcible rape	32,060	Weapons; carrying, possessing, etc.	218,900
Robbery	132,450	Prostitution and commercialized vice	101,600
Aggravated assault	534,920	Sex offenses (except forcible rape and prostitution)	101,900
Burglary	356,000	Drug abuse violations	1,583,600
Larceny-theft	1,472,600	Gambling	15,900
Motor vehicle theft	167,000	Offenses against family and children	155,800
Arson	20,000	Driving under the influence	1,477,300
		Liquor laws	636,400
Violent crime[3]	717,750	Drunkenness	734,800
Property crime[4]	2,015,600	Disorderly conduct	811,100
		Vagrancy	28,800
Crime Index total[5]	2,733,400	All other offenses	3,884,600
Other assaults	1,395,800	Suspicion (not included in totals)	6,500
Forgery and counterfeiting	120,100	Curfew and loitering law violations	182,700
Fraud	414,600	Runaways	196,100

[1] Arrest totals are based on all reporting agencies and estimates for unreported areas.
[2] Because of rounding, figures may not add to total.
[3] Violent crimes are offenses of murder, forcible rape, robbery, and aggravated assault.
[4] Property crimes are offenses of burglary, larceny-theft, motor vehicle theft, and arson.
[5] Includes arson.

Source: *Crime in the United States, 1997*, Federal Bureau of Investigation, Washington, DC, 1998

TABLE 3.5

State prisoners held in local jails because of prison crowding, by State, yearend 1997 and 1996

| | State prisoners held in local jails | | | |
| | Number | | As a percent of State inmates | |
	1997	1996	1997	1996
U.S. total	33,736	30,741	3.0%	2.9%
Louisiana	10,795	9,147	36.9%	34.2%
Virginia	3,753	2,506	13.2	9.1
New Jersey	2,864	4,367	10.1	15.9
Colorado	1,886	1,163	14.0	9.4
Alabama	1,824	1,168	8.2	5.4
Mississippi	1,463	3,242	9.5	23.4
Tennessee	1,428	1,958	8.6	12.5
Arkansas	1,376	1,201	13.7	12.8
Indiana	1,323	1,194	7.4	7.0
Kentucky	1,144	778	7.8	6.0
New York	918	0	1.3%	--
Oklahoma	802	285	3.9	1.5
West Virginia	775	286	24.4	10.4
New Mexico	557	307	11.9	6.5
Massachusetts	484	554	4.1	4.7
South Carolina	400	413	1.9	2.0
Utah	348	308	8.1	7.8
Wisconsin	284	338	1.9	2.6
North Carolina	282	516	0.9	1.7
Montana	217	85	9.7	3.7
Arizona[a]	211	124	0.9%	0.5%
Michigan[a]	151	330	0.3	0.8
Oregon	72	91	0.9	1.1
North Dakota	68	91	8.5	12.6
New Hampshire	66	65	3.0	3.2
Missouri	55	0	0.2	--
Alaska	55	0	1.3	--
Minnesota[b]	50	208	0.9	4.0
Idaho	31	0	0.8	--
Wyoming	29	16	1.9	1.1
Pennsylvania	25	0	0.1	--

--Not calculated.

[a]For States without jail backups in their counts, the percentage is based on the total of State inmates in jail and prison.

[b]Held in a private facility.

Source: *Prisoners in 1997*, Bureau of Justice Statistics, Washington, DC, 1998

of rated capacity). (See below for rated capacity.) Even though jail admissions increased 7.4 percent over a three-year period, by 1994, only 35 percent of the jail administrators thought their facilities were overcrowded. The building of new jail facilities had alleviated the problems.

Capital budgets for jail construction more than doubled during the period 1990 to 1992, compared to the years from 1987 to 1989. From 1987 to 1989, jails added an average of 159 new beds to their facilities, compared to 220 new beds from 1990 to

1992. In 1997, over 12,000 new beds were added to the nation's jails. Approximately 9,000 beds were in new facilities, and more than 3,200 were added through renovation of or new additions to existing facilities. As of January 1, 1998, 7,411 more beds were planned. Jail crowding has been eased at some jails because of the imposition of maximum capacities by the courts, establishment of weekend sentences, implementation of alternative sanctions, and other approaches.

The survey asked the administrators at the 103 jails (35 percent) with crowded conditions what factors had contributed to their problems. The administrators considered arrests for drug offenses, arrests for violent crimes, probation and parole violators, length of jail sentences, and incarceration for persons convicted of felonies as major factors. More than half saw arrests for drug possession and drug sales as major contributors to jail crowding. (See Table 3.6.)

PROBLEMS DUE TO INCREASED NUMBERS

Harsher penalties for crimes such as driving under the influence and failure to pay child support have also helped increase the numbers of inmates in the nation's jails. In addition, many jails are housing more hardened criminals than previously. The warehousing of federal and state prisoners has not only led to an overcrowding in many jails, but also added security issues because these prisoners are more hard-core and often afflicted with drug abuse or mental health problems. Dean Moser of the National Sheriffs' Association, in an interview in the *New York Times,* commented that "You're seeing a very volatile situation. It's almost like a pressure valve in [the jails]. You're taking a county jail that was meant for 12-month sentences and less and you're making it into a prison setting."

JUVENILES IN JAIL

On June 30, 1998, an estimated 8,090 persons under age 18 were housed in adult jails (Table 3.3). Approximately 8 of 10 of these juveniles had been convicted or were being held for trial as adults in

TABLE 3.6
Factors Associated with Jail Crowding
(N = 103)

	Percent of Respondents		
Crowding Contributor	Major Contributor	Moderate Contributor	Not a Contributor
Arrests for drug possession	53.0	41.0	6.0
Arrests for drug sales	51.0	43.0	6.0
Arrests for violent crimes	40.0	50.0	10.0
Domestic violence	9.1	59.6	30.3
Insufficent alternative sentence programs	17.8	34.7	43.6
Insufficient pretrial release options	21.8	33.7	41.6
Jail incarceration for persons convicted of felonies	30.3	42.4	22.2
Lack of community alternatives for mentally ill	15.2	43.4	36.4
Length of sentences to jail	23.2	45.5	28.3
Mandatory jail sentences for driving while intoxicated	24.2	40.4	31.3
Parole violations	24.0	48.0	27.0
Prison system delay in accepting convicted felons	34.7	19.8	38.6
Probation violations	29.0	55.0	16.0

Source: *National Assessment Program: 1994 Results*, National Institute of Justice, Washington, DC, 1995

criminal court. Most states define a juvenile as a person under age 18 subject to juvenile court jurisdiction, but exceptions can be made, usually depending on the severity of the offense or the offender's criminal history.

LARGEST JAIL JURISDICTIONS

In 1998, the country's 25 largest jail jurisdictions accounted for 27 percent of all jail inmates. On June 30, 1998, the 25 largest jurisdictions held 157,098 inmates, an increase of 3,673 (2 percent) from a year earlier. Eighteen jurisdictions reported increases in their populations; 7 reported decreases. (See Table 3.7.)

These large jail systems were in 12 states: California (7), Florida (5), Texas (4), and 1 each in New York, Illinois, Louisiana, Tennessee, Arizona, Pennsylvania, Georgia, Maryland, and Wisconsin. (See Table 3.7.) New York City's system, with 15 institutions, had the largest number of facilities. The two jurisdictions with the most inmates, Los Angeles County and New York City, together held more than 38,900 inmates or 7 percent of the national total. San Bernardino County (Los Angeles metropolitan area), California (up 37.5 percent), Orange County (Orlando),

Florida (up 13.3 percent), and Broward County (Fort Lauderdale), Florida (up 12.5 percent) reported the largest increases among the 25 largest jail jurisdictions. The four jurisdictions reporting the largest declines were Bexar County (San Antonio), Texas (down 8.6 percent); Harris County (Houston), Texas (down 7.7 percent); and Fulton County (Atlanta), Georgia; and Dade County (Miami), Florida (each down 3.9 percent).

RATED CAPACITY

Rated capacity is the maximum number of beds or inmates allocated by state or local rating officials to each jail facility. At midyear 1998, the rated capacity of the nation's local jails was 612,780, with an occupancy rate of 97 percent. (See Table 3.8 and Figure 3.1.) As a ratio of all inmates housed in jail facilities to total capacity, the percentage occupied decreased by 12 percentage points from 1990 to 1996. However, since 1996, the growth in inmate population has been greater than the growth in jail capacity. From July 1, 1996 to June 30, 1998, the local jail population increased approximately 73,970, while capacity rose by 49,809 beds.

Jail jurisdictions with the largest average daily populations reported the highest occupancy rates. At midyear 1998, occupancy was 103 percent of rated capacity in jail jurisdictions with an average daily population of 1,000 or more inmates, compared to 77 percent in small jails with fewer than 50 inmates. (See Table 3.9.) In fact, most jails with fewer than 1,000 prisoners were below capacity. According to the Criminal Justice Institute (*The Corrections Yearbook — 1998*, see above), the average rated capacity of jails in 1998 was 105.2 percent, with Newport News, Virginia, having the highest rated capacity (234.3 percent) and Palm Beach, Florida, the lowest (44.8 percent).

TABLE 3.7

The 25 largest local jail jurisdictions: Number of inmates held, average daily population, and rated capacity, midyear 1996-98

Jurisdiction	Number of inmates held[a]			Average daily population[b]			Rated capacity[c]			Percent of capacity occupied at midyear[d]		
	1996	1997	1998	1996	1997	1998	1996	1997	1998	1996	1997	1998
Los Angeles County, CA	18,627	21,962	21,268	18,167	19,931	21,136	20,099	21,416	21,366	93%	103%	100%
New York City, NY	19,890	17,528	17,680	18,382	19,205	17,524	20,862	22,634	22,584	95	77	78
Cook County, IL	8,713	9,189	9,321	9,169	9,100	9,297	9,617	9,376	9,776	91	98	95
Dade County, FL	6,357	7,320	7,036	6,499	7,157	7,836	6,387	6,237	6,005	100	117	117
Harris County, TX	7,703	8,224	7,587	7,140	8,153	7,781	8,698	8,657	8,657	89	95	88
Dallas County, TX	6,380	6,439	6,941	5,862	6,528	7,000	8,374	8,182	8,182	76%	79%	85%
Maricopa County, AZ	5,679	6,732	7,019	5,542	6,520	6,910	6,252	6,252	6,252	91	108	112
Orleans Parish, LA	5,368	6,537	6,670	5,433	6,270	6,398	7,174	7,174	7,174	75	91	93
Philadelphia County, PA	5,695	5,563	5,990	5,341	5,600	5,753	5,600	5,600	6,179	102	99	97
San Diego County, CA	5,549	5,709	6,040	5,522	5,588	5,745	4,653	5,539	5,815	119	103	104
Shelby County, TN	5,264	5,568	5,808	5,153	5,297	5,627	6,364	6,532	6,583	83%	85%	88%
Orange County, CA	5,326	5,368	5,546	5,143	5,246	5,374	3,821	3,821	3,821	139	140	145
San Bernardino County, CA	3,958	4,156	5,713	4,119	4,500	5,103	4,957	5,000	5,000	80	83	114
Santa Clara County, CA	4,213	4,588	4,658	4,314	4,317	4,722	3,774	3,774	3,774	112	122	123
Broward County, FL	3,528	4,125	4,640	3,470	4,129	4,289	3,656	3,736	3,756	96	110	124
Fulton County, GA	2,489	3,982	3,827	2,395	3,401	4,276	2,320	2,987	2,987	107%	133%	128%
Alameda County, CA	3,994	4,098	4,164	3,954	4,109	3,823	4,264	4,218	4,590	94	97	91
Baltimore City, MD	3,309	3,598	3,881	3,300	3,636	3,791	2,933	2,933	2,966	113	123	131
Orange County, FL	3,120	3,411	3,865	3,332	3,321	3,547	3,329	3,234	3,234	94	105	120
Tarrant County, TX	2,881	3,366	3,572	2,876	3,291	3,529	4,193	4,193	4,739	69	80	75
Sacramento County, CA	3,093	3,505	3,654	3,217	3,329	3,507	3,700	3,871	3,871	84%	91%	94%
Bexar County, TX	3,058	3,683	3,368	2,821	3,491	3,398	3,640	3,670	3,670	84	100	92
Hillsborough County, FL	2,661	3,155	3,101	2,679	2,973	3,062	2,757	2,877	2,909	97	110	107
Milwaukee County, WI	2,653	2,876	2,850	2,695	2,757	2,918	2,274	2,274	2,466	117	126	116
Duval County, FL	2,384	2,743	2,899	2,473	2,687	2,755	3,300	3,100	3,000	72	88	97

Note: Jurisdictions are ordered by their average daily population in 1998.
[a]Number of inmates held in jail facilities.
[b]Based on the average daily population for the year ending June 30. The average daily population is the sum of the number of inmates in jail each day for a year, divided by the number of days in the year.
[c]Rated capacity is the number of beds or inmates assigned by a rating official to facilities within each jurisdiction.
[d]The number of inmates divided by the rated capacity multiplied by 100.

Source: Darrell K. Gilliard, *Prison and Jail Inmates at Midyear 1998*, Bureau of Justice Statistics, Washington, DC, 1999

Renting out Space

The building boom in the construction of private and local prisons and jails has alleviated the overcrowding in many jurisdictions. In fact, some systems have too many beds and are advertising to house inmates from other areas for a fee. With a $3 billion building program for prisons providing more than 150,000 beds, many local jails had empty beds for rent. By 1996, more than 10 states had contracted with county and private jails in Texas to take their inmates, with 13 Texas counties housing out-of-state prisoners.

Although more than 3,700 out-of-state inmates had already been sent to Texas, the state still had another 12,800 beds empty. (By 1997, 5,500 out-of-state inmates resided in Texas jails.) Costs ranged from $37 to $75 per inmate per day, depending on the programs offered by the jail and the special needs of the inmates. In an interview in the *Dallas Morning News*, Andy Kahan, Houston's crime victims' service coordinator, commented that "it's ironic that we go from having no space to being Motel 6.... We're becoming the leading importer of convicted felons in the nation." However, that may be changing.

Negative Spotlight on Texas Jails

In 1997, a videotape used to train Texas prison guards was discovered. In the year-old tape, guards were shown kicking Missouri inmates, using a stun gun, and commanding dogs to bite the prisoners. As a result, Missouri cancelled its contract with Texas and brought 415 prisoners back to Missouri. This was not the first time out-of-state prisoners

TABLE 3.8
Rated capacity of local jails and percent of capacity occupied, 1990-98

Year	Rated capacity[a]	Amount of capacity added[b]	Percent of capacity occupied[c]
1998	612,780	26,216	97%
1997	586,564	23,593	97
1996	562,971	17,208	92
1995	545,763	41,439	93
1994	504,324	29,100	96%
1993	475,224	26,027	97
1992	449,197	27,960	99
1991	421,237	32,066	101
1990	389,171	21,402	104
Average annual increase, 6/30/90-6/30/98	5.8%	30,626	--

Note: Capacity data for 1990-92 and 1994-98 are survey estimates subject to sampling error. See the appendix table for sampling errors.
--Not available.
[a]Rated capacity is the number of beds or inmates assigned by a rating official to facilities within each jurisdiction.
[b]The number of beds added during the 12 months before June 30 of each year.
[c]The number of inmates divided by the rated capacity times 100. For 1990-93 the ratio may include some inmates under supervision who were not confined in a jail facility. For 1994-98 the ratio includes only those held in jail.

FIGURE 3.1

Local jails
(primarily holding unconvicted persons and those with a sentence of a year or less)

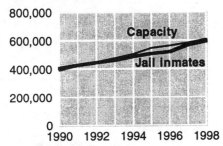

Source of table and figure: Darrell K. Gilliard, *Prison and Jail Inmates at Midyear 1998*, Bureau of Justice Statistics, Washington, DC, 1999

TABLE 3.9
Jail occupancy as a percent of capacity

Size of jurisdiction*	Percent of capacity occupied
Total	97%
Fewer than 50 inmates	77%
50-99	86
100-249	93
250-499	99
500-999	94
1,000 or more	103

*Based on the average daily population in the year ending June 30, 1998

Source: Darrell K. Gilliard, *Prison and Jail Inmates at Midyear 1998*, Bureau of Justice Statistics, Washington, DC, 1999

A privately run Texas facility, which housed Montana and Hawaii inmates, is also under investigation. Prisoners in this facility complained about strip searches and the guards' use of warning gun shots when giving orders. Inadequate food, medical care, and counseling services were also found at the prison. State correction officials deny charges of abuse and poorer living conditions in Texas jails than those in other states. They point out that jails are designed for shorter stays than prisons and, therefore, have fewer services and recreational facilities.

Some out-of-state prisoners have filed civil-rights lawsuits because they are serving their time out-of-state, which can make access to their families and attorneys far more difficult. In addition, at least one Missouri inmate filed a civil lawsuit asking $100,000 in damages for being kicked by guards and bitten by a jail dog.

INMATE CHARACTERISTICS

Over the past decade, about 9 of 10 prisoners have been male. (See Table 3.10.) An estimated 1 in every 185 adult men and 1 in every 1,626 adult women were held in local jails on June 30, 1998.

Most local jail inmates were minorities. At midyear 1998, non-Hispanic Whites made up 41.3 percent of the jail population; non-Hispanic Blacks, 41.2 percent; Hispanics, 15.5 percent; and other races

were brought back to their home states. Oklahoma took back its prisoners after complaints about the overuse of pepper spray.

TABLE 3.10

Sex, race, and Hispanic origin of local jail inmates, midyear 1990-98

Characteristic	Percent of jail inmates								
	1990	1991	1992	1993	1994	1995	1996[a]	1997	1998
Total	100 %	100 %	100 %	100 %	100 %	100 %	100 %	100 %	100 %
Sex									
Male	90.8%	90.7%	90.8%	90.4%	90.0%	89.8%	89.2%	89.4%	89.2%
Female	9.2	9.3	9.2	9.6	10.0	10.2	10.8	10.6	10.8
Race/Hispanic origin[b]									
White, non-Hispanic	41.8%	41.1%	40.1%	39.3%	39.1%	40.1%	41.6%	40.6%	41.3%
Black, non-Hispanic	42.5	43.4	44.1	44.2	43.9	43.5	41.1	42.0	41.2
Hispanic	14.3	14.2	14.5	15.1	15.4	14.7	15.6	15.7	15.5
Other[c]	1.3	1.2	1.3	1.3	1.6	1.7	1.7	1.8	2.0

Note: Detail may not add to total because of rounding.
[a]Data for 1996 were based on all persons under jail supervision.
[b]Data on race/Hispanic origin were reported for 89.7% of all inmates in 1990, 91.1% in 1991, 97.6% in 1992, 85.1% in 1993, 95.8% in 1994, 97.1% in 1995, 99.3% in 1996-97, and 99.6% in 1998.
[c]Includes American Indians, Alaska Natives, Asians, and Pacific Islanders.

Source: Darrell K. Gilliard, *Prison and Jail Inmates at Midyear 1998*, Bureau of Justice Statistics, Washington, DC, 1999

(Asians, Pacific Islanders, American Indians, and Alaska Natives), 2 percent per 100,000 U.S. residents of each racial/ethnic group (Table 3.10). Non-Hispanic Blacks were six times more likely than non-Hispanic Whites, over twice as likely as Hispanics, and almost eight times more likely than persons of other races to have been held in a local jail on June 30, 1998. (See Table 3.11.)

Adult Conviction Status

On June 30, 1998, fewer than half (43 percent) of all adults under supervision by jail authorities had been convicted of their current charges. Convicted inmates included those awaiting sentencing, serving a sentence, or returned to jail for a violation of pro-

bation or parole. (See Table 3.12.)

CONFINEMENT STATUS

In 1995, for the first time, the *Annual Survey of Jails* (Bureau of Justice Statistics, Washington, DC) obtained the count of the number of offenders under community supervision. Respondents were asked if their jail jurisdictions operated any community-based programs and how many persons participated in them.

Among persons under community supervision by jail staff in 1998, about one-third (34 percent) were required to perform community service (17,518) or to participate in an alternative work program (7,089). Nearly 1 in 4 was in a weekend reporting program (17,249). About 5,702 offenders under jail supervision were in drug, alcohol, mental health, or other medical treatment programs. Another 10,827 offenders were under home detention using electronic monitoring. (See Table 3.13.)

PRIVATIZATION OF JAILS

One suggestion to solve the overcrowding of jails has been to allow the private sector to construct, ad-

TABLE 3.11

Racial characteristics of jail inmates, June 30, 1998

	Estimated count	Per 100,000 residents in each group
Total	592,500	219
White*	244,900	125
Black*	244,000	747
Hispanic	91,800	302
Other	11,800	100

Note: Inmate counts were estimated and rounded to the nearest 100.
*Non-Hispanic only.

TABLE 3.12

Over half of adult jail inmates were awaiting trial

	Number of adult jail inmates, midyear 1998
Total	584,372
Convicted	252,600
Male	224,700
Female	27,900
Unconvicted	331,800
Male	295,900
Female	35,900

Note: Detail may not add to total because of rounding.

Source of both tables: Darrell K. Gilliard, *Prison and Jail Inmates at Midyear 1998*, Bureau of Justice Statistics, Washington, DC, 1999

minister, and operate jails. In "Private Jails: Locking Down the Issues" (*American Jails*, vol. 11, no. 1, March/April 1997), Dale K. Sechrest and David Shichor found that proponents of privatization believe that by following profit motives, private companies can perform most services cheaper and more effectively than the public sector. They point out that private companies can pay less for products and supplies because they do not have to deal with long-term contracts like the government does. Supporters of privatization believe that private companies are better at management and at budgeting and accounting for expenditures than civil service employees. They also feel that competition with the public sector will encourage government employees to work harder and perform their jobs better.

Those who oppose privatization, according to Sechrest and Shichor, believe that cost-savings have not yet been proved, and fear that cost-cutting may lead to substandard goods and services. They also voice concern over the issue of private companies finding qualified employees or using a smaller and less qualified workforce to make a profit. They point out that poorly qualified and underpaid staff can lead to a large turnover, and a stable workforce is necessary to maintain order and security in a facility that may house difficult and sometimes violent inmates, those with mental problems, and drug addicts.

There is also the issue of control. The public has elected the sheriffs. They are responsible for dispensing punishment, keeping the public safe, acting in accordance with local laws and regulations, taking legal responsibility for running the facility properly, and using deadly force when necessary. Opponents of privatization wonder how much power the government would allow a private corporation to use in order to run the jail and how private performance would be monitored. Finally, a sheriff's department that relies on private jail management must have proper backup to take charge in an emergency situation where the use of deadly force may be required.

Privatization of Health Care

In *Estelle v. Gamble* (429 U.S. 97, 1976), the Supreme Court ruled that inmates had a constitutional right to adequate health services. To improve the health services, jail authorities turned to contract services. Although part-time doctors and dentists had already been used by jails, contracting with private firms for more health services was controversial. Opponents feared that for-profit firms would not deliver quality service. Administrators were afraid of having less control without losing the responsibility and liability. Supporters of privatization thought that the system would have better staff and would be able to retain the staff, the jails could transfer legal liability to the firms, and the budget would be fixed. The generally accepted opinion arising from various court cases is that, while jail systems may lessen their liability, they cannot contract it away to private firms.

As long ago as 1973, Rikers Island (New York) contracted with Montefiore Hospital to provide all health services (except psychiatric, dental, and some other services not available at Montefiore). In 1978,

---

TABLE 3.13

Persons under jail supervision, by confinement status and type of program, midyear 1995-98

Confinement status and type of program	Number of persons under jail supervision			
	1995	1996	1997	1998
Total	541,913	591,469	637,319	664,847
Held in jail	507,044	518,492	567,079	592,462
Supervised outside a jail facility[a]	34,869	72,977	70,239	72,385
Electronic monitoring	6,788	7,480	8,699	10,827
Home detention[b]	1,376	907	1,164	370
Day reporting	1,283	3,298	2,768	3,089
Community service	10,253	17,410	15,918	17,518
Weekender programs	1,909	16,336	17,656	17,249
Other pretrial supervision	3,229	2,135	7,368	6,048
Other work programs[c]	9,144	14,469	6,631	7,089
Treatment programs[d]	--	10,425	6,693	5,702
Other	887	517	3,342	4,493

--Not available.
[a]Excludes persons supervised by a probation or parole agency.
[b]Includes only those without electronic monitoring.
[c]Includes persons in work release programs, work gangs/crews, and other work alternative programs administered by the jail jurisdiction.
[d]Includes persons under drug, alcohol, mental health, and other medical treatment.

Source: Darrell K. Gilliard, *Prison and Jail Inmates at Midyear 1998*, Bureau of Justice Statistics, Washington, DC, 1999

Delaware County and Baltimore City also contracted out their health services. By the mid-1990s, 110 jails in 25 states with an average inmate population of 86,950 had contracted out medical services.

A major reason for contracting health services is to save money. Appropriated funds are often scattered among various departments before privatization, so jail authorities have no accurate way of knowing the exact costs of health care before privatization. Since privatization often causes a change in the number of services offered to meet higher standards, it makes it harder to compare costs.

In "Privatization of Jail Health Care Services: The First Twenty Years" (*American Jails,* January/February 1995), Barbara Cotton concluded that the saying holds true that one gets what one pays for and that contracting for services is only one option and must fit the needs of the situation. She believes that the "delivery of inmate health services is and must be a team effort, a partnership of health services" and contract services and that "competition had had a positive influence on inmate health services."

PAYING FOR SERVICES

Jails in some jurisdictions are now requiring their inmates to pay for their room and board and health care. According to the National Institute of Corrections (*Fees Paid by Jail Inmates: Findings from the Nation's Largest Jails*, U.S. Department of Justice, Longmont, Colorado, 1997), at least 41 states have passed legislation authorizing assessment of inmate fees for jail services and operations. The legislation most often identifies specific functions for which fees can be collected, such as room and board, medical services, or programs. (See Table 3.14 for the statutory authority for jail fees in each state.)

In November 1996, the National Institute of Corrections distributed surveys to more than 130 of the largest jails, with a response rate of 77 percent. About 16 jails had inmate populations of

2,500 or greater; 7 had populations of fewer than 250 inmates. Fees were imposed in four major areas:

- Medical services — collecting co-payments or other fees for medical care.

- Per diem fees — requiring jail inmates to reimburse the county for all or a portion of their daily incarceration costs, including housing, food, and basic programs.

- Other non-program functions — charging for services such as bonding, telephone use, haircuts, release escort, and drug testing.

- Participation in programs — imposing a fee or collecting a portion of any compensation earned by inmates in programs, such as work release, weekend incarceration, and electronic monitoring; or charging for participation in rehabilitation programs, such as education or substance abuse treatment.

More than three-quarters of the agencies surveyed charged fees for one or more programs and/or services or are implementing systems for doing so. At least seven jails initiated fees-for-services operations in 1996 or 1997. Inmates are most commonly charged fees for medical care (56 agencies) and participation in work release programs (46 agencies). Most jails charging inmates fees impose them for more than one service or function, although 13 agencies in the survey sample charge inmate fees only for medical services.

Major functions generating the most revenues in 1996 included telephone services (averaging $54,400 per year), work release programs (averaging $230,500 per year), and home detention programs (averaging $161,000 annually).

Medical Services

Fees for medical services ranged from $3 to $15 for each medical visit. The most common fee amount was $3. Most jails used a scale on which cost is determined by type of treatment. For ex-

TABLE 3.14

Statutes on Charging Fees to Jail Inmates

	Statutes Provide Authority to Charge Fees For:					No Statutory Authority Indicated
	General costs of incarceration	Medical services	Per diem	Specific programs	Other specific functions	
Alabama[1]	(Legislation is specific to individual counties; intent varies)					
Alaska	(No data available)					
Arizona		✔				
Arkansas						✔
California		✔	✔	✔	✔	
Colorado				✔		
Connecticut	✔					
Delaware		✔				
D.C.						✔
Florida		✔	✔	✔		
Georgia		✔				
Hawaii		✔		✔		
Idaho		✔				
Illinois[1]		✔	✔			
Indiana[1]		✔				
Iowa			✔			
Kansas				✔		
Kentucky		✔		✔		
Louisiana	(No data available)					
Maine		✔				
Maryland		✔				
Massachusetts						✔
Michigan		✔	✔			
Minnesota		✔				
Mississippi		✔				
Missouri		✔		✔		
Montana		✔	✔			
Nebraska				✔		
Nevada		✔	✔			
New Hampshire		✔	✔	✔		
New Jersey		✔		✔		
New Mexico						✔
New York						✔[2]
North Carolina		✔	✔			
North Dakota				✔		
Ohio		✔	✔		✔	
Oklahoma[1]		✔	✔			
Oregon		✔		✔		
Pennsylvania						✔
Rhode Island		✔	✔	✔	✔	
South Carolina		✔				
South Dakota		✔	✔	✔	✔	
Tennessee		✔				
Texas		✔	✔	✔		
Utah						✔
Vermont						✔
Virginia		✔		✔		
Washington	✔					
West Virginia[1]		✔				
Wisconsin		✔	✔	✔		
Wyoming		✔	✔		✔	
United States Code						✔

1. Statutory data for these states was supplemented by information from the National Conference of State Legislatures ("Selected Laws on Offender Fees," January 1997).
2. Jail standards in New York permit the charging of a per diem fee for work release participation; statutes permit payment of medical charges by third-party insurance.

Source: *Fees Paid by Jail Inmates: Findings from the Nation's Largest Jails*, National Institute of Corrections, Longmont, CO, 1997

ample, a jail might charge $6 for care from a nurse or physician's assistant, $20 to see a doctor, and $12 for a dental exam. Annual revenues from medical fees tended to be modest ($22,800 average annual revenues). This reflects the fact that, in most cases, medical fees were charged to control the numbers of visits rather than cover or offset expenses.

Impact of Medical Fees

Three-quarters of the agencies that collected medical fees found that inmates' use of medical services had declined since the fees were begun. Most of these declines were attributed to reductions in inmates' frivolous medical requests. As one respondent commented, "The demand for sick call has been greatly reduced, as fewer inmates are using this avenue as a way to get out of their cells for a couple of hours." Laramie County, Wyoming, officials noted that medical co-pay requirements have cut sick calls by two-thirds.

Care for Indigent Inmates

Seventeen agencies disregarded the medical fee for inmates who could not pay. In 32 jurisdictions, staff debited the inmates' accounts, creating a negative balance, and collected the fees if additional funds were received. Some jurisdictions maintained these records after the inmate was released and collected the funds if the inmate was rebooked into the jail.

Per Diem Fees

Thirteen jails in the survey charged inmates all or a portion of the daily cost of their incarceration. Since the expense of housing and caring for prisoners has traditionally been viewed as a public responsibility, charging inmates is somewhat controversial. Sixteen states have enacted laws that specifically authorize jails to charge inmates for all or a portion of the county's actual costs of room and board. Statutes in two other states authorize fees to offset "general costs of incarceration."

Ability to pay is considered in most state laws that authorize charging inmates for costs of incarceration. A Texas statute, effective September 1997, provides that if the county and inmate do not agree on the amount of the inmate's liability, either may file a civil action in a district court to determine the amount of liability. Under Florida's 1996 statute (see below), the local jail determines the financial status of inmates based on their income, assets, and obligations.

Per diem fees charged ranged from a token $2 per day in Palm Beach to the substantial $60 per day in Oakland County (Pontiac), Michigan. Annual revenues from per diem charges ranged from $3,000 in Wayne County (Detroit metropolitan area), Michigan, to $4.9 million in Pierce County (Tacoma), Washington. Average revenues, excluding the dramatically higher Pierce County figure, were $125,000.

Florida

In 1996, Florida passed a law (Florida Statute 951.033) allowing county jails to charge inmates for daily room and board (*American Jails*, Susan W. McCampbell, "Room with a View, at a Price," *American Jails*, March/April 1997). Officials must consider the prisoners' ability to pay and establish a process by which inmates can show reasons why they cannot pay the fees. In August 1996, jail inmates in Broward County (Fort Lauderdale), Florida, began paying $2.00 a day for their room and board and a $10.00 fee for processing.

On October 21, 1996, a class action lawsuit was filed against the sheriff's office to overturn the state law and prevent the county from collecting any more fees. The lawsuit claims that the procedures are illegal because inmates who have not been convicted are being charged and that poor inmates also must pay the fee. At the time the lawsuit was filed, no other Florida jails had implemented these fees. Jail officials in many states, however, have requested information from Broward County. In 1999, according to the General Legal Section of the

Florida Attorney General's office, the class action lawsuit was still in litigation.

JAIL INDUSTRIES

The National Institute of Justice defines a jail industry as one that uses inmate labor to create a product or provide a service that has value to a public or private client and for which the inmates receive compensation, whether it be pay, privileges, or other benefits. This definition describes a variety of activities. If a convict cuts the grass in front of the jail and thereby earns permission to watch television an extra hour, the elements of labor, service provision, value, and compensation are all present. At the other end are those jail inmates who work for private sector industry and earn real dollars.

Jail officials hoped these programs would develop inmate work habits and skills, generate revenues or reduce costs for the county, reduce inmate idleness, and meet needs in the community. The 1984 Justice Assistance Act (PL 98-473) removed some of the long-standing restrictions on interstate commerce of prisoner-made goods, thereby opening new opportunities for prison labor to work for the private sector. Both state prisons and county jails have entered into private-sector work programs.

In most programs, inmates receive no or low wages. Their work often serves the public sector, and they are usually credited with "good time." Thus the offenders pay for their crimes with public service labor, and their early release makes scarce bed space available for other offenders.

The Future

The future of jail work and industries programs is bright, according to Rod Miller in "Inmate Labor in the 21st Century: You Ain't Seen Nothin' Yet" (*American Jails*, vol. 11, no. 1, March/April 1997). He sees a gradual shift toward inmate labor as the public and the private sector turn to the inmate workforce because of cost-savings and the demand that inmates work rather than be idle.

Miller predicts pretrial detainees will be put to work while sentenced offenders work away from jail. Inmates will be involved in more diverse work projects, including high-tech projects using computers, telephones, and the Internet, which may prepare them for finding jobs after they complete their sentences. Some work will be performed 24 hours per day, seven days per week. Facility kitchens, for example, will produce goods and services for customers outside the facility.

Work assignments and activities will be related to an inmate's education and training. Eligibility for preferred programs will be based on completion of educational programs and treatment plans. Jails will begin to consider post-confinement job performance by providing employment-related programs to inmates prior to their release.

New Challenges

As the jail workforce grows, opponents and proponents of inmate work and industry programs will watch developments closely. Managers will be more accountable for the programs, and many work programs will be under pressure to become profitable, or at least self-sufficient. Inmates will raise issues with the courts including job classification, work assignments, working conditions, discipline, removal from work assignments, and fairness of work opportunities. There may be conflicts with "work-fare" programs set up for welfare recipients. Some of the welfare and jail programs and activities will overlap.

CHAPTER IV

PRISONS AND PRISONERS — AN INCREASING NUMBER

In my experience, prisons and jails fill up as fast as they are built. — Judge Braxton Kittree, Mobile, Alabama, 1990

SENTENCING

State courts convicted 997,970 felons during 1996 (year of the most recent data), and one-third of the convictions was for drug offenses. Seventeen percent of those convicted of a felony in state courts were sentenced for committing a violent offense; 30 percent for property offenses of burglary, larceny, fraud, and forgery; 34.5 percent for drug offenses; and 3 percent for weapons offenses. (See Table 4.1.)

More Than Four in Ten Convicted Felons Went to Prison

In 1996, 69 percent of all convicted felons were sentenced to a period of confinement — 31 percent were sentenced to local jails, usually for a year or less, and 38 percent were sentenced to prisons. The remaining 31 percent were sentenced to probation with no jail or prison time to serve (Table 4.2). Felons sentenced to state prisons in 1996 were sentenced to an average of just over five years.

The mean (average) prison sentence for murder was about 21.5 years. (See Table 4.3.) Among persons convicted of murder or nonnegligent manslaughter, 26 percent were sentenced to life in prison and 2 percent were sentenced to death. As of June 30, 1998, more than 1.8 million U.S. residents were incarcerated in a jail or prison.

TABLE 4.1

Number of felony convictions in State courts, by offense and type of conviction, 1996

Most serious conviction offense	Number of felons convicted by —				
	Total	Trial			Guilty plea
		Total	Jury	Bench	
All offenses	997,970	92,015	37,541	54,474	905,957
Violent offenses	167,824	29,319	17,671	11,648	138,508
Murder[a]	11,430	5,298	4,519	780	6,133
Sexual assault[b]	30,057	5,568	3,414	2,154	24,489
Robbery	42,831	6,985	4,128	2,858	35,844
Aggravated assault	69,522	9,390	4,653	4,737	60,134
Other violent[c]	13,984	2,077	958	1,119	11,908
Property offenses	298,631	19,380	5,536	13,844	279,251
Burglary	93,197	7,282	2,705	4,577	85,915
Larceny[d]	123,201	7,327	2,155	5,172	115,874
Fraud[e]	82,233	4,771	676	4,095	77,462
Drug offenses	347,774	28,587	9,843	18,744	319,185
Possession	135,270	12,228	2,908	9,321	123,040
Trafficking	212,504	16,359	6,935	9,424	196,145
Weapons offenses	33,337	2,880	1,217	1,663	30,456
Other offenses[f]	150,404	11,849	3,274	8,575	138,557

Note: Detail may not add to the total because of rounding.
Data on type of conviction were available for 629,593 cases.
Table includes estimates for cases missing a designation of type of conviction.
[a]Includes nonnegligent manslaughter.
[b]Includes rape.
[c]Includes offenses such as negligent manslaughter and kidnaping.
[d]Includes motor vehicle theft.
[e]Includes forgery and embezzlement.
[f]Composed of nonviolent offenses such as receiving stolen property and vandalism.

Source: Jodi M. Brown, Patrick A. Langan, and David J. Levin, *Felony Sentences in State Courts, 1996*, Bureau of Justice Statistics, Washington, DC, 1999

PRISON POPULATION PASSES 1.2 MILLION

On December 31, 1997, over 1.2 million men and women were incarcerated in state and federal correctional institutions. State jurisdictions held 1,131,581 inmates, and federal institutions housed 112,973. (See Table 4.4 and Figure 4.1.) The prisoner population grew 5.2 percent in 1997, somewhat less than the average annual growth of 7 percent since 1990. (See Table 4.5.) The 1997 increase was the equivalent of 1,177 more inmates per week.

In 1997, the incarceration rate of state prisoners sentenced to more than a year reached a record 410 prisoners per 100,000 U.S. residents, up sharply from 272 per 100,000 in 1990. The number of sentenced federal prisoners per 100,000 U.S. residents increased from 20 in 1990 to 35 in 1997. (See Table 4.4.) As of June 30, 1998, the total incarceration rate for state and federal inmates held in prisons and jails was 668 inmates per 100,000 U.S. residents, more than double the rate incarcerated in 1985 (313 per 100,000). (See Chapter III, Table 3.1.) That meant that 1 in every 150 U.S. residents were incarcerated.

Reasons for Growth

Factors underlying the growth in state prison population between 1990 and 1996 (year of the latest data available) include

- A 43 percent increase among sentenced males and a 65 percent increase among sentenced females per 100,000 U.S. residents.

- A 66 percent increase in rates among persons ages 35 to 39, a 75 percent increase for those

ages 40 to 44, and a 71 percent increase for those persons ages 45 to 54 years.

Sources of Population Growth Among State Inmates

- Violent offenders accounted for most of the growth from 1990 to 1996 among males (52 percent) and among all racial and ethnic groups — Whites (46 percent), Blacks (50 percent), and Hispanics (54 percent).

- A sharp rise in violent offenders among White inmates accounted for 42 percent of the 10-year increase in White prisoners. The rise in drug offenders among Black inmates accounted for 42 percent of their increase.

TABLE 4.2

Types of felony sentences imposed by State courts, by offense, 1996

Most serious conviction offense	Total	Percent of felons sentenced to —			
		Incarceration			Probation
		Total	Prison	Jail	
All offenses	100%	69%	38%	31%	31%
Violent offenses	100%	79%	57%	22%	21%
Murder[a]	100	95	92	3	5
Sexual assault[b]	100	79	63	16	21
Robbery	100	87	73	14	13
Aggravated assault	100	72	42	30	28
Other violent[c]	100	73	38	34	27
Property offenses	100%	62%	34%	28%	38%
Burglary	100	71	45	26	29
Larceny[d]	100	63	31	32	37
Fraud[e]	100	50	26	24	50
Drug offenses	100%	72%	35%	37%	28%
Possession	100	70	29	41	30
Trafficking	100	73	39	33	27
Weapons offenses	100%	67%	40%	27%	33%
Other offenses[f]	100%	63%	31%	32%	37%

Note: For persons receiving a combination of sentences, the sentence designation came from the most severe penalty imposed — prison being the most severe, followed by jail, then probation. Prison includes death sentences. Data on sentence type were available for 997,906 cases.
[a]Includes nonnegligent manslaughter.
[b]Includes rape.
[c]Includes offenses such as negligent manslaughter and kidnaping.
[d]Includes motor vehicle theft.
[e]Includes forgery and embezzlement.
[f]Composed of nonviolent offenses such as receiving stolen property and vandalism.

Source: Jodi M. Brown, Patrick A. Langan, and David J. Levin, *Felony Sentences in State Courts, 1996*, Bureau of Justice Statistics, Washington, DC, 1999

31

- Drug offenders accounted for 30 percent of the growth among Blacks, 23 percent among Hispanics, and 16 percent among Whites.

- Drug offenders were the greatest source of growth for female prisoners (45 percent of the total increase).

The incarceration rate (prisoners per 100,000 U.S. residents) has continued to increase despite the decrease in crime. The major explanation for this rise in the number of prisoners while the crime rate decreased since 1992 is that the largest increase in incarceration is due to the sale and possession of drugs. In 1997, Professor Blumstein, a professor of criminology at Carnegie-Mellon University, estimated that drug offenders accounted for about half the growth in the prison population in the past decade.

STATES WITH THE MOST PRISONERS

In 1997, two states, California (157,547) and Texas (140,729), together accounted for almost 1 in 4 inmates (23.9 percent) in the country. The 10 states with the largest prison populations held 61 percent of the nation's total prison population.

The states with the highest incarceration rates were Texas (717 per 100,000 residents), Louisiana (672), and Oklahoma (617). From 1992 to 1997, the sentenced inmate population in state prisons grew 41.5 percent and in federal prisons, 44.6 percent. During this period, 10 states reported increases of at least 50 percent, led by West Virginia (up 89.5 percent) and Wisconsin (up 79.2 percent). (See Tables 4.6 and 4.7.)

TABLE 4.3

Lengths of felony sentences imposed by State courts, by offense and type of sentence, 1996

Most serious conviction offense	Maximum sentence length in months for felons sentenced to —				
		Incarceration			
	Total	Total	Prison	Jail	Probation
Mean					
All offenses	39 mo	38 mo	62 mo	6 mo	41 mo
Violent offenses	72 mo	78 mo	105 mo	7 mo	48 mo
Murder[a]	241	249	257	8	72
Sexual assault[b]	92	98	120	8	66
Robbery	84	87	101	10	52
Aggravated assault	43	43	69	6	41
Other violent[c]	36	34	59	6	44
Property offenses	33 mo	30 mo	49 mo	6 mo	40 mo
Burglary	43	41	60	6	46
Larceny[d]	27	22	40	6	38
Fraud[e]	31	24	43	5	39
Drug offenses	32 mo	28 mo	51 mo	6 mo	42 mo
Possession	24	20	41	5	37
Trafficking	36	34	55	7	45
Weapons offenses	31 mo	29 mo	45 mo	5 mo	35 mo
Other offenses[f]	30 mo	24 mo	42 mo	6 mo	40 mo
Median					
All offenses	24 mo	16 mo	36 mo	6 mo	36 mo
Violent offenses	36 mo	38 mo	60 mo	6 mo	36 mo
Murder[a]	254	288	300	8	60
Sexual assault[b]	60	60	72	6	60
Robbery	60	60	72	9	60
Aggravated assault	24	23	48	6	36
Other violent[c]	23	12	36	6	36
Property offenses	24 mo	13 mo	36 mo	6 mo	36 mo
Burglary	30	24	48	6	36
Larceny[d]	23	12	24	6	36
Fraud[e]	24	12	30	4	36
Drug offenses	23 mo	12 mo	36 mo	6 mo	36 mo
Possession	12	9	24	5	36
Trafficking	24	16	36	6	36
Weapons offenses	24 mo	16 mo	30 mo	4 mo	36 mo
Other offenses[f]	24 mo	12 mo	32 mo	5 mo	36 mo

Note: Means exclude sentences to death or to life in prison. Sentence length data were available for 997,906 incarceration and probation sentences.
[a]Includes nonnegligent manslaughter.
[b]Includes rape.
[c]Includes offenses such as negligent manslaughter and kidnaping.
[d]Includes motor vehicle theft.
[e]Includes forgery and embezzlement.
[f]Composed of nonviolent offenses such as receiving stolen property and vandalism.

Source: Jodi M. Brown, Patrick A. Langan, and David J. Levin, *Felony Sentences in State Courts, 1996,* Bureau of Justice Statistics, Washington, DC, 1999

TABLE 4.4

Trend in Prison Population, 1990-1997

December 31	Number of inmates		Sentenced prisoners per 100,000 resident population		Population housed as a percent of highest capacity	
	Federal	State	Federal	State	Federal	State
1990	65,526	708,393	20	272	151%	115%
1991	71,608	753,951	22	287	146	116
1992	80,259	802,241	26	305	137	118
1993	89,587	880,857	29	330	136	118
1994	95,034	959,668	30	356	125	117
1995	100,250	1,025,624	32	379	126	114
1996	105,544	1,077,824	33	394	125	116
1997	112,973	1,131,581	35	410	119	115

Source: Darrell K. Gilliard and Alan J. Beck, *Prisoners in 1997*, Bureau of Justice Statistics, Washington, DC, 1998

CHARACTERISTICS OF PRISONERS

Age

In 1997, according to the Criminal Justice Institute (Camille Graham Camp and George M. Camp, *The Corrections Yearbook — 1998*, Middletown, Connecticut, 1998), the average age for admission to prison was 31.2 years of age — males, 30.8; and females, 32.4.

Gender

At midyear 1998, women accounted for 6.4 percent of all prisoners nationwide, up from 5.7 percent in 1990 and 4.1 percent in 1980. In 1997, women accounted for 7.4 percent of the prisoners in Federal Bureau of Prisons custody. At midyear 1998, the rate for inmates serving a sentence of more than 1 year was 866 males per 100,000 U.S. male residents and 55 females per 100,000 U.S. female residents (Table 4.8). On June 30, 1998, 1 in every 185 men and 1 in every 1,626 women were under the jurisdiction of state or federal correctional authorities.

Women

The number of women in state and federal prisons has increased over the last decade. In the 1980s,

FIGURE 4.1

From yearend 1985 to midyear 1998, the number of inmates in the Nation's prisons and jails grew more than 1,058,000, an annual increase of 7.3%

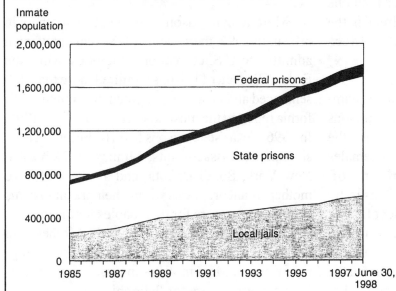

Source: Darrell K. Gilliard, *Prison and Jail Inmates at Midyear 1998*, Bureau of Justice Statistics, Washington, DC, 1999

TABLE 4.5

Change in the State and Federal prison populations, 1990-97

Year	Number of inmates	Annual increase	
		Number	Annual percent change
1990	773,919		
1991	825,559	51,640	6.7%
1992	882,500	56,941	6.9
1993*	970,444	64,992	7.4
1994	1,054,702	84,258	8.7
1995	1,125,874	71,172	6.7
1996	1,183,368	57,494	5.1
1997	1,244,554	61,186	5.2
Average annual increase, 1990-97		63,955	7.0%

Note: All counts are for December 31 of each year and may reflect revisions of previously reported numbers.
*Includes the jurisdiction populations in Massachusetts and Texas for the first time. The 1993 count (947,492), excluding the noncustody population in Texas and Massachusetts, may be used for comparisons.

Source: Darrell K. Gilliard and Alan J. Beck, *Prisoners in 1997*, Bureau of Justice Statistics, Washington, DC, 1998

TABLE 4.6

The 10 highest and lowest jurisdictions for selected characteristics of the prison population, yearend 1997

Prison population	Number of inmates	Incarceration rates, 12/31/97	Sentenced prisoners per 100,000 State residents*	1-year growth, 1996-97	Percent change	5-year growth, 1992-97	Percent change
10 highest:							
California	157,547	Texas	717	Hawaii	23.4%	West Virginia	89.5%
Texas	140,729	Louisiana	672	West Virginia	15.4	Wisconsin	79.2
Federal	112,973	Oklahoma	617	Alaska	13.6	Texas	75.3
New York	70,026	South Carolina	536	Maine	13.6	Idaho	74.9
Florida	64,565	Mississippi	531	Vermont	13.5	Mississippi	73.5
Ohio	48,002	Nevada	518	Kentucky	13.1	Hawaii	69.1
Michigan	44,771	Alabama	500	Wisconsin	13.0	North Dakota	67.1
Illinois	40,788	Arizona	484	Mississippi	11.5	Utah	58.7
Georgia	36,450	California	475	North Dakota	10.4	North Carolina	54.7
Pennsylvania	34,964	Georgia	472	Iowa	9.4	Iowa	53.6
10 lowest:							
North Dakota	797	North Dakota	112	Oregon	-7.6%	District of Columbia	-14.0%
Vermont	1,270	Minnesota	113	Montana	-2.2	Maine	6.6
Wyoming	1,566	Maine	124	New Mexico	-0.8	Maryland	11.3
Maine	1,620	Vermont	140	District of Columbia	-0.2	New York	13.4
New Hampshire	2,164	West Virginia	174	New York	0.5	South Carolina	13.6
South Dakota	2,239	New Hampshire	184	Maryland	0.8	Michigan	14.5
Montana	2,242	Nebraska	200	Pennsylvania	1.2	Arkansas	21.0
West Virginia	3,172	Utah	205	Florida	1.3	Oregon	21.5
Rhode Island	3,371	Rhode Island	213	Massachusetts	1.3	Rhode Island	21.5
Nebraska	3,402	Oregon	232	Kansas	2.0	New Hampshire	21.8

*Prisoners with a sentence of more than a year. The Federal Bureau of Prisons and the District of Columbia are excluded.

Source: Darrell K. Gilliard and Alan J. Beck, *Prisoners in 1997*, Bureau of Justice Statistics, Washington, DC, 1998

the number of women prisoners increased yearly, and the number of women incarcerated in the 1990s has tripled the 1980s incarceration rates. In 1985, 21,345 females were imprisoned; by 1995, that number had more than tripled to 68,544. In 1996, 74,730 women were in prison, and by midyear 1998, 82,716 women were incarcerated (Table 4.8), 91 percent serving a sentence of longer than one year (Figure 4.2 illustrates the upward trend in the number of women incarcerated in prison between 1985 and 1995.)

Some studies show that the increase in the number of women serving sentences in state prisons may be due to drug offenses. In recent years, the proportion of drug offenses committed by females has surpassed violent offenses and property offenses. The proportion of violent offenses by women have declined, while public order offenses (weapons possession, driving while intoxicated, escape from custody, offenses against morals and decency, and prostitution) have remained about the same. (See Table 4.9.) In 1998, according to "Female Offenders" (*Corrections Compendium,* vol.

23, March 1998), most women were held in minimum (29,181 inmates) and medium (19,601 inmates) security facilities. About 4,479 female offenders were housed in maximum security facilities, while approximately 5,318 female offenders were supervised in community corrections or treatment facilities.

More female prisoners mean more mothers in prison. In 1996, there were 1,778 pregnant women admitted to U.S. correctional facilities, while the Federal Bureau of Prisons admitted more than 200 sentenced and unsentenced pregnant women. California reported the most prison births (353) in 1995. In 1996, Texas state prisons had 161 births. At least six states (Massachusetts, Minnesota, Nebraska, New York, South Dakota, and Tennessee) have mother-infant programs within their prison systems to help women care for their babies for the infant's first year. The federal system has the Mothers and Infants Together (MINT) program to help pregnant women. Most mothers in prison rely on family members to care for their children.

Race

Blacks accounted for approximately 49 percent and Whites for about 48 percent of sentenced prisoners under state or federal jurisdiction in 1996. (See Table 4.10.) About 58 percent of those in the Federal Bureau of Prisons custody were White; 39 percent, Black; and 2 percent each, Asian and American Indian. Three of 10 (30.9 percent) were of Hispanic origin. (See Table 4.11.)

The number of prisoners with sentences of more than one year rose over 396,800 (54 percent) between 1990 and 1996. The number of White males grew 46 percent; the number of Black males, 55 percent; the number of White females, 67 percent; and the number of Black females, 72 percent. (See Table 4.10.)

In 1996, approximately 2.8 percent of all adult residents of the United States were in prisons and jails, up from 1.6 percent in 1985. In 1996, about 9 percent of Black adults, 2 percent of White adults, and 1.3 percent of adults of other races were incarcerated.

Hispanics, who may be of any race, represent the fastest-growing minority group being imprisoned, increasing 54 percent from 1990 to 1996. (See Table

TABLE 4.7

Prisoners under the jurisdiction of State or Federal correctional authorities, by region and jurisdiction, yearend 1996 and 1997

Region and jurisdiction	Total			Sentenced to more than 1 year			Incarceration rate, 1997[a]
	Advance 1997	1996	Percent change, 1996-97	Advance 1997	1996	Percent change, 1996-97	
U.S. total	1,244,554	1,183,368	5.2%	1,197,590	1,138,984	5.1%	445
Federal	112,973	105,544	7.0%	94,987	88,815	6.9%	35
State	1,131,581	1,077,824	5.0	1,102,603	1,050,169	5.0	410
Northeast	172,244	169,261	1.8%	163,836	161,324	1.6%	317
Connecticut[b,c]	18,521	17,851	3.8	13,005	12,465	4.3	397
Maine	1,620	1,426	13.6	1,542	1,351	14.1	124
Massachusetts[d]	11,947	11,796	1.3	10,847	10,880	-0.3	278
New Hampshire	2,164	2,062	4.9	2,164	2,062	4.9	184
New Jersey[e]	28,361	27,490	3.2	28,361	27,490	3.2	351
New York	70,026	69,709	0.5	70,026	69,709	0.5	386
Pennsylvania	34,964	34,537	1.2	34,963	34,535	1.2	291
Rhode Island[b]	3,371	3,271	3.1	2,100	2,031	3.4	213
Vermont[b,f]	1,270	1,119	13.5	828	801	3.4	140
Midwest	216,757	204,657	5.9%	216,391	203,701	6.2%	346
Illinois[e,f]	40,788	38,852	5.0	40,788	38,852	5.0	342
Indiana	17,903	16,960	5.6	17,730	16,791	5.6	301
Iowa[e,f]	6,938	6,342	9.4	6,938	6,342	9.4	243
Kansas[e]	7,911	7,756	2.0	7,911	7,756	2.0	304
Michigan[f]	44,771	42,349	5.7	44,771	42,349	5.7	457
Minnesota	5,326	5,158	3.3	5,306	5,158	2.9	113
Missouri	23,998	22,003	9.1	23,980	22,003	9.0	442
Nebraska	3,402	3,287	3.5	3,329	3,223	3.3	200
North Dakota	797	722	10.4	715	650	10.0	112
Ohio[e]	48,002	46,174	4.0	48,002	46,174	4.0	429
South Dakota	2,239	2,063	8.5	2,239	2,063	8.5	303
Wisconsin	14,682	12,991	13.0	14,682	12,340	19.0	283
South	491,956	469,252	4.8%	480,061	458,671	4.7%	506
Alabama	22,290	21,760	2.4	21,680	21,108	2.7	500
Arkansas	10,021	9,407	6.5	9,936	8,992	10.5	392
Delaware[b]	5,435	5,110	6.4	3,264	3,119	4.6	443
District of Col.[b]	9,353	9,376	-0.2	8,814	8,668	1.7	1,682
Florida[f]	64,565	63,763	1.3	64,540	63,746	1.2	437
Georgia[f]	36,450	35,139	3.7	35,722	34,328	4.1	472
Kentucky	14,600	12,910	13.1	14,600	12,910	13.1	372
Louisiana	29,265	26,779	9.3	29,265	26,779	9.3	672
Maryland	22,232	22,050	0.8	21,088	20,980	0.5	413
Mississippi	15,447	13,859	11.5	14,548	13,143	10.7	531
North Carolina	31,638	30,647	3.2	27,726	27,751	-0.1	370
Oklahoma[e]	20,542	19,593	4.8	20,542	19,593	4.8	617
South Carolina	21,173	20,446	3.6	20,264	19,758	2.6	536
Tennessee[e]	16,659	15,626	6.6	16,659	15,626	6.6	309
Texas[e]	140,729	132,383	6.3	140,729	132,383	6.3	717
Virginia	28,385	27,655	2.6	27,524	27,062	1.7	407
West Virginia	3,172	2,749	15.4	3,160	2,725	16.0	174
West	250,624	234,654	6.8%	242,315	226,473	7.0%	405
Alaska[b]	4,220	3,716	13.6	2,571	2,335	10.1	420
Arizona[e]	23,484	22,493	4.4	22,353	21,523	3.9	484
California	157,547	146,049	7.9	154,368	142,865	8.1	475
Colorado	13,461	12,438	8.2	13,461	12,438	8.2	342
Hawaii[b]	4,949	4,011	23.4	3,424	2,954	15.9	288
Idaho	3,946	3,832	3.0	3,946	3,832	3.0	323
Montana	2,242	2,293	-2.2	2,242	2,293	-2.2	255
Nevada	9,024	8,439	6.9	8,884	8,439	5.3	518
New Mexico	4,688	4,724	-0.8	4,450	4,506	-1.2	256
Oregon	7,999	8,661	-7.6	7,589	7,316	3.7	232
Utah	4,284	3,972	7.9	4,263	3,946	8.0	205
Washington	13,214	12,527	5.5	13,198	12,527	5.4	233
Wyoming	1,566	1,499	4.5	1,566	1,499	4.5	326

Note: The advance count of prisoners is conducted in January and may be revised.
[a]The number of prisoners with sentences of more than 1 year per 100,000 U.S. residents.
[b]Prisons and jails form one integrated system. NPS data include jail and prison populations.
[c]Jurisdiction data are reported for the first time. Comparisons to past counts are inapplicable.
[d]Includes an estimated 6,200 inmates sentenced to more than 1 year but held in county facilities.
[e]Sentenced inmates may include some inmates sentenced to a year or less.
[f]Population figures are based on custody counts.

Source: Darrell K. Gilliard and Alan J. Beck, *Prisoners in 1997*, Bureau of Justice Statistics, Washington, DC, 1998

35

TABLE 4.8

Number of prisoners under the jurisdiction of State or Federal correctional authorities, by sex of inmate, 6/30/97 and 6/30/98

	Men	Women
Total		
6/30/98	1,195,150	82,716
6/30/97	1,141,413	78,363
Percent change	4.7%	5.6%
Sentenced to more than 1 year		
6/30/98	1,145,078	75,396
6/30/97	1,095,162	71,488
Percent change	4.6%	5.5%
Sentenced prisoners per 100,000 U.S. residents*	866	55

*The total number of male and female prisoners with a sentence of more than 1 year in the United States per 100,000 males and females in the resident population.

Source: Darrell K. Gilliard, *Prison and Jail Inmates at Midyear 1998*, Bureau of Justice Statistics, Washington, DC, 1999

4.12.) During this period the number of Hispanic males in prison rose 53 percent, and the number of Hispanic females grew by 71 percent.

Abuse Reported by Inmates

According to the Bureau of Justice Statistics, recent surveys indicate that 19 percent of state prison inmates and 10 percent of federal inmates were physically or sexually abused before their current sentence. Nearly half of the women and 1 in 10 men in correctional facilities said they had been abused in the past. Between 6 percent and 14 percent of male offenders and between 23 percent and 37 percent of female offenders claimed they had been physically or sexually abused before age 18. (See Table 4.13.) In the general adult population, 5 percent to 8 percent of males and 12 percent to 17 percent of females said they were abused as children. More men who reported abuse said they were age 17 or younger when the abuse took place. Women, on the other hand, were abused as juveniles and

as adults. One-fourth of the women in state prisons claimed they were abused as both juveniles and adults, as were 14 percent of those in federal prisons. In nearly all cases, the abuser was an adult (Table 4.13).

Allegedly abused prisoners in state prisons in 1997 were more apt to be serving sentences for violent offenses than those who had not been abused. Six of 10 (61 percent) of abused male state prisoners were serving sentences for violent offenses, while 46.1 percent of those not reporting abuse were serving sentences for violent crimes. One-third (33.5 percent) of abused women were serving sentences for violent offenses, and 20.9 percent of women not abused were imprisoned for violent crime offenses. (See Table 4.14.)

Abused state prisoners reported somewhat more illegal drug use and regular drinking than those inmates who had not been abused. About 76 percent of abused men and 79.7 percent of abused women had used illegal drugs regularly, compared to 67.9 percent of men and 65 percent of women who had not experienced abuse. About 69 percent of abused men and 57.5 percent of abused women reported regular drinking at some time in their lives, compared to 59.8 percent of men and 38.2 percent of women who had not suffered abuse (Table 4.14).

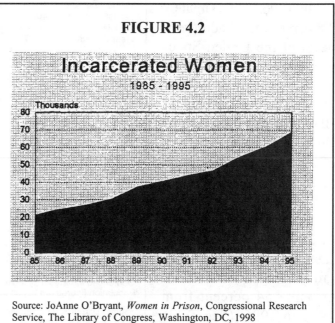

FIGURE 4.2

Source: JoAnne O'Bryant, *Women in Prison*, Congressional Research Service, The Library of Congress, Washington, DC, 1998

36

TABLE 4.9

Percent and Number of Females Incarcerated by Type of Offense

Offense	1986	1991	1992	1997
Violent	40.7%	32.2%	16.4%	23,108
Property	41.2%	28.7%	36.5%	18,425
Drug	12.0%	32.8%	40.3%	23,571
Public-order	5.1%	5.7%	5.6%	3,014

Source: JoAnne O'Bryant, *Women in Prison*, Congressional Research Service, The Library of Congress, Washington, DC, 1998

Incarceration Rates

When incarceration rates are estimated separately for men and women, Black males in their twenties and thirties are found to have very high rates compared to other groups. In 1996, 8.3 percent of Black males ages 25 to 29 were in prison, compared to 2.6 percent of Hispanic males ages 25 to 29 and about 0.8 percent of White males ages 25 to 29. (See Table 4.15.) Although incarceration rates drop with age, nearly 2.8 percent of Black males ages 45 to 54 were in prison in 1996.

In State Prisons

The reasons for state inmate incarceration vary among different racial and ethnic groups. Between 1990 and 1996, the number of Black inmates serving time for drug offenses rose from 79,800 to 133,400 (an increase of 67 percent), while the number of White inmates incarcerated for drug offenses increased from 29,600 to 46,300 (56.5 percent). The number of Hispanic inmates held for drug offenses rose from 38,700 to 52,300 (35 percent). The number of violent offenses increased more among Black inmates (60.5 percent) and Hispanic inmates (74 percent) than among White inmates (42 percent). (See Table 4.16.)

In Federal Prisons

Prisoners sentenced for drug offenses made up the largest group of federal prisoners (59.6 percent) in 1996, up from 52.6 percent in 1990. In 1996, federal inmates incarcerated for violent offenses made up 12.4 percent, down from 18 percent in 1990. During that same period, however, the number of federal prisoners held for weapons and immi-

TABLE 4.10

Number of sentenced prisoners under State or Federal jurisdiction, by sex and race, 1990-96

		Number of sentenced prisoners					
		Male			Female		
Year	Total	All[a]	White[b]	Black[b]	All[a]	White[b]	Black[b]
1990	739,980	699,416	350,700	340,300	40,564	20,200	19,700
1991	789,610	745,808	369,200	366,500	43,802	21,100	22,000
1992	846,277	799,776	394,500	393,700	46,501	22,200	23,600
1993	932,074	878,037	428,700	434,900	54,037	25,800	27,300
1994	1,016,691	956,566	465,300	474,800	60,125	28,800	30,200
1995	1,085,022	1,021,059	487,400	509,800	63,963	30,500	31,900
1996	1,138,984	1,069,257	510,900	528,200	69,727	33,800	33,900

Note: Previously published estimates by sex and race have been revised. Sentenced prisoners are those with a sentence of more than 1 year.
[a]Includes Asians, Pacific Islanders, American Indians, Alaska Natives, and other racial groups.
[b]The numbers for sex and race were estimated and rounded to the nearest 100. In each year Hispanics were identified among inmates of unknown racial origin. The race of these inmates was then estimated using inmate self-reported identification from the 1991 and 1997 State inmate surveys. For non-Hispanic inmates of unknown racial origin, race was estimated using the reported racial distribution in NPS.

Source: Darrell K. Gilliard and Alan J. Beck, *Prisoners in 1997*, Bureau of Justice Statistics, Washington, DC, 1998

TABLE 4.11

FEDERAL BUREAU OF PRISONS FACTS
March 1999

NUMBER OF INSTITUTIONS	94		AVERAGE INMATE AGE	37

TOTAL POPULATION*	127,168	SENTENCE IMPOSED (BOP only)	
In BOP Facilities	115,138	Less than 1 year	1.8%
In Contract Facilities	12,030	1-3 years	13.5%
		3-5 years	13.7%
SENTENCED POPULATION	95,522	5-10 years	29.5%
		10-15 years	19.8%
INMATES BY SECURITY LEVEL (BOP Only)		15-20 years	8.9%
Minimum	26.9%	More than 20 years	9.9%
Low	36.2%	Life	2.9%
Medium	23.4%		
High	13.5%	TYPE OF OFFENSE (BOP Only)	
		Drug Offenses	52.4%
		Robbery	7.5%
GENDER		Firearms, Explosives,	
Male	92.5%	Arson	8.1%
Female	7.5%	Extortion, Fraud, Bribery	4.7%
		Property Offenses	5.1%
RACE		Violent Offenses	2.2%
White	58.1%	Immigration	5.4%
Black	38.6%	Continuing Criminal	
Asian	1.7%	Enterprise	0.6%
Native American	1.6%	White Collar	0.6%
		Courts or Corrections	0.5%
ETNICITY		National Security	0.1%
Hispanic	30.9%	Miscellaneous	2.4%
CITIZENSHIP			
United States	70.5%	PERSONNEL	30,458
Mexico	13.7%	STAFF BY GENDER	
Colombia	3.4%	Male	73.0%
Cuba	2.3%	Female	27.0%
Other	10.1%		
		STAFF BY RACE/ETHNICITY	
		White (non-Hispanic)	66.4%
		Black	20.0%
		Hispanic	10.2%
		Other	3.4%

*The total population includes all inmates in BOP custody: those in BOP facilities and those in contract facilities. BOP facilities — penitentiaries, federal correctional institutions, federal prison camps, federal medical centers, and others — are operated by the BOP. Contract facilities, usually community corrections centers or detention facilities, are operated by non-BOP staff. The BOP contracts with these facilities to house federal offenders on a per capita basis. The data presented here relate to offenders in BOP facilities only unless otherwise noted.

Source: Federal Bureau of Prisons, Washington, DC, 1999

gration offenses more than doubled. The number of weapons offenders rose from 3,234 (5.4 percent) in 1990 to 7,480 (8.1 percent) in 1996. Immigration offenders increased from 1,645 (2.8 percent) in 1990 to 4,476 (4.8 percent) in 1996. (See Table 4.17.)

Black prisoners comprise an increasing proportion of federal prisoners. Between 1990 and 1996, the percentage of Black federal inmates rose from 30 percent to 38 percent, while the percentage of White federal inmates declined from 38 percent to 30 percent. The percentage of Hispanic federal inmates remained unchanged at 28 percent.

As a proportion of the total growth, drug offenses accounted for a larger share of the increases among Black inmates (82 percent) than among

TABLE 4.12

Number of sentenced Hispanic prisoners under State or Federal jurisdiction, by sex, 1990-96

Year	Reported in NPS	Estimated from BJS surveys and inmate self-identification		
		Total	Male	Female
1990	98,500	130,000	123,500	6,500
1991	107,600	137,800	131,000	6,800
1992	119,900	148,500	141,600	6,900
1993	133,400	160,100	152,400	7,800
1994	151,300	175,600	167,400	8,200
1995	168,000	190,100	181,300	8,800
1996	179,800	200,400	189,300	11,100

Note: Sentenced prisoners are those with a sentence of more than 1 year. The total number of Hispanic inmates was estimated in each year by multiplying the percent identifying as Hispanic in the 1991 and 1997 surveys by the NPS sentenced inmate counts. Estimates have been rounded to the nearest 100.

Source: Darrell K. Gilliard and Alan J. Beck, *Prisoners in 1997*, Bureau of Justice Statistics, Washington, DC, 1998

Hispanic (67 percent) or White inmates (65 percent). Altogether, Black and Hispanic inmates made up three-fourths of the total increase in federal inmates.

HIV and AIDS

In 1991, 17,551 state and federal prisoners were HIV-positive; by 1995, 24,226 were HIV-positive, a 38 percent increase. (See Table 4.18.) In 1995, 2.3 percent of federal and state prison inmates were infected with the human immunodeficiency virus (HIV). (See Table 4.18.) Of the total prison population, 5,099 prisoners (0.5 percent) had confirmed AIDS, and 18,165 prisoners were HIV-positive without having confirmed AIDS. (See Table 4.19.)

Between 1991 and 1995, the number of HIV-positive inmates grew at about the same rate as the overall prison population (38 percent compared to 36 percent). As a result, the percentage of all prisoners infected with HIV stayed the same (2.2 in 1991 and 2.3 percent in 1995; Table 4.18).

The rates of confirmed AIDS cases have been much higher in prisons than in the general population. At the end of 1995, approximately 0.51 percent of all prisoners had confirmed AIDS, compared to 0.08 percent of the U.S. population. The rate of death because of AIDS is higher in the prison population ages 15 to 54 than in the total U.S. population ages 15 to 54. In 1995, about 1 in every 3 prisoner deaths was attributable to AIDS-related cases, compared to 1 in 10 deaths in the general population ages 15 to 54.

All states, the District of Columbia, and the Federal Bureau of Prisons have guidelines for testing inmates for HIV. Forty-five jurisdictions tested prisoners if they had HIV-related symptoms or if inmates requested tests. In 1995, 24 states tested prisoners after they were involved in incidents such as fights, and 15 states tested inmates who were classified as "high-risk." Sixteen jurisdictions

TABLE 4.13

Physical or sexual abuse before admission, by sex of inmate or probationer

Before admission	State inmates		Federal inmates		Jail inmates		Probationers	
	Male	Female	Male	Female	Male	Female	Male	Female
Ever abused	16.1%	57.2%	7.2%	39.9%	12.9%	47.6%	9.3%	40.4%
Physically[a]	13.4	46.5	6.0	32.3	10.7	37.3	7.4	33.5
Sexually[a]	5.8	39.0	2.2	22.8	5.6	37.2	4.1	25.2
Both	3.0	28.0	1.1	15.1	3.3	26.9	2.1	18.3
Age of victim at time of abuse								
17 or younger[b]	14.4%	36.7%	5.8%	23.0%	11.9%	36.6%	8.8%	28.2%
18 or older[b]	4.3	45.0	2.7	31.0	2.3	26.7	1.1	24.7
Both	2.5	24.7	1.3	14.2	1.3	15.8	0.5	12.5
Age of abuser								
Adult	15.0%	55.8%	6.9%	39.0%	12.1%	46.0%	8.5%	39.2%
Juvenile only	0.9	1.0	0.2	0.3	0.8	1.3	0.6	1.2
Rape before admission	4.0%	37.3%	1.4%	21.4%	3.9%	33.1%	--	--
Completed	3.1	32.8	1.0	17.9	3.0	26.6	--	--
Attempted	0.8	4.3	0.3	3.2	0.7	5.6	--	--

--Not available.
[a]Includes those both physically and sexually abused.
[b]Includes those abused in both age categories.

Source: Caroline Wolf Harlow, *Prior Abuse Reported by Inmates and Probationers*, Bureau of Justice Statistics, Washington, DC, 1999

TABLE 4.14

Current and past violent offenses and past alcohol and drug use, by whether abused before admission to State prison, 1997

Offense history and drug and alcohol use	Percent of State prison inmates					
	Reported being abused			Reported being not abused		
	Total	Males	Females	Total	Males	Females
Current or past violent offense	70.4%	76.5%	45.0%	60.2%	61.2%	29.1%
Current violent offense	55.7%	61.0%	33.5%	45.3%	46.1%	20.9%
Homicide	15.9	16.3	13.9	12.7	12.8	7.3
Sexual assault	15.6	18.8	2.0	6.9	7.1	0.4
Robbery	12.5	13.5	7.8	14.5	14.7	6.1
Assault	9.5	9.9	7.6	9.3	9.4	5.7
Used an illegal drug						
Ever	88.6%	88.5%	88.9%	81.8%	81.9%	77.4%
Ever regularly	76.3	75.5	79.7	67.9	67.9	65.0
In month before offense	61.4	59.7	68.6	55.3	55.3	54.0
At time of offense	39.6	38.0	46.2	30.7	30.7	32.0
Drank alcohol						
Ever regularly	66.9%	69.1%	57.5%	59.0%	59.8%	38.2%
At time of offense	41.6	43.6	33.1	36.1	36.6	23.5

Source: Caroline Wolf Harlow, *Prior Abuse Reported by Inmates and Probationers*, Bureau of Justice Statistics, Washington, DC, 1999

and women who often come from segments of the community with high rates and risk of TB because of such factors as poverty, poor living conditions, substance abuse, and HIV/AIDS.

Little data is available on how many inmates and guards have tested positive for TB since few of the state/federal systems and city/county systems report on TB in their facilities. Therefore, it is hard to know the actual severity of the TB problem.

Hepatitis C

tested all prisoners upon admission. Three states and the Federal Bureau of Prisons also tested prisoners upon release. (See Table 4.20.)

HIV testing of prisoners is controversial in many states due to confidentiality laws requiring that medical test results be kept secret. In Washington state, concern for prison guards prompted the passage of a new bill in 1996 that allows corrections workers who have been exposed to a prisoner's body fluids to find out if that prisoner tested positive for sexually transmitted diseases (STDs), including AIDS.

A significant proportion of inmates (some experts have estimated as high as 40 percent) may be infected with hepatitis C, a deadly, infectious disease for which there is no sure cure. Hepatitis C attacks the liver after lying dormant for many years. The disease is spread through contact with contaminated blood and is rampant among prison populations because intravenous drug users are among the most common carriers. Health officials worry because almost all prisoners eventually leave prison, and when they do, many of them will bring the disease out with them.

Tuberculosis

Tuberculosis (TB) is a particularly serious problem in prisons because the germ is airborne and close physical contact is not necessary for the disease to spread. Crowded conditions without adequate ventilation and poor sanitary conditions can quickly lead to the spread of the disease. In addition, correctional facilities house men

TABLE 4.15

Number of sentenced prisoners under State or Federal jurisdiction per 100,000 residents, by sex, race, Hispanic origin, and age, 1996

Age	Number of sentenced prisoners per 100,000 residents of each group							
	Male				Female			
	Total	White	Black	Hispanic	Total	White	Black	Hispanic
Total	809	370	3,098	1,278	51	23	188	78
18-19	771	263	2,615	1,303	27	17	74	32
20-24	1,886	762	6,740	2,774	71	35	203	115
25-29	2,024	829	8,319	2,609	123	54	415	186
30-34	1,845	862	7,052	2,547	160	73	597	200
35-39	1,615	759	6,601	2,278	134	61	518	193
40-44	1,244	606	4,824	2,308	82	38	326	126
45-54	692	380	2,768	1,313	42	20	161	93
55 or older	151	96	505	413	5	3	18	9

Source: Darrell K. Gilliard and Alan J. Beck, *Prisoners in 1997*, Bureau of Justice Statistics, Washington, DC, 1998

TABLE 4.16

Estimated number of sentenced prisoners under State jurisdiction, by offense, race, and Hispanic origin, 1990 and 1996

Offenses	White 1990	White 1996	Black 1990	Black 1996	Hispanic 1990	Hispanic 1996
Total	243,400	350,700	314,700	490,500	115,300	175,500
Violent offenses	117,600	167,200	146,100	234,400	43,700	76,100
Murder	28,400	36,300	32,100	56,300	10,000	17,100
Manslaughter	5,100	6,000	5,700	7,000	2,400	3,200
Rape	11,700	18,100	9,900	16,400	2,000	2,800
Other sexual assault	24,700	38,200	9,000	15,300	4,800	7,800
Robbery	24,600	29,800	59,100	85,600	14,200	21,700
Assault	17,300	31,300	25,500	44,100	8,800	18,800
Other violent	5,800	10,300	4,800	7,800	1,500	3,800
Property offenses	75,200	105,100	70,900	96,200	24,200	33,700
Burglary	38,300	48,600	33,800	44,600	13,700	15,700
Larceny	13,700	19,400	16,300	22,500	4,200	6,600
Motor vehicle theft	5,800	8,600	5,800	7,800	2,600	4,800
Fraud	9,800	14,500	8,200	10,400	1,500	2,600
Other property	7,600	13,700	6,700	11,200	2,200	4,100
Drug offenses	29,600	46,300	79,800	133,400	38,700	52,300
Public-order offenses	19,700	31,400	16,600	24,700	8,300	12,600
Other/unspecified	1,300	700	1,400	1,900	400	800

Source: Darrell K. Gilliard and Alan J. Beck, *Prisoners in 1997*, Bureau of Justice Statistics, Washington, DC, 1998

ESTIMATED TIME SERVED

The amount of time convicted felons actually serve in prison is typically a fraction of their sentences. There are two important reasons for the gap between sentences received and time served. In states that impose indeterminate sentences, a judge specifies the minimum and/or maximum sentence length, but a parole board decides when the prisoner will actually be released. In most states, prisoners gain early release through time credits that they receive automatically or that are granted them for good behavior or special achievements — provisions that are intended to help correctional officials manage institutional populations.

For both types of sentence reduction, released offenders usually serve the remaining portion of their sentences under supervision in the community. According to the Bureau of Justice Statistics, in 1996, inmates released from state prisons and jails served an average of 30 months (44 percent) of their total sentences in prison, and violent offenders served an average of 45 months (53 percent) of their total sentences.

Today, many states have enacted truth-in-sentencing laws, which require offenders to serve a large portion of their sentences, therefore reducing the difference between the sentence imposed and actual time served in prison. A prisoner admitted in 1996 will serve 85 percent of his or her sentence in most states.

Not all states have adopted the federal 85 percent standard, however. Maryland and Texas require violent offenders to serve 50 percent of their sentences, and Nebraska and Indiana require all offenders to serve 50 percent of their sentences. Arkansas requires certain offenders to serve 70 per-

TABLE 4.17

Number and percent of sentenced inmates in Federal prisons, by offense, 1990 and 1996

	Federal inmates of any sentence length			
	Number		Percent	
	1990	1996	1990	1996
Total	59,526	92,672	100.0%	100.0%
Violent offenses	10,728	11,523	18.0%	12.4%
Homicide	1,316	1,084	2.2	1.2
Robbery	7,804	8,334	12.3	9.0
Assault	808	645	1.4	0.7
Other violent	1,300	1,460	2.2	1.6
Property offenses	8,307	7,781	14.0%	8.4%
Burglary	412	181	0.7	0.2
Fraud	5,386	5,807	9.0	6.3
Other property	2,509	1,793	4.2	1.9
Drug offenses	31,300	55,194	52.6%	59.6%
Public-order offenses	8,826	17,227	14.8%	18.6%
Immigration	1,645	4,476	2.8	4.8
Weapons	3,234	7,480	5.4	8.1
Other public-order	3,947	5,271	6.6	5.7
Other/unknown	365	947	0.6%	1.0%

Note: Data for December 31, 1990, and September 30, 1996, were obtained from the BJS Federal justice database.

Source: Darrell K. Gilliard and Alan J. Beck, *Prisoners in 1997*, Bureau of Justice Statistics, Washington, DC, 1998

41

cent, while Colorado requires violent offenders with two prior violent convictions to serve 75 percent — 56 percent with one prior violent conviction. Massachusetts requires that inmates serve 75 percent of a minimum prison sentence. (See Table 4.21.)

RECIDIVISM OF PRISONERS

According to the *Corrections Yearbook — 1998,* the average recidivism (rearrest) rate among 40 jurisdictions was 34.2 percent in 1997. Utah had the highest recidivism rate (70 percent) and Michigan had the lowest (14.6 percent).

As a rule, recidivism rates are higher among men, Blacks, Hispanics, and persons who have not completed high school than among women, Whites, non-Hispanics, and high school graduates. Recidivism is inversely related to the age of the prisoner at time of release; the older the prisoner, the lower the rate of recidivism. About half of 17- to 25-year-olds are reincarcerated compared to 35 percent of adults 40 years and more.

LIFETIME LIKELIHOOD OF GOING TO STATE OR FEDERAL PRISON

The lifetime likelihood of incarceration represents the percentage of all U.S. residents expected to be jailed in a prison at some time during their lives. Such a measure is hypothetical and is based on the assumption that recent rates of incarceration (and death rates) will not change in the future. Using incarceration rates recorded in 1991 as a model, an estimated 1 of every 20 persons (5.1 percent) in the United States will be confined in a state or federal prison during his/her lifetime. (See Table 4.22.)

Men (9 percent) are eight times more likely than women (1.1 percent) to be incarcerated in prison at least once during their lives. Among men, Blacks (28.5 percent) are twice as likely as Hispanics (16 percent) and six times more likely than Whites (4.4 percent) to be admitted to prison during their lives. (See Table 4.22.) At 1991 levels of

TABLE 4.18

HIV-positive State and Federal prison inmates

Year	Number	Percent of custody population
1991	17,551	2.2%
1992	20,651	2.5
1993	21,475	2.4
1994	22,717	2.4
1995	24,226	2.3

TABLE 4.19

Trend in HIV Infection, Prison Population, 1991-1995

Year	Confirmed AIDS cases	Other than confirmed AIDS cases
1991	1,682	15,797
1992	2,644	18,087
1993	3,765	17,773
1994	4,849	17,864
1995	5,099	18,165

Note: Care should be exercised when comparing the number of reported cases over time. In January 1993 the Centers for Disease Control and Prevention revised the HIV classification system and expanded the surveillance case definition for AIDS to include specific CD4+ T-lymphocyte criteria and three additional clinical conditions — pulmonary tuberculosis, recurrent pneumonia, and invasive cervical cancer. This expansion resulted in a substantial increase in the number of reported AIDS cases during 1993.

Source of both tables: Laura Maruschak, *HIV in Prisons and Jails*, Bureau of Justice Statistics, Washington, DC, 1997

incarceration, a Black male in the United States has greater than a 1 in 4 chance of going to prison during his lifetime, while a Hispanic male has a 1 in 6 chance and a White male has a 1 in 23 chance of serving time. (See Table 4.22 and Figure 4.3.) Black women (3.6 percent) have nearly the same chance as White men (4.4 percent) of serving time in prison.

The chances of going to prison decline with age regardless of sex, race, or Hispanic origin. Among U.S. residents who are age 30 and have not been previously incarcerated, an estimated 2.1 percent are expected to go to prison at some time before they die. Among those 35 years old, an estimated 1.4 percent will go to prison; among those age 40, fewer than 1 percent. (See Table 4.22.)

42

TABLE 4.20

Prison system testing policies for the antibody to the human immunodeficiency virus, by jurisdiction, 1995

Jurisdiction	All inmates		High-risk group	Inmate request	Clinical indica-tion	Involve-ment in incident	Random sample	Other
	In Entering custody	Upon release						
Federal		■		■	■		■	
Northeast								
Connecticut			■	■	■			
Maine				■				
Massachusetts			■	■			■	
New Hampshire	■			■	■	■		
New Jersey			■	■	■	■		
New York			■	■	■	■	■	■
Pennsylvania				■				
Rhode Island	■	■		■				
Vermont								
Midwest								
Illinois			■	■	■	■		
Indiana			■					
Iowa	■							
Kansas				■	■	■		
Michigan	■			■	■	■		
Minnesota			■					
Missouri	■	■	■					
Nebraska	■							
North Dakota	■							
Ohio			■	■		■		■
South Dakota				■				
Wisconsin								■
South								
Alabama	■	■	■		■			
Arkansas			■	■	■	■	■	
Delaware				■	■			
District of Columbia			■	■	■			
Florida			■		■			
Georgia	■			■	■	■		
Kentucky				■	■			
Louisiana				■	■	■		
Maryland				■	■			
Mississippi	■		■	■	■	■		■
North Carolina				■	■	■		
Oklahoma	■			■	■	■		
South Carolina				■	■			■
Tennessee			■	■	■			
Texas			■					
Virginia				■	■			
West Virginia				■	■			
West								
Alaska				■	■	■		
Arizona				■	■			
California				■	■			■
Colorado	■				■			■
Hawaii				■	■			
Idaho	■				■			
Montana			■		■			
Nevada	■	■						■
New Mexico				■	■			
Oregon				■	■	■		
Utah	■	■						■
Washington				■	■			
Wyoming	■	■						

Source: Laura Maruschak, *HIV in Prisons and Jails*, Bureau of Justice Statistics, Washington, DC, 1997

INTERNATIONAL COMPARISONS

The Sentencing Project, a prisoner advocacy group based in Washington, DC, compares the international rates of imprisonment in *Americans Behind Bars: The International Use of Incarcera-* *tion, 1995* (Marc Mauer, Washington, DC, 1997). According to the Sentencing Project, Russia now has passed the United States in the rate of citizens imprisoned, with 690 residents per 100,000 incarcerated, compared to the U.S. rate of 600 (Figure 4.4). (This includes both prison and jail populations as most countries do not distinguish between the two.) Russia is experiencing severe problems of organized crime, political instability, and uncertain economic times.

Among the 52 nations surveyed, the United States was second in the world in the rate of prisoners incarcerated. It had 5 to 10 times the rate of most industrialized nations. (See Figure 4.4.) American Black males faced imprisonment at more than 4 times the rate of Black males in South Africa (3,822 per 100,000 as compared to 851 per 100,000).

Various reasons exist why one nation has a high incarceration rate and another does not. A country with a high rate might have a high crime rate, a repressive government, a strict sentencing system, or a combination of these factors. Nations with low incarceration rates might not necessarily be lenient or have low crime rates, but just may not have enough money to build prisons. Furthermore, having a low incarceration rate does not mean that conditions inside the prisons are not brutal. For example, in 1994, Zaire had an incarceration rate of 88 per 100,000, but approximately 7.5 percent of the inmates died each year from malnutrition and poor health care (*Prison Conditions in Zaire*, Human Rights Watch, Washington, DC, 1994).

TABLE 4.21

Truth-in-sentencing requirements, by State

Meet Federal 85% requirement		50% requirement	100% of minimum requirement	Other requirements
Arizona	Missouri	Indiana	Idaho	Alaska[c]
California	New Jersey	Maryland	Nevada	Arkansas[d]
Connecticut	New York	Nebraska	New Hampshire	Colorado[e]
Delaware	North Carolina	Texas		Kentucky[f]
District of Col.	North Dakota			Massachusetts[g]
Florida	Ohio			Wisconsin[h]
Georgia	Oklahoma[b]			
Illinois[a]	Oregon			
Iowa	Pennsylvania			
Kansas	South Carolina			
Louisiana	Tennessee			
Maine	Utah			
Michigan	Virginia			
Minnesota	Washington			
Mississippi				

[a]Qualified for Federal funding in 1996 only.
[b]Effective July 1, 1999, offenders will be required to serve 85% of the sentence.
[c]Two-part sentence structure (⅔ in prison; ⅓ on parole); 100% of prison term required.
[d]Mandatory 70% of sentence for certain violent offenses and manufacture of methamphetamine.
[e]Violent offenders with 2 prior violent

convictions serve 75%; 1 prior violent conviction, 56.25%.
[f]Effective July 15, 1998, offenders are required to serve 85% of the sentence.
[g]Requires 75% of a minimum prison sentence.
[h]Effective December 31, 1999, 2-part sentence: offenders serve 100% of the prison term and a sentence of extended supervision at 25% of the prison sentence.

Source: Paula M. Ditton and Doris James Wilson, *Truth in Sentencing in State Prisons*, Bureau of Justice Statistics, Washington, DC, 1999

INMATE VIOLENCE

Inmate violence has always been a concern. In a recent census of American prisons, the Bureau

TABLE 4.22

Chances of going to State or Federal prison at some time during the rest of life, by age, sex, race, and Hispanic origin

	Percent expected to go to State or Federal prison at some time during the rest of life among persons not previously incarcerated, by age —						
	Birth	20	25	30	35	40	45
Total	5.1%	4.5%	3.1%	2.1%	1.4%	.9%	.6%
Sex							
Male	9.0%	7.9%	5.5%	3.7%	2.5%	1.6%	1.0%
Female	1.1	1.0	.8	.6	.3	.2	.1
Race/Hispanic origin							
White*	2.5%	2.3%	1.7%	1.2%	.9%	.6%	.4%
Male	4.4	4.1	3.0	2.1	1.5	1.1	.8
Female	.5	.5	.4	.3	.2	.1	.1
Black*	16.2%	14.1%	9.6%	6.0%	3.6%	2.0%	1.2%
Male	28.5	25.3	17.3	10.8	6.5	3.6	2.1
Female	3.6	3.5	2.8	1.9	1.1	.6	.4
Hispanic	9.4%	8.7%	6.4%	4.9%	3.8%	2.3%	1.6%
Male	16.0	14.8	11.1	8.6	6.8	4.3	3.0
Female	1.5	1.5	1.2	.9	.6	.4	.2

Note: Estimates were obtained by subtracting the cumulative percent first incarcerated for each age from the lifetime likelihood of incarceration.
*Excludes persons of Hispanic origin.

Source: Thomas P. Bonczar and Alan J. Beck, *Lifetime Likelihood of Going to State or Federal Prison*, Bureau of Justice Statistics, Washington, DC, 1997

of Justice found that, in 1995, 25,948 inmates were assaulted — up 20 percent since 1990. However, the number per 1,000 inmates dropped from 31 assaults in 1990 to 27 in 1995. The staff incurred another 14,165 assaults. It is likely that a significant number of assaults are not reported.

In 1997, according to the *Corrections Yearbook — 1998* (see above), inmates committed 40,364 incidents of recorded assaults; 35.6 percent were against staff and 64.4 percent against other inmates. In 1993, Stop Prisoner Rape, a national organization, estimated that more than 290,000 male prisoners are raped annually. The victims of rape are usually the youngest, the smallest, the nonviolent, the first-timers, and those charged with less serious crimes. With the increase in the number of women serving time, rape of female prisoners, both by male inmates and guards, has become a growing concern.

One reason for the recent concern about prisoner violence is that prisoners convicted of violent crimes are serving longer sentences. For example, since 1987, federal prisoners are not eligible for parole until they serve 85 percent of their sentences, and the sentences can be reduced only by a maximum of 54 days annually for good behavior. Without good time, prisoners have less incentive to behave. In a *New York Times* interview, the United States Attorney for the Northern District of Georgia commented, "There are more violent offenders in the system. They are serving longer sentences, and they feel they've got nothing to lose."

In many prisons, gang affiliations can threaten the safety of inmates. For example, in July 1994, a gang fight at the Robinson Correctional Institution in Enfield, Connecticut, turned into a riot in which two inmates were killed. Some prisons deal with the problem of gangs by tolerating them; others ban gang colors and watch the members closely, transferring leaders to other facilities when trouble occurs. In 1986, after two years in which inmates

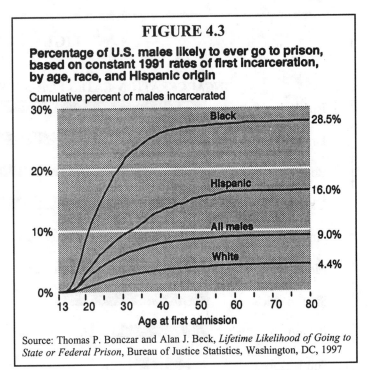

FIGURE 4.3

Percentage of U.S. males likely to ever go to prison, based on constant 1991 rates of first incarceration, by age, race, and Hispanic origin

Source: Thomas P. Bonczar and Alan J. Beck, *Lifetime Likelihood of Going to State or Federal Prison*, Bureau of Justice Statistics, Washington, DC, 1997

killed 51 other prisoners and assaulted thousands of guards, Texas started putting gang members into high-security cellblocks for their entire sentence. Connecticut has also put violent gang members into a maximum security prison.

Guard violence towards inmates can also be a problem. For example, at Clinton, a maximum security prison in New York, inmates have won seven federal cases claiming excessive force by correctional staff members from 1990 through 1995. The state settled 10 other brutality lawsuits rather than defend them in court. In 1997, an inmate abused in the aftermath of the Attica (New York) uprising in 1973 received a several million dollar settlement. Other cases are still under litigation.

REINTRODUCTION OF CHAIN GANGS

The reintroduction of chain gangs into American prisons, part of a prison movement to make prisons more efficient and less comfortable for inmates, is hotly debated. Politicians, responding to public demands to "get tough on crime," consider harsher measures to be popular with voters. Advocates of a get-tough approach claim that tougher prison conditions will act both as a deterrent to new offenders and keep prior offenders from com-

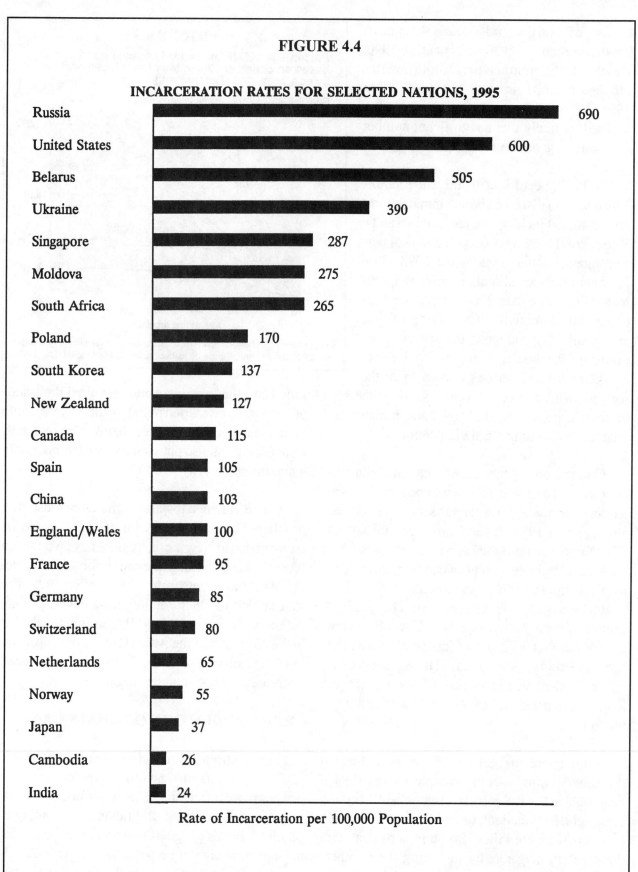

FIGURE 4.4

INCARCERATION RATES FOR SELECTED NATIONS, 1995

Nation	Rate
Russia	690
United States	600
Belarus	505
Ukraine	390
Singapore	287
Moldova	275
South Africa	265
Poland	170
South Korea	137
New Zealand	127
Canada	115
Spain	105
China	103
England/Wales	100
France	95
Germany	85
Switzerland	80
Netherlands	65
Norway	55
Japan	37
Cambodia	26
India	24

Rate of Incarceration per 100,000 Population

Source: Marc Mauer, *Americans Behind Bars: U.S. and International Use of Incarceration, 1995*, The Sentencing Project, Washington, DC, 1997

mitting new crimes. Some states are denying television, visitation, and exercise rooms to inmates; others plan to clothe inmates in old-fashioned striped uniforms to humiliate them. Opponents claim that chaining inmates and putting them along highways is dangerous because of the possibility of traffic accidents or inmate violence.

Chain gangs, although not work gangs, were eliminated in the 1940s because of accounts of brutality. In May 1995, Alabama brought back the chain gang, mainly to help lower the state's budget deficit. One guard with a shotgun could watch twice as many chained prisoners than unchained prisoners. A short time later, the Arizona Department of Corrections began using chain gangs along the state highways. Florida and Iowa passed laws allowing chain gangs in 1995.

At least six other states (California, Indiana, Missouri, Oklahoma, Washington and Wisconsin) introduced legislation in 1996. However, in June 1996, Alabama banned the chain gang order after lawyers reached an agreement for prisoners, state prison officials, and the governor. Inmates will still work on roadside cleanup projects and can still have their legs shackled, but they cannot be attached to someone else. Richard Cohen, a lawyer with the Southern Poverty Law Center, which had challenged the chain gangs as cruel punishments, commented that the correctional officials "realized that chaining them together was inefficient, that it was unsafe...."

In 1999, what is believed to be the first Massachusetts chain gang painted an iron fence at a drug treatment center under surveillance by armed guards. The men were shackled to each other with five feet of chain. The inmates who work on these "tandem work crews" are volunteers, according to Bristol County (New Bedford) Sheriff Thomas Hodgson. The prisoners are all dressed in red shirts and pants, and see benefits to working on chain gangs, such as relieving stress, helping the community, and being out in the fresh air. Only inmates convicted of nonviolent crimes may volunteer for the program.

OTHER "GET TOUGH" POLICIES

As the number of convicts has increased, many people have demanded that prison life become tougher. Responding to advocates for a no-frills policy, many prison administrators have banned television privileges and abolished weight-lifting equipment and computers. In 1994, Congress eliminated Pell grants, which helped prisoners pay for college courses. Governor George E. Pataki of New York ended the Sing Sing Correctional program of state tuition assistance programs. In Illinois, officials shut down college classes and vocational schools at three of its correctional institutions, and the state did not budget any more money for these programs.

In South Carolina, the prison director removed air conditioning and televisions from cells, stopped intramural sports, banned long hair and beards, and required uniforms. The new rules prompted an uprising at one facility. The inmates who began the uprising were identified as either Muslims or Rastifarians, who objected to the new rules on religious grounds. Currently, Arizona, Mississippi, Louisiana, California, Wisconsin, Florida, New York, North Carolina, Ohio, and Texas are among the states that have laws restricting prisoners' access to recreational activities. By 1996, at least half of all state prisons had cut their educational programs. The federal government passed the Prison Security Act of 1995 to prevent federal prisoners from participating in activities that could increase their strength or fighting ability.

Convicts, prisoner rights advocates, and many prison administrators view these cutbacks as shortsighted. Many prisons already do not comply with minimal health and safety standards. With the popular characterization of prisons as resorts and the desire to cut public spending, the health and safety conditions of prisons might deteriorate even further. The prisoner rights advocates and prison administrators further noted that prisoners who gain an education are usually less likely to commit new crimes when they are released.

A study by Anne Piehl, an assistant professor at the John F. Kennedy School of Government at Harvard, found that male inmates in Wisconsin who enrolled in high school classes were 10 percent less likely to be rearrested four years after their release than prisoners who had not taken classes. Reducing the prison population by 10 percent, according to Piehl, would save the United States $29 billion annually. In 1995, commenting on the states having to build more prisons, Malcolm Young, director of the Sentencing Project advocacy group said, "If you've got the drug treatment, job training and other programs, you won't need the prisons."

NATIONAL CORRECTIONS EXECUTIVE SURVEY

W. Wesley Johnson, Katherine Bennett, and Timothy Flanagan of Sam Houston State University at Huntsville, Texas ("Getting Tough on Prisoners: Results from the National Corrections Executive Survey, 1995," *Crime & Delinquency*, vol. 43, no. 1, January 1997, pp. 24-41), analyzed the data gathered from the *1995 Corrections Executive Survey of Wardens of State Adult Correctional Facilities.* Most wardens favored reducing or eliminating martial arts instruction (93 percent), boxing (71 percent), cosmetic surgery (89 percent), conjugal visits (85 percent), condom distribution (72 percent), non-regulation personal clothing (72 percent), and tobacco smoking (62 percent) and chewing (58 percent). (See Table 4.23.)

On the other hand, none of the wardens wanted basic literacy education reduced, and only 4 percent favored reducing or eliminating vocational training. Just 16 percent wanted television and

VCRs reduced or eliminated, while 15 percent favored eliminating intramural leagues. (See Table 4.23.)

The researchers found that wardens who thought rehabilitation was the more important goal of prisons did not want to reduce prison amenities as much as those who ranked rehabilitation low

TABLE 4.23

Support for Reduction or Elimination of Prison Programs and Services among State Prison Wardens

	Should Be Reduced or Eliminated (percentage responding "yes")
Education services	
Vocation training/certification	4
High school education/GED[a]	1
College education	41
Basic literacy education	0
Library services	6
Legal services	
Access to law library material	24
Copy privileges	45
Mutual legal assistance among inmates	44
State-funded legal services	50
Health care services	
Physical therapy	10
Disability benefits[b]	70
Organ transplant[b]	45
AIDS treatment/AZT	9
Condom distribution[b]	72
Cosmetic surgery[b]	89
Cosmetic dentistry[b]	83
Recreation programs/equipment	
Weight lifting	32
Boxing[b]	71
Intramural leagues	15
Martial arts instruction[b]	93
Jogging	4
Full-time recreation director/therapist(s)	13
Crafts/hobby programs	20
Ball games	7
Other amenities	
Television and VCR	16
Radios/tape and CD players	23
Musical instruments	24
Sexually oriented reading material	75
Personal, nonregulation clothing	72
Tobacco smoking	62
Tobacco chewing	58
Special diets (religion or health related)	27
Air conditioning[b]	33
Telephone calls	30
Mail privileges	12
Conjugal visitation[b]	85

a. GED = general equivalency diploma.
b. Percentages for this item should be interpreted with caution, as more than 20% of respondents gave the "N/A" response.

Source: W. Wesley Johnson, Katherine Bennett, and Timothy J. Flanagan, "Getting Tough on Prisoners: Results from the National Corrections Executive Survey, 1995," *Crime and Delinquency* (vol. 43, no. 1, January 1997), pp. 24-41, copyright © 1997 by Sage Publications. Reprinted by permission of Sage Publications, Inc.

on their agendas. Only 21 percent of the wardens felt that conditions should be harsher at their institutions. Those who did, of course, were more likely to want the number of amenities reduced.

Johnson et al. found that wardens were not "soft on crime" or sympathetic to the prisoners. Indeed, the 1995 survey, compared to past surveys, found that wardens "have become more punitive" in their views towards corrections. Nonetheless, wardens view amenities in "functional terms." As a result, only 1 percent felt that the impetus to reduce amenities came from the wardens themselves, while 37 percent and 34 percent, respectively, thought the public and the legislatures were behind the get-tough movement.

Wardens who thought an amenity helped them run a prison more smoothly favored keeping it. For example, television watching, hobbies, and crafts keep prisoners occupied during uncommitted time. Any program that helped the prisoners and staff prevent boredom helped the wardens run the prisons more efficiently and safely. Also, privileges that prisoners value can be given to them in exchange for obeying the rules or be taken away for violating the rules. For example, amenities, such as cable television, that the public rails against are the very programs that the wardens favor for control purposes.

Senate Survey

Budget cutbacks and get-tough policies have eliminated or reduced the size of many prison programs. However, in a 1994 survey conducted by the Subcommittee on the Constitution, wardens were nearly unanimous in calling for an expansion of rehabilitation programs in prisons. Ninety-three percent recommended the expansion of literacy and other educational programs to help reduce recidivism. Nine of 10 favored more drug treatment programs (89 percent) and vocational training (92 percent). Almost three-fourths (74 percent) wanted more psychological counseling.

Despite the cutbacks, the 1995 census of prisons (Bureau of Justice Statistics, *Census of State and Federal Correctional Facilities*, 1995, Washington, DC, 1997) found that 80 percent of all prisons offered a general equivalency diploma or other secondary program, and almost one-quarter of all prisoners were enrolled. About 70 percent of all facilities offered psychological or psychiatric inmate counseling.

Politicians view prisons differently from the wardens. They see prisons in "ideological" terms. Prisons are "places for punishment as opposed to imprisonment as punishment," meaning that harsh conditions in the prison should be the punishment, rather than the denial of freedom that comes with locking up offenders. This view, along with concern about budgets, makes prison amenities vulnerable to attack by politicians and easily eliminated by legislatures.

LIMITS ON HEALTH CARE SERVICES

In an effort to reduce the cost of housing inmates, states such as Alabama, Florida, and Nevada have introduced medical care copayment systems in which the inmates pay for part of their care. The prisons and jails established flat fees, which they deducted from inmates' personal accounts, for sick call visits, doctor calls, and prescriptions. The correction systems do not charge for initial admission-related examinations, emergency care, or staff-requested follow-up visits.

Supporters of the copayment plan maintain that charging fees makes the inmates consider whether they really need to see a doctor. Prisons that have instituted the flat-rate fee found a dramatic reduction in medical requests by inmates. Opponents of the fees contend that inmates may neglect going to the doctor when needed because they are spending their funds on other necessities, causing serious medical problems to go undetected and/or the spread of communicable diseases to increase.

Managed Health Care

Because of rising costs, more jails and prisons are contracting out their health care. In the past, inmates were usually young males who needed little medical care. With mandatory drug sentencing, many prisoners are drug users, and many have tested positive for HIV. More women are in prison because of the drug laws and, as a result, prisons have had to add gynecology and prenatal care to their health care services. Courts ordered some jails and prisons to close their internal health services because their medical care was so bad that it violated the Eighth Amendment, which prohibits cruel and unusual punishment. Many of these facilities turned to contracted medical services.

Some experts believe that the number of inmates cared for by private medical companies is increasing by approximately 20 percent annually. By the end of 1996, the largest company, Correctional Medical Services, had contracts with jails and prisons in 28 states and cared for the health needs of 162,000 inmates, double the number it cared for in 1992. An analyst with Equitable Securities in Nashville estimated that private companies cared for about 261,000 inmates in 1994 and 370,000 inmates in 1996.

Many critics of privatization of prison health care worry that the quality of health care given to the inmates will decrease. State and local governments pay a set fee no matter what type of care the inmates receive. Like managed care everywhere, the companies have strict rules on what tests are given, when inmates can be hospitalized, or when a specialist will be called in.

Some correctional officials think the service received has improved. According to Sheriff Frank Drew of Virginia Beach, Virginia, in 1996, the private company with which his jail had contracted gave better care to the inmates than "the public gets." On the other hand, other officials ended their contracts with private firms when inmates died, allegedly due to the companies' failures to provide necessary care.

CHAPTER V

CHARACTERISTICS OF PRISON INMATES

Prisoners overwhelmingly represent societal "failures," young men (and a small percentage of women and older men) who have had unsuccessful experiences in their families, schools, military services, and labor force. They suffer disproportionately from child abuse, alcohol and drug abuse, poor self-concept, and deficient social skills. They tend to be hostile to others, and especially to authority. — James B. Jacobs, "Inside Prisons" (*Crime File Study Guide*, National Institute of Justice, Washington, DC, not dated)

RACE, ETHNICITY, AGE, AND GENDER

In 1990 and 1996, non-Hispanic Blacks were more than twice as likely as Hispanics and eight times more likely than non-Hispanic Whites to be in state or federal prison. At year-end 1996, 1,571 sentenced Black inmates per 100,000 Blacks in the United States were imprisoned, compared to 688 Hispanic inmates per 100,000 Hispanics and 193 White inmates per 100,000 Whites. (See Table 5.1.)

In 1996, 60 percent of convicted prison inmates belonged to racial or ethnic minorities, down somewhat from 65 percent in 1991 but the same as in 1986. Non-Hispanic Whites made up 39.7 percent of the inmate population; non-Hispanic Blacks, 38.9 percent; other non-Hispanics, 3.2 percent; and Hispanics, 18.3 percent. (Hispanics, an ethnic category, may be of any racial group.)

In 1997, slightly more than half (56.8 percent) of inmates were under age 35, down from 65.8 percent in 1991 and 73 percent in 1986. More than one-third (37.9 percent) were between 25 and 34 years of age, with one-fifth (18.5 percent) between 18 and 24 years of age. Three of 10 (29.6 percent) were 35 to 44 years old, and 13.6 percent were older than 45. (See Table 5.2.) According to the Criminal Justice Institute (Camille Graham Camp and George M. Camp, *The Corrections Yearbook*

TABLE 5.1

Number of sentenced prisoners under State or Federal jurisdiction per 100,000 U.S. residents, by sex, race, Hispanic origin, and age, 1990 and 1996

Number of sentenced prisoners per 100,000 U.S. residents in each population group[a]

Age	Total 1990	Total 1996	Male 1990	Male 1996	Female 1990	Female 1996	White[b] 1990	White[b] 1996	Black[b] 1990	Black[b] 1996	Hispanic 1990	Hispanic 1996
Total	292	422	564	809	31	51	139	193	1,067	1,571	548	688
18-19	271	407	518	771	13	27	90	143	1,084	1,337	360	688
20-24	652	995	1,220	1,886	61	71	295	406	2,296	3,385	972	1,514
25-29	799	1,078	1,493	2,024	95	123	354	442	2,949	4,131	1,341	1,488
30-34	708	1,006	1,327	1,845	87	160	336	469	2,640	3,671	1,185	1,446
35-39	526	875	989	1,615	67	134	245	412	1,973	3,398	1,069	1,279
40-44	375	658	715	1,244	41	82	196	322	1,433	2,431	779	1,233
45-54	211	360	410	692	21	42	137	198	590	1,347	535	690
55 or older	49	69	109	151	3	5	32	44	168	218	142	188

[a]Based on estimates of the U.S. resident population on July 1 of each year and adjusted for the census undercount.
[b]Excludes Hispanics.

Source: Darrell K. Gilliard and Allen J. Beck, *Prisoners in 1997*, Bureau of Justice Statistics, Washington, DC, 1998

TABLE 5.2

Middle-aged inmates comprise a growing part of the Nation's prison populations

	Percent of inmates held in State or Federal prison*	
	1991	1997
Total	100.0%	100.0%
17 or younger	0.6	0.4
18-19	2.9	2.7
20-24	17.4	15.8
25-29	23.6	18.7
30-34	21.3	19.2
35-39	14.4	17.5
40-44	9.1	12.1
45-54	7.2	10.3
55 or older	3.4	3.3

*Based on data from the 1991 and 1997 surveys of State and Federal prison inmates.

Source: Darrell K. Gilliard and Allen J. Beck, *Prisoners in 1997*, Bureau of Justice Statistics, Washington, DC, 1998

— *1998*, Middletown, Connecticut, 1998), men in prison were slightly older in 1997 than in the past. In 1997, the average male prisoner was 33.4, and the average female prisoner was 33.8 years. Although more younger people commit crimes, the average age of inmates will continue to rise as more prisoners serve longer sentences.

Women

In 1997, women accounted for 6.4 percent of inmates, up slightly from 5 percent in 1991. Women in prisons in 1997 were most likely to be non-Hispanic Blacks and between the ages of 25 and 34. Compared to 1986, the female prison population had higher percentages of Hispanics and women older than 25. (For more information on race, gender, and age, see Chapter IV.)

In 1996, men were 16 times more likely to be in prison than women. By year-end 1996, 809 males per 100,000 U.S. males were imprisoned, compared to 51 women per 100,000 U.S. females (Table 5.1). Black women were 8 times more likely than White women and 2.5 times more likely than Hispanic women to be in prison.

TYPES OF CRIMES

State Prisoners

The percentage of state prisoners serving time for violent crimes barely increased from 45.8 percent in 1990 to 47.3 percent in 1996, but the number rose sharply from 315,900 in 1990 to 495,400 in 1996. One of

TABLE 5.3

Estimated number of sentenced prisoners under State jurisdiction, by offense and sex, 1990 and 1996

Offenses	All prisoners		Male		Female	
	1990	1996	1990	1996	1990	1996
Total	689,600	1,048,000	652,800	984,600	36,700	63,400
Violent offenses	315,900	495,400	304,800	477,900	11,100	17,500
Murder[a]	72,500	112,700	68,400	107,700	4,100	5,000
Manslaughter	13,300	16,900	12,000	15,400	1,300	1,600
Rape	24,700	39,200	24,600	38,800	100	300
Other sexual assault	39,400	63,200	39,000	62,600	400	600
Robbery	99,900	142,000	97,200	137,800	2,700	4,200
Assault	53,700	98,600	51,600	94,400	2,100	4,200
Other violent	12,500	22,700	11,900	21,400	600	1,400
Property offenses	175,000	240,000	163,300	222,600	11,700	17,500
Burglary	87,800	111,100	86,200	108,100	1,600	3,100
Larceny	35,100	49,800	31,000	43,700	4,100	6,200
Motor vehicle theft	14,500	21,600	14,300	20,800	200	800
Fraud	20,300	27,800	16,500	21,700	3,800	6,100
Other property	17,200	29,600	15,200	28,300	2,000	1,300
Drug offenses	149,700	237,600	137,900	213,900	11,800	23,700
Public-order offenses[b]	45,800	71,300	43,900	67,000	1,900	4,400
Other/unspecified[c]	3,100	3,700	2,900	3,400	200	300

Note: Offense distributions for yearend 1990 and 1996 were estimated using *stock-flow method* procedures that combine data from the 1991 and 1997 surveys of State prison inmates with estimates of admissions and releases obtained in the National Corrections Reporting Program, 1990-96.

[a]Includes nonnegligent manslaughter.
[b]Includes weapons, drunk driving, court offenses, commercialized vice, morals and decency charges, liquor law violations, and other public-order offenses.
[c]Includes juvenile offenses and unspecified felonies.

Source: Darrell K. Gilliard and Allen J. Beck, *Prisoners in 1997*, Bureau of Justice Statistics, Washington, DC, 1998

4 (22.9 percent) of the inmates was serving time for property offenses in 1996, a decrease from 25.4 percent in 1990. The percentage of inmates in prison for a drug crime remained about the same in 1990 (21.7 percent) and in 1996 (22.7 percent). (See Table 5.3 and Figure 5.1.)The number of prisoners serving time for drug charges rose sixfold from 38,500 in 1986 to 237,600 in 1996.

Gender

From 1990 to 1996, the percentage of women in state prison for drug offenses increased slightly, while the percentage in state prison for property offenses decreased somewhat. More than one-third (37.4 percent) of females were serving a

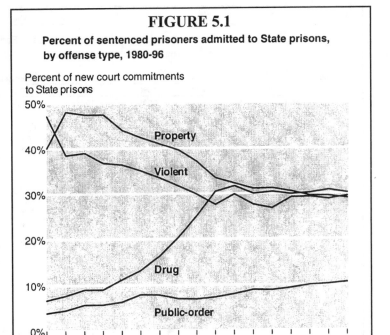

FIGURE 5.1

Percent of sentenced prisoners admitted to State prisons, by offense type, 1980-96

Percent of new court commitments to State prisons

Source: *Correctional Populations in the United States, 1996,* Bureau of Justice Statistics, Washington, DC, 1999

TABLE 5.4

Number of sentenced inmates in Federal prisons, by the most serious offense, 1990-96

Most serious offense	Number of inmates in Federal prison[a]						
	1990	1991	1992	1993	1994	1995	1996
Total	56.989	65.802	72.851	82.698	84.672	88.101	92.672
Violent offenses	9,557	9,852	9,506	11,058	10,855	11,321	11,523
Homicide[b]	1,233	1,166	917	867	889	966	1,084
Assault[c]	1,964	2,101	2,009	2,365	2,601	2,633	645
Robbery	5,158	5,410	5,409	6,561	6,174	6,341	8,334
Other violent[d]	1,202	1,175	1,171	1,265	1,191	1,381	1,460
Property offenses	7,935	8,518	8,617	8,718	7,445	7,524	7,781
Burglary	442	384	313	252	157	164	181
Fraud[e]	5,113	5,504	5,799	6,146	5,454	5,629	5,807
Larceny/theft/other property[f]	2,380	2,630	2,505	2,320	1,834	1,731	1,793
Drug offenses	30,470	36,782	42,879	48,997	49,507	51,737	55,194
Public-order offenses	8,585	10,011	11,253	13,276	13,536	15,762	17,227
Immigration	1,728	1,988	1,927	2,170	2,435	3,612	4,476
Weapons	3,073	3,826	4,996	6,515	6,735	7,519	7,480
Escape/court[g]	417	441	382	380	378	367	325
Other public-order[h]	3,367	3,756	3,948	4,202	3,988	4,264	4,946
Other[i]	442	639	596	658	473	0	0
Unknown	0	0	0	0	2,856	1,757	947

Note: All data are from the BJS Federal justice database. Data for 1990-95 are for December 31.
Data for 1996 are for September 30. Numbers may differ from the Federal Bureau of Prisons'
count because the Federal Justice Statistics Program includes prisoners in transit.
[a]Includes prisoners of any sentence length.
[b]Includes murder, nonnegligent manslaughter, and negligent manslaughter.
[c]In1996 assaults with intent to commit robbery were coded as robbery.
[d]Includes kidnaping, rape, other sexual assault, threats against the President, and other offenses.
[e]Includes embezzlement, counterfeiting, forgery, bankruptcy, and fraud (excluding tax fraud but including securities fraud).
[f]Includes motor vehicle theft, trespassing, destruction of property, and transport of stolen property.
[g]Includes flight to avoid prosecution, escape, parole and probation violation, and other court offenses.
[h]Includes liquor laws, national security laws, income tax, selective service acts, bribery, gambling, traffic offenses, and other public-order offenses.
[i]Includes offenses not classifiable or not a violation of the United States Code.

Source: *Correctional Populations in the United States, 1996,* Bureau of Justice Statistics, Washington, DC, 1999

TABLE 5.5

Percent of sentenced inmates in Federal prisons, by the most serious offense, 1990-96

Most serious offense	Percent of inmates in Federal prison[a]						
	1990	1991	1992	1993	1994[b]	1995[b]	1996[b]
Total	100%	100%	100%	100%	100%	100%	100%
Violent offenses	16.8%	15.0%	13.0%	13.4%	13.3%	13.1%	12.6%
Homicide[c]	2.2	1.8	1.3	1.0	1.1	1.1	1.2
Assault[d]	3.4	3.2	2.8	2.9	3.2	3.0	0.7
Robbery	9.1	8.2	7.4	7.9	7.5	7.3	9.1
Other violent[e]	2.1	1.8	1.6	1.5	1.5	1.6	1.6
Property offenses	13.9%	12.9%	11.8%	10.5%	9.1%	8.7%	8.5%
Burglary	0.8	0.6	0.4	0.3	0.2	0.2	0.2
Fraud[f]	9.0	8.4	8.0	7.4	6.7	6.5	6.3
larceny/theft/other property[g]	4.2	4.0	3.4	2.8	2.2	2.0	2.0
Drug offenses	53.5%	55.9%	58.9%	59.2%	60.5%	59.9%	60.2%
Public-order offenses	15.1%	15.2%	15.4%	16.1%	16.5%	18.3%	18.8%
Immigration	3.0	3.0	2.6	2.6	3.0	4.2	4.9
Weapons	5.4	5.8	6.9	7.9	8.2	8.7	8.2
Escape/court[h]	0.7	0.7	0.5	0.5	0.5	0.4	0.4
Other public-order[i]	5.9	5.7	5.4	5.1	4.9	4.9	5.4
Other[j]	0.8%	1.0%	0.8%	0.8%	0.6%	0.0%	0.0%

Note: All data are from the BJS Federal justice database. Data for 1990-95 are for December 31.
Data for 1996 are for September 30.
[a]Includes prisoners of any sentence length.
[b]Percents are based on prisoners for whom most serious offense was known.
[c]Includes murder, nonnegligent manslaughter, and negligent manslaughter.
[d]In 1996 assaults with intent to commit robbery were coded as robbery.
[e]Includes kidnaping, rape, other sexual assault, threats against the President, and other offenses.
[f]Includes embezzlement, counterfeiting, forgery, bankruptcy, and fraud (excluding tax fraud but including securities fraud).
[g]Includes motor vehicle theft, trespassing, destruction of property, and transport of stolen property.
[h]Includes flight to avoid prosecution, escape, parole and probation violation, and other court offenses.
[i]Includes liquor laws, national security laws, income tax, selective service acts, bribery, gambling, traffic offenses, and other public-order offenses.
[j]Includes offenses not classifiable or not a violation of the United States Code.

TABLE 5.6

Percent of sentenced prisoners returned to State prisons for a parole violation, by the most serious offense, 1990-96

Most serious offense	Percent of parole violators returned to State prisons[a]						
	1990	1991	1992	1993	1994	1995	1996
Total	100%	100%	100%	100%	100%	100%	100%
Violent offenses	24.8%	24.1%	24.0%	24.2%	24.5%	24.0%	24.6%
Murder[b]	1.7	1.8	1.6	1.5	1.5	1.5	1.4
Negligent manslaughter	0.5	0.5	0.5	0.5	0.5	0.5	0.4
Sexual assault[c]	3.0	4.0	4.0	3.0	4.0	3.0	4.0
Robbery	13.5	11.8	12.2	12.5	11.9	11.1	10.9
Aggravated assault	5.4	5.6	5.6	5.8	6.1	6.2	6.7
Other violent	0.7	0.7	0.8	0.8	1.0	1.1	1.1
Property offenses	46.1%	43.4%	40.3%	38.6%	37.4%	36.5%	34.7%
Burglary	23.4	21.2	20.0	18.8	17.8	17.1	15.1
Larceny/theft	12.4	11.9	10.8	10.5	10.2	9.9	9.9
Motor vehicle theft	4.2	4.2	3.6	3.7	3.8	3.8	4.4
Fraud	4.1	4.2	3.6	3.3	3.1	3.1	2.7
Other property	2.0	1.9	2.3	2.3	2.5	2.6	2.6
Drug offenses	23.1%	26.0%	26.4%	27.7%	28.9%	30.2%	31.1%
Public-order offenses	5.8%	6.3%	6.8%	7.1%	7.3%	7.6%	8.2%
Other	0.2%	0.2%	2.5%	2.4%	1.9%	1.7%	1.4%

Note: Data are from the National Corrections Reporting Program and are based on the most serious offense as reported by participating States. Data may not sum to total due to rounding.
[a]Includes only those with sentences of more than 1 year.
[b]Includes nonnegligent manslaughter.
[c]Includes rape and other sexual assault.

Source of both tables: *Correctional Populations in the United States, 1996*, Bureau of Justice Statistics, Washington, DC, 1999

sentence for drug offenses in 1996, up from 32.2 percent in 1990. In 1996, a smaller proportion of women were incarcerated for property crime (27.6 percent) than in 1990 (31.9 percent). The number of women serving time for drug offenses doubled while the number in prison for property offenses rose 50 percent. (See Table 5.3.)

Male incarceration for drug offenses remained about the same — approximately 21 percent for both years. The number of men in prison for drug offenses rose 59 percent from 1990 though 1996 and 37 percent for property crimes. In 1996, males were more likely to be imprisoned for violent crimes (48.5 percent) than women (27.6 percent). (See Table 5.3.)

Federal Prisoners

The percentage of federal prisoners serving time for violent crimes fell from 16.8 percent in 1990 to 12.6 percent in 1996, but the number increased from 9,557 in 1990 to 11,523 in 1996. In 1996, about 8.5 percent of federal inmates were serving time for property offenses, a decrease from 13.9 percent in 1990. In 1996, more than twice as many prisoners (17,227) were serving public-order offenses (mainly immigration and weapons offenses) as in 1990 (8,585). The percentage of inmates in federal prison for a drug crime rose from 53.5 percent in 1990 to about 60 percent in 1996. Nearly twice as many federal inmates were serving a prison sentence for a drug charge in 1996 (55,194) as in 1990 (30,470). (See Tables 5.4 and 5.5.)

Sentences

Women served shorter maximum sentences than men, mainly because of the differences in types of crimes they committed. Women were more likely than men to be imprisoned for drug and property offenses, which generally have shorter average sentences than violent offenses. The median (half had more, half had less) maximum sentence for women was 60 months, while the median for men was 120 months. Excluding life in prison or death sentences, women in prison received sentences, on average, 48 months shorter than those

TABLE 5.7

Physical or sexual abuse before admission, by sex of inmate or probationer

Before admission	State inmates Male	State inmates Female	Federal inmates Male	Federal inmates Female
Ever abused	16.1%	57.2%	7.2%	39.9%
Physically[a]	13.4	46.5	6.0	32.3
Sexually[a]	5.8	39.0	2.2	22.8
Both	3.0	28.0	1.1	15.1
Age of victim at time of abuse				
17 or younger[b]	14.4%	36.7%	5.8%	23.0%
18 or older[b]	4.3	45.0	2.7	31.0
Both	2.5	24.7	1.3	14.2
Age of abuser				
Adult	15.0%	55.8%	6.9%	39.0%
Juvenile only	0.9	1.0	0.2	0.3
Rape before admission	4.0%	37.3%	1.4%	21.4%
Completed	3.1	32.8	1.0	17.9
Attempted	0.8	4.3	0.3	3.2

--Not available.
[a]Includes those both physically and sexually abused.
[b]Includes those abused in both age categories.

Source: Caroline Wolf Harlow, *Prior Abuse Reported by Inmates and Probationers*, Bureau of Justice Statistics, Washington, DC, 1999

of men (mean sentences of 105 and 153 months, respectively).

Returning to Prison Because of a Parole Violation

The total number of prisoners returned to either state or federal prison for parole violations in 1996 was 175,305 — 2,672 prisoners were returned to federal prison, and 172,633 prisoners were returned to state prison. In 1996, 24.6 percent of state prisoners were returned to state prison for committing a violent offense — the same proportion as in 1990. One-third (34.7 percent) of those who were returned to prison in 1996 had committed a property offense, down from 46.1 percent in 1990, and another third (31.1 percent) were back behind bars for a drug offense, up from 23.1 percent in 1990. (See Table 5.6.)

INMATES WHO WERE ABUSED IN THE PAST

The Bureau of Justice Statistics recently surveyed prison inmates (*Prior Abuse Reported by*

TABLE 5.8

Relationship to abuser, by the inmate or probationer reporting abuse

Relationship of victim to abuser	Percent of those persons who reported experiencing physical or sexual abuse before admission			
	State inmates		Federal inmates	
	Male	Female	Male	Female
Knew abuser	**89.5%**	**90.6%**	**86.3%**	**95.4%**
Family	66.6	40.1	56.7	34.8
Parent or guardian	54.1	27.2	49.0	24.3
Other relative	22.9	21.0	15.1	15.4
Intimate	5.8	61.3	6.5	66.3
Spouse/ex-spouse	2.2	36.5	1.9	41.0
Boyfriend/girlfriend	4.4	36.0	4.8	36.0
Friend/acquaintance	22.6	26.2	24.4	17.2
Other	17.4	15.8	18.7	10.5
Knew none of abusers	**10.5%**	**9.4%**	**13.7%**	**4.6%**

Note: Detail does not add to totals because some were abused by more than 1 person.

Source: Caroline Wolf Harlow, *Prior Abuse Reported by Inmates and Probationers*, Bureau of Justice Statistics, Washington, DC, 1999

Inmates and Probationers, 1999) and found that 19 percent of state prisoners and 10 percent of federal prisoners claimed that they had been physically or sexually abused prior to committing their current offense. (The survey relied on respondents to define physical and sexual abuse for themselves.)

More than half (57.2 percent) of female state prisoners and 39.9 percent of female federal prisoners reported ever being either physically or sexually abused prior to admission to prison. Far fewer male prisoners (16.1 percent of state prisoners and 7.2 percent of federal prisoners) reported ever being either physically or sexually abused prior to admission to prison. (See Table 5.7.)

An estimated 28 percent of female state inmates and 15.1 percent of female federal inmates reported they had been both sexually and physically abused prior to admittance to prison. Only 3 percent of male state prisoners and 1.1 percent of male federal prisoners reported both physical and sexual abuse before entering prison. (See Table 5.7.)

For male inmates, physical and sexual abuse tended to abate around age 18. About 2.5 percent of male state prisoners and 1.3 percent of male federal prisoners reported being abused both before and after age 18. On othe other hand, about 1 in 7 male state prisoners (14.4 percent) and 5.8 percent

of male federal prisoners claimed they had been physically or sexually abused before age 18. (See Table 5.7.) Of males abused before age 18, 11.9 percent of state prison inmates and 5 percent of federal inmates reported that they had been physically abused before age 18, while 5 percent of state inmates and 1.9 percent of federal inmates said they had been sexually abused before age 18.

The percentages were higher for female prisoners. Some 36.7 percent of female state prisoners and 23 percent of female federal prison inmates reported physical or sexual abuse before age 18. One-fourth (24.7 percent) of female state inmates and 14.2 percent of female federal inmates reported being abused both before age 18 and after age 18. (See Table 5.7.) About 25.4 percent of female state prisoners and 15 percent of female federal prisoners reported being physically abused before age 18, and 25.4 percent of female state prison inmates and 14.7 percent of female federal prisoners reported sexual abuse before age 18.

TABLE 5.9

While growing up —	Percent of State inmates reporting abuse	
	Male	Female
Prisoners lived with		
Both parents	14.0%	54.7%
One parent	16.4	57.3
Foster/agency/other	43.6	86.7
Parent abused alcohol or drugs	29.4%	75.7%
Did not abuse	10.0	45.9
At any time —		
Family* incarcerated	20.2%	63.9%
Not incarcerated	12.3	46.9

*Includes boyfriends or girlfriends with whom the inmate had lived before admission.

Source: Caroline Wolf Harlow, *Prior Abuse Reported by Inmates and Probationers*, Bureau of Justice Statistics, Washington, DC, 1999

TABLE 5.10
Current and past violent offenses and past alcohol and drug use,
by whether abused before admission to State prison, 1997

Offense history and drug and alcohol use	Percent of State prison inmates					
	Reported being abused			Reported being not abused		
	Total	Males	Females	Total	Males	Females
Current or past violent offense	70.4%	76.5%	45.0%	60.2%	61.2%	29.1%
Current violent offense	55.7%	61.0%	33.5%	45.3%	46.1%	20.9%
Homicide	15.9	16.3	13.9	12.7	12.8	7.3
Sexual assault	15.6	18.8	2.0	6.9	7.1	0.4
Robbery	12.5	13.5	7.8	14.5	14.7	6.1
Assault	9.5	9.9	7.6	9.3	9.4	5.7

Source: Caroline Wolf Harlow, *Prior Abuse Reported by Inmates and Probationers*,
Bureau of Justice Statistics, Washington, DC, 1999

The Abusers

Most of the people who abused state and federal inmates were adults. About 9 of 10 (87.9 percent of men and 93 percent of women) survey participants knew their abuser(s). Men were primarily abused by family members, while women mainly suffered at the hands of husbands or boyfriends. (See Table 5.8.)

About half (51.6 percent) of male state and federal prison inmates claimed they were abused by a parent or guardian, while one-fifth (19 percent) were assaulted by another relative. One-fourth of males (23.5 percent) were abused by friends or acquaintances, while about 3 percent identified wives, ex-wives, and girl- or boyfriends (Table 5.8).

Family Background

State prisoners who grew up in foster care reported more abuse than those who lived with parents, unless the parents used alcohol or drugs heavily or a family member had been incarcerated. About half (54.7 percent) of female inmates who lived with both parents or one parent (57.3 percent) reported that they had been abused. Meanwhile, 86.7 percent of female prisoners who grew up in a foster family or agency reported abuse. Three-fourths of women inmates whose parents abused alcohol or drugs said they had been abused. Of those female prisoners who had a relative (including boyfriend or girlfriend) who had been in-

carcerated, 63.9 percent reported being abused. (See Table 5.9.)

As with female prisoners, there was not much difference in abuse among male inmates who grew up with both parents (14 percent) or one parent (16.4 percent), while a much larger percentage (43.6 percent) of male inmates growing up in a foster home or agency reported abuse. About 3 of 10 male prisoners (29.4 percent) living with a parent who abused alcohol or drugs reported maltreatment. One-fifth (20.2 percent) of male prisoners who lived with a relative (including boyfriend or girlfriend) who had ever served time reported having been abused (Table 5.9).

Associating Violent Crime and Past Abuse of State Prisoners

Abused state prisoners were more likely than prisoners not abused to be serving a sentence for violent crime. In 1997, 55.7 percent of state prisoners serving a sentence for a violent crime reported that they were abused, while 45.3 percent of prisoners serving a sentence for violent crime reported they had not been abused. About 61 percent of males imprisoned for committing a violent offense claimed they were abused, compared to

TABLE 5.11

	Executions, 1977-97				
Method of execution	White	Black	His- panic	Amer- ican Indian	Asian
Total	241	160	26	3	2
Lethal injection	161	94	24	3	2
Electrocution	69	63	2	0	0
Lethal gas	6	3	0	0	0
Hanging	3	0	0	0	0
Firing squad	2	0	0	0	0

Source: Tracy L. Snell, *Capital Punishment — 1997*,
Bureau of Justice Statistics, Washington, DC, 1998

FIGURE 5.2

Persons under sentence of death, by race, 1968-97

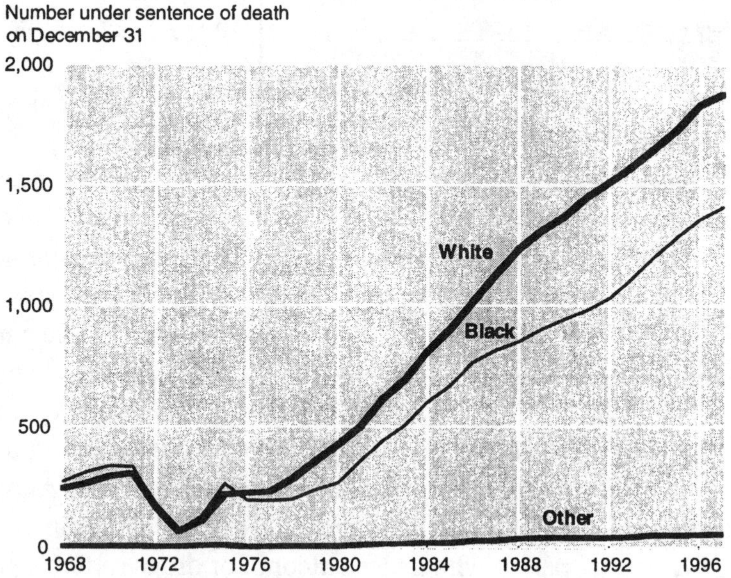

Number under sentence of death
on December 31

Source: Tracy L. Snell, *Capital Punishment — 1997*, Bureau of Justice Statistics, Washington, DC, 1998

TABLE 5.12

Persons under sentence
of death, by sex, race,
and Hispanic origin, 12/31/97

	White	Black	Other
Male	1,846	1,392	53
Hispanic	262	12	7
Female	30	14	0
Hispanic	1	1	0

Source: Tracy L. Snell, *Capital Punishment — 1997*, Bureau of Justice Statistics, Washington, DC, 1998

46.1 percent who reported no past abuse. One-third (33.5 percent) of women who had committed a violent offense reported that they had been abused, compared to 20.9 percent who indicated they had not been abused. (See Table 5.10.)

Crimes of sexual assault and homicide, in particular, are associated with past abuse. A larger proportion of men (16.3 percent) serving sentences for homicide had been abused in the past than were men (12.8 percent) who had not been abused. Furthermore, nearly twice the proportion of abused women (13.9 percent) as non-abused women (7.3 percent) were serving time for homicide. (See Table 5.10.)

Sexual assault was committed by 18.8 percent of previously abused male inmates, but by just 7.1 percent of non-abused male inmates. Few female inmates were in prison for crimes of sexual assault, but again, the proportion of abused women who committed a crime of sexual assault was much larger (2 percent)

TABLE 5.13

Demographic characteristics of prisoners under sentence of death, 1997

Characteristic	Prisoners under sentence of death, 1997		
	Yearend	Admissions	Removals
Total number under sentence of death	3,335	256	163
Sex			
Male	98.7%	99.2%	96.9%
Female	1.3	0.8	3.1
Race			
White	56.3%	57.0%	63.2%
Black	42.2	41.4	35.6
Other	1.6	1.6	1.2
Hispanic origin			
Hispanic	9.2%	12.0%	4.5%
Non-Hispanic	90.8	88.0	95.5
Education			
8th grade or less	14.2%	13.3%	16.2%
9th-11th grade	37.6	34.1	34.6
High school graduate/GED	38.0	45.0	40.4
Any college	10.1	7.6	8.8
Median	11th grade	12th grade	11th grade
Marital status			
Married	24.5%	23.9%	32.5%
Divorced/separated	21.3	20.0	19.5
Widowed	2.6	4.3	5.8
Never married	51.5	51.7	42.2

Note: Calculations are based on those cases for which data were reported. Missing data by category were as follows:

	Yearend	Admissions	Removals
Hispanic origin	258	39	6
Education	504	45	27
Marital status	304	26	9

Source: Tracy L. Snell, *Capital Punishment — 1997*, Bureau of Justice Statistics, Washington, DC, 1998

than for non-abused women (0.4 percent). (See Table 5.10.)

About 76.5 percent of male state prisoners reporting past abuse had been convicted of one or more violent crimes, compared to 61.2 percent of non-abused males. Abused women (45 percent) were twice as likely as non-abused women (29.1 percent) to have ever committed a violent crime (Table 5.10).

CHARACTERISTICS OF PRISONERS UNDER SENTENCE OF DEATH

In 1997, 17 states executed 74 prisoners, all of whom were men. Of those, 41 were non-Hispanic Whites, 26 non-Hispanic Blacks, four Hispanic Whites, one Hispanic Black, one Native American, and one Asian. Most (68 percent) of the executions were carried out by lethal injection, while six prisoners were electrocuted. Table 5.11 shows the methods of execution used from 1977 through 1997. In 1998, 18 states executed 68 prisoners. Among them were 48 Whites, 18 Blacks, one Native American, and one Asian. Two women were executed in 1998, the first year since 1984 that any women had been executed.

In 1997, 29 state prison systems reported receiving 253 prisoners under sentence of death, and the Federal Bureau of Prisons received 3 inmates, all of whom had been convicted of murder. White men accounted for 56.3 percent (144) of those prisoners and Black men for 41.4 percent (106). Only four prisoners were Native American men, and two

prisoners were women, both of whom were White. Of the 256 new admissions, 26 (10 percent) were Hispanic men.

As of December 31, 1997, 34 states and the federal prison system held a total of 3,335 prisoners under sentence of death. (See Figure 5.2.) Table 5.12 shows the numbers of persons awaiting death by race/ethnicity and gender at the end of 1997.

Demographic Characteristics

Gender, Race, and Ethnicity

In 1997, 3,291 men accounted for 98.7 percent of all prisoners on death row, and 44 women accounted for 1.3 percent. More than half (56.3 percent) were White, 42.2 percent were Black, and 9.2 percent were Hispanic. (See Table 5.13.) Other races included Native Americans (28 persons) and Asians (17 persons).

TABLE 5.14

Age at time of arrest for capital offense and age of prisoners under sentence of death at yearend, 1997

| Age | Prisoners under sentence of death | | | |
| | At time of arrest | | On December 31, 1997 | |
	Number*	Percent	Number	Percent
Total number under sentence of death on 12/31/97	2,975	100 %	3,335	100 %
17 or younger	69	2.3	0	
18-19	311	10.5	14	0.4
20-24	824	27.7	275	8.2
25-29	685	23.0	497	14.9
30-34	471	15.8	578	17.3
35-39	315	10.6	727	21.8
40-44	155	5.2	521	15.6
45-49	85	2.9	354	10.6
50-54	35	1.2	216	6.5
55-59	16	0.5	88	2.6
60 or older	9	0.3	65	1.9
Mean age	28 yrs		37 yrs	
Median age	26 yrs		37 yrs	

Note: The youngest person under sentence of death was a black male in Alabama, born in November 1979 and sentenced to death in October 1997. The oldest person under sentence of death was a white male in Arizona, born in September 1915 and sentenced to death in June 1983.
*Excludes 360 inmates for whom the date of arrest for capital offense was not available.

Source: Tracy L. Snell, *Capital Punishment — 1997*, Bureau of Justice Statistics, Washington, DC, 1998

Education

At the end of 1997, of those prisoners under sentence of death for whom information on education was available, three-fourths had either graduated from high school (38 percent) or completed ninth, tenth, or eleventh grade (37.6 percent). One of 7 (14.2 percent) inmates had not gone beyond eighth grade, and just 1 of 10 had attended college. The median level of education for prisoners on death row was the eleventh grade (Table 5.13).

Marital Status

In 1997, among inmates under a capital sentence with available information on marital status, half (51.5 percent) had never married. One-fourth (24.5 percent) were married, 21.3 percent were divorced or separated, and 2.6 percent were widowed (Table 5.13).

Age

Of those inmates on death row for whom date of arrest information was available, more than half (50.7 percent) were between the ages of 20 and 29 at the time of their arrest. About 1 of 8 (12.8 percent) was under the age of 20, and less than 1 percent was older than age 55. (See Table 5.14.) At the end of 1997, the youngest inmate waiting on death row was 18 years old; the oldest, 82 years of age.

Past Criminal History

At the end of 1997, about two-thirds (65.3 percent) of inmates on death row for whom criminal history information was available had past felony convictions, including 8.6 percent with at least one previous conviction for homicide. Among those awaiting execution, 19.5 percent had been on parole and 10.1 percent had been on probation. More than half (58 percent) had no legal status at the time they committed their capital offense. (See Table 5.15.)

Race/Ethnicity

Criminal history differed by race and Hispanic origin. Blacks (69.5 percent) were somewhat more likely than Whites (63 percent) or Hispanics (59.5 percent) to have had prior felony convictions. Hispanics (25.7 percent) and Blacks (21.8 percent) were slightly more likely than Whites (16.4 percent) to be on parole when arrested

TABLE 5.15

Criminal history profile of prisoners under sentence of death, by race and Hispanic origin, 1997

	Prisoners under sentence of death							
	Number				Percent[a]			
	All[b]	White	Black	Hispanic	All[b]	White	Black	Hispanic
U.S. total	3,335	1,613	1,393	283	100%	100%	100%	100%
Prior felony convictions								
Yes	2,011	939	895	153	65.3%	63.0%	69.5%	59.5%
No	1,068	552	393	104	34.7	37.0	30.5	40.5
Not reported	256							
Prior homicide convictions								
Yes	281	127	125	22	8.6%	8.0%	9.2%	8.1%
No	2,980	1,457	1,234	251	91.4	92.0	90.8	91.9
Not reported	74							
Legal status at time of capital offense								
Charges pending	225	121	86	16	7.6%	8.4%	7.0%	6.5%
Probation	301	141	132	25	10.1	9.7	10.7	10.2
Parole	578	237	270	63	19.5	16.4	21.8	25.7
Prison escapee	38	25	10	2	1.3	1.7	0.8	0.8
Incarcerated	76	35	35	4	2.6	2.4	2.8	1.6
Other status	30	16	12	1	1.0	1.1	1.0	0.4
None	1,721	872	691	134	58.0	60.3	55.9	54.7
Not reported	366							

[a]Percentages are based on those offenders for whom data were reported. Detail may not add to total because of rounding.
[b]Includes persons of other races.

Source: Tracy L. Snell, *Capital Punishment — 1997*, Bureau of Justice Statistics, Washington, DC, 1998

for their current capital offense. About the same percentage of Blacks (9.2 percent), Hispanics (8.1 percent), and Whites (8 percent) had prior homicide convictions (Table 5.15).

GANG MEMBERSHIP

The Bureau of Justice Statistics defines gangs as groups that commit illegal acts and have five or six of these characteristics:

- Formal membership with a required initiation or rules for members.

- A recognized leader or certain members whom others follow.

- Common clothing or group colors, symbols, tattoos, or special language.

- A group name.

- Members from the same neighborhood, street, or school.

- Turf or territory where the group is known and where group activities usually take place.

In 1997, about 6 percent of prison inmates had belonged to groups that engaged in illegal activities and that had five or six gang characteristics. Another 6 percent had engaged in illegal activities with groups that had three or four gang character-

istics. Among inmates who were gang members, half had belonged for 36 months or more and belonged at the time they were arrested for their current offenses. One-third (32 percent) were still members.

PROGRAM PARTICIPATION

Nearly all inmates had participated in work, education, or other programs since their admission to prison. A third of all inmates had participated in a drug treatment program after entering prison. (See Chapter XII for more information.)

In a 1995 census of prisons, the Bureau of Justice found that 80 percent of all prisons offered a general equivalency diploma or other secondary program, and almost one-quarter of all prisoners were enrolled. About 70 percent of all facilities offered psychological or psychiatric inmate counseling. Recent funding cuts by state legislatures are expected to lead to a cutback in many of these programs.

In 1995, the census of prisons also found that fewer convicts than in previous years were involved in pre-release organizations and activities, designed to help prisoners return to noninstitutional life. These included classes to improve skills, outside community programs, or ethnic or racial programs, such as the National Association for the Advancement of Colored People (NAACP) or the Hispanic Committee.

CHAPTER VI

PRISONS AND PRISON OVERCROWDING

If you cram people in prison, create forced idleness without the supervision that's needed, you can expect the situation to get out of hand. It's an unbelievable burden on corrections staff to manage people in inhumane conditions. — Stephen B. Bright, Executive Director for Human Rights

FACILITIES

The Bureau of Justice Statistics (BJS) conducts a census of state and federal adult correctional facilities every five years (*Census of State and Federal Correctional Facilities, 1995*, Washington, DC, 1997). Confinement facilities include prisons, prison hospitals, boot camps, and other institutions from which prisoners are not free to leave. Community-based facilities, such as halfway houses and pre-release centers, typically hold inmates who are nearing the completion of their sentences and are permitted to leave to work or study in the community. The census excluded the nation's approximately 3,300 locally operated jails and county or municipal detention centers.

In 1995, the BJS counted 1,196 state and federal confinement institutions and 304 community-based facilities. The states operated 1,375 facilities and the federal Bureau of Prisons operated 125 facilities. These prisons had a capacity of 976,000 beds — up 41 percent in the five-year period. The number of state and federal correctional facilities in operation increased 17 percent, from 1,287 at midyear 1990, when the last census was conducted, to 1,500 at midyear 1995. (See Table 6.1.)

As of January 1, 1998, there were 1,387 adult correctional facilities in operation in the United States. Texas had the most facilities (107) and North Dakota, with only two facilities, had the fewest.

Facility Types and Security Levels

In both 1990 and 1995, confinement facilities accounted for 80 percent of all facilities, and commu-

---

TABLE 6.1

168 State facilities and 45 Federal facilities were added between 1990 and 1995

Facility characteristic	Community and confinement facilities			
	State		Federal	
	1990	1995	1990	1995
Number	1,207	1,375	80	125
Confinement	957	1,084	80	112
Community-based	250	291	0	13
Rated capacity	650,600	909,908	42,183	65,811
Inmates in custody	658,828	941,642	56,821	81,930
Percent of capacity occupied	101%	103%	135%	124%
Private facilities	67	98	0	12
Average number of inmates held	7,771	15,408	0	1,018
Security level				
Maximum/close/high	223	289	11	9
Medium	368	438	37	25
Minimum/low	616	648	32	91
Court orders/consent decrees*				
For any reason	323	378	0	113
To limit population	264	228	0	1
For specific conditions	242	321	0	112
For the totality of conditions	212	149	0	0

*Specific reasons add to more than "For any reason" because some facilities were under court order or consent decree for more than one reason.

Source: James J. Stephan, *Census of State and Federal Correctional Facilities, 1995*, Bureau of Justice Statistics, Washington, DC, 1997

TABLE 6.2

State and Federal facilities held 1,023,572 inmates in 1995, up from 715,649 in 1990

Inmate characteristic	State and Federal correctional facilities	
	1990	1995
Number of Inmates		
Total	715,649	1,023,572
Under age 18	3,600	5,309
Noncitizen inmates^a	25,250	51,500
Type of facility		
Confinement	698,570	992,333
Community-based	17,079	31,239
Custody level		
Maximum/close/high	150,205	202,174
Medium	292,372	415,688
Minimum/low	219,907	366,227
Not classified	53,165	39,483
Number of assaults^b		
On other inmates	21,590	25,948
On staff	10,731	14,165
Rate of assault per 1,000 inmates		
All confinement facilities	46.8	40.8
Maximum security	60.7	61.5
Medium security	46.5	33.9
Minimum security	18.7	17.8

^aData from 1995 were based on reporting from 81% of facilities.
^bIn confinement facilities during the 12 months preceding the

Source: James J. Stephan, *Census of State and Federal Correctional Facilities, 1995*, Bureau of Justice Statistics, Washington, DC, 1997

nity-based institutions accounted for about 20 percent. The distribution of inmates by type of facility remained virtually unchanged from 1990 to 1995. In 1990, all but 2 percent of prisoners were housed in confinement facilities, and in 1995, all but 3 percent. (See Table 6.2.)

On all security levels, more state facilities were in operation in 1995 than five years earlier. By contrast, the federal system operated more minimum-security facilities and fewer maximum and medium security institutions. (See Table 6.1.)

In 1998, according to the Criminal Justice Institute (*The Corrections Yearbook — 1998*), of all adult correctional facilities, multi-level security facilities were the most numerous (334), followed by medium (330), minimum (299), community (219), and maximum (96).

PRISON OVERCROWDING

More and More Prisoners

The nation's courts are sentencing and admitting more offenders into America's prisons than the facilities can hold. (See Chapter IV for statistics on the number of prisoners.) At the beginning of 1995, 39 states plus the District of Columbia, Puerto Rico, and the Virgin Islands were under court order to relieve overcrowding and/or unconstitutional conditions (*Status Report: State Prisons and the Courts*, The National Prison Project of the American Civil Liberties Union Foundation, Washington, DC, 1995).

According to the 1995 BJS census (see above), approximately 1 in 4 state correctional facilities was under a court order or consent decree to limit population or to address specific confinement conditions. Nonetheless, the number of state facilities ordered by courts to limit their populations declined somewhat from 183 in 1990 to 174 in 1995.

The American Correctional Association guidelines call for a standard cell area of 60 square feet for inmates spending no more than 10 hours per day in their cells. In many prisons, inmates are double-bunked in cells designed for one or sleep on mattresses in unheated prison gyms or on the floors of dayrooms, halls, or basements. Some are housed in tents; others sleep in the same bunks at different times of the day.

As room for prisoners has diminished, it has become harder to segregate violent from nonviolent prisoners, causing tension and often leading to injuries. Overcrowding has also contributed to the spread of communicable diseases such as tuberculosis. Many taxpayers do not consider overcrowding a problem because they believe that discomfort should be part of the punishment.

BUILDING MORE PRISONS — RUNNING TO STAY IN PLACE

Most states have been dealing with growth in their prison populations by building more facilities. The 1995 BJS census found that state and federal officials built

213 new prisons — 168 state and 45 federal facilities — with more than 280,000 beds between 1990 and 1995 to try to keep pace with the growing prison population. This new prison construction resulted in an increase in the percentage of facilities less than 20 years old — growing from 37 percent in 1990 to more than 50 percent in 1995. Almost 40 percent of all prison inmates in 1995 were held in facilities built after 1985.

The Criminal Justice Institute (*The Corrections Yearbook — 1998*) reported that, in 1997, 15 correction agencies opened 31 new institutions, adding 25,248 beds at an average cost of $48,601 (only 13 agencies reported costs). Some states have trouble building prisons fast enough to meet court orders to correct conditions. For example, the corrections office of New Mexico admitted that it could not open new prisons until at least 1998, although the state was ordered by the courts to close its aging, inadequate main facility by October 1997. While waiting for the new prisons, New Mexico put more prisoners in local jails or sent them to out-of-state jails.

Because building prisons and adding new beds is costly, states are looking for other ways to manage overcrowding, such as early release programs, electronic monitoring, keeping prisoners in local jails, and having offenders pay restitution to their victims. Early release gives officials a way to allow prisoners to leave before their sentences are completed. In New York, "presumptive release" permits the parole board to release offenders on parole after they have served their minimum sentences if they have not caused any problems. Good-time or merit-time allows the reduction of sentence time for every day of good behavior or participation in particular programs.

Felons were sentenced to an average of just over 5 years (62 months) in 1996. State prisoners actually served about 45 percent of that sentence, or 28

TABLE 6.3

State prisoners held in local jails because of prison crowding, by State, yearend 1997 and 1996

| | State prisoners held in local jails | | | |
| | Number | | As a percent of State inmates | |
	1997	1996	1997	1996
U.S. total	33,736	30,741	3.0%	2.9%
Louisiana	10,795	9,147	36.9%	34.2%
Virginia	3,753	2,506	13.2	9.1
New Jersey	2,864	4,367	10.1	15.9
Colorado	1,886	1,163	14.0	9.4
Alabama	1,824	1,168	8.2	5.4
Mississippi	1,463	3,242	9.5	23.4
Tennessee	1,428	1,958	8.6	12.5
Arkansas	1,376	1,201	13.7	12.8
Indiana	1,323	1,194	7.4	7.0
Kentucky	1,144	778	7.8	6.0
New York	918	0	1.3%	--
Oklahoma	802	285	3.9	1.5
West Virginia	775	286	24.4	10.4
New Mexico	557	307	11.9	6.5
Massachusetts	484	554	4.1	4.7
South Carolina	400	413	1.9	2.0
Utah	348	308	8.1	7.8
Wisconsin	284	338	1.9	2.6
North Carolina	282	516	0.9	1.7
Montana	217	85	9.7	3.7
Arizonaª	211	124	0.9%	0.5%
Michiganª	151	330	0.3	0.8
Oregon	72	91	0.9	1.1
North Dakota	68	91	8.5	12.6
New Hampshire	66	65	3.0	3.2
Missouri	55	0	0.2	--
Alaska	55	0	1.3	--
Minnesotaᵇ	50	208	0.9	4.0
Idaho	31	0	0.8	--
Wyoming	29	16	1.9	1.1
Pennsylvania	25	0	0.1	--

--Not calculated.
ªFor States without jail backups in their counts, the percentage is based on the total of State inmates in jail and prison.
ᵇHeld in a private facility.

Source: Darrell K. Gilliard and Allen J. Beck, *Prisoners in 1997*, Bureau of Justice Statistics, Washington, DC, 1998

TABLE 6.4

| States housing prisoners in other States or Federal facilities | Prisoners held in other States or Federal facilities | |
	Number	As a percent of all State prisoners
U.S. total	5,877	0.5%
Colorado	1,009	7.5
Oklahoma	941	4.6
Wisconsin	819	5.6
Idaho	608	15.4
Hawaii	600	12.1
New Mexico	486	10.4
Montana	381	17.0
Alaska	332	7.9
Massachusetts	318	2.7
Alabama	104	0.5
Wyoming	99	6.3
New Hampshire	73	3.4
Indiana	69	0.4
Michigan	38	0.1

Source: Darrell K. Gilliard and Allen J. Beck, *Prisoners in 1997*, Bureau of Justice Statistics, Washington, DC, 1998

months, before release. The danger in releasing inmates to make room for new admissions is that some prisoners who should not be released, such as violent offenders, might be let out.

STATE PRISONERS IN LOCAL JAILS

At the end of 1997, 31 jurisdictions reported that a total of 33,736 state prisoners were held in local jails or other facilities because of crowding in state facilities (Table 6.3). Louisiana accounted for 36.9 percent of its prisoners sentenced to prison but housed locally. Seven states (Louisiana, Virginia, New Jersey, Colorado, Arkansas, New Mexico, and West Virginia) held at least 10 percent of their prison population in local jails. Overall, because of prison crowding, 3 percent of the state prison population was confined in local jails in 1997, about the same (2.9 percent) as in 1996, but down from the 5.4 percent of state prisoners held in local jails on December 31, 1993. (For jail overcrowding, see Chapter III.)

In addition to housing inmates in local jails, 14 states and the District of Columbia eased prison crowding by placing inmates in other states or in federal facilities. On December 31, 1997, 5,877 prisoners nationwide were held under such arrangements—less than 1 percent of all state prisoners. Colorado placed the most inmates in federal and out-of-state facilities (1,009). At year-end 1997, Idaho, Montana, and Hawaii had more than 12 percent of their total prison population in other state or federal facilities. (See Table 6.4.)

In 1993, Texas had more than 10 percent of its prison population in jails,

TABLE 6.5

Reported Federal and State prison capacities, yearend 1997

| Region and jurisdiction | Type of capacity measure | | | Population as a percent of | |
	Rated	Operational	Design	Highest capacity	Lowest capacity
Federal[a]	85,387	...	...	119%	119%
Northeast					
Connecticut[b]	...	...	...	...	...
Maine	1,437	1,590	1,437	102%	113%
Massachusetts[a,c]	...	...	8,138	137	137
New Hampshire[c]	1,841	1,644	1,744	110	123
New Jersey[a,c]	...	...	15,906	160	160
New York	60,947	65,823	53,463	106	131
Pennsylvania[a,c]	...	22,875	23,156	151	153
Rhode Island	3,774	3,774	3,774	89	89
Vermont	1,140	1,140	1,023	111	124
Midwest					
Illinois	28,797	28,797	25,135	142%	162%
Indiana[c]	13,611	16,892	...	98	121
Iowa	4,951	4,951	4,951	140	140
Kansas	8,168	...	...	97	97
Michigan[a]	...	45,146	...	99	99
Minnesota	5,327	5,327	5,327	98	98
Missouri[a,c]	...	22,317	...	107	107
Nebraska[a]	...	2,517	2,013	135	169
North Dakota[c]	579	579	579	126	126
Ohio[a]	34,706	...	...	138	138
South Dakota[a]	...	...	2,329	96	96
Wisconsin	10,288	10,288	10,288	129	129
South					
Alabama[c,d]	20,412	20,412	20,412	100%	100%
Arkansas[a,c]	8,760	8,760	8,760	99	99
Delaware[a]	...	4,206	3,192	129	170
District of Col.[e]	7,251	9,729	9,419	72	97
Florida[a]	77,425	71,276	52,865	83	122
Georgia	36,610	...	...	100	100
Kentucky[a,c]	10,774	10,827	8,934	124	151
Louisiana[a,c]	18,470	18,467	...	100	100
Maryland[a]	...	22,921	...	97	97
Mississippi[c]	...	14,428	15,187	92	97
North Carolina	26,887	...	26,887	117	117
Oklahoma	11,439	15,414	...	104	140
South Carolina[c]	...	22,474	21,731	92	96
Tennessee[a,c]	16,150	15,808	...	94	96
Texas	143,928	143,928	146,779	96	98
Virginia[a,c]	16,111	16,111	16,111	153	153
West Virginia[c]	2,378	2,404	2,370	100	101
West					
Alaska[c]	2,603	2,603	2,603	147%	147%
Arizona[a]	...	24,137	21,370	97	110
California	...	...	76,352	206	206
Colorado[a,c]	...	9,046	7,643	115	137
Hawaii[a,c]	...	2,912	1,991	149	218
Idaho[a,c]	2,483	3,437	2,483	96	133
Montana[c]	...	1,400	896	117	183
Nevada[a]	8,851	...	6,557	102	138
New Mexico[c]	...	4,435	...	82	82
Oregon[a,c]	...	7,548	...	105	105
Utah	4,495	4,261	...	88	92
Washington[c]	7,963	10,971	10,971	108	148
Wyoming[c]	1,231	1,243	1,047	116	137

...Data not available.
[a]See *NPS jurisdiction notes.*
[b]Connecticut no longer reports capacity because of a law passed in 1995. See *NPS jurisdictional notes.*
[c]Population housed as a percent of capacity was calculated excluding jail backups and inmates held in another State from yearend counts.
[d]The capacity of community programs is not included.
[e]Population housed as a percent of capacity was calculated excluding inmates held in Federal facilities.

Source: Darrell K. Gilliard and Allen J. Beck, *Prisoners in 1997*, Bureau of Justice Statistics, Washington, DC, 1998

65

but since late 1995, Texas has experienced excess correctional capacity. By 1995, the state had built 43 of 75 planned new facilities. Therefore, because Texas state prisons had room for their own prisoners, Texas jails were able to lease space to other states. Consequently, nearly 5,500 inmates from 12 other states were housed in 21 Texas institutions — mostly local and county jails. (See Chapter III.)

For many states, it is cheaper to send prisoners away to be housed in other states' prisons and jails. For example, the corrections commissioner of Massachusetts observed that $42 per inmate per day to house an inmate in Dallas, Texas, was half the cost of incarceration in Massachusetts. (See Chapter II for more information on costs.)

Prisoner advocates criticize the transfers of prisoners to other states because they make the lives of the prisoners and their families far more difficult. Jill Brotman, head of the American Friends Service Committee in Cambridge, Massachusetts, said, "It's not possible for them [family and friends] to visit. Having family members incarcerated is difficult enough, but to have the person 1,800 miles away, suddenly, is absolutely devastating." In addition, the inmates complain about difficulties meeting their lawyers and arranging for work and housing upon their release.

PRISON CAPACITY

The extent of crowding in the nation's prisons is difficult to determine because of the absence of uniform measures for defining capacity. The 52 reporting jurisdictions apply a wide variety of standards to reflect both available space to house inmates and the ability to staff and operate an institution. To estimate the capacity of the nation's prisons, jurisdictions are asked to supply three measures — rated, operational, and design capacities. Rated capacity is the number of beds or inmates assigned by a rating official to institutions within the jurisdiction. Operational capacity is the number of inmates that can be accommodated based on a facility's staff, existing programs, and services. Design capacity is the number of inmates that planners or architects intended for the facility.

Of the 52 reporting jurisdictions, 33 supplied rated capacities, 41 provided operational capacities, and 37 submitted design capacities. Twenty-three jurisdictions reported one capacity measure or gave the same figure for each capacity measure they reported. (See Table 6.5.)

Most Operate Above Capacity

Prisons generally require reserve capacity to operate efficiently. Prison dormitories and cells need to be maintained and repaired periodically, special housing is needed for protective custody and disciplinary

TABLE 6.6	
State prison population as a percent of capacity, yearend 1997	
	State prisons[a]
Highest capacity	947,750
Lowest capacity	874,792
Net change in capacity, 1996-97	
Highest	53,998
Lowest	38,520
Population as a percent of capacity[b]	
Highest	
1990	115
1991	116
1992	118
1993	118
1994	117
1995	114
1996	116
1997	115
Lowest	
1990	127
1991	131
1992	131
1993	129
1994	129
1995	125
1996	124
1997	124

Note: States were asked to report their rated, operational, and design capacities. Data reflect the highest and lowest of the three capacities for 1990-97.
[a]Data include estimated capacity figures for Connecticut at yearend 1995-97.
[b]Excludes inmates sentenced to prison but held in local jails because of crowding.

Source: Darrell K. Gilliard and Allen J. Beck, *Prisoners in 1997*, Bureau of Justice Statistics, Washington, DC, 1998

cases, and space may be needed to cope with emergencies. At the end of 1997, 17 states and the District of Columbia reported they were operating at or below 99 percent of their highest capacity. (See Table 6.5.)

On the other hand, in 1997, 36 states and the federal prison system reported operating at 100 percent or more of their lowest capacity. New Mexico, which was operating at 82 percent of its lowest capacity, had the least crowded prison system. California, operating at over twice its highest reported capacity (206 percent), had the most crowded prison system. By 1997, officials estimated that the federal system was operating at 19 percent over capacity (Table 6.5) and state prisons at 15 percent above their highest capacities and 24 percent of their lowest capacities. (See Table 6.6.)

RISING STATE PRISON POPULATIONS

More People Coming to Court

There are a number of reasons why the nation's state prison population has been growing. First is the simple increase in the number of prisoners. The Bu-

TABLE 6.7

Estimated number of felony convictions in State courts, 1996

Most serious conviction offense	Felons convictions in State court	
	Number	Percent
All offenses	997,970	100%
Violent offenses	167,824	16.8%
Murder[a]	11,430	1.1
Murder	8,564	0.9
Manslaughter	2,866	0.3
Sexual assault[b]	30,057	3.0
Rape	13,559	1.4
Other sexual assault	16,498	1.7
Robbery	42,831	4.3
Armed	12,041	1.2
Unarmed	12,155	1.2
Unspecified	18,635	1.9
Aggravated assault	69,522	7.0
Other violent[c]	13,984	1.4
Property offenses	298,631	29.9%
Burglary	93,197	9.3
Residential	10,605	1.1
Nonresidential	18,220	1.8
Unspecified	64,371	6.5
Larceny[d]	123,201	12.3
Motor vehicle theft	17,794	1.8
Other theft	105,406	10.6
Fraud[e]	82,233	8.2
Fraud	41,480	4.2
Forgery	40,753	4.1
Drug offenses	347,774	34.8%
Possession	135,270	13.6
Trafficking	212,504	21.3
Marijuana	20,618	2.1
Other	68,985	6.9
Unspecified	122,901	12.3
Weapons offenses	33,337	3.3%
Other offenses[f]	150,404	15.1%

Note: Detail may not sum to total because of rounding. Data specifying the conviction offense were available for 997,970 cases.
[a]Manslaughter is defined as nonnegligent manslaughter only. A small number of cases were classified as nonnegligent manslaughter when it was unclear if the conviction offense was murder or nonnegligent manslaughter.
[b]Includes rape.
[c]Includes offenses such as negligent manslaughter and kidnaping.
[d]Includes a small number of convictions with unspecified offenses.
[e]Includes embezzlement.
[f]Composed of nonviolent offenses such as receiving stolen property and vandalism.

Source: Jodi M. Brown, Patrick A. Langan, and David J. Levin, *Felony Sentences in State Courts, 1996*, Bureau of Justice Statistics, Washington, DC, 1999

TABLE 6.8

	Number of felony convictions
1988	667,366
1990	829,344
1992	893,630
1994	872,217
1996	997,970

FIGURE 6.1

Number of felony convictions in State courts

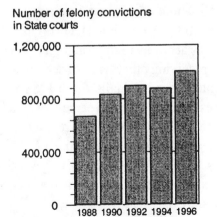

Source of above table and figure: Jodi M. Brown, Patrick A. Langan, and David J. Levin, *Felony Sentences in State Courts, 1996*, Bureau of Justice Statistics, Washington, DC, 1999

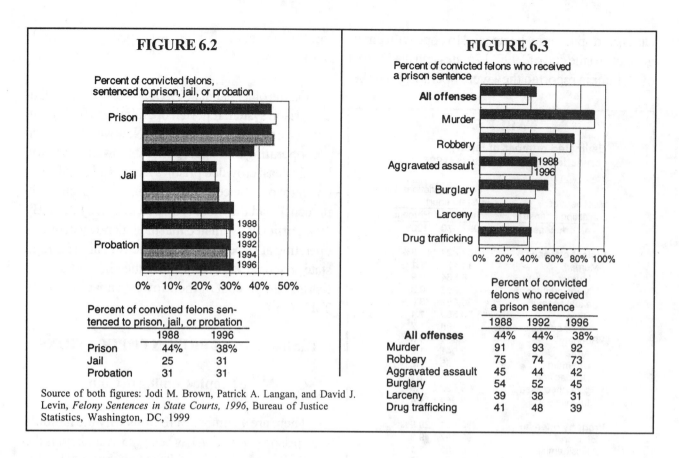

FIGURE 6.2

Percent of convicted felons, sentenced to prison, jail, or probation

Prison

Jail

Probation

1988
1990
1992
1994
1996

0% 10% 20% 30% 40% 50%

Percent of convicted felons sentenced to prison, jail, or probation

	1988	1996
Prison	44%	38%
Jail	25	31
Probation	31	31

FIGURE 6.3

Percent of convicted felons who received a prison sentence

All offenses
Murder
Robbery
Aggravated assault
Burglary
Larceny
Drug trafficking

1988
1996

0% 20% 40% 60% 80% 100%

Percent of convicted felons who received a prison sentence

	1988	1992	1996
All offenses	44%	44%	38%
Murder	91	93	92
Robbery	75	74	73
Aggravated assault	45	44	42
Burglary	54	52	45
Larceny	39	38	31
Drug trafficking	41	48	39

Source of both figures: Jodi M. Brown, Patrick A. Langan, and David J. Levin, *Felony Sentences in State Courts, 1996*, Bureau of Justice Statistics, Washington, DC, 1999

reau of Justice Statistics reported that, in 1996, state courts convicted 997,970 adults of a felony, 50 percent greater than the number convicted in 1988 (667,366). Since 1988, the general trend has been upward. (See Tables 6.7 and 6.8 and Figure 6.1.)

The state courts are sentencing more people to prison because more people are being brought to court, not because the courts are becoming more likely to sentence them to prison. From 1988 to 1994, the percentage of felons receiving a state prison sentence remained at about 45 percent, but in 1996, that percentage fell to 38 percent. The drop in prison sentences was accompanied by an increase in the percentage receiving other types of sentences, particularly sentences to local jails. From 1988 to 1994, jail sentences made up about 25 percent of all felony sentences. In 1996, the percentage receiving a jail sentence rose to 31 percent. (See Figure 6.2.) Of all felony offenses, burglary had one of the largest decreases in the percentage sentenced to prison between 1988 and 1996 (Figure 6.3).

From 1985 to 1990, admissions to state prisons increased 91 percent, and from 1990 through 1995,

admissions rose another 13 percent. As Figure 6.4 shows, the total incarceration rate tripled from 145 inmates for every 100,000 U.S. residents in 1980 to 428 inmates per 100,000 in 1995. Meanwhile, the incarceration rate for federal inmates more than tripled from 11 inmates per 100,000 U.S. residents in 1980 to 38 inmates per 100,000 U.S. residents in 1995. (See Chapter IV, Figure 4.1 for the growth of the total incarcerated population from 1985 to midyear 1998.)

An Increasing Number in Prison for Violent and Drug Offenses

Much of the growth in the state prison population can be attributed to the increase in the number of people sent to prison for drug and violent offenses. As a percentage of the total growth, violent offenders accounted for 50 percent of the total growth; drug offenders, 25 percent; property offenders, 18 percent; and public order offenders, 7 percent. From 1990 to 1996, the number of White violent offenders grew 42 percent, and the number of White drug offenders increased 56 percent. Among Black prisoners, the increase was 60 percent for violent offenders and 67 percent for drug offenders. (See Table 6.9.)

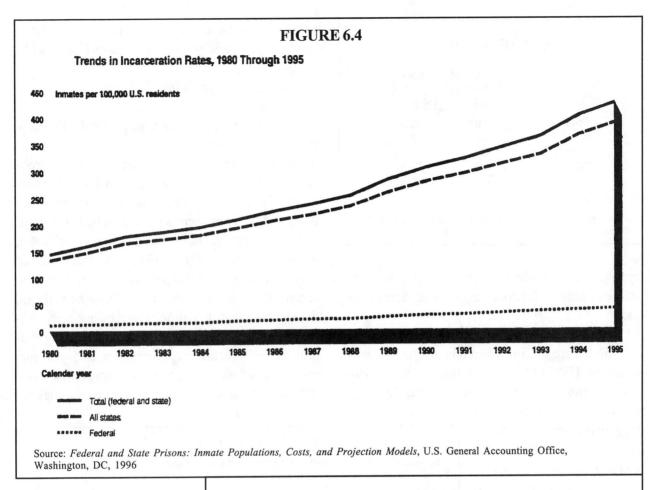

FIGURE 6.4

Trends in Incarceration Rates, 1980 Through 1995

450 Inmates per 100,000 U.S. residents

400

350

300

250

200

150

100

50

0

1980 1981 1982 1983 1984 1985 1986 1987 1988 1989 1990 1991 1992 1993 1994 1995

Calendar year

——— Total (federal and state)
— — — All states
•••••• Federal

Source: *Federal and State Prisons: Inmate Populations, Costs, and Projection Models*, U.S. General Accounting Office, Washington, DC, 1996

From 1985 to midyear 1998, the size of the state prison population more than doubled from 451,812 to 1.1 million. Meanwhile, the distribution of the four major offense categories that sent these people to prison — violent, property, drug, and public-order offenses — changed dramatically in the nation's prison population. As a percentage of all state prisoners, violent offenders fell from 54 percent in 1985 to 47 percent in 1996, while property offenders dropped from 31 percent to 23 percent. Meanwhile, the proportion of drug offenders rose from 9 percent to 23 percent, and public-order offenders increased somewhat from 5 percent to 7 percent. Most of this dramatic change occurred between 1985 and 1990, since, as Table 6.10 illustrates, between 1990 and 1996, the apportionment of the four major of-

TABLE 6.9

Estimated number of sentenced prisoners under State jurisdiction, by offense, race, and Hispanic origin, 1990 and 1996

Offenses	White		Black		Hispanic	
	1990	1996	1990	1996	1990	1996
Total	243,400	350,700	314,700	490,500	115,300	175,500
Violent offenses	117,600	167,200	146,100	234,400	43,700	76,100
Murder	28,400	36,300	32,100	56,300	10,000	17,100
Manslaughter	5,100	6,000	5,700	7,000	2,400	3,200
Rape	11,700	18,100	9,900	16,400	2,000	2,800
Other sexual assault	24,700	38,200	9,000	15,300	4,800	7,800
Robbery	24,600	29,800	59,100	85,600	14,200	21,700
Assault	17,300	31,300	25,500	44,100	8,800	18,800
Other violent	5,800	10,300	4,800	7,800	1,500	3,800
Property offenses	75,200	105,100	70,900	96,200	24,200	33,700
Burglary	38,300	48,600	33,800	44,600	13,700	15,700
Larceny	13,700	19,400	16,300	22,500	4,200	6,600
Motor vehicle theft	5,800	8,600	5,800	7,800	2,600	4,800
Fraud	9,800	14,500	8,200	10,400	1,500	2,600
Other property	7,600	13,700	6,700	11,200	2,200	4,100
Drug offenses	29,600	46,300	79,800	133,400	38,700	52,300
Public-order offenses	19,700	31,400	16,600	24,700	8,300	12,600
Other/unspecified	1,300	700	1,400	1,900	400	800

Source: Darrell K. Gilliard and Allen J. Beck, *Prisoners in 1997*, Bureau of Justice Statistics, Washington, DC, 1998

TABLE 6.10

Percent of sentenced
State inmates*

	1990	1996
Total	100%	100%
Violent	46	47
Property	25	23
Drug	22	23
Public-order	7	7

Source: Darrell K. Gilliard and Allen J. Beck, *Prisoners in 1997*, Bureau of Justice Statistics, Washington, DC, 1998

fense groups — violent, property, drug, and public-order offenses — did not change among state prisoners.

There were six times as many drug offenders in prison in 1996 (237,600) as there were in 1985 (38,900). But there were far more violent criminals in prison in 1996 (495,400) than drug offenders (237,600). (See Table 6.11.) The number of criminals convicted of violent crime grew by 211,400 between 1985 and 1995, more than the 186,000 increase in the number of persons convicted of drug crimes.

Overall, violent criminals continue to make up the major proportion (47 percent) of those in prison. Yet those convicted of drug offenses, only ten years ago a small percentage of the prison population, now account for as many prisoners as those sentenced for property crimes (23 percent each), as shown in Table 6.10. From 1990 through 1996, the number of female inmates serving time for drug offenses doubled, and the number of male inmates in for drug offenses rose 55 percent. The number serving time for vio-

lent offenses rose at about the same pace — 57 percent for men and 58 percent for women (Table 6.11).

More Time Served

In 1996, state prisoners released for the first time served 25 months in prison, compared to 22 months in 1990. (See Table 6.12.) There is a serious problem, however, with using this data to determine how long a prisoner serves. These data reflect the time actually served by prisoners who have been released. Some prisoners will never be released but will die in prison, and others with very long sentences will not show up among released prisoners for many years. As a result, these measurements of time served tend to understate the actual time served by persons entering prison. The National Corrections Reporting Program (NCRP) is currently completing its 5-year survey, which includes the sentences of all prisoners. While preliminary findings suggest that state prisoners are

TABLE 6.11

Estimated number of sentenced prisoners under State jurisdiction, by offense and sex, 1990 and 1996

	All prisoners		Male		Female	
Offenses	1990	1996	1990	1996	1990	1996
Total	689,600	1,048,000	652,800	984,600	36,700	63,400
Violent offenses	315,900	495,400	304,800	477,900	11,100	17,500
Murder[a]	72,500	112,700	68,400	107,700	4,100	5,000
Manslaughter	13,300	16,900	12,000	15,400	1,300	1,600
Rape	24,700	39,200	24,600	38,800	100	300
Other sexual assault	39,400	63,200	39,000	62,600	400	600
Robbery	99,900	142,000	97,200	137,800	2,700	4,200
Assault	53,700	98,600	51,600	94,400	2,100	4,200
Other violent	12,500	22,700	11,900	21,400	600	1,400
Property offenses	175,000	240,000	163,300	222,600	11,700	17,500
Burglary	87,800	111,100	86,200	108,100	1,600	3,100
Larceny	35,100	49,800	31,000	43,700	4,100	6,200
Motor vehicle theft	14,500	21,600	14,300	20,800	200	800
Fraud	20,300	27,800	16,500	21,700	3,800	6,100
Other property	17,200	29,600	15,200	28,300	2,000	1,300
Drug offenses	149,700	237,600	137,900	213,900	11,800	23,700
Public-order offenses[b]	45,800	71,300	43,900	67,000	1,900	4,400
Other/unspecified[c]	3,100	3,700	2,900	3,400	200	300

Note: Offense distributions for yearend 1990 and 1996 were estimated using *stock-flow method* procedures that combine data from the 1991 and 1997 surveys of State prison inmates with estimates of admissions and releases obtained in the National Corrections Reporting Program, 1990-96.

[a]Includes nonnegligent manslaughter.
[b]Includes weapons, drunk driving, court offenses, commercialized vice, morals and decency charges, liquor law violations, and other public-order offenses.
[c]Includes juvenile offenses and unspecified felonies.

Source: Darrell K. Gilliard and Allen J. Beck, *Prisoners in 1997*, Bureau of Justice Statistics, Washington, DC, 1998

TABLE 6.12

Mean sentence length and time served for first releases from State prison, 1990 and 1996

Most serious offense	Mean maximum sentence length[a]		Mean time served for first releases				Total time served[c]		Percent of sentence served[d]	
			Jail[b]		Prison					
	1990	1996	1990	1996	1990	1996	1990	1996	1990	1996
All offenses	69 mo	62 mo	6 mo	5 mo	22 mo	25 mo	28 mo	30 mo	38.0%	44.4%
Violent offenses	99 mo	85 mo	7 mo	6 mo	39 mo	39 mo	46 mo	45 mo	43.8%	49.6%
Murder[e]	209	180	9	11	83	84	92	95	43.1	50.9
Negligent manslaughter	88	97	5	6	31	41	37	47	41.0	46.6
Rape	128	116	7	6	55	61	62	66	45.5	52.6
Other sexual assault	77	81	5	5	30	39	36	45	43.8	51.7
Robbery	104	92	7	6	41	40	48	46	42.8	47.0
Assault	64	61	6	6	23	28	30	33	43.9	51.7
Other violent	80	67	6	6	33	29	38	35	43.5	48.9
Property offenses	65 mo	56 mo	6 mo	5 mo	18 mo	22 mo	24 mo	26 mo	34.4%	43.0%
Burglary	79	68	6	5	22	26	29	31	33.9	42.4
Larceny/theft	52	47	6	4	14	18	20	22	35.5	43.2
Motor vehicle theft	56	45	7	5	13	19	20	24	33.1	49.1
Fraud	56	51	6	4	14	18	20	22	33.2	38.2
Other property	55	48	4	4	18	20	22	24	37.6	46.1
Drug offenses	57 mo	57 mo	6 mo	5 mo	14 mo	20 mo	20 mo	24 mo	32.9%	39.8%
Possession	61	55	6	4	12	17	18	22	29.0	37.6
Trafficking	60	62	6	5	16	22	22	26	34.8	39.3
Other/unspecified drug	42	45	4	5	12	17	16	23	34.8	46.7
Public-order offenses	40 mo	41 mo	5 mo	4 mo	14 mo	17 mo	18 mo	21 mo	42.6%	45.9%
Other offenses	51 mo	50 mo	6 mo	6 mo	16 mo	19 mo	23 mo	25 mo	39.2%	45.6%
Total	212,166	252,238	174,161	203,167	214,871	254,217				

Note: Includes only offenders with a sentence of more than 1 year released for the first time on the current sentence. Excludes prisoners released from prison by escape, death, transfer, appeal or detainer. Data were reported on maximum sentence length for 93.4% of the 227,100 first releases reported to NCRP in 1990 and 97.6% of the 258,480 first releases reported in 1996. Data were reported on time served in jail for 76.7% in 1990 and 78.6% in 1996, and time served in prison for 94.6% in 1990 and 98.4% in 1996.

[a]Maximum sentence length an offender may be required to serve for the most serious offense. Excludes sentences of life without parole, life plus additional years, life and death.
[b]Average time spent in jail credited towards the current offense.
[c]Based on mean time served in jail and mean time served in prison by offense.
[d]Based on the mean total time served and mean total sentence length by offense. Details may not add to total because of rounding.
[e]Includes nonnegligent manslaughter.

Source: Paula M. Ditton and Doris James Wilson, *Truth in Sentencing in State Prisons*, Bureau of Justice Statistics, Washington, DC, 1999

serving more time, this information will not be known until the survey is completed and its findings released.

According to the Bureau of Justice Statistics in *Felony Sentences in State Courts, 1996* (Washington, DC, 1999), inmates released from state prison in 1988 had served an average of one-third of the sentence imposed on them by the court. In 1996, inmates were released after serving approximately half of their court-imposed sentences. This means that, while prisoners are serving a growing percentage of their court-imposed sentence, the average court-imposed sentence has been decreasing.

In 1988, the typical felon received a six-year sentence and would normally serve one-third, or two years, of that sentence before being released. (This is assuming a person sentenced in 1988 served the same proportion of the sentence as was typical of those persons released in 1988.) In contrast, in 1996, the typical felon received a five-year sentence (assuming a person sentenced in 1996 served the same proportion of the sentence as was typical of those persons released in 1996), but would serve half of that sentence, or 2.5 years. (See Table 6.13.)

Truth-in-Sentencing Laws

Over the past decade, sentencing requirements and release policies have become more restrictive, largely in response to prevailing "get tough on crime" attitudes throughout the country. States enacted truth-in-sentencing laws that require offenders to serve a substantial portion of their prison sentences and reduce

TABLE 6.13

	Average imposed prison sentence length (in months)		
	1988	1992	1996
All offenses	76 mo	79 mo	62 mo
Murder	239	251	257
Robbery	114	117	101
Aggravated assault	90	87	69
Burglary	74	76	60
Larceny	50	53	40
Drug trafficking	66	72	55

	Percent of imposed prison sentence actually served		
	1988	1992	1996
All offenses	32%	38%	45%
Murder	33	44	50
Robbery	39	46	47
Aggravated assault	36	48	54
Burglary	30	35	42
Larceny	29	33	44
Drug trafficking	30	34	42

	Estimated actual time to be served in prison (in months)		
	1988	1992	1996
All offenses	24 mo	30 mo	28 mo
Murder	79	110	128
Robbery	38	54	48
Aggravated assault	32	42	38
Burglary	22	27	25
Larceny	15	17	17
Drug trafficking	20	24	23

Jodi M. Brown, Patrick A. Langan, and David J. Levin, *Felony Sentences in State Courts, 1996*, Bureau of Justice Statistics, Washington, DC, 1999

TABLE 6.14

Truth-in-sentencing requirements, by State

Meet Federal 85% requirement		50% requirement	100% of minimum requirement	Other requirements
Arizona	Missouri	Indiana	Idaho	Alaska[c]
California	New Jersey	Maryland	Nevada	Arkansas[d]
Connecticut	New York	Nebraska	New Hampshire	Colorado[e]
Delaware	North Carolina	Texas		Kentucky[f]
District of Col.	North Dakota			Massachusetts[g]
Florida	Ohio			Wisconsin[h]
Georgia	Oklahoma[b]			
Illinois[a]	Oregon			
Iowa	Pennsylvania			
Kansas	South Carolina			
Louisiana	Tennessee			
Maine	Utah			
Michigan	Virginia			
Minnesota	Washington			
Mississippi				

[a]Qualified for Federal funding in 1996 only.
[b]Effective July 1, 1999, offenders will be required to serve 85% of the sentence.
[c]Two-part sentence structure (2/3 in prison; 1/3 on parole); 100% of prison term required.
[d]Mandatory 70% of sentence for certain violent offenses and manufacture of methamphetamine.
[e]Violent offenders with 2 prior violent convictions serve 75%; 1 prior violent conviction, 56.25%.
[f]Effective July 15, 1998, offenders are required to serve 85% of the sentence.
[g]Requires 75% of a minimum prison sentence.
[h]Effective December 31, 1999, two-part sentence: offenders serve 100% of the prison term and a sentence of extended supervision at 25% of the prison sentence.

Source: Paula M. Ditton and Doris James Wilson, *Truth in Sentencing in State Prisons*, Bureau of Justice Statistics, Washington, DC, 1999

the disparity between the sentence imposed and actual time served in prison. Under these laws, parole eligibility and good-time credits were restricted or eliminated. The definition of truth in sentencing, the percent of sentence required to be served, and the crimes covered vary among the states. (See Table 6.14.) Most states have focused on violent offenders under truth in sentencing.

As a result of truth-in-sentencing laws, state prison populations increased sharply between 1990 and 1997. From 1990 to 1997, the state prison custody population increased by 57 percent, reaching a high of 1,075,052 inmates in 1997, up from 684,544 in 1990. As shown in Figure 6.5, the growth has not been the result of offenders entering state prisons. The number of offenders admitted during the 1990s has remained fairly constant. (Admissions to state prisons increased about 17 percent from 1990 to 1997, rising to 540,748 from 460,739.) Rather, the growth is due to the increasing amount of time served by offenders under states' truth-in-sentencing laws. Under these policies, the more serious offenders with long sentences are being kept in prison, and less serious offenders with shorter sentences make up an increasingly larger percentage of released prisoners.

RISING FEDERAL PRISON POPULATIONS

It is much easier to determine the cause of the increase in the number of inmates in the nation's federal prisons. Between 1990 and 1996, the number of federal prisoners rose from 59,526 to 92,672, an increase of 33,146 prisoners. Over this period, the number of people incarcerated for drug crimes rose from 31,300 to 55,194 (Table 6.15), an

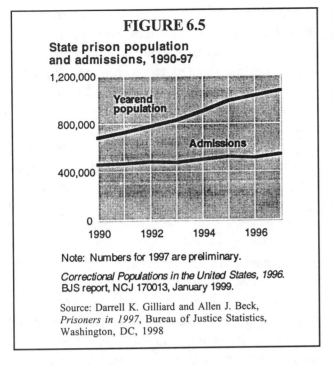

FIGURE 6.5

State prison population and admissions, 1990-97

Note: Numbers for 1997 are preliminary.

Correctional Populations in the United States, 1996. BJS report, NCJ 170013, January 1999.

Source: Darrell K. Gilliard and Allen J. Beck, *Prisoners in 1997*, Bureau of Justice Statistics, Washington, DC, 1998

increase of 23,894, accounting for 72 percent of the growth in the number of inmates.

Most of the remaining increase can be attributed to public-order offenses, mainly weapons and immigration offenses, which nearly doubled from 8,826 to 17,227. In 1996, those in prison for drug offenses made up 59.6 percent of all the federal inmates, up from 52.6 percent in 1990, and those imprisoned for public-order offenses made up 18.6 percent, up from 14.8 percent in 1990. Within this category, weapons offenses accounted for 8.1 percent of all federal inmates (Table 6.15).

NATIONAL ASSESSMENT PROGRAM (NAP)

The 1995 National Assessment Program survey of wardens indicates concern about overcrowding. Of the 361 warden responses, 135 wardens (37 percent) reported that their prisons were crowded (they housed more than 100 percent of rated capacity). Thirteen wardens indicated their inmate population was at less than 90 percent of rated capacity, 147 wardens claimed their population was between 90 and 100 percent of rated capacity,

and 54 wardens had inmate populations between 101 and 110 percent of rated capacity.

Wardens with crowded conditions gave several reasons for their problems, including drug crime offenders (cited by 88 percent of wardens), violent crime offenders (80 percent), longer sentences for offenders (78 percent), parole violators (72 percent), and insufficient alternatives to prisons (71 percent). Observations from wardens supported these conclusions:

- Drug offenders with heavy sentences fill up about 75 percent of the available cells.

- Approximately 85 percent of female inmates have a history of substance abuse. Whether directly convicted of a drug crime or committing crimes to support drug habits, these offenses account for the highest increase in population.

- Increasing commitments in mandatory drug sentences drive the rapid increase in the growth of female offenders.

TABLE 6.15

Number and percent of sentenced inmates in Federal prisons, by offense, 1990 and 1996

	Federal inmates of any sentence length			
	Number		Percent	
	1990	1996	1990	1996
Total	59,526	92,672	100.0%	100.0%
Violent offenses	10,728	11,523	18.0%	12.4%
Homicide	1,316	1,084	2.2	1.2
Robbery	7,304	8,334	12.3	9.0
Assault	808	645	1.4	0.7
Other violent	1,300	1,460	2.2	1.6
Property offenses	8,307	7,781	14.0%	8.4%
Burglary	412	181	0.7	0.2
Fraud	5,386	5,807	9.0	6.3
Other property	2,509	1,793	4.2	1.9
Drug offenses	31,300	55,194	52.6%	59.6%
Public-order offenses	8,826	17,227	14.8%	18.6%
Immigration	1,645	4,476	2.8	4.8
Weapons	3,234	7,480	5.4	8.1
Other public-order	3,947	5,271	6.6	5.7
Other/unknown	365	947	0.6%	1.0%

Note: Data for December 31, 1990, and September 30, 1996, were obtained from the BJS Federal justice database.

Source: Darrell K. Gilliard and Allen J. Beck, *Prisoners in 1997*, Bureau of Justice Statistics, Washington, DC, 1998

- More offenders are being sentenced for violent crimes, and more are given life sentences that are now 40 years or more without parole.

- Essentially, the increasing number of drug-related offenders has backlogged the system to the point that hundreds of inmates who should be at reduced security facilities end up in prisons.

- The number of violent criminals who are also substance abusers or drug sellers has increased. They are younger and more difficult to control. Consequently, they stay in prison longer as parole officials are not inclined to release them.

- Prison crowding especially impacts negatively on classification of inmates for program needs. As the numbers increase, the emphasis shifts from treatment and programming to containment. Resources normally allocated to programs are diverted to security. Prison crowding, combined with the states' fiscal austerity, makes for an atmosphere of hard choices, and the first mission becomes confinement.

- Lines for everything are longer — inmate canteen, inmate meals, backlog to get into specialty programs, and backlog for transfers to minimum security facilities. There is also not enough disciplinary segregation space. Patience wanes; tempers flare. Staff is more stressed as inmates become more demanding of individual attention and acknowledgment.

PRIVATIZATION OF PRISONS

Many conservatives believe that the government could save money by allowing private businesses to perform some government functions (privatization). This policy has also affected the corrections system, especially as states and the federal government face deteriorating conditions of older public prisons, an increasing number of prisoners, and, as a result, a growing need to build more prisons. Proponents of privatization think that private firms would be more flexible than government bureaucracies in meeting changing needs and that competing firms would both improve the quality of services and reduce the costs.

More than 30 types of services are provided by the private sector. The services most frequently supplied by private enterprise are health services, community treatment centers, facility construction, educational programs, drug treatment, staff training, counseling, and vocational training.

In the 1980s, some prison systems allowed the private sector to own and manage prisons. In 1984, President Reagan allowed private holding cells for illegal aliens. According to the National Conference of State Legislatures, in 1995, approximately 20 private companies were running 84 state institutions, with a rated capacity of 43,508 inmates. The 1995 BJS census (see above) found that about 2 percent of all state and federal inmates were held in facilities operated by private contractors (Table 6.1). The census counted 81 privately run community-based facilities and 29 confinement institutions. In 1998, according to the Criminal Justice Institute (*Corrections Yearbook — 1998*), 50,484 inmates were incarcerated in 80 privately operated facilities.

Concerns involving privatization of ownership and management include

- It is the right of the state to punish. The American Civil Liberties Union commented, "No one but the state should possess the awesome responsibility or power to take away an individual's freedom; freedom should not be contracted to the lowest bidder."

- The profit motive might bring about abuses in the system. The National Association of Criminal Justice Planners commented, "Does the government want to emphasize such a mercenary value as profit in its response to a social problem, as opposed to values such as fairness, equity, and personal accountability?" Proponents of privatization counter that with government monitoring, the private sector should be able to manage corrections.

- The government is still liable for any suits that are brought against the company.

- Cost savings and improved quality of services are still not proven.

One of the major corporations in private industry, Corrections Corporation of America, based in Nashville, Tennessee, ran 60 correctional institutions in 17 states in 1997. It asserts private prisons can make profits. The company pays the prevailing local wages, but is not unionized. It also does not offer pension plans. The wardens assert that keeping prisoners from being troublesome makes the largest gains. While drug rehabilitation and recreational programs cost more at the beginning, they pay for themselves by keeping the prisoners satisfied, thus reducing tension and violence in prison. With less stress on the employees, turnover is less, reducing training costs.

According to one of the wardens, a dissatisfied prisoner in a state prison can destroy his cell, costing the state money in repairs. In privately run facilities, better-quality goods are bought up front. For example, a costly $40 hard-to-destroy plastic chair is bought by a private corporation, while a state-run prison might be required to buy a cheaper, more easily destroyed, wooden chair, which has to be replaced.

Do Private Prisons Really Save Money?

A number of studies conducted by the General Accounting Office and other research firms have found that trying to determine whether or not using private prisons saves money is difficult, because there is little information available that is widely applicable to a broad variety of correctional settings.

However, such findings have not slowed the growth of the private prison industry, which surpassed $1 billion in revenues in 1997, up sharply from $650 million in 1996. The federal government and 27 states have privatized some of their prisons and detention centers. In 1997, 120 prisons and jails (including some under construction) were privately run. In 1987, barely 3,000 prisoners were held in private facilities. By 1996, about 3 percent of all U.S. prisoners, or 85,000 inmates, were incarcerated in private facilities.

In 1996, the General Accounting Office conducted a study of public and private prisons in five states. (*Private and Public Prisons — Studies Comparing Operational Costs and/or Quality of Service*, Washington, DC). Of the five states studied in the GAO report (California, New Mexico, Tennessee, Texas, and Washington), the GAO considered the Tennessee study, conducted in 1995, to be the most sound of all the reports. The Tennessee study, conducted in two parts — one for operational costs and one for quality of service — by the Tennessee state legislature, compared three of Tennessee's multicustody (minimum-to maximum-security) prisons for male inmates over a period of five years. One prison was privately managed, and the other two were state-run facilities. That study did not find much difference in the cost per inmate per day among the three similar facilities: one private and two government-run institutions. The three facilities were analyzed over a five-year period. The prisons run by the government had an average per diem rate per prisoner (adjusted for differences in prison population) of $33.18, compared to $33.78 for the privately run prison.

On the Other Hand . . .

A 1997 study prepared by two Louisiana State University professors showed that, in their state, private prisons do save money. The two professors, William G. Archambeault, a criminologist, and Donald R. Deis, a professor of accounting, found that private prisons were better managed and less expensive. The report considered cost savings and performance of three prisons over a five-year period. Two of the institutions were managed by private companies, and one by the state. Archambeault and Deis reported that the private facilities averaged $22.93 and $23.49 per diem for each prisoner, while the publicly run prison cost $26.60.

Some officials want to continue experimenting with privatization even though there may be no cost savings by private companies. According to Donald Campbell, Commissioner of the Tennessee Department of Corrections, "…as long as it does not cost any more than it costs the state, then we should consider privatization. We should compare and explore the options out there that would save the taxpayers money."

The industry is growing internationally as well as within the United States. Great Britain and Australia have contracts with private companies, and Ontario,

Canada, has expressed interest in private prisons. South Africa plans a project that would include the construction of four prisons with a total capacity of 5,300 beds.

Another Option

Many states have moved toward privatization even though studies on the cost of private prisons and their quality of service are mixed. Moreover, some critics claim that the profit motive has no place in corrections.

Some observers have been suggesting another choice — the private, not-for-profit prison. A privately owned and operated not-for-profit institution could be incorporated as a tax-exempt organization, similar to a church or hospital. Such a facility would not necessarily save money but would be exempt from income and property taxes, be eligible for tax-deductible donations, and be free of shareholders to answer to. A private, not-for-profit prison would not be tied to government rules or union and benefits packages.

There are nonprofit organizations that provide treatment and counseling on a contractual basis already involved in the criminal justice system. A few such groups have successfully managed juvenile detention centers. Some supporters of private, nonprofit prisons feel that a nonprofit penitentiary might be able to recruit professionals who are principally committed to penal reform and making changes.

PRISON WORK PROGRAMS AND INDUSTRIES

Work in fields, laundries, and kitchens has always been a part of many inmates' lives; some even participate in work-release programs. According to the 1995 BJS census of correctional facilities, more than 94 percent of all prisons operated inmate work programs. About 63 percent of state inmates and 90 percent of federal inmates participated in some type of work program.

According to the Criminal Justice Institute (*The Corrections Yearbook — 1998*), among the report-ing jurisdictions (including the District of Columbia and the federal government), 76,080 inmates (6.7 percent) worked in prison industries, which produced goods or services that could be sold. Almost 29,854 (4.8 percent) worked on prison farms, and another 393,275 (44.5 percent) did other work assignments, such as laundry, which helped run the prisons. Another 156,888 (16.3 percent) were receiving full-time academic or vocational training.

State and local governments prevent prisoners from working at some jobs generally because they would be in competition with private enterprise or workers. In 1936, Congress barred convicts from working on federal contracts worth more than $10,000. In 1940, Congress made it illegal to transport convict-made goods in interstate commerce. Many states have laws prohibiting the sale of prisoner-made products within the state borders.

Some states allow prisoners to make goods for sale to governmental agencies only. In 1979, Congress allowed prisoners to work in other types of industries if they were paid the prevailing wage and local labor was not affected. Since 1990, 30 states have permitted the contracting out of prison labor to private companies.

According to the American Correctional Association, the number of inmates employed in prison industries varies from 1 percent in some states to 30 percent in others, with an average of 9 percent. They usually work at producing furniture, license plates, and textiles and at printing and farming.

Wages

Some private industries pay minimum wage, but many prisons take most of it to pay for room and board, restitution, family support, and taxes. The Criminal Justice Institute found that, in 1997, the average daily pay of inmates working for state prison industries ranged from a daily average low of $1.60 to an average high of $7.06. Inmates in Georgia received no wages, while Nevada prisoners got up to $48.75 per day. Private industry generally paid higher wages to the inmates, an average of $24.27 to $38.23 per day. Florida paid inmates the lowest daily wages ($0.20) for private industry work, while Nebraska paid the highest ($67.50). According to the Criminal Justice Institute, 48 jurisdictions reported annual prison industry gross sales of $1.5 billion for agency-operated industries.

Reasons for Work Programs

Prison administrators favor work programs. In a *New York Times* interview, J. Michael Quinlan, former director of the Federal Bureau of Prisons, indicated that work programs are "absolutely the most important ingredient in managing a safe and secure institution to keep the inmates productively occupied, in either work or education or drug treatment or structured recreation." He believes work programs also help prepare prisoners for reentry into the noninstitutionalized world.

A Federal Bureau of Prisons study found that inmates who worked in industry were less likely to cause problems in prison or be rearrested after release than convicts who had not participated. Thomas Townsend, president of the Corrections Industry Association, observed, "It is a matter of public safety: inmates who have worked in prison and gained new skills have a significantly better chance of not returning to crime and prison."

Businesses favor prison industries also. As Bob Tessler, owner of DPAS, a California company, commented, "We don't have to pay health and welfare on top of wages; we don't have to pay vacation or sick pay." However, Jack Henning, executive secretary-treasurer of California's Federation of Labor, asserted that even the paying of minimum hourly wages for some jobs like data entry destabilizes higher-paid labor on the open market. Even though the California law says that industries should consult labor unions before establishing their prison industries, most do not.

Many inmates like the opportunity to work. It gives them relief from boredom and some extra money. When

working conditions are substandard, though, convicts cannot protest. They do not have the right to talk to the media, to strike, or to change jobs.

UNICOR

UNICOR is the trade name for Federal Prison Industries, Inc., the government corporation that employs inmates in federal prisons. UNICOR should not be confused with state prison industry programs that are administered by the states. Under UNICOR, established in 1934, federal inmates get job training by producing goods and services for federal agencies. In 1999, items produced by the inmates included metal products (lockers, storage cabinets, shelving), clothing and textile products (draperies, canvas goods, military clothing), graphics and services (data entry, text editing, road signs), plastics, electronics (cable assemblies, connectors, power distribution systems), and furniture products and accessories.

UNICOR products and services must be purchased by federal agencies and are not for sale in interstate commerce or to non-federal entities. UNICOR is not permitted to compete with private industry. If UNICOR cannot make the needed product or provide the required service, federal agencies may buy the product from the private sector through a waiver issued by UNICOR. According to JoAnne O'Bryant and Keith Bea in "Prison Industries: UNICOR," a 1999 Congressional Report for Congress, approximately 18 percent of all inmates incarcerated in federal prisons are employed by UNICOR in 100 factories located in about 25 states.

UNICOR is a self-supporting government corporation that may borrow funds from the U.S. Treasury and use the proceeds to purchase equipment, pay wages to inmates and staff (over 1,600 staffers who are not inmates are employed), and invest in expansion of facilities. No funds are appropriated for UNICOR operations. Inmates earn between $0.25 per hour and $1.15 per hour.

CHAPTER VII

JUVENILE CONFINEMENT

The children detained in our correctional facilities represent a significant challenge to our Nation. As a result of acts of crime and violence that contradict our ideals of childhood and adolescence, these youth require strong intervention that serves public order and safety. However, while we must protect society from their misconduct, we must also enable these young offenders to adopt more conventional attitudes and behaviors. — Shay Bilchik, Administrator, Office of Juvenile Justice and Delinquency, 1993

Serious juvenile crime, particularly violent offenses, grew rapidly from the mid-1980s to the mid-1990s and began to decline slightly in 1995. In response to the rise in juvenile crime between 1985 and 1994, state legislators increased the severity of punishments for violent or habitual juvenile offenders. In addition, many states have made it easier to sentence serious juvenile offenders as adults.*

The Office of Juvenile Justice and Delinquency Prevention (OJJDP) was established in 1974. It is part of the U.S. Department of Justice, and its goal is to provide national leadership in addressing the issues of juvenile delinquency and improving juvenile justice.

According to the OJJDP, a juvenile may be taken into custody for

- Violating or allegedly violating a federal, state, or local delinquency or criminal statute or local ordinance regarding noncriminal misbehavior.

- Violating a judicial order, decree, or condition of supervision (either probation or aftercare).

- Being the subject of dependency, neglect, or child abuse allegation, investigation, or petition.

The purpose for custody may include providing care, protection, treatment, supervision, control, and punishment. (See Table 7.1.) Table 7.1 also defines the types of custody facilities in which a juvenile may be placed.

In 1995, almost half (47.8 percent) of the respondents surveyed by the Survey Research Program (College of Criminal Justice, Sam Houston State University, Huntsville, Texas) thought that the purpose of sending a juvenile to detention was to "train, educate, and counsel offenders." Three of 10 (30 percent) of those interviewed thought that the purpose was to "give offenders the punishment they deserve." (See Table 7.2.)

NUMBER OF ADMISSIONS

In 1995, the year of the most recent census of state and federal correctional facilities, with 81 percent of all facilities reporting, there were 5,309 jail inmates under the age of 18, a 47 percent increase

_____

* For more information on arrests and sentencing procedures for juveniles, see *Crime — A Serious American Problem*, Information Plus, Wylie, Texas, 1998.

TABLE 7.1

Juveniles Taken Into Custody: Working Definitions

Juveniles taken into custody are those youth who are younger than age 18, or who are 18 or older under juvenile court jurisdiction, and who are admitted to a juvenile custody facility or to an adult facility in which they are held under (staff) supervision.

Authority for Custody

The taking of a juvenile into custody may be the result of:

■ An order to take or place a juvenile into physical custody issued by a law enforcement agent (police, sheriff, immigration agent, marshall, or prosecutor); by a court (probation officer, magistrate, judge); or, by a social service agency (Child Protective Services, Welfare) that has wardship over the juvenile.

■ A formal diversion agreement authorized by the parent, the juvenile's legal custodian, or the juvenile.

■ A voluntary admission by the juvenile.

Purpose for Custody

The juvenile may be taken into custody for the purposes of providing care, protection, treatment, supervision, and control or punishment.

Reasons for Being Taken Into Custody

The juvenile may be taken into custody for the following reasons:

■ For violating, or allegedly violating, a Federal, State, or local delinquency or criminal statute or local ordinance regarding noncriminal misbehavior; a judicial order, decree, or condition of supervision (either probation or aftercare) pursuant to a diversion agreement or dispositional order (including those youth 18 years or older who are still under juvenile court authority).

■ For being the subject of a dependency, neglect or child abuse allegation, investigation, or petition.

Custody Facility

A custody facility is one that admits juveniles into custody for at least 6 hours, during which the juvenile is under the supervision of facility staff. The facility may:

■ Be operated by a Federal, State, or local government agency.

■ Be operated by a private nonprofit or proprietary agency under contract to a Federal, State, or local government agency to provide physical custody to juveniles.

■ Be a facility that is architecturally designed or operated to prevent juveniles from leaving the facility without legal authorization (generally secure).

■ Be a facility that does not rely on physically restrictive architecture or devices to prevent juveniles from leaving, but permits access to the community (generally nonsecure).

Source: James Austin et al., *Juveniles Taken into Custody: Fiscal Year 1993*, Office of Juvenile Justice and Delinquency Prevention, Washington, DC, 1995

from the 3,600 juveniles incarcerated in 1990. At mid-year 1998, 8,090 juveniles were incarcerated in local jails throughout the U.S.; 6,542 were held as adults and 1,548 were held as juveniles.*

---

* The admissions reported may reflect multiple counting of youth. For example, if a single youth entered several facilities as part of one legal process or if the youth was taken into custody more than once in a particular admissions year, this would result in multiple counting. The offense profile of the population on the one-day counts is also not representative. Although the admissions data overestimate the number of youth taken into custody, the one-day counts underestimate the number of juveniles who enter custody each year. The more serious offenders have a higher probability of being included in the one-day census because they are more likely to be held for a longer period of time.

TABLE 7.2

Attitudes toward most important purpose in sentencing adults and juveniles

By demographic characteristics, United States, 1995

Question: "Please tell me which of these four purposes do you think should be the most important in sentencing adults? Which of these four purposes do you think should be the most important in sentencing juveniles?"

	Adults				Juveniles			
	Discourage others from committing crime	Separate offenders from society	Train, educate, and counsel offenders	Give offenders the punishment they deserve	Discourage others from committing crime	Separate offenders from society	Train, educate, and counsel offenders	Give offenders the punishment they deserve
National	12.4%	12.5%	19.9%	50.8%	14.6%	4.0%	47.8%	30.0%
Sex								
Male	13.3	11.0	20.5	51.2	15.3	5.0	45.7	30.4
Female	11.5	13.8	19.4	50.5	14.0	3.1	49.8	29.7
Race								
White	13.2	13.6	17.3	51.4	15.0	3.9	46.5	31.3
Black	7.5	6.6	29.2	52.8	16.2	2.9	46.7	29.5
Hispanic	9.6	9.6	28.8	47.9	9.6	5.5	61.6	19.2
Age								
18 to 29 years	10.9	8.6	27.1	48.4	16.7	5.9	48.6	25.2
30 to 39 years	13.6	11.8	17.9	55.2	16.5	2.2	47.1	32.0
40 to 59 years	13.6	16.8	17.7	47.8	13.5	3.8	51.3	27.7
60 years and older	9.2	12.1	18.4	52.9	10.5	5.2	43.6	35.5
Education								
College graduate	12.5	20.0	21.8	42.5	13.3	3.6	59.1	21.5
Some college	17.2	11.6	19.3	48.1	17.9	4.2	46.0	29.1
High school graduate	10.2	9.5	19.1	56.6	13.5	4.0	43.7	34.8
Less than high school graduate	4.9	5.8	22.3	62.1	10.0	5.0	40.0	40.0
Income								
Over $60,000	12.8	16.6	25.7	42.8	13.4	5.9	56.5	22.0
Between $30,000 and $60,000	13.3	12.2	19.1	51.2	16.3	1.7	49.2	30.1
Between $15,000 and $29,999	10.9	14.2	15.5	57.3	13.3	6.3	42.5	35.8
Less than $15,000	11.9	6.8	25.4	50.8	10.9	0.8	51.3	28.6
Community								
Urban	9.7	18.1	14.8	49.7	11.5	3.8	51.9	28.8
Suburban	11.7	15.5	21.6	47.3	11.8	5.7	50.2	28.5
Small city	13.8	13.8	24.9	43.4	16.5	4.3	50.5	26.1
Rural/small town	12.6	8.1	18.6	58.0	16.2	2.9	45.3	33.0
Region								
Northeast	14.2	13.6	15.9	49.4	14.9	4.0	48.6	28.0
Midwest	8.5	11.0	26.7	48.7	12.2	4.6	45.0	32.8
South	11.7	10.9	16.6	57.6	17.2	3.2	43.6	33.8
West	15.8	15.4	21.2	44.4	12.5	4.6	56.7	23.8
Politics								
Republican	16.7	16.0	13.9	50.7	17.3	3.1	46.9	29.9
Democrat	8.9	10.7	23.8	53.7	13.2	2.5	48.9	31.8
Independent/other	11.7	12.2	22.6	47.3	13.8	5.3	49.6	28.4

Note: The "don't know" and "refused" categories have been omitted; therefore percents may not sum to 100.

Table constructed by SOURCEBOOK staff from data provided by the Survey Research Program, College of Criminal Justice, Sam Houston State University.

Source: Kathleen Maguire and Ann L. Pastore, eds., *Sourcebook of Criminal Justice Statistics 1995*, Bureau of Justice Statistics, Washington, DC, 1996

On February 15, 1995, the reference day for the *1995 Children in Custody* census of public and private detention, correctional, and shelter facilities, more than 108,700 juveniles were in detention, correctional, or shelter facilities. (See Table 7.3.) Of those, 84 percent were held for law violations; 77 percent were charged with delinquency offenses, and 28 percent were person offenses. The remaining 16 percent were non-offenders — youth referred for abuse, neglect, emotional disturbance, mental retardation, or voluntarily admitted juveniles (often referred by school officials or parents).

Minorities

The provisions of the Juvenile Justice and Delinquency Prevention Act of 1974 (PL 93-415) regarding "disproportionate minority confinement" require that states determine whether or not the proportion of minorities in confinement exceeds their proportion in the

TABLE 7.3

Juveniles in Custody

	Juveniles in public and private custody on February 15, 1995	
	Count	Percent
Total population	108,746	100%
Law violation	91,505	84
Delinquency	84,020	77
Person	30,969	28
Violent Index	18,011	17
Status offense	7,485	7
Nonoffenders	17,241	16

Source: Melissa Sickmund, Howard N. Snyder, and Eileen Poe-Yamagata, *Juvenile Offenders and Victims: 1997 Update on Violence*, Office of Juvenile Justice and Delinquency Prevention, Washington, DC, 1997

general population. If it does, the state must implement efforts to reduce such overrepresentation.

In 1995, 32 percent of the U.S. population between 10 and 17 years of age was classified as minorities. Minorities made up 68 percent of the detention center population of February 15, 1995, up from 65 percent in February 1991 and 53 percent in February 1983. Similarly, the minority proportion of the custody population in public long-term institutional facilities, such as training schools, rose from 56 percent in 1983 to 69 percent in 1991. In 1995, the minority proportion in these facilities remained virtually the same at 68 percent.

PUBLIC AND PRIVATE CUSTODY

In October 1997, the Office of Juvenile Justice and Delinquency Prevention (OJJDP) conducted the most recent *Census of Juveniles in Residential Placement, 1997* (CJRP). More than 94 percent of all facilities that hold or can hold alleged or adjudicated (tried and found guilty) juvenile delinquents or status* offenders responded to the census, which collected information on each juvenile offender in residence on October 29, 1997.

On October 29, 1997, there were 125,805 youths assigned beds in 1,121 public and 2,310 private residential facilities. Of the 3,431 residential facilities, 2,844 had at least one juvenile who met the criteria below. Of the residents in these facilities, 105,790 (84 percent) were

• Under the age of 21.

• Charged with or court-adjudicated for an offense.

• Placed at the facility because of the offense.

(Non-offenders accounted for the other 16 percent.)

Most (72.2 percent) of the juvenile offenders lived in 1,108 public facilities on October 29, 1997. Public facilities are owned and operated exclusively by state or local government agencies and include detention centers, shelters, reception centers, training schools, ranches or camps, and halfway houses. The remaining 27.8 percent were held in 1,736 private facilities. Private facilities are owned and operated by various nongovernmental organizations that provide services to juvenile offenders. At least 10 percent of a private facility's population is offenders, while a significant percentage of the private facility population may include youth referred for abuse, neglect, emotional disturbance, or mental retardation, as well as youngsters who were voluntarily admitted by parents or school officials. In 1997, 41 percent of the population of private facilities was made up of non-offenders. Private facilities have traditionally specialized in one particular method of treatment or one type of offender. For example, a private facility might hold only status offenders or juveniles who require more intensive psychiatric treatment.

Race and Ethnic Patterns

Most offenders were Black (40 percent) or White (37.5 percent). Nearly one-fifth (18.5 percent) were Hispanic, 1.8 percent were Asian American, 1.5 per-

---

*Status offenses are acts that are illegal only because the persons committing them are juveniles. In other words, an adult cannot be arrested for status offenses. Status offenses include being a runaway, truancy, ungovernability, and underage liquor law violations.

cent were Native American, and 0.3 percent were Pacific Islander.

Gender and Age Patterns

Most (86.5 percent) offenders were male. The average age for males in placement was 16 years; the average age for females was 15.4 years. (See Table 7.4.)

Reasons for Incarceration

Most (42.4 percent) juveniles were in residential facilities for a serious personal or property offense. Of these, nearly one-fourth (23.5 percent) of the inmates were there because of an aggravated assault, violent sexual assault, kidnapping, or robbery, and about one-fifth (18.9 percent) were charged with, or convicted of, arson, auto theft, or burglary. Nearly 2 percent were charged with or found guilty of homicide or murder. (See Table 7.5.)

Only a few (6.5 percent) juvenile inmates were housed in a facility because of a status offense (Table 7.5). Status offense classifications differ from state to state. Many states do not consider running away to be subject to juvenile court action, and in those states, runaways were not counted in the census. Only youths that committed an act for which they had to go to court were included in the census.

CROWDING IN JUVENILE CUSTODY FACILITIES

As the juvenile custody population has increased, so have crowded conditions in juvenile facilities. Since most juveniles in custody are maintained in secure public facilities, such as detention centers and training schools, even small increases affect a large number of incarcerated youth.

Detention Centers

Detention centers are used to house youth in a restrictive facility between referral to court and case disposition. In 1995, half of all public detention centers were operating above their capacity. These

TABLE 7.4

Age and Sex of Young Offenders in Residential Placement

Age	Male Number	Male Percent	Female Number	Female Percent	Total Number	Total Percent
<13	1,782	82.3	382	17.7	2,164	2.0
13	3,639	78.6	988	21.4	4,627	4.3
14	9,160	79.1	2,424	20.9	11,584	10.9
15	17,568	82.7	3,683	17.3	21,251	20.0
16	24,455	86.5	3,829	13.5	28,284	26.7
17	22,355	90.3	2,399	9.7	24,754	23.3
>17	12,512	95.3	614	4.7	13,126	12.4
Total	91,471	86.5	14,319	13.5	105,790	100.0

Note: Percentages may not add to 100% due to rounding.

TABLE 7.5

Juveniles in Residential Facilities, by Offense

	Number	Percent
Personal Crimes	**35,357**	**33.4**
Murder/manslaughter	1,927	1.8
Violent sex offense	5,590	5.3
Kidnaping	326	0.3
Robbery	9,451	8.9
Aggravated assault	9,530	9.0
Simple assault	6,630	6.3
Other person offense	1,903	1.8
Property Crimes	**31,991**	**30.2**
Household burglary	12,560	11.9
Auto theft	6,525	6.2
Arson	915	0.9
Property damage	1,758	1.7
Theft	7,294	6.9
Other property offense	2,939	2.8
Drug Offenses	**9,286**	**8.8**
Drug trafficking	3,045	2.9
Drug possession	5,693	5.4
Other drug offense	548	0.5
Public Order Offenses	**9,718**	**9.2**
Driving under the influence	260	0.2
Obstruction of justice	1,754	1.7
Nonviolent sex offense	1,739	1.6
Weapons offense	4,191	4.0
Other public order offense	1,774	1.7
Probation or Parole Violation	**12,549**	**11.9**
Other Delinquent Offenses	**12**	**.0**
Status Offenses	**6,877**	**6.5**
Curfew violation	193	0.2
Incorrigibility	2,849	2.7
Running away	1,497	1.4
Truancy	1,332	1.3
Under age alcohol offense	320	0.3
Other status offense	686	0.6
Total	**105,790**	**100.0**

Source of both tables: Catherine A. Gallagher, "Juvenile Offenders in Residential Placement, 1997," *OJJDP Fact Sheet*, no. 96, March 1999

crowded centers held nearly three-fourths of public detention center residents. In 1991, one-third of detention centers was crowded.

Institutional Facilities

Institutional facilities, such as training schools, house juvenile inmates for long-term placement. The proportion of institutional facilities that were operating above their capacity remained the same (about 45 percent in 1991 and 1995), but the number of residents held in crowded facilities increased. There were 10,000 more residents in over-capacity training schools and other public long-term institutional facilities in 1995 than in 1991 — an increase of 55 percent. Over-capacity public long-term institutional facilities held more than 70 percent of public long-term institutional residents in 1995, compared to 62 percent in 1991.

In 1995, public facilities were more crowded than private facilities. An average public facility that held more than 350 residents was operating 88 percent over capacity, while an average private facility holding more than 350 residents was operating at 33 percent over capacity. A public facility designed to hold fewer than 31 residents was 21 percent over capacity in 1995, compared to a small private facility holding 31 or fewer residents at 7 percent over capacity in 1995. (See Table 7.6.)

Nine of 10 residents (91 percent) held in large public facilities (more than 350 residents) were held in overcrowded facilities, compared to 32 percent of residents held in large private facilities. While 29 percent of inmates in small (fewer than 31 residents) public facilities lived in over-crowded conditions, only 10 percent of inmates in small private facilities lived that way (Table 7.6).

SECURITY LEVEL

In 1995, there were no inmates in federal facilities under the age of 18, although 64 juveniles were housed under contract outside the federal system. In 1995, state correctional facilities held 5,309 juvenile inmates, about one-half of one percent of all state inmates. Most (47 percent) were admitted to maximum security facilities, while 42 percent were admitted to medium, and 11 percent to minimum security facilities. (See Table 7.7.)

TABLE 7.6

69% of public facility residents were held in facilities operating above their design capacity on February 15, 1995

| Design capacity | All public facilities | | Residents | |
	Total	Percent operating above design capacity	Total	Percent held in facilities operating above design capacity
All public facilities	1,080	40%	69,929	69%
Fewer than 31 residents	595	21	8,543	29
31–110 residents	324	58	18,506	59
111–200 residents	90	63	13,141	66
201–350 residents	39	82	10,075	82
More than 350 residents	32	88	19,664	91

Compared with public facilities, a substantially smaller proportion of private facilities were crowded on February 15, 1995

| Design capacity | All private facilities | | Residents | |
	Total	Percent operating above design capacity	Total	Percent held in facilities operating above design capacity
All private facilities	1,989	8%	39,706	15%
Fewer than 31 residents	1,694	7	17,377	10
31–110 residents	259	14	14,078	16
111–200 residents	25	20	3,672	17
201–350 residents	5	20	1,345	19
More than 350 residents	6	33	3,234	32

Note: Design capacity is the number of residents a facility is constructed to hold without double bunking in single rooms and without using areas not designed as sleeping quarters to house residents.

Source: Melissa Sickmund, Howard N. Snyder, and Eileen Poe-Yamagata, *Juvenile Offenders and Victims: 1997 Update on Violence*, Office of Juvenile Justice and Delinquency Prevention, Washington, DC, 1997

PROBLEMS IN THE LOUISIANA JUVENILE SYSTEM

Since 1996, Louisiana's juvenile prison system has been under investigation by the U.S. Department of Justice for civil-rights abuses. In November 1998, the Department of Justice sued the state demanding changes in the "systemic and life-threatening abuse" of offenders in four of the state's five secure juvenile institutions. (The case is scheduled to be tried in 1999.) Stories of sexual abuse by guards and other inmates along with charges of common and often brutal abuse, particularly at Tallulah Correctional Center for Youth, have been confirmed by corrections experts and former inmates. According to the Department of Justice, Louisiana's juvenile prison system lacks sufficient medical care and educational opportunities. The Justice Department also cites chronic breakdowns in authority leading to extensive sexual and physical abuse.

State officials agree that there have been problems with the Louisiana's juvenile system, but claim that they have remedied most of the worst of them. However, one state official acknowledged that the time had come for Louisiana to make changes.

Many of the complaints involve the Tallulah facility, a privately operated secure juvenile prison, located in Tallulah, Louisiana. Critics assert that the fault lies with Trans-American Development Associates, the management company that built Tallulah and had a contract to run it. Trans-American, critics say, in an attempt to make a profit, forced inmates to endure substandard conditions and hired underpaid and inexperienced guards who abused them. When Trans-American was awarded the Tallulah contract, it had had no previous experience constructing or maintaining prisons. According to Trans-American's lawyer, Trans-American had contracted management responsibilities to an experienced company that could not handle the responsibility.

In December 1998, state officials hired Florida-based Correctional Services Corporation to take over management at Tallulah. Unlike Trans-American Development, Correctional Services Corporation has had previous experience running juvenile facilities.

THE DEATH PENALTY

It is rare for the death penalty to be imposed on juveniles 17 or younger. (See Table 7.8 for a list of those who were executed between January 1, 1973, and June 30, 1996, for crimes committed when they were under 18 years old.) The Supreme Court, reversing the sentence of a 16-year-old in *Eddings v. Oklahoma* (455 U.S. 104, 1982), noted that adolescents are not mature, responsible, or self-disciplined enough to consider the long-range implications of their actions. The court also held that a defendant's young age and mental and emotional development should be considered an important mitigating factor when decided whether to apply the death penalty. Nonetheless, the High Court failed to indicate the age at which a defendant would receive the death penalty, indicating only that it was not 16 years.

Between January 1, 1973, and June 30, 1996, 143 death sentences were handed down to 130 persons younger than 18 at the time of their crime. Most

TABLE 7.10

Minimum age authorized for capital punishment, 1997

Age 16 or less	Age 17	Age 18	None specified
Alabama (16)	Georgia	California	Arizona
Arkansas (14)[a]	New Hampshire	Colorado	Idaho
Delaware (16)	North Carolina[b]	Connecticut[c]	Louisiana
Florida (16)	Texas	Federal system	Montana
Indiana (16)		Illinois	Pennsylvania
Kentucky (16)		Kansas	South Carolina
Mississippi (16)[d]		Maryland	South Dakota[e]
Missouri (16)		Nebraska	Utah
Nevada (16)		New Jersey	
Oklahoma (16)		New Mexico	
Virginia (14)[f]		New York	
Wyoming (16)		Ohio	
		Oregon	
		Tennessee	
		Washington	

Note: Reporting by States reflects interpretations by State attorney generals' offices and may differ from previously reported ages.
[a]See Ark. Code Ann. 9-27-318(b)(2)(Repl. 1991).
[b]Age required is 17 unless the murderer was incarcerated for murder when a subsequent murder occurred; then the age may be 14.
[c]See Conn. Gen. Stat. 53a-46a(g)(1).
[d]The minimum age defined by statute is 13, but the effective age is 16 based on interpretation of U.S. Supreme Court decisions by the State attorney general's office.
[e]Juveniles may be transferred to adult court. Age can be a mitigating factor.
[f]The minimum age for transfer to adult court by statute is 14, but the effective age is 16 based on interpretation of U.S. Supreme Court decisions by the State attorney general's office.

Source: Tracy L. Snell, *Capital Punishment 1997*, Bureau of Justice Statistics, Washington, DC, 1998

---

prisoned for life. The law does not allow the death penalty for those children, but it does permit youths serving life sentences for murder to be eligible for parole. The bill was passed in response to the 1998 Jonesboro school shootings in which two young boys murdered five people and wounded another 10.

Survey

In 1995, 2 of 3 respondents (63 percent) surveyed by the Survey Research Program (College of Criminal Justice, Sam Houston State University) thought that "a juvenile charged with a serious property crime should be tried as adult." An even greater proportion of those surveyed (87 percent) believed those charged with a serious violent crime should be tried as adult. (See Table 7.12.) In 1998, when teenagers were asked where juveniles who committed violent crimes should be tried, more than half (56 percent) said they should be tried in adult court. (See Table 7.13.)

Admissions to Adult Facilities

While information is not available on the effect of the recent changes in transfer laws, earlier data indicate that an increasing number of young inmates were already being confined in adult prisons. In 1982, about 2,600 people ages 17 and younger were admitted to prisons in 30 states, about 2.6 percent of all admissions.

By 1991, 35 states reported 4,350 prison admissions for people ages 17 or younger. About 5,150 people admitted in 1992 to state prisons were younger than 18. A substantial but undetermined number were nominally "adults;" that is, they were committed in states in which the age of majority was 17. The rest were juveniles transferred to adult courts, which convicted and sentenced them.

However, although the number of juveniles in adult prisons is increasing, the percentage is not. In 1991,

---

Act (Act 1192 of 1999), which is an example of blended sentencing. The law allows for extended juvenile jurisdiction (also known as blended sentencing), in which juvenile offenders first could be sent to the Division of Youth Services. Then, before they turn 18, a second hearing could be held, and a judge would decide whether or not to transfer them to adult prison. The new law could keep children of any age who have committed crimes of capital or first-degree murder im-

---

TABLE 7.11

Oldest age of original juvenile court jurisdiction in delinquency matters, 1995

Age	States
15	Connecticut, New York, North Carolina
16	Georgia, New Hampshire, Illinois, Louisiana, Massachusetts, Michigan, Missouri, South Carolina, Texas, Wisconsin
17	All other States and the District of Columbia

Source: Melissa Sickmund, Howard N. Snyder, and Eileen Poe-Yamagata, *Juvenile Offenders and Victims: 1997 Update on Violence*, Office of Juvenile Justice and Delinquency Prevention, Washington, DC, 1997

FIGURE 7.1

Blended sentencing options create a "middle ground" between traditional juvenile and adult sanctions

Blended sentencing option	State
Juvenile-Exclusive Blend: The juvenile court may impose a sanction involving either the juvenile or adult correctional systems.	New Mexico

Juvenile-Inclusive Blend: The juvenile court may impose both juvenile and adult correctional sanctions. The adult sanction is suspended pending a violation and revocation.	Connecticut Minnesota Montana

Juvenile-Contiguous Blend: The juvenile court may impose a juvenile correctional sanction that may remain in force beyond the age of its extended jurisdiction, at which point the offender may be transferred to the adult correctional system.	Colorado¹ Massachusetts Rhode Island South Carolina Texas

Juvenile Court ——— Juvenile — Adult

Criminal-Exclusive Blend: The criminal court may impose a sanction involving either the juvenile or adult correctional systems.	California Colorado² Florida Idaho Michigan Virginia

Criminal-Inclusive Blend: The criminal court may impose both juvenile and adult correctional sanctions. The adult sanction is suspended pending a violation and revocation.	Arkansas Missouri

Criminal Court — Juvenile / and \ Adult

Note: Blends apply to a subset of juveniles specified by State statute.

¹ Applies to those designated as "aggravated juvenile offenders."
² Applies to those designated as "youthful offenders."

Authors' adaptation of P. Torbet's *State responses to serious and violent juvenile crime.*

Source: Melissa Sickmund, Howard N. Snyder, and Eileen Poe-Yamagata, *Juvenile Offenders and Victims: 1997 Update on Violence*, Office of Juvenile Justice and Delinquency Prevention, Washington, DC, 1997

With the increases in sentence length and time actually served the number of aging adults will increase faster than the number of younger adults and juveniles in the prison population.

Differences by State

Prison admissions for young and very young offenders vary greatly among the states. According to the most recent data available, of the 5,207 people age 17 or younger who were admitted to state adult prisons in 1993, the majority (79 percent) came from 10 states, with North Carolina alone accounting for 23.5 percent of juvenile admissions (Table 7.14).

Only 102 very young inmates (ages 13 to 15) were in custody of state adult correctional agencies on June 30, 1994. Of these, almost three-fourths were in four states (Table 7.15). Of inmates ages 16 to 17, 4,730 were in nonfederal adult correctional populations. Of these, almost three-fourths were held in nine jurisdictions (Table 7.16). In the age group 18 to 21, 65,575 were in state adult correctional populations, with 62 percent of them held in nine states (Table 7.17).

Managing Young Offenders in Adult Prisons

It is likely that the number of young inmates sentenced to confinement in adult prisons will increase. As the number grows, state correctional officials will face decisions about some important management issues.

Housing

In 1994, 36 jurisdictions placed young inmates in housing with adult inmates (half as a general practice and half only in certain circumstances). Nine states

young offenders accounted for just 1.8 percent of all prison admissions; by mid-1996, they accounted for less than 1 percent. The median age of all people admitted to prison between 1982 and 1991 rose from 25 to 26 years. According to the Criminal Justice Institute, in 1995, the average age was almost 31 years.

housed young inmates with those 18 to 21 but not with older inmates. Only six states never housed young inmates with people 18 and older; they either transferred young inmates to their state juvenile training schools until they reached the age of majority (age considered adults) or housed them in segregated living units within an adult prison.

Some believe that housing young inmates with older populations ensures they will be victimized, assaulted, and abused, both physically and sexually. Others will learn criminal behavior from career criminals. Young inmates who cannot survive in such a situation have little choice but to enter protective custody, which is usually a separate, secure housing unit in which they spend a great deal of time in isolation — a setting that is especially conducive to suicidal behavior.

Programs

Another issue is ensuring that young inmates are able to participate in the educational and physical programs they need, and receive the nutrition they require. Young inmates may be subject to state mandatory education laws as well as federal mandates for special education. In addition, they have dietary needs different from those of adult inmates; yet their food allowance (in caloric value and type of food) is likely to be the same as that of adult inmates. Misconduct by young inmates is, to some extent, linked to their development as adolescents. Staff responses based on adult patterns of misconduct are likely to be less effective in managing juveniles.

BOOT CAMPS

Boot camps for juvenile offenders are a relatively recent phenomenon. (See Chapter IX for information on the purpose of boot camps and the adult application.) The oldest program, in Orleans Parish, Louisiana, began in 1985. Three of the programs (Cleveland, Ohio; Denver, Colorado; and Mobile, Alabama) were funded through the Office of Juvenile Justice and Delinquency Prevention. OJJDP also sponsored a two-year evaluation from April 1992 to March 1994 of the three sites. Table 7.18 lists the programs and their key characteristics.

Boot camps for juveniles are typically intended for "midrange" offenders — those who have failed with lesser sanctions like probation but are not yet hardened criminals. Juvenile programs typically exclude some types of offenders, such as sex offenders, armed rob-

TABLE 7.12

Attitudes toward treating juveniles as adults if charged with serious property crime, selling drugs, or serious violent crime

By demographic characteristics, United States, 1995

Question: "Please tell me for each of the following statements whether you strongly agree, agree, neither agree nor disagree, disagree or strongly disagree."

(Percent responding "strongly agree" or "agree")

	A juvenile charged with a serious property crime should be tried as an adult	A juvenile charged with selling illegal drugs should be tried as an adult	A juvenile charged with a serious violent crime should be tried as an adult
National	62.6%	69.1%	86.5%
Sex			
Male	68.3	69.6	87.8
Female	57.4	68.6	85.2
Race			
White	63.1	69.7	86.9
Black	57.7	65.4	81.7
Hispanic	66.2	66.7	86.3
Age			
18 to 29 years	60.2	68.0	86.1
30 to 39 years	60.4	67.5	86.0
40 to 59 years	64.0	68.8	87.7
60 years and older	68.2	74.0	86.6
Education			
College graduate	57.7	65.5	85.0
Some college	60.7	70.6	86.3
High school graduate	65.3	71.4	87.4
Less than high school graduate	71.6	67.3	85.1
Income			
Over $60,000	64.0	71.5	86.1
Between $30,000 and $60,000	62.3	68.7	88.4
Between $15,000 and $29,999	65.4	72.4	85.4
Less than $15,000	60.2	64.2	82.2
Community			
Urban	60.5	67.1	85.4
Suburban	60.1	66.9	87.5
Small city	62.8	67.6	86.2
Rural/small town	64.7	72.0	85.9
Region			
Northeast	60.5	66.3	83.0
Midwest	60.8	68.5	86.1
South	67.8	71.6	88.3
West	58.9	68.0	86.7
Politics			
Republican	65.3	70.7	86.4
Democrat	57.9	65.0	86.7
Independent/other	62.9	70.0	85.4

Table constructed by SOURCEBOOK staff from data provided by the Survey Research Program, College of Criminal Justice, Sam Houston State University.

Source: Kathleen Maguire and Ann L. Pastore, eds., *Sourcebook of Criminal Justice Statistics 1996*, Bureau of Justice Statistics, Washington, DC, 1997

bers, and youths with a record of serious violence. But definitions of terms like "nonviolent" vary from program to program.

Most juvenile boot camps share the 90- to 120-day duration typical of military boot camps. They employ military customs and have uniformed drill instructors, use a platoon sergeant, and subject participants to verbal harassment, summary punishment, and group punishment under some circumstances.

Besides military discipline, all juvenile boot camps except the one in Orleans Parish included some type of work detail. Because of state-mandated education rules, all programs spent a minimum of three hours on academic education. Most programs also included some vocational education, work-skills training, or job preparation. All of the programs except Alabama's state-run boot camp included some form of drug and alcohol counseling or treatment, and all but California's included other forms of rehabilitative counseling. Upon graduation, most boot camp programs for juveniles assigned their graduates to a period of intensive community supervision (aftercare programs).

Recent Evaluations

The three demonstration programs were to develop camps and aftercare programs for male juveniles. Their goals were to

- Serve as an effective alternative to institutionalization.

- Promote discipline through physical conditioning and teamwork.

- Instill moral values and a work ethic.

- Promote literacy and increase academic achievement.

- Reduce drug and alcohol abuse.

- Encourage participants to become productive, law-abiding citizens.

- Ensure that offenders are held accountable for their actions.

High percentages of first-year youths completed the residential phase of boot camp, ranging from 94 percent in Cleveland to 82 percent in Mobile and 80 percent in Denver. Most youths not completing the programs were terminated for noncompliance or attempting to escape. One-third of Denver's dropouts, however, left boot camp for medical reasons. (See Table 7.19.)

TABLE 7.13

Teenagers' attitudes toward juveniles who commit violent crimes being tried as adults
By sex and age, United States, 1998

Question: "Do you think that juveniles who are 13 years old who are accused of committing a violent crime should be tried in the same court as adult offenders, or in juvenile court?"

	Adult court	Juvenile court	Depends
National	56%	37%	6%
Sex			
Male	59	35	6
Female	54	39	7
Age			
13 to 15 years	56	37	7
16 and 17 years	59	36	6

Note: The "don't know/no answer" category has been omitted; therefore percents may not sum to 100.

Table adapted by SOURCEBOOK staff from data provided by the New York Times Poll/CBS News Poll.

Source: Kathleen Maguire and Ann L. Pastore, eds., *Sourcebook of Criminal Justice Statistics 1997*, Bureau of Justice Statistics, Washington, DC, 1998

TABLE 7.14

Juvenile* Admissions to State Correctional Agencies, 1993

State	Number	Percent
Total U.S.**	**5,207**	**100.0**
North Carolina	1,226	23.5
New York	834	16.0
Illinois	405	7.8
Florida	380	7.3
Texas	348	6.7
Alabama	191	3.7
Georgia	189	3.6
Puerto Rico	187	3.6
Michigan (tie)	170	3.3
Missouri (tie)	170	3.3

National Institute of Corrections, *Offenders under Age 18 in State Adult Corrections Systems: A National Picture*, Special Issues in Corrections, Number 1, National Institute of Corrections, Washington, D.C., 1995.
*Age 17 and younger.
**Excludes New Jersey.

Source: Dale Parent et al., "Key Legislative Issues in Criminal Justice: Transferring Serious Juvenile Offenders to Adult Courts," *National Institute of Justice Research in Action*, January 1997

Two programs were disrupted by high staff turnover (Cleveland and Mobile) due to burnout and low salaries. Staff reported that the programs had some difficulty achieving a healthy balance between adhering to the strict requirements of a military model and addressing the unique correctional needs of juveniles. Staff with military backgrounds cited the frustration of trying to adjust to youths that were younger, more defiant, and less accustomed to structure than military recruits. On the other hand, staff without military experience were not familiar with military procedures and drills, and many favored rehabilitation over the military model.

Data suggest that youths improved their educational performance, physical fitness, and behavior, and most participants graduated at each site. In Cleveland and Mobile, where staff tested educational achievement at entry and at graduation, youths gained an average of one grade level or more over the 90-day term. Drill instructor ratings of participants' respect for authority, self-discipline, teamwork, and physical appearance also improved substantially, particularly in Denver and Mobile. More importantly, youths surveyed shortly before they returned to the community and entered aftercare believed that boot camps had significantly changed the direction of their lives.

Aftercare

Sites differed widely in the types of aftercare services they offered. In Cleveland and Denver, youths attended aftercare centers created for them by the programs, while in Mobile, graduates were "mainstreamed" to seven local Boys and Girls Clubs. Denver's aftercare services focused on academic instruction and were

TABLE 7.15

People Ages 13–15 in State Adult Correctional Populations, June 30, 1994

State	Number	Percent
Total U.S.*	102	100.0
Florida	39	38.2
North Carolina	18	17.6
Arkansas	11	10.8
Georgia	8	7.8

National Institute of Corrections, *Offenders under Age 18 in State Adult Corrections Systems: A National Picture,* Special Issues in Corrections, Number 1, National Institute of Corrections, Washington, D.C., 1995.
* Excludes New Jersey.

TABLE 7.16

People Ages 16–17 in State Adult Correctional Populations, June 30, 1994

State	Number	Percent
Total U.S.*	4,730	100.0
South Carolina	870	18.4
Florida	740	15.6
New York	487	10.3
North Carolina	451	9.5
Connecticut	334	7.1
Illinois	168	3.6
Georgia	163	3.4
Arkansas	140	3.0
Puerto Rico	138	2.9

National Institute of Corrections, *Offenders under Age 18 in State Adult Corrections Systems: A National Picture,* Special Issues in Corrections, Number 1, National Institute of Corrections, Washington, D.C., 1995.
* Excludes New Jersey.

TABLE 7.17

People Ages 18–21 in State Adult Correctional Populations, June 30, 1994

State	Number	Percent
Total U.S.*	65,575	100.0
California	8,514	13.0
Florida	6,007	9.2
New York	5,953	9.1
Illinois	4,966	7.6
Ohio	3,805	5.8
Michigan	3,401	5.2
North Carolina	2,982	4.5
Georgia	2,890	4.4
Virginia	1,961	3.0

National Institute of Corrections, *Offenders under Age 18 in State Adult Corrections Systems: A National Picture,* Special Issues in Corrections, Number 1, National Institute of Corrections, Washington, D.C., 1995.
* Excludes New Jersey.

Source of all tables: Dale Parent et al., "Key Legislative Issues in Criminal Justice: Transferring Serious Juvenile Offenders to Adult Courts," *National Institute of Justice Research in Action,* January 1997

offered in an atmosphere resembling a small private school. Youths were referred to other providers for non-academic services, such as drug counseling. Cleveland's center, on the other hand, was the hub of

TABLE 7.18

Key Characteristics of Boot Camps for Juvenile Offenders

Program	Operated by:	Year began	Capacity	Program duration (in days)	Age limits	Limited to:				% of time devoted:[1]		Level of supervision after boot camp
						Nonviolent offenders	First serious offense	First custodial commitment	volunteers	Physical training, drill, and work	Education and counseling	
High Intensity Treatment, Chalkville, AL	State	1990	100[2]	30	12–18			•		36	64	Depends on risk
Environmental Youth Corps, Mobile, AL	County/Private	1992	52	90	13–17	•	•	•		43	57	Intensive
LEAD, CA	State	1992	60	120	16–20		•		•	34	66	Intensive
Drug Treatment Boot Camp, Los Angeles, CA	County	1990	210	140	16–18					NA	NA	Intensive
Camp Foxfire, Denver, CO	State/Private	1992	24	90	14–18	•				58	42	Intensive
Orleans Parish Prison, New Orleans, LA	Parish	1985	275	Depends on sentence	13–16					NA	NA	None, usually
Mississippi Rehabilitative Camp, Raymond, MS	State	1992	175	168[3]	10–20					24	76	Minimal
Youth Leadership Academy, South Kortwright, NY	State	1992	30	120	15–16			•	•	44	56	Intensive
Camp Roulston, Cleveland, OH	County/Private	1992	30	90	14–17				•	38	63	Intensive

1 = Available only for programs in the ICR/Rutgers survey (Toby and Pearson, 1992).
2 = Includes 25 beds for females.
3 = Average actual completion time.
NA = Not Available

Source: *Boot Camps for Adult and Juvenile Offenders: Overview and Update*, National Institute of Justice, Washington, DC, 1994

TABLE 7.19

Completion Rates for Boot Camps: Year 1 Platoons

	Cleveland		Denver		Mobile	
	No.	Percentage	No.	Perce ge	No.	Percentage
Graduated boot camp	112	94.1	61	80.3	100	82.0
Terminated	7	5.9	15	19.7	22	18.0
Disruptive or noncompliant	3	2.5	6	7.9	7	5.7
Escape	4	3.4	3	3.9	12	9.8
Medical problems	0	0.0	5	6.6	3	2.5
Other	0	0.0	1	1.3	0	0.0
Total Youths	119	100.0	76	100.0	122	100.0

Source: Blair B. Bourque et al., "Boot Camps for Juvenile Offenders: An Implementation Evaluation of Three Demonstration Programs," *National Institute of Justice Research in Brief*, May 1996

daily counseling and support services, in addition to operating an alternative school.

What appeared to be a promising prognosis for youths' adjustment during the residential phase (boot camp) changed when they returned home. Without the 24-hour surveillance and regimentation of boot camp, most youths soon reverted to old patterns of behavior. All three programs reported high attrition rates for noncompliance, absenteeism, and new arrests. No site graduated more than 50 percent of its aftercare participants. (See Table 7.20.) One factor in this lackluster performance was the program's inability to keep graduates involved in activities. None of the aftercare programs found effective incentives to attract regular attendance, and absenteeism was a significant problem at each site.

Moreover, the programs did not maintain the intensive discipline and regimentation of the boot camp phase, the withdrawal of which was associated with the breakdown in graduates' focus and motivation. Youths who went on to aftercare and remained in the demonstration for at least eight months reported that their attitudes and behavior changed for the better in every cat-

egory surveyed (Table 7.21). These findings were based on a small sample, however, and responses may have been biased toward socially acceptable answers.

Costs

Only rough estimates of the programs' daily costs, which ranged from $75 per youth in Cleveland to $66 in Mobile, were possible. They indicate, however, that the daily operating costs of boot camps were less than those of alternative state and local facilities. (See Table 7.22.) Ohio estimated the average daily cost of state

TABLE 7.20

Completion Rates of Youths Entering Aftercare

	Cleveland (n=112)		Denver (n=61)		Mobile (n=100)	
	No.	Percentage	No.	Percentage	No.	Percentage
Youths Graduated from Aftercare	50	44.6	16	26.2	49	49.5
Youths Still in Aftercare	6	5.4	2	3.3	23	23.2
Youths Terminated	56	50	43	70.5	28	28.3
Failure to comply	7	6.3	5	8.2	6	6.1
AWOL–no known offense	10	8.9	20	32.8	2	2.0
Arrested for criminal offense	37	33.0	18	29.5	20	20.2
Deceased	2	1.8	—		—	

Source: Blair B. Bourque et al., "Boot Camps for Juvenile Offenders: An Implementation Evaluation of Three Demonstration Programs," *National Institute of Justice Research in Brief*, May 1996

TABLE 7.21

Youths' Ratings of Boot Camp Program at the 8-Month Mark

Compared to before boot camp . . .		Percentages of youths		
		Cleveland (n=19)	Denver (n=15)	Mobile (n=33)
How well do you think you can control your behavior and stay out of trouble?	More (Less)	57.9 (21.1)	66.7 (0)	69.7 (18.2)
How well do you get along with other people?	Better (Worse)	52.6 (5.3)	26.7 (13.3)	48.5 (6.1)
How do you feel about yourself?	Better Worse	63.2 (5.3)	66.7 (6.7)	60.6 (3.0)
How responsible are you in terms of what you say you will do and taking care of yourself?	More (Less)	68.4 (10.5)	93.3 (0)	60.6 (9.1)
How honest and truthful are you?	More (Less)	52.6 (5.3)	60.0 (6.7)	57.6 (0)
How well do you work with others?	Better (Worse)	63.2 (0)	40.0 (6.7)	51.5 (0)
How often do you use drugs or alcohol?	Less (More)	78.9 (5.3)	73.3 (0)	63.3 (15.2)
How often do you commit crimes?	Less (More)	94.7 (0)	100.0 (0)	84.4 (0)

Source: Blair B. Bourque et al., "Boot Camps for Juvenile Offenders: An Implementation Evaluation of Three Demonstration Programs," *National Institute of Justice Research in Brief*, May 1996

institutionalization at $99, and Denver's higher security and community residential facilities averaged $138 and $92, respectively, per day.

Conclusions

The evaluation team could not draw any conclusions about the programs' long-term ability to change offenders' behaviors or to save money and space for the country's overburdened juvenile system. Since typical detention sentences for juveniles are short, the researchers doubted whether putting youths in boot camps would save much money. (The shorter term of adult boot camps, compared to the time served in prison, does save money.)

Postprogram (boot camp) recidivism was not tracked, and recidivism in aftercare was studied only to the extent that a rearrest prompted a juvenile's termination from the program. Until more information is available on recidivism and the cost of alternatives to institutionalization, the impact of juvenile camps on correctional crowding will be difficult to determine.

Problems in Boot Camps

Trouble in a Texas Boot Camp

In June 1999, a 14-year-old asserted that he had been hit, kicked, and dragged on the ground when he could not perform calisthenics in a weekend boot camp in Dallas, Texas. Camp officials claim that the youth was physically restrained only because he tried to run away from the facility.

Following an investigation that found an officer at the camp had used unnecessary restraint, a Texas juvenile department official said that procedures at the camp would be tightened. In addition, officers at the camp will be required to take a refresher course in restraint and will hone their skills in how to handle confrontation without touching an inmate. New officers will be required to take the course before working with the youngsters. A ratio of one officer per 12 inmates will be strictly enforced, and a county liaison will be in attendance whenever youngsters are at the camp.

TABLE 7.22

Annual Demonstration Program Costs

	Cleveland	Denver	Mobile
Boot Camp			
Personnel	$567,112	$457,840	$551,425
Other expenses	258,954	160,608	217,500
Subtotal: Boot Camp	$826,066	$618,448	$768,925
Aftercare			
Personnel	$441,748	$159,120	$69,525
Other Expenses	359,104[1]	63,221	21,000
Subtotal: Aftercare	$800,852	$222,341	$90,525
Total: Boot Camp and Aftercare	**$1,626,918**	**$840,789**	**$859,450**
Estimated Annual Cost of Maintaining a Single Program Bed/Slot			
Boot Camp[2]	$27,536	$25,769	$24,029
Aftercare[3]	8,898	4,632[4]	943
Estimated Daily Cost for Participant			
Boot Camp	$75	$71	$66
Aftercare	24	13[5]	3
Estimated Program Cost per Participant (Assuming Program Completion)			
Boot Camp[6]	$6,750	$6,390	$5,940
Aftercare[7]	6,576	2,379[8]	822

[1] Includes $138,800 for contract with an alternative school.

[2] Based on daily capacity of 30 beds in Cleveland, 24 beds in Denver, and 32 beds in Mobile.

[3] Based on daily capacity of 90 youths in Cleveland, 48 youths in Denver, and 96 youths in Mobile.

[4] Excludes cost of teachers.

[5] Excludes cost of teachers.

[6] Assumes standard program length of 90 days in boot camp at all sites.

[7] Assumes standard length of stay in aftercare of 9 months (274 days) in Cleveland and Mobile, 6 months (183 days) in Denver.

[8] Excludes cost of teachers.

Source: Blair B. Bourque et al., "Boot Camps for Juvenile Offenders: An Implementation Evaluation of Three Demonstration Programs," *National Institute of Justice Research in Brief*, May 1996

Arizona Drops Boot Camp Programs

In 1996, after seven years, Arizona decided to end juvenile boot camp programs. Although state officials once believed boot camps were a way to save money and reduce crowded prisons, they concluded that the "break-them-down-and-build-them-back-up" philosophy does not work. The Arizona Department of Corrections found that the success rate of the boot camp program was small. A study conducted just prior to closing down the program showed that only 22.6 percent of those admitted to the boot camps successfully completed the program. The remainder either dropped out of the program or were returned to prison for another offense — about half the success rate of those sentenced to traditional jail time.

CHAPTER VIII

PROBATION AND PAROLE

Any society that depends on only two sentencing options — confinement or nothing at . all — is unsafe and unjust. We need a full array of effective sentencing tools that actually suit our various sentencing purposes. — Michael Smith, Vera Institute of Justice

During 1997, the number of adults on probation or parole increased to record levels. State and federal agencies reported 3.3 million adult offenders on probation and 685,033 on parole, a 22.2 percent and 28.9 percent increase, respectively, since 1990. It should be noted, however, that these increases are well below the growth in the jail (38.4 percent) and prison (59.5 percent) populations over the same period. (See Table 8.1.) About 2.9 percent of all American adults — 1 in every 35 — were incarcerated or on probation or parole.

Approximately 7 of 10 (69.3 percent) of the total corrections population were under community supervision — 57 percent were on probation, 12 percent were on parole, and 31 percent were confined in jail or prison. (See Table 8.1.)

TABLE 8.1

Number of adults under community supervision or incarcerated, 1990-97

| Year | Total estimated correctional population[a] | Community supervision | | Incarceration | | Adults under community supervision as a percent of — | |
		Probation	Parole	Jail	Prison	Total correctional population	All U.S. adult residents
1990[b]	4,348,000	2,670,234	531,407	403,019	743,382	73.6%	2.3%
1991[b]	4,535,600	2,728,472	590,442	424,129	792,535	73.2	2.4
1992[b]	4,762,600	2,811,611	658,601	441,781	850,566	72.9	2.5
1993[b]	4,944,000	2,903,061	676,100	455,500	909,381	72.4	2.6
1994	5,141,300	2,981,022	690,371	479,800	990,147	71.4	2.7
1995	5,335,100	3,077,861	679,421	499,300	1,078,542	70.4%	2.7%
1996	5,475,600	3,161,205	676,045	510,400	1,127,528	70.1	2.8
1997[c]	5,694,400	3,261,888	685,033	557,974	1,185,800	69.4	2.9
Percent change							
1996-97	3.9%	3.2%	1.3%	9.3%	5.2%		
1990-97	30.9	22.2	28.9	38.4	59.5		
Average annual percent change							
1990-97	3.9%	2.9%	3.7	4.8%	6.9%		

Note: Counts are for December 31, except for jail counts, which are for June 30. Counts of adults in jail facilities for 1993-96 were estimated and rounded to the nearest 100. Parole counts for 1996 dropped from the previously reported 704,709 because of reporting changes in New Jersey, Florida, California, and the Federal system. Prisoner counts are for inmates in custody.
[a]A small number of individuals have multiple correctional statuses; consequently, the total of persons under correctional supervision is an overestimate.
[b]The estimated jail population for 1990-93 includes an unknown number of persons supervised outside jail facilities.
[c]The prison population in custody is estimated.

Source: Press release, *Nation's Probation and Parole Population Reached New High Last Year*, Bureau of Justice Statistics, Washington, DC, 1998

TABLE 8.2

Adults on probation, 1997

Region and jurisdiction	Probation population, 1/1/97	1997 Entries	1997 Exits	Probation population, 12/31/97	Percent change in probation population during 1997	Number on probation on 12/31/97 per 100,000 adult residents
U.S. total	3,161,030	1,725,834	1,628,403	3,261,888	3.2%	1,647
Federal	34,202	14,756	16,331	32,627	-4.6%	16
State	3,126,828	1,711,078	1,612,072	3,229,261	3.3	1,630
Northeast	551,727	249,991	229,955	572,594	3.8%	1,470
Connecticut	55,978	38,275	38,264	55,989	0	2,260
Maine^a	7,753	:	:	8,584	10.7	909
Massachusetts	44,858	39,021	37,449	46,430	3.5	995
New Hampshire	4,414	3,585	3,123	4,876	10.5	556
New Jersey	125,881	59,651	54,967	130,565	3.7	2,153
New York	174,406	47,634	36,159	185,881	6.6	1,369
Pennsylvania	110,532	47,366	45,405	112,493	1.8	1,229
Rhode Island	20,446	8,473	9,271	19,648	-3.9	2,607
Vermont	7,459	5,986	5,317	8,128	9.0	1,833
Midwest	704,965	491,274	465,678	730,005	3.6%	1,579
Illinois	115,503	63,296	59,318	119,481	3.4	1,370
Indiana	93,509	81,799	78,263	97,045	3.8	2,222
Iowa	15,386	15,428	13,980	16,834	9.4	791
Kansas^{b,c}	15,732	19,502	19,029	16,205	3.0	850
Michigan^{a,d}	147,598	124,731	117,525	154,236	4.5	2,122
Minnesota^a	90,202	55,258	55,509	90,707	0.6	2,641
Missouri^{d,e}	42,368	20,718	16,785	46,301	9.3	1,159
Nebraska	14,363	14,696	14,534	14,525	1.1	1,198
North Dakota	2,599	1,498	1,440	2,657	2.2	559
Ohio^{a,d}	116,865	64,512	61,957	118,761	1.6	1,423
South Dakota^{a,f}	3,548	4,768	4,764	3,467	-2.3	641
Wisconsin^g	47,292	25,068	22,574	49,786	5.3	1,302
South	1,272,488	667,472	651,235	1,292,339	1.6%	1,850
Alabama^{a,d}	37,865	2,153	1,669	35,723	-5.7	1,100
Arkansas	25,178	8,529	7,315	26,392	4.8	1,419
Delaware^{a,e}	16,528	:	:	17,872	8.1	3,225
District of Columbia	9,740	9,875	8,818	10,797	10.9	2,560
Florida^{a,d}	237,117	196,263	196,902	239,932	1.2	2,146
Georgia^d	143,457	65,452	60,489	148,420	3.5	2,699
Kentucky^h	11,689	6,087	5,683	12,093	3.5	410
Louisiana	35,375	11,815	11,737	35,453	0.2	1,122
Maryland	70,553	39,163	35,104	74,612	5.8	1,950
Mississippi^{a,b,c}	10,376	3,547	3,926	10,997	6.0	556
North Carolina	102,483	59,327	56,394	105,416	2.9	1,899
Oklahoma^{a,d}	28,090	13,812	13,131	28,733	2.3	1,178
South Carolina	42,417	15,046	15,059	42,404	0	1,512
Tennessee^d	37,002	20,305	19,056	38,251	3.4	946
Texasⁱ	429,329	193,128	193,364	429,093	-0.1	3,095
Virginia^e	29,620	22,970	22,588	30,002	1.3	589
West Virginia^{a,d,e}	5,669	:	:	6,149	8.5	438
West	597,648	302,341	265,204	634,323	6.1%	1,473
Alaska	3,999	2,038	1,659	4,378	9.5	1,040
Arizona^{d,e}	40,607	29,604	25,398	44,813	10.4	1,368
California	286,526	164,882	146,877	304,531	6.3	1,306
Colorado^{a,d,e}	42,688	20,153	16,051	45,447	6.5	1,580
Hawaii	14,027	7,521	6,147	15,401	9.8	1,742
Idaho^j	5,855	2,308	1,796	6,367	8.7	741
Montana^{h,k}	4,473	1,257	1,052	4,678	4.6	720
Nevada^a	9,760	:	:	10,902	11.7	884
New Mexico^d	8,903	7,470	7,478	8,895	-0.1	723
Oregon	42,292	16,210	14,522	43,980	4.0	1,808
Utah	9,306	4,107	3,952	9,461	1.7	690
Washington^{a,d}	125,780	44,511	38,016	132,014	5.0	3,177
Wyoming	3,432	2,280	2,256	3,456	0.7	993

:Not known.

^aBecause of nonresponse or incomplete data, the population on December 31, 1997, does not equal the population on January 1, 1997, plus entries, minus exits.
^bData do not include absconders.
^cData do not include out-of-State cases.
^dMultiple agencies reporting.
^eAll data are estimated.

^fData are for year ending June 30, 1997.
^gData are provisional, pending further review by the State.
^hData do not include inactive cases.
ⁱData are for year ending August 31, 1997.
^jTotal entries are estimated.
^kTotal exits are estimated.

Source: Press release, *Nation's Probation and Parole Population Reached New High Last Year*, Bureau of Justice Statistics, Washington, DC, 1998

TABLE 8.3

Community corrections among the States, yearend 1997

10 States with the largest 1997 community corrections populations	Number supervised	10 States with the largest percent increase	Percent increase	10 States with the highest rates of supervision, 1997	Persons supervised per 100,000 adult U.S. residents*	10 States with the lowest rates of supervision, 1997	Persons supervised per 100,000 adult U.S. residents*
Probation:							
Texas	429,093	Nevada	11.7%	Delaware	3,225	Kentucky	410
California	304,531	Maine	10.7	Washington	3,177	West Virginia	438
Florida	239,932	New Hampshire	10.5	Texas	3,095	Mississippi	556
New York	185,881	Arizona	10.4	Georgia	2,699	New Hampshire	556
Michigan	154,236	Hawaii	9.8	Minnesota	2,641	North Dakota	559
Georgia	148,420	Alaska	9.5	Rhode Island	2,607	Virginia	589
Washington	132,014	Iowa	9.4	Connecticut	2,260	South Dakota	641
New Jersey	130,565	Missouri	9.3	Indiana	2,222	Utah	690
Illinois	119,481	Vermont	9.0	New Jersey	2,153	Montana	720
Ohio	118,761	Ildaho	8.7	Florida	2,146	New Mexico	723
Parole:							
Texas	109,437	Colorado	25.7%	Pennsylvania	833	Maine	6
California	104,409	North Dakota	19.0	Texas	789	Washington	12
Pennsylvania	76,232	South Dakota	18.6	Oregon	691	North Dakota	25
New York	59,670	Idaho	18.5	Louisiana	630	Connecticut	40
Illinois	30,348	Alaska	17.1	California	448	Nebraska	57
Georgia	21,915	New Jersey	16.2	New York	439	West Virginia	64
Louisiana	19,927	New Mexico	14.0	Maryland	412	Mississippi	70
New Jersey	16,903	Utah	13.7	Georgia	399	Rhode Island	70
Oregon	16,815	Indiana	13.0	Illinois	348	Minnesota	71
Maryland	15,763	Virginia	8.0	Kansas	323	Florida	76

Note: The District of Columbia as a wholly urban jurisdiction is excluded.
*Rates are computed using U.S. adult resident population on July 1, 1997.

Source: Press release, *Nation's Probation and Parole Population Reached New High Last Year*, Bureau of Justice Statistics, Washington, DC, 1998

Three-quarters of probationers and parolees were required to maintain regular contact with a supervisory agency. The other offenders were not required to have regular contact (9 percent), and 9 percent had failed to report and could not be located.

PROBATION

Probation is the suspension of a sentence of a person convicted, but not yet imprisoned, on condition of continued good behavior and regular reporting to a probation officer. The whole sentence might be served under probation, or probation might be combined with a short sentence in a prison or jail.

Rates and Numbers

In 1997, almost 1,650 adults per 100,000 adult U.S. residents were on probation. The probation population rate in the South was the highest at 1,850 per 100,000 adults. Texas, Washington, and Delaware each had more than 3,000 persons on probation per 100,000 adult residents. Georgia, Minnesota, Rhode Island, Florida, Connecticut, Indiana, New Jersey, Michigan, and the District of Columbia each had more than 2,000 persons on probation per 100,000 adult residents. (See Tables 8.2 and 8.3.)

At the end of 1997, Texas had the largest number of adults on probation (429,093). Eleven other states (California, Florida, New York, Michigan, Georgia, New Jersey, Washington, Ohio, Illinois, Pennsylvania, and North Carolina) had more than 100,000 people on probation. (See Tables 8.2 and 8.3.)

Characteristics

Women made up about 21 percent of the nation's probationers in 1997. Approximately 64 percent of the adults on probation were White and 35 percent were Black. Hispanics, who may be of any race, made up 16 percent of probationers. (See Table 8.4.)

More than half (54 percent) of all offenders on probation in 1997 were on probation for a felony. A quarter (28 percent) were on probation for a misdemeanor. One in every 7 probationers (14 percent) had been convicted of driving while intoxicated or under the influence of alcohol. (See Table 8.4.)

According to the Criminal Justice Institute (*The Corrections Yearbook, 1998*, Middletown, Connecticut, 1998), the caseload for a regular probation officer averaged 175 probationers (93 for combination probation and parole agencies). For intensive supervision, the caseload was 34 people per probation officer (25 for combination). Other caseloads were 20 for electronic supervision (24 for combination) and 62 for special caseloads (37 for combination).*

In 1997, 22.9 percent of the probationers who had their freedom revoked returned to jail or prison because they committed new crimes. Six of 10 (60.1 percent) were reincarcerated due to other reasons, such as not reporting to their parole officers, and 16.9 percent were returned for both committing a new crime and for other reasons.

Conditions Imposed

Felons released on probation to the community are required, as a condition of their freedom, to comply with the orders of the court. These orders frequently include having the probationer meet with the probation officer on a periodic basis, maintain steady employment, remain in school, or avoid certain places or people. Judges may also impose special conditions, often tailored to specific offender characteristics, such as drug treatment, community service, restitution, or mental health counseling.

TABLE 8.4

Characteristics of adults on probation, 1990 and 1997

Characteristic of adults on probation	1990	1997
Sex		
Male	82 %	79 %
Female	18	21
Race		
White	68 %	64%
Black	31	35
Other races	1	1
Hispanic origin		
Hispanic	18 %	16 %
Non-Hispanic	82	84
Status of supervision		
Active supervision	83 %	79 %
Inactive supervision	9	8
Absconded from supervision	6	10
Supervised out of State	2	2
Other	**	2
Entries		
Probation without incarceration	87 %	76 %
Probation with incarceration	8	17
Probation of other types	5	6
Exits		
Successful completions	69%	62%
Returned to incarceration	14	18
With new sentence	3	5
With the same sentence	11	13
Other unsuccessful	9	12
Death	--	1
Other	7	7
Type of offense		
Felony	48 %	54%
Misdemeanor	31	28
Driving while intoxicated	21	14
Other infractions	1	4

Note: For every characteristic there were persons of unknown status or type.
**Not available.
--Less than 0.5%.

Source: Press release, *Nation's Probation and Parole Population Reached New High Last Year*, Bureau of Justice Statistics, Washington, DC, 1998

In *Characteristics of Adults on Probation, 1995* (1997), the Bureau of Justice Statistics (BJS) reported that 82 percent of probationers were given three or more conditions on their sentences. Nearly all probationers (98.6 percent) had one or more conditions to their sentence. Almost all (98.4 per-

---

* Special supervision includes programs such as boot camps, substance abuse treatment programs, or other services. Regular supervision establishes a set number of visits or reports, while intensive supervision involves a greater number of visits or reports. Electronic supervision includes electronic monitoring devices.

cent) felony probationers had at least one special condition imposed. (See Table 8.5.) Seventeen percent of probationers had one or two conditions, 36 percent had three or four conditions, and nearly half (46 percent) had five or more.

A monetary requirement was the most common condition, affecting 84.3 percent of all probationers. Types of financial penalties included victim restitution (30.3 percent), court costs (54.5 percent), fines (55.8 percent), and supervision fees (61 percent). Performing community service as a condition was required for 25.7 percent of probationers, and 40.3 percent had to have jobs or enroll in an education or training program (Table 8.5).

One-tenth of all probationers were monitored or had their movements restricted. This means that they might have been required to stay away from certain places (bars or particular businesses) or might have been subject to electronic monitoring, house arrest, or curfew. Another 10.4 percent were restricted from contacting their victim or victims (Table 8.5).

Probationers Pay for Their Own Supervision

With correctional costs skyrocketing, many government officials have decided that offenders should help pay for their supervision and rehabilitation. Currently, most jail and prison work programs require inmates to contribute a portion of their earnings to their own upkeep. A more recent approach to recouping taxpayers' dollars is to require offenders on probation and who are capable of working to pay for at least some of the cost of

TABLE 8.5

Conditions of sentences of adult probationers, by severity of offense, 1995

Condition of sentence	Total	Severity of offense	
		Felony	Misdemeanor
Any condition	98.6%	98.4%	98.9%
Fees, fines, court costs	84.3%	84.2%	85.1%
Supervision fees	61.0	63.9	59.8
Fines	55.8	47.4	67.9
Court costs	54.5	56.4	54.5
Restitution to victim	30.3%	39.7%	17.6%
Confinement/monitoring	10.1%	12.9%	6.3%
Boot camp	.5	.8	.1
Electronic monitoring	2.9	3.2	2.0
House arrest without electronic monitoring	.8	1.1	.5
Curfew	.9	1.6	0
Restriction on movement	4.2	5.3	2.9
Restrictions	21.1%	24.0%	16.0%
No contact with victim	10.4	11.8	8.2
Driving restrictions	5.3	4.3	5.8
Community service	25.7%	27.3%	24.0%
Alcohol/drug restrictions	38.2%	48.1%	23.7%
Mandatory drug testing	32.5	43.0	17.1
Remain alcohol/drug free	8.1	10.4	5.2
Substance abuse treatment	41.0%	37.5%	45.7%
Alcohol	29.2	21.3	41.0
Drug	23.0	28.3	14.8
Other treatment	17.9%	16.1%	20.9%
Sex offenders program	2.5	3.9	.2
Psychiatric/psychological counseling	7.1	8.9	4.7
Other counseling	9.2	4.4	16.4
Employment and training	40.3%	45.4%	34.4%
Employment	34.7	40.9	27.3
Education/training	15.0	15.5	15.1
Other special conditions	16.5%	19.0%	12.6%
Number of probationers*	2,558,981	1,470,696	982,536

Note: Detail may not sum to total because probationers may have more than one condition on their sentences and totals may include items not shown in the table.
*Excludes 61,579 probationers (2% of all adults on probation) for whom information on conditions of probation was not reported.

Source: Thomas P. Bonczar, *Characteristics of Adults on Probation, 1995*, Bureau of Justice Statistics, Washington, DC, 1997

their supervision. More than half the states allow local probation departments to charge fees to probationers. The amount of fees states collect varies widely. In 1997, according to the Criminal Justice Institute, the jurisdictions responding to its survey charged an average monthly fee of $29.62.

The increasing use of probation fees has prompted heated debate among correctional professionals. Some critics argue that correctional fees are not an efficient way to generate revenue because many correctional clients are indigent and the cost of collecting fees may exceed the amount

TABLE 8.6		
Disciplinary Hearings: Months Served		
Months served on probation	Number of probationers*	Percent of probationers who had at least one disciplinary hearing
All probationers	2,553,052	18.4%
Less than 6 months	557,238	4.8
6 to 11	594,726	11.0
12 to 23	697,545	21.8
24 to 35	344,361	26.1
36 or more	359,183	37.6

*Excludes 67,508 probationers (3% of all adults on probation) for whom information on formal disciplinary hearings or time served on probation

TABLE 8.7	
Disciplinary Hearings: Employment and Prior Sentences	
	Percent of adults on probation with disciplinary hearing
Employment	
Employed	15.9%
Not employed	22.9
Severity of offense	
Felony	21.1%
Misdemeanor	14.8
Prior sentence	
No prior sentence	14.9%
Probation or incarceration	23.2

Source of both tables: Thomas P. Bonczar, *Characteristics of Adults on Probation, 1995*, Bureau of Justice Statistics, Washington, DC, 1997

of money earned. Others assert that it is unethical or even illegal to force convicted offenders to pay for services they are required to receive.

Opponents of the idea allege that creating incentives to accumulate probation fees may cause probation officers to neglect their supervisory responsibilities. Finally, they warn that collecting fees may cause government officials to lose control over local probation departments if these departments achieve significant fiscal independence from the states and counties.

Disciplinary Action

According to the *Characteristics of Adults on Probation* survey (above), nearly 1 of 5 (18.4 percent) of all probationers faced one or more disciplinary hearings while on probation. (See Table 8.6.) Probationers may face such a hearing if they violate a condition of their probation or are arrested for a new offense. A disciplinary hearing might result in an arrest warrant being issued for the probationer (if he or she has disappeared), the probationer being sent back to prison, or probation being reinstated with or without new conditions.

The longer a probationer was on probation, the more likely it was that he or she had experienced at least one disciplinary hearing. More than one-third (37.6 percent) of probationers who had been on probation for 36 months or more had faced a

disciplinary hearing, compared to 4.8 percent who had served less than six months (Table 8.6). The survey did not include those probationers who were incarcerated at the time of the survey.

Probationers who were employed were less apt to face a disciplinary hearing than those who were not working (15.9 percent and 22.9 percent, respectively). Probationers who had no prior sentence were less likely to have a disciplinary hearing than those who had a prior sentence (14.9 percent and 23.2 percent, respectively). (See Table 8.7.)

Reasons for Facing a Hearing

The most common reason for a probationer having to face a disciplinary hearing was failure to contact the probation officer (41.1 percent). This was followed by arrest or conviction for a new crime (38.4 percent), failure to pay fines or restitution (37.9 percent), failure to attend or complete an alcohol or drug treatment program (22.5 percent), a positive drug test (11.2 percent), or failure to complete a community service requirement (8.5 percent.) (See Table 8.8.)

Overall, felons were more likely than misdemeanants to fail to maintain contact with the probation officer (43.3 and 37.6 percent, respectively) and to be arrested or convicted for a new offense. On the other hand, misdemeanants (43 percent) were more apt than felons (34.1 percent)

TABLE 8.8

Reasons for disciplinary hearings of adult probationers, by severity of most serious offense, 1995

Reason for disciplinary hearing[a]	Total	Severity of offense	
		Felony	Misdemeanor
Absconded/failed to maintain contact	41.1%	43.3%	37.6%
New offense	38.4%	43.2%	31.0%
Arrested	30.4	34.9	23.5
Convicted	13.9	15.8	10.5
Failure to pay fines or restitution	37.9%	34.1%	43.0%
Drug/alcohol violation			
Failure to attend/complete treatment program	22.5%	17.5%	33.0%
Positive drug test	11.2	14.3	5.6
Alcohol abuse	2.7	2.9	2.7
Violation of confinement restrictions			
Failure to do jail time/return from furlough	2.5%	2.5%	2.8%
Violation of home confinement	1.3	1.6	.6
Other violations			
Failure to complete community service	8.5%	9.5%	6.7%
Other	6.8	6.9	6.7
Number of probationers[b]	457,279	297,481	144,550

[a]Detail adds to more than total because some probationers had more than one disciplinary hearing, while others had a single hearing with more than one reason.
[b]Excludes probationers who never had a disciplinary hearing or for whom information on disciplinary hearings was not reported.

Source: Thomas P. Bonczar, *Characteristics of Adults on Probation, 1995*, Bureau of Justice Statistics, Washington, DC, 1997

followed by larceny/theft (9.9 percent), drug possession (9.8 percent), drug trafficking (9.7 percent), and assault (9.2 percent). (See Table 8.9.)

In 1995, 58 percent of all adults on probation had been convicted of a felony. Half of those had been convicted of a violent (19.5 percent) or drug (30.7 percent) offense. Drug trafficking (15.4 percent) was the most frequent offense among felons on probation, followed by drug possession (13.1 percent), larceny/theft (11.1 percent), and burglary (9.7 percent.) (See Table 8.9.)

to fail to pay fines or restitution and to fail to complete drug or alcohol treatment programs (33 percent and 17.5 percent, respectively; Table 8.8).

Results of the Hearings

Of those probationers who had faced one or more disciplinary hearings, 42 percent were permitted to continue their probation, but with additional conditions. One of three (29 percent) were incarcerated in jail or prison, another 29 percent had their probation reinstated without any new conditions, and 4 percent had charges that were not sustained. (The percentages for hearing outcomes add to more than 100 percent, because some probationers faced more than one hearing or outcome.)

Types of Crimes

In 1995, 17.3 percent of probationers had been convicted of violent offenses and 21.4 percent for drug offenses. Almost equal proportions had been sentenced for property offenses (28.9 percent) and for public-order offenses (31.1 percent). Driving while intoxicated (DWI; 16.7 percent) was the most frequent single offense among those on probation,

TABLE 8.9

Most serious offense of adults on probation, by severity of offense, 1995

Most serious current offense	Total[a]	Severity of offense[b]	
		Felony	Misdemeanor
Violent offenses	17.3%	19.5%	13.5%
Homicide	.7	1.0	.2
Sexual assault	3.6	5.6	.4
Robbery	1.9	3.2	0
Assault	9.2	7.6	11.1
Other violent	2.0	2.1	1.7
Property offenses	28.9%	36.6%	18.2%
Burglary	5.8	9.7	.3
Larceny/theft	9.9	11.1	8.5
Motor vehicle theft	1.4	2.0	.4
Fraud	7.2	9.6	4.2
Stolen property	1.7	2.3	.9
Other property	2.7	1.9	3.8
Drug offenses	21.4%	30.7%	7.6%
Possession	9.8	13.1	4.6
Trafficking	9.7	15.4	1.6
Other/unspecified	1.9	2.3	1.4
Public-order offenses	31.1%	12.1%	59.6%
Weapons	2.3	2.5	2.1
Obstruction of justice	2.2	1.3	3.3
Traffic	4.7	.9	10.2
Driving while intoxicated	16.7	5.2	35.2
Drunkenness/morals	2.1	.5	4.5
Other public-order	3.0	1.7	4.3
Other	1.3%	1.0%	1.2%
Number of probationers	2,595,499	1,479,904	988,033

[a]Excludes 25,061 probationers (1% of all adults on probation) for whom information on the most serious offense was not reported.
[b]Based on 2,543,925 probationers for whom information on most serious offense and severity of offense is known. Excludes 75,988 probationers sentenced for an offense other than a felony or a misdemeanor.

Source: Thomas P. Bonczar, *Characteristics of Adults on Probation, 1995*, Bureau of Justice Statistics, Washington, DC, 1997

Most misdemeanants on probation (59.6 percent) had been convicted of a public-order offense. In fact, one-third (35.2 percent) of all misdemeanor probationers were convicted of DWI, 10.2 percent for other traffic offenses, and 4.5 percent for drunkenness or morals offenses (Table 8.9). Approximately 14 percent of probationers convicted of a misdemeanor had also committed a violent offense (most often, assault). Nearly 1 of 5 (18.2 percent) had been convicted of a property offense and 7.6 percent, of a drug offense (Table 8.9).

Types of offenses committed by probationers differed between genders and racial/ethnic categories. More men (19.4 percent) than women (9.5 percent) had been sentenced for a violent offense, but nearly as many women (20.1 percent) as men (21.7 percent) had been sentenced for a drug offense. DWI was the most frequent offense (17.4 percent) for men, followed by assault and drug possession (10.3 percent each) and drug trafficking (9.7 percent). Women most often were sentenced for property offenses (42.6 percent), espe-

cially fraud (20.8 percent) and larceny/theft (16.5 percent). About 14 percent of female probationers (nearly as many as men) were convicted of driving while intoxicated. (See Table 8.10.)

Blacks (30.9 percent) were more likely than Hispanics (23.1 percent) or Whites (17 percent) to have been sentenced for drug offenses. White (21.2 percent) and Hispanic (17.3 percent) probationers were more likely than Black (7.7 percent) probationers to have been sentenced for driving while intoxicated. Virtually equal percentages of Whites (16.5 percent) and Blacks (17.1 percent) were on probation for violent offenses as well as for property offenses (29.9 percent and 28.6 percent, respectively.) (See Table 8.10.)

Characteristics of Probationers

Women made up 20.9 percent of probationers. Non-Hispanic Whites accounted for 58.3 percent of all probationers, 55.4 percent of felons, and 61.8 percent of misdemeanants. Non-Hispanic Blacks

TABLE 8.10

Most serious offense of adults on probation, by sex, race/Hispanic origin, and age, 1995

Most serious current offense	Sex		Race/Hispanic origin			Age			
	Male	Female	White	Black	Hispanic	24 or younger	25-34	35-44	45 or older
Violent offenses	19.4%	9.5%	16.5%	17.1%	19.4%	16.5%	17.0%	17.4%	20.3%
Homicide	.6	.9	1.0	.3	.3	.4	.6	.9	1.1
Sexual assault	4.3	.6	4.9	1.2	2.4	1.8	3.0	3.8	9.1
Robbery	2.0	1.4	1.0	3.1	2.4	3.1	1.3	2.0	.7
Assault	10.3	5.1	7.6	11.0	11.6	9.0	10.3	8.7	7.1
Other violent	2.2	1.5	2.0	1.6	2.7	2.2	1.8	2.0	2.3
Property offenses	25.3%	42.6%	29.9%	28.6%	23.8%	38.7%	27.0%	22.9%	24.7%
Burglary	6.6	2.8	6.3	5.5	4.3	10.4	5.2	3.5	2.2
Larceny/theft	8.2	16.5	10.0	10.9	8.4	13.6	9.3	8.2	7.2
Motor vehicle theft	1.5	.8	1.1	1.0	2.7	2.5	1.4	.7	.1
Fraud	3.7	20.8	7.4	7.4	5.6	4.6	7.9	7.7	10.3
Stolen property	2.0	.8	2.0	1.3	1.5	3.0	1.4	1.3	1.0
Other property	3.2	.9	3.2	2.5	1.3	4.6	1.8	1.6	3.8
Drug offenses	21.7%	20.1%	17.0%	30.9%	23.1%	19.7%	23.9%	23.2%	13.4%
Possession	10.3	8.0	8.1	13.4	10.9	8.0	10.7	11.2	8.1
Trafficking	9.7	9.7	7.8	14.2	9.7	10.2	10.8	9.8	4.7
Other/unspecified	1.7	2.4	1.1	3.4	2.4	1.5	2.3	2.2	.6
Public-order offenses	32.3%	26.5%	35.6%	22.2%	30.4%	22.1%	31.5%	35.7%	40.7%
Weapons	2.8	.7	1.8	3.2	2.5	3.9	2.3	.9	1.8
Obstruction of justice	2.3	1.7	2.1	2.4	2.1	2.6	2.7	1.3	1.4
Traffic	4.7	4.7	4.7	5.0	4.7	4.2	5.5	4.6	3.2
Driving while intoxicated	17.4	14.2	21.2	7.7	17.3	7.1	16.4	22.7	27.7
Drunkenness/morals	2.0	2.5	2.0	2.3	1.6	1.5	2.0	2.7	2.3
Other public-order	3.1	2.8	3.9	1.6	2.2	2.7	2.6	3.5	4.3
Other	1.3%	1.3%	1.0%	1.2%	3.2%	3.1%	.6%	.7%	.8%
Number of probationers	2,057,405	538,094	1,521,161	717,389	295,243	700,261	957,412	641,015	296,811

Note: Excludes an estimated 25,061 probationers (1% of all adults on probation) for whom information on type of offense was not reported.

Source: Thomas P. Bonczar, *Characteristics of Adults on Probation, 1995*, Bureau of Justice Statistics, Washington, DC, 1997

TABLE 8.11

Characteristics of adults on probation, by severity of most serious offense, 1995

Characteristic	Total	Severity of offense	
		Felony	Misdemeanor
Sex			
Male	79.1%	79.1%	78.4%
Female	20.9	20.9	21.6
Race/Hispanic origin			
White non-Hispanic	58.3%	55.4%	61.8%
Black non-Hispanic	27.9	30.8	24.5
Hispanic	11.3	11.2	11.4
Other	2.4	2.6	2.3
Age			
17 or younger	.5%	.5%	.5%
18-24	26.4	27.6	24.7
25-34	36.8	36.6	37.0
35-44	24.7	24.6	25.2
45-54	8.4	8.2	8.7
55 or older	3.2	2.6	3.9
Marital status			
Married	26.2%	26.8%	24.7%
Widowed	.9	.9	.9
Separated	7.0	6.9	7.8
Divorced	14.5	14.6	13.4
Never married	51.4	50.8	53.2
Education completed			
8th grade or less	7.5%	8.0%	7.0%
Some high school	34.9	37.6	30.4
High school graduate/GED	39.9	37.6	43.2
Some college or more	17.7	16.8	19.5
Number of probationers	2,620,560	1,491,670	991,161

Note: Estimates are based on complete data on sex and race/Hispanic origin and reported data on marital status (82%) and education (81%).

Source: Thomas P. Bonczar, *Characteristics of Adults on Probation, 1995*, Bureau of Justice Statistics, Washington, DC, 1997

made up 27.9 percent of all probationers, 30.8 percent of felons, and 24.5 percent of misdemeanants. Hispanics, who may be of any race, made up 11 percent of both felons and misdemeanants. About half (51.4 percent) of probationers were never married, and a great proportion (42.4 percent) had not completed high school. (See Table 8.11.)

Substance Abuse and Treatment of Adults on Probation

According to *Substance Abuse and Treatment of Adults on Probation, 1995* (Bureau of Justice Statistics, 1998), nearly 70 percent of adult probationers admitted to using drugs in the past, and half of probationers who used alcohol or drugs had received treatment during their current probation sentence. This is the first survey ever conducted to collect data on drug abuse and treatment in the probation population. Personal interviews were conducted with more than 2,000 adult probationers under active supervision in 1995.

Drugs and Alcohol

More than two-thirds (67.3 percent) of all probationers claimed to have been involved with drugs or alcohol. Male probationers (70.9 percent) were more likely than female probationers (53.7 percent) to have used drugs or alcohol. A somewhat higher proportion of non-Hispanic White probationers (70.6 percent) than non-Hispanic Black probationers (64 percent) or Hispanic probationers (58.8 percent) reported using alcohol or drugs. A greater percentage (73 percent) of those between the ages of 25 and 44 used alcohol or drugs than those of any other ages. (See Table 8.12.)

The Bureau of Justice Statistics analyzed probationers' use of drugs or alcohol based on whether they had been under the influence of drugs or alcohol ever in the past, in the month before committing the offense, or at the time of the offense. Over 69 percent said they had ever used drugs in the past, 31.8 percent said they had used drugs in the month prior to the offense, and 13.5 percent admitted using drugs at the time the offense was committed. About 4 of 10 probationers (39.9 percent) said they were under the influence of alcohol at the time they committed the offense. (See Table 8.13.)

TABLE 8.12

Selected characteristics of alcohol- or drug-involved probationers, 1995

	Percent of probationers reporting alcohol or drug involvement
All probationers	67.3%
Sex	
Male	70.9%
Female	53.7
Race/Hispanic origin	
White non-Hispanic	70.6%
Black non-Hispanic	64.0
Hispanic	58.8
Other	59.1
Age	
24 or younger	57.5%
25-34	72.5
35-44	73.4
45-54	60.2
55 or older	66.6

Source: Christopher J. Mumola and Thomas P. Bonczar, *Substance Abuse and Treatment of Adults on Probation, 1995*, Bureau of Justice Statistics, Washington, DC, 1998

TABLE 8.13

Levels of prior drug use, by selected characteristics of adult probationers, 1995

| | | Percent of probationers | | | | | | |
| | | Probationers' level of prior drug use | | | | Probationers' prior alcohol abuse | | |
Characteristic	Number of probationers	Ever in the past	Used regularly[a]	In the month prior to offense	At the time of offense	Under the influence of alcohol at time of offense	Ever had a binge drinking experience[b]	Had three or more positive CAGE responses
All probationers	2,065,896	69.4%	43.4%	31.8%	13.5%	39.9%	35.3%	24.0%
Sex								
Male	1,636,017	69.9%	44.7%	33.7%	14.0%	43.5%	40.4%	25.5%
Female	429,879	67.7	38.4	24.6	11.6	26.2	16.1	18.1
Race/Hispanic origin								
White non-Hispanic	1,264,990	72.8%	46.0%	33.1%	13.6%	46.6%	43.3%	28.6%
Black non-Hispanic	509,919	68.1	43.8	34.7	14.7	26.2	19.2	15.8
Hispanic	228,399	56.4	32.3	23.3	10.7	32.7	27.7	15.8
Other	62,588	59.3	29.0	14.5	13.8	41.5	34.5	27.0
Age								
24 or younger	556,760	69.9%	42.3%	38.3%	16.4%	26.1%	35.0%	14.4%
25-34	713,204	76.9	47.3	34.9	14.5	42.8	35.1	24.0
35-44	523,583	75.4	52.8	32.5	14.0	47.4	37.6	32.5
45-54	191,382	44.1	22.4	11.6	5.3	41.6	33.1	32.3
55 or older	80,967	21.4	6.8	3.8	1.1	55.5	30.2	14.2
Education								
8th grade or less	114,818	49.6%	32.1%	25.8%	15.0%	42.7%	28.2%	26.4%
Some high school	509,091	71.5	43.2	33.8	14.6	35.1	35.7	21.5
GED	224,007	83.6	57.7	44.6	17.4	43.1	44.7	31.0
High school graduate	595,715	65.0	40.0	30.5	12.4	38.8	35.8	22.1
Some college or more	586,236	70.6	44.4	27.3	11.7	43.8	33.0	25.6

[a]Regular use is defined as once a week or more for at least a month.
[b]Binge drinking is defined as having consumed a fifth of liquor in a single day, equivalent to 20 drinks, 3 bottles of wine, or 3 six-packs of beer.

Source: Christopher J. Mumola and Thomas P. Bonczar, *Substance Abuse and Treatment of Adults on Probation, 1995*, Bureau of Justice Statistics, Washington, DC, 1998

Drug Testing and Treatment

Probationers were also asked if they had ever received drug treatment in the past. Nearly half (49 percent) had been tested for drug use while on their current probation sentence, but only 17.4 percent received treatment while on probation. The longer a person was on probation, the more likely he or she was to be tested and to receive treatment. (See Table 8.14.)

Probationers who had received treatment for drugs took part in different types of programs. Moreover, some probationers who had received drug treatment more than once may not have participated in the same type of treatment program each time. The most common types of drug treatment programs were outpatient care (used by 16.5 percent of those being treated), followed by self-help programs (used by 13.7 percent). More probationers (51.2 percent) who had used drugs in the month prior to committing the offense received treatment than those who used drugs regularly (45.9 percent) or those who had ever used drugs in the past (31.6 percent.) (See Table 8.15.)

Alcohol Testing and Treatment

A significantly larger proportion (40.6 percent) of probationers with a history of alcohol use had received treatment than those who had used drugs (22.1 percent). Nearly three-fourths (72.5 percent) of probationers under the influence of alcohol at the time of the offense sought treatment, as did 62.9 percent of those who had binged on alcohol and 65.3 percent of those who had gotten into a physical fight because of their drinking. (See Table 8.16.) It is important to remember when using these statistics that alcohol and drug abusers tend to underestimate the amount of alcohol and/or drugs they use.

Nearly 8 of 10 (78.1 percent) of those who had had three or more positive CAGE responses had received some kind of treatment. (See Table 8.16.) A CAGE questionnaire is a diagnostic device used

TABLE 8.14

Drug testing and treatment of adult probationers, by level of prior drug use and time served, 1995

Level of prior drug use	Number of probationers	Percent of probationers tested for drug use during probation sentence			Percent of probationers receiving drug treatment during probation sentence		
		Total	Time served on probation		Total	Time served on probation	
			Less than 1 year	1 year or more		Less than 1 year	1 year or more
All probationers	2,065,896	49.0%	40.5%	56.3%	17.4%	15.9%	18.7%
Used drugs —							
Ever	1,425,528	54.8	45.4	63.2	24.7	21.9	27.1
Regularly*	892,108	61.2	52.7	68.4	35.8	32.5	38.7
In the month before offense	653,327	65.2	55.5	72.7	42.2	38.0	45.3
At the time of offense	277,778	69.8	58.6	77.2	52.6	51.2	53.3
Committed offense to get drug money	136,892	73.3	51.4	84.0	47.9	48.8	47.5
Ever used a needle to inject drugs	142,687	74.4	69.0	76.5	62.0	71.7	58.2

*Regular use is defined as once a week or more for at least a month.

Source: Christopher J. Mumola and Thomas P. Bonczar, *Substance Abuse and Treatment of Adults on Probation, 1995*, Bureau of Justice Statistics, Washington, DC, 1998

to detect a person's history of alcohol abuse or dependence. CAGE is an acronym for the four questions asked on the questionnaire — attempts to (C)ut back on drinking, (A)nnoyance at others' criticism of one's drinking, feelings of (G)uilt about drinking, and needing a drink first thing in the morning as an (E)ye opener to steady the nerves. The number of positive responses to these four questions determines a person's likelihood of alcohol abuse.

One-third (31.5 percent) of probationers received alcohol treatment through self-help groups, while one-fourth (25.5 percent) received help through outpatient care. Fewer participated in counseling (12.4 percent), crisis/emergency care (12 percent), and inpatient care (8.1 percent.) (See Table 8.16.)

PAROLE

Parole is the release of a prisoner before his or her sentence has expired, on condition of future good behavior. The sentence is not set aside, and the parolee remains under the supervision of a parole board. There are three kinds of releases from prisons.

- *Supervised mandatory release* is most common in jurisdictions with determinate (set) sentencing, conditionally releasing inmates at the end of their sentence (with time off for good behavior) into a parole portion of their sentence.

- *Discretionary parole release* is a decision made by a parole board based on statutory (state law) or administrative (parole board rules) determination of eligibility.

- An *unconditional prison release* is given when the offender's obligation to serve a sentence has been fully satisfied — the prisoner has served his or her time.

Because of prison overcrowding, parole boards routinely release prisoners to make room for new prisoners. At the same time, because of the public's fear of violent crime, many states are imposing sentences without parole. For example, North Carolina has prison room for 21,500 inmates but has 30,000 annual admissions to prison. The state spent $550 million from 1985 into the mid-1990s to add 16,600 new beds and more than doubled its prison budget from $195 million in 1985 to $472 million in 1993.

At the same time, the state wanted to end the "revolving door" for felons. Starting in January 1995, parole was abolished, and a sentencing system was set up to establish sentences based on the type of crime, the mitigating circumstances, and available room in the prisons. Offenders who fell into certain levels of less serious crimes would be put under probation or house arrest, placed in boot camp or a drug treatment program, or made to pay restitution. Such sentences for low-level offenders would allow for more prison space for offenders convicted of more serious crimes.

In 1997, the Midwest had the lowest ratio of parolees to adult residents (192 per 100,000 adults), while the Northeast had the highest ratio of parolees to residents at 413 per 100,000. Among individual jurisdictions, the District of Columbia had the highest ratio, 1,676 per 100,000, and Pennsylvania reported the second highest ratio, 833 per 100,000 adults. At the end of 1997, Texas maintained the largest parole population of any reporting jurisdiction, with 109,437 adults, followed by California, with 104,409. (See Table 8.17.)

In 1997, 11 percent of individuals on parole were female, 54 percent were White, 45 percent were Black, and 21 percent were Hispanic, who may be of any race (Table 8.18). In 1997, according to the Criminal Justice Institute, the average daily cost to maintain an individual on parole was $4.63; for intensive supervision parole, $7.85; and for electronic supervision, $10.83. The average caseload was 69 parolees for regular supervision, 29 for intensive supervision, and 18 for electronic supervision.

The Criminal Justice Institute reported that individuals on regular supervision made up 80.3 percent of those on parole in 1997, while intensive supervision was 15.3 percent, and electronic su-

pervision was less than 1 percent of the parolees. Special cases made up 3.6 percent of the caseloads.

Abolishing Parole

Abolishing Parole: Why the Emperor Has No Clothes (Lexington, Kentucky, 1995), a report commissioned by the American Probation and Parole Association and the Association of Parole Authorities, International, concluded that states that abolished parole have less control over violent offenders who have been released.

The report claimed that, in states that have abolished parole, "public confidence in the system has plummeted, costs have skyrocketed, prison populations have grown out of control, and violent and dangerous offenders have been routinely released without any judgement or accountability." In other

---

TABLE 8.15

Types of drug treatment ever received by adult probationers, by prior drug use, 1995

Drug treatment program	Percent of probationers			
	All	Probationers with prior drug use		
		Ever in the past	Regularly*	In the month prior to offense
Any kind of treatment	22.1%	31.6%	45.9%	51.2%
Crisis/emergency care	7.9	11.4	17.1	19.3
Self-help group	13.7	19.8	30.2	33.9
Counseling	8.4	12.0	18.3	19.1
Outpatient care	16.5	23.7	34.7	40.5
Inpatient care	7.9	11.3	17.7	20.7
Number of probationers	2,065,896	1,425,528	892,108	653,327

Note: Probationers may have received more than one type of treatment in the past.
*Regular use is defined as once a week or more for at least a month.

TABLE 8.16

Types of alcohol treatment ever received by adult probationers, by prior alcohol use levels, 1995

Type of alcohol treatment program	Percent of probationers				
	All	Under the influence of alcohol at time of offense	Ever had a binge drinking experience*	Ever gotten into physical fight because of drinking	Had three or more positive CAGE responses
Any kind of treatment	40.6%	72.5%	62.9%	65.3%	78.1%
Crisis/emergency care	12.0	23.1	23.3	26.2	36.7
Self-help group	31.5	56.8	52.6	55.3	67.9
Counseling	12.4	22.8	24.2	23.4	33.5
Outpatient care	25.5	48.3	43.0	45.3	55.9
Inpatient care	8.1	14.9	15.9	18.1	24.7
Number of probationers	2,065,896	821,030	727,253	665,300	494,933

*Binge drinking is defined as having consumed as much as a fifth of liquor in a single day, equivalent to 20 drinks, 3 bottles of wine, or 3 six-packs of beer.

Source of both tables: Christopher J. Mumola and Thomas P. Bonczar, *Substance Abuse and Treatment of Adults on Probation, 1995*, Bureau of Justice Statistics, Washington, DC, 1998

TABLE 8.17

Region and jurisdiction	Parole population, 1/1/97	1997 Entries	1997 Exits	Parole population, 12/31/97	Percent change in parole population during 1997	Number on parole on 12/31/97 per 100,000 adult residents
U.S. total	675,986	420,615	410,839	685,033	1.3%	346
Federal[a]	56,591	23,884	21,648	58,827	4%	30
State	619,395	396,731	389,191	626,206	1.1	316
Northeast	154,959	78,667	72,493	160,737	3.7%	413
Connecticut	1,083	1,058	1,145	996	-8	40
Maine	57	4	2	59	3.5	6
Massachusetts[b]	4,836	3,809	3,653	4,596	-5	98
New Hampshire	1,066	872	855	1,083	1.6	124
New Jersey	14,545	14,608	12,250	16,903	16.2	279
New York	57,137	27,096	24,563	59,670	4.4	439
Pennsylvania	75,013	30,211	28,992	76,232	1.6	833
Rhode Island	573	587	629	531	-7.3	70
Vermont	649	422	404	667	2.8	150
Midwest	87,987	62,604	61,922	88,683	0.8%	192
Illinois	30,064	23,595	23,311	30,348	0.9	348
Indiana[c,d]	3,580	4,549	4,085	4,044	13	93
Iowa[b]	2,200	2,343	2,506	2,051	-6.8	96
Kansas[c]	6,004	4,650	4,504	6,150	2.4	323
Michigan	14,609	8,758	9,016	14,351	-1.8	197
Minnesota	2,377	2,632	2,563	2,446	2.9	71
Missouri	13,087	4,720	5,293	12,514	-4.4	313
Nebraska	688	770	770	688	0	57
North Dakota	100	212	193	119	19	25
Ohio	6,331	5,258	4,786	6,803	7.5	81
South Dakota	725	675	540	860	18.6	159
Wisconsin[e]	8,222	4,442	4,355	8,309	1.1	217
South	241,668	98,173	104,626	234,780	-2.9%	336
Alabama[b,f,g]	4,966	0	0	4,742	-4.5	146
Arkansas[f]	5,459	3,225	2,817	5,867	7.5	315
Delaware[f]	591	196	196	591	--	107
District of Columbia	7,120	2,310	2,363	7,067	-0.7	1,676
Florida	9,243	3,596	4,362	8,477	-8.3	76
Georgia[b]	21,146	11,567	10,587	21,915	3.6	399
Kentucky	4,621	2,853	3,241	4,233	-8.4	144
Louisiana	19,082	10,819	9,974	19,927	4.4	630
Maryland	16,246	9,732	10,215	15,763	-3	412
Mississippi[c,d,h]	1,326	1,233	1,181	1,378	3.9	70
North Carolina	12,358	8,774	12,984	8,148	-34.1	147
Oklahoma	2,159	442	673	1,928	-10.7	79
South Carolina	5,036	1,343	1,369	5,010	-0.5	179
Tennessee[d]	8,934	4,294	4,535	8,693	-2.7	215
Texas[f]	112,594	27,682	30,839	109,437	-2.8	789
Virginia[f]	9,918	9,538	8,746	10,710	8	210
West Virginia	869	569	544	894	2.9	64
West	134,781	157,287	150,150	142,006	5.4%	330
Alaska	642	466	356	752	17.1	179
Arizona	3,785	6,141	6,548	3,378	-10.8	103
California[g]	99,578	134,345	129,514	104,409	4.9	448
Colorado	3,294	3,744	2,899	4,139	25.7	144
Hawaii	1,733	699	639	1,793	3.5	203
Idaho	692	600	472	820	18.5	95
Montana[c,h,i]	771	444	409	806	4.5	124
Nevada[b]	3,216	:	:	3,304	2.7	268
New Mexico	1,426	1,617	1,417	1,626	14	132
Oregon	15,800	6,649	5,634	16,815	6.4	691
Utah	2,920	2,329	1,930	3,319	13.7	242
Washington[f]	560	32	112	480	-14.3	12
Wyoming	364	221	220	365	0.3	105

: Not known.
-- Not calculated.
[a] Defined as persons received for supervision upon release from prison. Includes supervised release, parole, military parole, special parole, and mandatory release.
[b] Because of nonresponse or incomplete data, the population on December 31, 1997, does not equal the population on January 1, 1997, plus entires, minus exits.
[c] Data do not include absconders.
[d] Data do not include out-of-State cases.
[e] Data are provisional, pending further review by the State.
[f] All data are estimated.
[g] Multiple agencies were reporting.
[h] Data do not include inactive cases.
[i] Total exits are estimated.

Source: Press release, *Nation's Probation and Parole Population Reached New High Last Year*, Bureau of Justice Statistics, Washington, DC, 1998

TABLE 8.18

Characteristics of adults on parole, 1990 and 1997

Characteristic of adults on parole	1990	1997
Sex		
Male	92%	89%
Female	8	11
Race		
White	52%	54%
Black	47	45
Other races	1	1
Hispanic origin		
Hispanic	18%	21%
Non-Hispanic	82	79
Status of supervision		
Active supervision	82%	80%
Inactive supervision	6	7
Absconded from supervision	6	7
Supervised out of State	6	5
Other	**	1
Entries		
Discretionary parole	59%	45%
Mandatory parole	41	50
Reinstatement	**	4
Other	**	1
Exits		
Successful completions	50%	44%
Returned to incarceration	46	41
With new sentence	17	13
With revocation pending	11	28
Other	18	1
Transferred to another State	1	2
Death	1	1
Other	2	11
Length of sentence		
Less than 1 year	5%	4%
One year or more	95	96

Note: For every characteristic there were persons of unknown status or type. Detail may not sum to total due to rounding error.
**Not available.

Source: Press release, *Nation's Probation and Parole Population Reached New High Last Year*, Bureau of Justice Statistics, Washington, DC, 1998

grant prisoners early release by earning good behavior credits. In these states, parole boards do not review whether a convict is a safe risk to be released into the community. Florida reinstated parole hearings after an inmate released under a credit system murdered a police officer.

COST OF PROBATION AND PAROLE

The Criminal Justice Institute estimated that the total administrative budgets for probation and parole for fiscal year 1998 were $1.2 billion for probation agencies, $1 billion for parole agencies, and $1.2 billion for those that combined their probation and parole agencies.

REASONS FOR THE INCREASING NUMBERS OF VIOLATORS AND ABSCONDERS

Given the growth in the probation and parole population, an increase in the number of violators would be expected, but not necessarily the violation rates. However, according to the National Institute of Justice, in *Responding to Probation and Parole Violations* (Washington, DC, 1994), about one-third of the states said their rates of violation also had risen. They cited several reasons believed to have caused this increase, including

• A shift in the purposes of community supervision — In the 1970s and 1980s, the idea of community supervision as a treatment to rehabilitate offenders declined, and the idea of sentencing alternatives, such as "community-based punishments" that could be applied in increments to match the seriousness of the offenders' crimes or their blameworthiness, took hold. If control and surveillance were objects of supervision, then detected violations and revocations were indicators of success. As one probation officer put it, his job was to "trail 'em, nail 'em, and jail 'em."

• An increase in probation and parole caseloads — As the parole and probation populations grew, the number of cases each officer super-

words, claimed the report, parole apparently provides community supervision for less violent prisoners and allows room in the prisons to maintain the more violent prisoners.

Eleven states (California, Delaware, Illinois, Indiana, Maine, Minnesota, New Mexico, North Carolina, Oregon, Virginia, and Washington) have abolished parole. Colorado, Connecticut, and Florida had abolished the system but reinstated it. Most states without parole still use systems that

vised increased, and the time the officer had for each case decreased. Rising caseloads, it is argued, cause the officers to focus their attention on rule enforcement generally and on individual offenders who have the most trouble following rules. As revocations increase, probation and parole officers spend more and more time on the procedures and paperwork linked to revocation and thus have even less time available to supervise offenders.

- An increase in the number of conditions probationers and parolees are expected to obey — Instead of facing a year of standard probation, an offender might now have to perform 200 hours of community service, participate in an outpatient drug-treatment program, and pay $500 restitution during the year of supervision. As the number of conditions grows, offenders have more chances to violate.

- The use of improved technology to detect violations — As emphasis on control increases, new technologies such as drug-use testing and electronic monitoring have made it easier to detect some violations.

- Changes in the types of offenders supervised on probation and parole — Many believe that more hardened, dangerous offenders are being placed on community supervision to avoid or reduce prison and jail crowding. Others argue that today's offenders are more likely to be involved with drugs and to resort to violence than offenders were in the past. Not all those involved in law enforcement agree with this view. Some believe that the officers' emphasis on control and their use of tools like improved criminal-history information systems, risk assessment, and drug testing merely make today's offenders seem tougher than in the past.

CHAPTER IX

ALTERNATIVE SENTENCING —
FROM MEDIATION TO WORK RELEASE

Lawmakers increasingly are looking to corrections to develop and demonstrate safe, cost-effective alternatives to prison as a step toward getting corrections spending under control.
— Donna Hunzeker, Program Manager for Criminal Justice, National Conference of State Legislatures

If we recognize gradations in the seriousness of criminal behavior, then we should have gradations in sanctions as well. That's why we need a portfolio of intermediate punishments.... Intermediate punishments can provide the means by which we can hold offenders accountable for their illegal actions and achieve our goal of increasing public safety. — Richard Thornburgh, former U.S. Attorney General, 1990

INCARCERATION VERSUS COMMUNITY SANCTIONS

Sentencing practices in this country suggest that offenses can be divided into two categories. When the crime is relatively serious, offenders are put behind bars; when it is less so, they are put on probation, often with very little supervision. This twofold division disregards the range of severity in crime. As a result, sentencing can often be either too harsh, incarcerating people whose crimes might not be serious enough to warrant imprisonment, or too lenient, putting people on probation whose crimes might call for more severe punishments.

Many penal reformers have called for a "continuum of punishments with probation at one end, more severe community-based sanctions in the middle, and incarceration at the most restrictive end" (*Americans Behind Bars*, The Edna McConnell Clark Foundation, New York City, New York, 1993). Over the past decade, many states have experimented with intermediate sanctions (alternative sentencing or community sanc-

tions), such as intensive supervision, as well as probation and parole techniques, to put nonviolent inmates back into the community. The community corrections authorities can provide punishment and rehabilitation while keeping an offender out of prison. They can restrict an offender's movements, impose treatment programs, and/or require restitution. (See Chapter VIII.)

Proponents believe that many offenders will not commit other crimes and deserve alternative sanctions so they will not become "hardened" and "embittered." They also hope that alternative sentencing will rehabilitate the criminal. In addition, some believe it can reduce prison and jail costs and relieve overcrowding. In January 1995, for example, George Pataki, governor of New York, proposed using alternative sentencing for nonviolent criminals to make room in prison for violent offenders. Opponents, on the other hand, see prison sentencing as the only "real punishment" for criminals. Figure 9.1 shows the average costs for various sentencing alternatives.

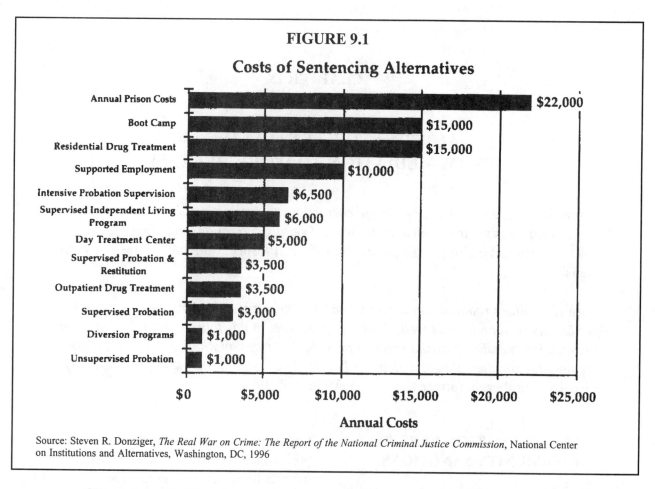

FIGURE 9.1

Costs of Sentencing Alternatives

Annual Prison Costs	$22,000
Boot Camp	$15,000
Residential Drug Treatment	$15,000
Supported Employment	$10,000
Intensive Probation Supervision	$6,500
Supervised Independent Living Program	$6,000
Day Treatment Center	$5,000
Supervised Probation & Restitution	$3,500
Outpatient Drug Treatment	$3,500
Supervised Probation	$3,000
Diversion Programs	$1,000
Unsupervised Probation	$1,000

Annual Costs

Source: Steven R. Donziger, *The Real War on Crime: The Report of the National Criminal Justice Commission*, National Center on Institutions and Alternatives, Washington, DC, 1996

Client-Specific Planning

In 1980, the National Center on Institutions and Alternatives proposed the idea of client-specific planning. In such programs, independent sentencing specialists provide judges background information on offenders and assess their potential for meeting the requirements of a community-based punishment plan. Based on this information, the specialist recommends penalties that can include probation, treatments, payment of restitution, or other conditions. The judge may use the plan, change it, or reject it.

Alternatives to Confinement in Jail

In 1998, 11 percent of the 664,847 persons under jail supervision were supervised outside of a jail facility. Among persons under community supervision, about half (48 percent) were required to perform community service or to participate in a weekend reporting program (24 percent each).

Another 15 percent were under home detention with electronic monitoring. An estimated 10 percent were in an alternative work program, and about 8 percent were supervised outside of a jail facility in a drug, alcohol, mental health, or other medical treatment program. (See Table 9.1.)

Felons Sentenced to Prison with Additional Penalties

Besides being sentenced to incarceration or probation, some convicted felons were also ordered to pay a fine, pay victim restitution, receive treatment, perform community service, or comply with some other additional penalty (for example, undergo house arrest or appear periodically for drug testing). A fine was imposed on at least 20 percent of convicted felons. Conservative estimates for other penalties were 14 percent, restitution; 6 percent, some form of treatment; and 6 percent, community service. (See Table 9.2.)

MEDIATION AND RESTITUTION

Started in Canada in 1974, mediation spread to the United States, where more than 20 states now use mediation. In mediation, the victim and the offender meet under the auspices of a community worker and work out a "reconciliation" between them, usually involving some type of restitution. The offender must take responsibility for his actions. This technique is used mainly for minor crimes and often involves private organizations; therefore, the judiciary does not always accept its resolution. Most often, restitution is not considered the complete punishment but part of a wider punishment, such as probation or working off the amount while in prison.

HALFWAY HOUSES AND RESIDENTIAL PROGRAMS

TABLE 9.1

Persons under jail supervision, by confinement status and type of program, midyear 1995-98

Confinement status and type of program	Number of persons under jail supervision			
	1995	1996	1997	1998
Total	541,913	591,469	637,319	664,847
Held in jail	507,044	518,492	567,079	592,462
Supervised outside a jail facility[a]	34,869	72,977	70,239	72,385
Electronic monitoring	6,788	7,480	8,699	10,827
Home detention[b]	1,376	907	1,164	370
Day reporting	1,283	3,298	2,768	3,089
Community service	10,253	17,410	15,918	17,518
Weekender programs	1,909	16,336	17,656	17,249
Other pretrial supervision	3,229	2,135	7,368	6,048
Other work programs[c]	9,144	14,469	6,631	7,089
Treatment programs[d]	--	10,425	6,693	5,702
Other	887	517	3,342	4,493

--Not available.
[a]Excludes persons supervised by a probation or parole agency.
[b]Includes only those without electronic monitoring.
[c]Includes persons in work release programs, work gangs/crews, and other work alternative programs administered by the jail jurisdiction.
[d]Includes persons under drug, alcohol, mental health, and other medical treatment.

Source: Darrell K. Gilliard, *Prison and Jail Inmates at Midyear 1998*, Bureau of Justice Statistics, Washington, DC, 1999

Halfway houses, also called community treatment centers, provide an intermediate place for offenders at the end of their prison sentence to ease themselves back into the life of a community. In 1997, according to the Criminal Justice Institute, the Federal Bureau of Prisons had the largest number of inmates (5,070) in the largest number of halfway houses (260). Twenty-five states had inmates in 272 community treatment centers operated by contractors. In 1997, 21,117 inmates were in halfway houses in 30 agencies. Alaska had the highest percentage of its inmates in halfway houses (16.9 percent), and Iowa operated the largest number of halfway houses (20).

In 1997, monitoring an offender in a halfway house cost $49.03 a day in a facility run by the Department of Corrections (up from $47.28 in 1990), compared to $42.97 to house an offender in a halfway house operated by a contractor (up from $36.66 in 1990). Offenders in federal halfway houses must pay 25 percent of their gross income to the government.

Residential programs house offenders in a structured setting. They work full time, maintain the residence center, perform community service, and can attend educational or counseling programs. They may leave the centers only for work or approved programs, such as substance-abuse treatment. One type of residential program, the restitution center, allows the offender to work to pay restitution and child-support payments. Centers also regularly test the residents for drugs.

Brooklyn, New York, established a program in which those arrested for drug sales who had no prior felonies could have their charges held in abeyance or deferred if they entered residential treatment for 15 to 24 months. If they completed treatment, the government dropped the charges and helped them find jobs and housing.

DAY REPORTING CENTERS

Developed in Great Britain, day reporting centers (DRCs) first appeared in the United States in the mid-1980s. A 1990 study by the National Institute of Justice found only 13 day reporting centers in the United States. By 1994, an updated (and still the most recent) study by the National Institute of Justice identified 114 DRCs operating in 22 states (Figure 9.2).

These programs require persons on pretrial release, probation, or parole to appear at day reporting centers on a frequent and regular basis in order to participate in services or activities provided by the center or other community agencies. Failure to report or participate could cause revocation of conditional release or community supervision. Many DRCs operate in distinct phases, in which offenders move from higher to lower levels of control based on their progress in treatment and compliance with supervisory guidelines. Most DRC programs last five to six months.

The primary goal of most DRCs is to provide offenders with access to treatment service, although older DRCs (those that opened before 1992) give greater emphasis to providing treatment and services than do newer programs. Most provide a wide array of on-site treatment and services (Table 9.3). The secondary goal of most DRCs is to reduce jail or prison crowding.

The average daily cost per offender of a DRC is $35.04. As would be expected, DRCs that provide few services cost less than those that provide many. The cost of operating DRCs grows with increasingly strin-gent surveillance practices. Day reporting appears to be less expensive than imprisonment, but is often more expensive than other community sanctions. As a rule, DRCs pay for 8 of the 10 most common categories of services. If DRCs cannot fund services themselves, other agencies usually finance the treatment provided. Seldom do offenders pay for services themselves. The average daily population of DRCs is 85.

DRCs do not generally exclude serious offenders, although many programs appear to be selecting nonserious drug- and alcohol-using offenders who do not require residential treatment. Two-thirds of the responding DRCs require offenders

TABLE 9.2
Felons sentenced to an additional penalty by State courts, by offense, 1996

Most serious conviction offense	Percent of felons with an additional penalty of —				
	Fine	Restitution	Treatment	Community service	Other
All offenses	20%	14%	6%	6%	3%
Violent offenses	14%	12%	5%	4%	3%
Murder[a]	8	9	1	1	2
Sexual assault[b]	13	9	8	3	4
Robbery	8	11	3	2	2
Aggravated assault	19	14	5	6	4
Other violent[c]	18	13	6	6	4
Property offenses	20%	25%	4%	7%	4%
Burglary	17	21	4	6	3
Larceny[d]	20	22	5	6	5
Fraud[e]	24	32	4	10	3
Drug offenses	22%	7%	7%	6%	2%
Possession	19	7	10	6	3
Trafficking	23	6	5	6	2
Weapons offenses	16%	6%	3%	4%	2%
Other offenses[f]	25%	12%	7%	6%	4%

Note: Where the data indicated affirmatively that a particular additional penalty was imposed, the case was coded accordingly. Where the data did not indicate affirmatively or negatively, the case was treated as not having an additional penalty. These procedures provide a conservative estimate of the prevalence of additional penalties. A felon receiving more than one kind of additional penalty appears under more than one table heading. Data on additional penalties were available for 997,970 cases.
[a]Includes nonnegligent manslaughter.
[b]Includes rape.
[c]Includes offenses such as negligent manslaughter and kidnaping.
[d]Includes motor vehicle theft.
[e]Includes forgery and embezzlement.
[f]Composed of nonviolent offenses such as receiving stolen property and vandalism.

Source: Jodi M. Brown, Patrick A. Langan, and David J. Levin, *Felony Sentences in State Court, 1996*, Bureau of Justice Statistics, Washington, DC, 1999

to perform community service, but the level and type of community service performed differs greatly from jurisdiction to jurisdiction. DRCs terminate a high rate of participants — an average of 50 percent — but vary widely (from 14 percent to 86 percent). Privately run DRCs are more likely than public ones to terminate enrolled offenders when they are charged with a new crime, fail to participate in treatment, or violate other DRC rules. No systematic research has been completed to answer important questions on cost effectiveness and recidivism reduction.

Chicago Day Reporting Center Study

The Department of Community Supervision and Intervention (DCSI), part of the Cook County (Chicago, Illinois) Sheriff's Office, established the Cook County Day Reporting Center (CCDRC) in 1993. CCDRC's social services are contracted to Treatment Alternatives for Safe Communities (TASC). Day reporting clients, nonviolent pretrial detainees, receive services on site.

In 1993, the Cook County Jail was operating at more than 150 percent of capacity. The major goal of establishing the CCDRC was to reduce the need for prison beds. Additional goals included providing clients with drug treatment and educational and vocational services, trying to make sure that program participants did not commit further crimes while awaiting trial and trying to make sure they appeared at scheduled court dates. Between 1993 (when the program began) and 1998, 7,200 participants — all male — went through CCDRC. Clients must have stable residences and phone ser-

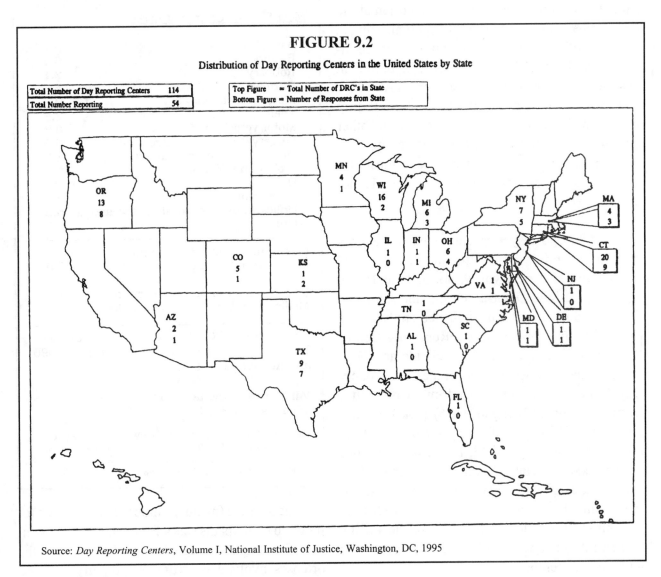

FIGURE 9.2

Distribution of Day Reporting Centers in the United States by State

| Total Number of Day Reporting Centers | 114 |
| Total Number Reporting | 54 |

Top Figure = Total Number of DRC's in State
Bottom Figure = Number of Responses from State

Source: *Day Reporting Centers*, Volume I, National Institute of Justice, Washington, DC, 1995

vices and are required to be in DSCI's electronic monitoring program prior to becoming eligible for the program. The DSCI staff chooses program participants who have nonviolent criminal records, no psychiatric histories, and bonds of less than $150,000.

The Center is open five days per week, and participants' schedules vary from three to eight hours each day. Every program participant receives three weeks of program orientation, including 90 hours of educational programming in the areas of drug and alcohol abuse, violence interruption, HIV/AIDS prevention, drug treatment readiness, and life skills management. TASC (see above) coordinates social services, including scheduling classes, counseling sessions, and other types of interventions, and oversees on-site drug treatment services. Program participants must submit urine samples regularly for drug and alcohol tests.

In "Chicago Day Reporting Center Reduces Pretrial Detention, Drug Use, and Absconding" (*Overcrowded Times*, vol. 9, no. 3, June 1998), Arthur J. Lurigio, David E. Olson, and James A. Swartz reported on an unpublished study of the Cook County (Chicago) Day Reporting Center (CCDRC). The study (D. C. McBride and C. J. VanderWaal, "An Assessment of the Cook County Day Reporting Center," Andrews University, Berrien Springs, Michigan, 1996) looked at case results of 2,253 clients discharged between October 1, 1996, and August 12, 1997. Most of those discharged were relatively young single males (average age, 27). Nearly 90 percent were Black, and more than 80 percent had never married. Less than one-third had completed high school or had a GED, 95 percent were unemployed, and 91 percent lived with family members.

TABLE 9.3
Types and Locations of Services Offered by DRC's

Type of Service	Percent of DRC's that Provide Services	Location of Service		
		At DRC	Elsewhere	Both
Job-seeking skills (N = 53)	98 %	79 %	13 %	8 %
Drug abuse education (N = 52)	96	69	17	14
Group counseling (N = 51)	96	80	12	8
Job placement services (N = 50)	93	62	34	4
Education (N = 49)	93	55	31	14
Drug treatment (N = 48)	92	31	54	15
Life skills training (N = 49)	91	92	6	2
Individual counseling (N = 47)	89	72	17	11
Transitional housing (N = 32)	63	13	81	6
Recreation and leisure (N = 31)	60	74	16	10

Source: *Day Reporting Centers*, Volume I, National Institute of Justice, Washington, DC, 1995

TABLE 9.4
Current Charges and Prior Record, Program Participants[a]

Most Serious Charge at Arrest

Assault	0.1 %
Battery	0.4
Robbery	2.1
Burglary	5.5
Motor vehicle burglary	0.9
Theft	2.8
Motor vehicle theft	0.9
Forgery/fraud/deceptive practices	0.4
Drug possession or delivery	71.0
Probation violation	2.0
DUI	1.8
Other motor vehicle offense	2.0
Unlawful use/possession of weapons	5.3
Other	2.0

Mean number of prior arrests	4.2
Median number of prior arrests	3.0

Mean number of prior convictions	1.4
Median number of prior convictions	1.0

Note: Data for CCDRC participants assessed by TASC case managers between October 1, 1996 and August 12, 1997.

[a]All figures in the table are percentages unless otherwise specified.

Source: D. C. McBride and C. J. VanderWaal, "An Assessment of the Cook County Day-Reporting Center," Unpublished report, Andrews University, Berrien Springs, MI, 1996 as in *Overcrowded Times*, vol. 9, no. 3, June 1998

The average (mean) number of prior arrests for program participants was 4.2, and the average number of previous convictions was 1.4. Most of the offenses involved drugs or were property offenses.

TABLE 9.5

Substance Use/Abuse Characteristics of Program Participants[a] (N = 2,253)

Primary Substance of Abuse

Heroin/opiates	27.8 %
Alcohol	8.9
Cocaine powder	4.8
Crack or freebase cocaine	4.6
Amphetamines	0.1
PCP	0.2
Inhalants	0.0
Marijuana	42.5
None	11.1
Missing	0.0

Frequency of Primary Substance Use

No use past month	1.4
Less than weekly	0.6
Once per week	9.0
Several times per week	24.3
Once daily	12.5
Two to three times daily	14.3
More than three times daily	15.5
Unknown/inapplicable	13.2
Missing	0.1

Severity of Primary Substance Use[b]

No abuse or dependence	1.4
Abuse	3.9
Mild dependence	28.5
Moderate dependence	43.4
Severe dependence	9.4
Unknown/inapplicable	11.1
Missing	2.4

Percentages of Subjects Abusing

Heroin/opiates	30.9
Alcohol	24.5
Cocaine powder	14.6
Crack or freebase cocaine	9.9
Marijuana	59.0
PCP	1.4
Injection use	2.4

Mean age at first drug use (years)	16.6
Median age at first drug use (years)	16.0

Note: Data for CCDRC participants assessed by TASC case managers between October 1, 1996 and August 12, 1997.

[a]All figures in the table are percentages unless otherwise specified.
[b]Based on assessors' ratings of participants' primary, secondary, and tertiary drugs of abuse.

Source: D. C. McBride and C. J. VanderWaal, "An Assessment of the Cook County Day-Reporting Center," unpublished report, Andrews University, Berrien Springs, MI, 1996 as in *Overcrowded Times*, vol. 9, no. 3, June 1998

Nearly three-fourths (71 percent) were charged with possession or delivery of a controlled substance. (See Table 9.4.)

According to TASC tests, most program participants were dependent on illicit drugs. Of those who were discharged, fewer than 2 percent had no symptoms of substance abuse or dependency upon entrance to the program or when they were discharged. Of those who tested positive for substance abuse, 42.5 percent abused marijuana, 27.8 percent used heroin, and 9.4 percent abused cocaine. Forty percent abused more than one drug. Over 42 percent of those who were abusing or dependent on drugs said they used drugs at least once daily, and 24.3 reported that they used drugs several times per week. Two-thirds (66.6 percent) used drugs at a minimum of several times per week. (See Table 9.5.) Most of the participants claimed that CCDRC had given them their first opportunity to face their substance abuse problems; fewer than 10 percent had ever been in substance abuse treatment programs prior to being placed in CCDRC.

Nearly two-thirds of program participants were successfully discharged during the period of the study. Of those who were unsuccessfully discharged, most were terminated for program violations, such as being absent without leave or violating administrative rules. Those with severe drug problems were more likely to be unsuccessfully terminated from the program. Prior criminal history was not a factor in a client being successfully or unsuccessfully discharged.

Less than 5 percent were rearrested for new crimes while enrolled in the program, compared to more than one-third in traditional programs who were rearrested for new crimes prior to settlement of their court cases.

One of CCDRC's goals is to reduce clients' drug use. During the study period, the percentage testing positive for any drug decreased for those who had participated in the program for at least 12 weeks: from 74 percent at the first week, to 47 percent at the sixth week, and to 39 percent at the twelfth week.

CCDRC also met its goal to reduce failure-to-appear court rates. Since the program's beginning, including the study period, CCDRC's failure-to-appear rate was just 2 percent, compared to 30 percent in other large jurisdictions throughout the United States.

CCDRC seems to have met its major goals, with two-thirds of participants successfully completing the program. Participation in the program decreased drug use among the detainees and ensured court appearances. However, it should be noted that CCDRC's clients were carefully screened before they were admitted to the program, making comparisons between CCDRC participants and other pretrial populations difficult.

DAY FINES

Most judges assess fixed, flat-fee fines sparingly. The fees are tied to the seriousness of the crimes and the criminal records of the offenders, and they bear no relationship to the wealth of the offender. As a result, judges often think the fixed fines are too lenient on wealthy offenders and too harsh on poor ones. Using the day fine alternative, however, permits judges to first determine how much punishment an offender deserves, which is defined in some unit other than money.

For example, a judge decides that the gravity of the offense is worth 15, 60, or 120 punishment units, without regard to income. Then the value of each unit is set at a percentage of the offender's daily income, and the total fine amount is determined by simple multiplication. European countries use day fines much more frequently than the courts in the United States.

COMMUNITY SERVICE

Started in the United States in Alameda County, California (Alameda is the major city), in 1966 as a penalty for traffic offenses, community service has spread throughout the United States. The penalty is most often a supplement to other penalties and mainly given to "white-collar" criminals, juvenile delinquents, and those who commit nonserious crimes. Offenders are usually required to work for government or private nonprofit agencies cleaning parks, collecting roadside trash, setting up chairs for community events, and helping out at nursing homes.

The Vera Institute of Justice's Community Service Sentencing Project in New York has been the most evaluated program. Offenders who could have had sentences of up to six months in jail usually work 70 hours of community service over a two-week period. In Stark County, (Canton) Ohio, because of jail overcrowding, municipal judges began using community service as a way to relieve the jail conditions. In the early 1990s, the typical judge handed down sentences totaling 350 hours of community service. By 1995, the average per judge increased to a total of 35,000 hours per year of community service.

TREATMENT PROGRAMS

Some jurisdictions have substance-abuse treatments, but many lack the resources. Attending a drug-treatment program is often a condition of probation. In a 1997 survey by the Bureau of Justice Statistics (BJS), 37 percent of felony probationers were required to be in alcohol or drug treatment programs. (See Chapter VIII for more on probation and parole.) A treatment program was required for 6 percent of felons convicted in 1996 (Table 9.2).

INTENSIVE SUPERVISION PROBATION

Increasingly, more of the probation population consists of people convicted of felonies rather than misdemeanors. Routine probation, however, was neither intended nor structured to handle this type of offender. Therefore, Intensive Supervision Probation/Parole (ISP) was developed as an alternative to prison or routine probation. Between 1980 and 1990, every state implemented some form of ISP.

Many use ISP to alleviate prison overcrowding and provide rigorous supervision of high-risk probationers, with the aim of reducing the risk to public safety posed by such offenders. In 1996, according to BJS, 92,559 adults on probation and 24,885 adults on parole were under intensive supervision.

The caseloads of supervising officers normally range from 30 to 50 ISP probationers, compared to traditional probation caseloads of 150 to 200, where supervision sometimes amounts to the probationer mailing a card to the supervisor monthly. ISP requires some combination of multiple weekly contacts with a supervising officer, random and unannounced drug testing, stringent enforcement of probation/parole conditions, and participation in relevant treatment, employment, and perhaps community service.

An Example of an ISP

An example of an ISP is described by the Oregon Department of Corrections:

> ... the offender will be visited by a probation officer two or three times per week, who will phone on the other days. The offender will be subject to unannounced searches of his home for drugs and have his urine tested regularly for alcohol and drugs. He must strictly abide by other conditions set by the court — not carrying a weapon, not socializing with certain persons — and he will have to perform community service and be employed or participate in training or education. In addition, he will be strongly encouraged to attend counseling and/or other treatment, particularly if he is a drug offender (Joan Petersilia, "When Probation Becomes More Dreaded Than Prison," *Federal Probation*, Washington, DC, 1990).

Joan Petersilia has evaluated ISP programs for the National Institute of Justice and RAND Corporation, a non-profit public policy research institute. She observes that an ISP is in the conflicting position of having to appear punitive enough to be acceptable to the "get-tough" public while appearing not too punitive to prisoners. When given the choice of serving time or taking ISP, one-third of nonviolent offenders in New Jersey chose prison. Petersilia points out that prison is not always the deterrent it is meant to be. Sanctions are most effective if social standing is injured and the offender feels that he or she may be excluded from his or her group. For some people, however, having a prison record is not the stigma it once was. In some social milieus, it is common for peers and family members to have done time.

Such a high proportion of Black men is incarcerated that, for some, prison is a part of life, not a terrible dishonor. In gangs, imprisonment can even confer status. Petersilia adds that, "the grim fact — and national shame — is that for most people who go to prison, the conditions inside are not all that different from the conditions outside." For some, it is even an improvement, providing regular food, shelter, medical care, and a community.

Ironically, social programs and job training are often more available inside prisons than outside. "Prisons are becoming the place where we provide services to our poor people," claims Robert Gangi, executive director of the Correctional Association of New York, a nonpartisan prison watchdog agency. Moreover, the offender often finds a large social network on "the inside." As the warden of a penitentiary described it, "When a new guy comes up here, it's almost a homecoming — undoubtedly there are people from his neighborhood and people who know him." On the other hand, an ISP does change one's social standing. To be isolated and restricted within your own community can be harder to handle than prison. The intrusions, lack of privacy, and curfews are more stressful to the offender within his normal community than within a prison, where such limitations are considered normal.

How Successful Are ISPs?

In "Key Legislative Issues in Criminal Justice: Intermediate Sanctions" (*Research in Action*, National Institute of Justice, January 1997), Dale Parent, Terence Dunworth, Douglas McDonald, and William Rhodes found that intermediate sanctions, such as ISPs, have not achieved the expected results. Appraising these programs nationally is difficult because they have developed independently in many different jurisdictions, and only a few programs in scattered jurisdictions have been evaluated. Nonetheless, it appears that ISPs and community service have not rehabilitated or kept program participants from committing more crimes any better than the traditional sentencing choices they replaced.

The costs of running ISPs have been found to be higher than expected, mostly because the costs to adjudicate the many technical violations that occur with intermediate sanction program participants and to reincarcerate such offenders can quickly use up any potential savings.

Parent et al. concluded that, despite mixed results in achieving hoped-for benefits of intermediate sanctions, they should be continued since they offer more alternatives than just confinement or probation.

HOUSE ARREST AND ELECTRONIC MONITORING

Some nonviolent offenders are sentenced to house arrest in which they are legally ordered to remain confined in their own homes. They are allowed to leave only for medical purposes or to go to work, although some curfew programs permit offenders to work during the day and have a few hours of free time before returning home at a specified time.

The most severe type of house arrest is home incarceration, where the offender's home is actually a prison that he or she cannot leave except for very special reasons, such as medical emergencies. Home-detention programs require the offender to be at home when he or she is not working. Some offenders are required to perform a certain number of hours of community service and, if they are employed, to repay the cost of probation and/or restitution.

Electronic monitoring is a recent and fast-growing addition to the house-arrest concept. In 1984, just three house-arrest programs in the United States existed; experts now estimate that agencies in all 50 states use electronic monitoring for over 45,000 people. In 1998, electronic monitoring accounted for 15 percent of persons supervised outside a jail facility (Table 9.1).

A small radio transmitter is attached to the offender in a nonremovable bracelet or anklet. Some systems send a signal to a small monitoring box, which is programmed to phone a Department of Corrections computer if the signal is broken; other systems randomly call probationers, and the computer makes a voice verification of the prisoner. In some cases, a special device in the electronic monitor sends a confirmation to the computer.

Electronic monitoring costs states much less than building a new prison cell or housing another inmate. In 1995, Florida corrections reported monitoring costs were $6.41 a day versus $38.14 to house, feed, and guard a prisoner. Florida requires monitored convicts to be employed to help keep their families off welfare and to pay taxes, restitution to victims, court costs, and $40 a month for the monitoring. Electronic monitoring cost New Jersey about $4,700 annually per detainee, compared to $26,000 in prison. (See Chapter VIII for additional information on costs and face-to-face contacts.)

WORK RELEASE

Work-release programs permit selected prisoners nearing the end of their terms to work in the community, returning to prison facilities or community residential facilities in nonworking hours. Such programs are designed to prepare inmates to return to the community in a relatively controlled environment while they are learning how to work productively. Work release also allows inmates to earn income, reimburse the state for part of their confinement costs, build up savings for their eventual full release, and acquire more positive living habits.

During the 1970s, prison work-release programs expanded considerably, but they have declined in recent years. Although 43 states have existing statutes authorizing work release, only about one-third of U.S. prisons report operating such programs, and fewer than 3 percent of U.S. inmates participate in them.

Washington State Evaluations

The National Institute of Justice sponsored two evaluations of Washington State's work release program, conducted between 1991 and 1994 (Susan Turner and Joan Petersilia, *Work Release: Recidivism and Corrections Costs in Washington State*, Washington, DC, 1996). The first study analyzed a group of 2,452 males released from Washington prisons in 1990, nearly 40 percent of whom spent a part of their sentences on work release. The second compared the recidivism of 218 offenders; approximately half participated in work release, and half completed their sentences in prison.

In contrast to the national decline of work release as a means of preparing imprisoned offenders for rejoining the community, Washington allocated more than one-third of its community corrections budget to work release. The releasees obtained daytime jobs, lived in community facilities, and contributed to their room and board costs.

Overall, the studies found that the program achieved its most important goal, preparing inmates for final release and facilitating their adjustment to the community. The program did not cost the state more than keeping the inmates in prison. The public safety risks were nearly nonexistent because almost no work releasee committed new crimes, and when they committed rule violations, they were quickly returned to prison. The results of the evaluation were mostly positive:

TABLE 9.6

Most Serious Infraction for "Unsuccessful" Work Release Participants

Reason for Return	Percent of 290 Offenders
Law Violation	**3.6**
Forgery	0.7
Theft	1.4
Other, unspecified	1.5
Medical Condition	**3.6**
Drug Possession	**34.9**
Program Rule Violation	**57.8**
Alcohol possession	12.2
Escape/curfew	20.1
Fighting	3.2
Failure to work	4.3
Failure to report income	2.5
Miscellaneous	15.5

Source: *Work Release: Recidivism and Corrections Costs in Washington State*, National Institute of Justice, Washington, DC, 1996

- Nearly one-quarter of all prisoners released in Washington made a successful transition to the community through work release.

- Less than 5 percent of the work releasees committed new crimes while on work release, 99 percent of which were less serious property offenses, such as forgery or theft. No one committed a violent felony. However, with heightened supervision under strict conditions, many work releasees incurred infractions (most for rule violations and drug possession).

- Middle-aged offenders and those convicted of property crimes were most likely to participate in work release. Hispanic offenders were less likely to go to work release than White or Black offenders.

- Fifty-six percent of the 965 work releasees in the group studies were termed "successful;" they incurred no program infractions or arrests. Another 13.5 percent were "moderately successful;" their infractions were not serious enough to return them to prison. Almost 30 percent were "unsuccessful;" they returned to prison. Most were returned for program rule violations (58 percent) or drug possession (35 percent). (Table 9.6 shows the crimes/infractions for which the offenders were returned to prison.)

- Older offenders were more successful than younger ones, and Whites were more successful than either Hispanics or Blacks. Success was also associated with having no prior criminal record.

- About 4 percent of both the nonwork releasees (control group) and the work releasees (experimental group) were returned to prison for a new crime during the year.

- An offender serving part of his or her sentence in prison and then participating in a work-release program cost the state the same ($25,883 average) as the inmate who served his or her entire sentence in prison ($25,949 average).

Conclusion of Studies

While in the program, inmates kept a job, reconnected with their local communities, and paid for their room and board; most remained drug-free. However, the work release program did not reduce offender recidivism or corrections costs. Critics of community corrections often argue that such programs should deliver all of the above (jobs, drug-free inmates, etc.), while showing a reduction in recidivism and costs.

Turner and Petersilia think that those expectations are unrealistic. Realistic measures of correction programs' effectiveness should account for what was accomplished and the constraints under which the programs operate. Realism, however, does not mean easy to achieve. Most participants in Washington's work-release program had lengthy criminal histories, serious substance abuse problems, and limited education and job skills. Yet, when supervised in this work-release program, they found jobs, paid rent, and refrained from crime.

According to Turner and Petersilia, although most corrections evaluations adopt recidivism as their primary outcome measure, few corrections officials believe that what they do chiefly determines recidivism rates. As John J. DiIulio observed in "Rethinking the Criminal Justice System: Toward a New Paradigm," (*Performance Measures for the Criminal Justice System*, Bureau of Justice Statistics, Washington, DC, 1993), most justice practitioners understand that they can rarely do for their clients what parents, teachers, friends, neighbors, clergy, or economic opportunities may have failed to do.

Adopting more realistic outcome measures may make it more possible to bridge the wide gap between public expectations for the justice system and what most practitioners recognize as the system's actual capacity to control crime. By documenting what corrections programs can accomplish, the systems can move toward integrating programs like work release into a more balanced corrections strategy. Such a strategy would successfully return low-risk inmates to the community, thereby making room to incarcerate the truly violent offenders.

CHAPTER X

ALTERNATIVE SENTENCING — BOOT CAMPS

The program's main thing is to teach you to stay out of trouble.

This is better than serving the 4 years of my regular sentence.... I will get out after 107 days.

This program teaches me to respect others and work with others. I learned confidence. — Interviews with inmates participating in the Intensive Motivational Program of Alternative Correction Treatment in Louisiana (*An Evaluation of Shock Incarceration in Louisiana,* National Institute of Justice, Washington, DC, 1993)

Our concern with 'boot camp' programs is that there is little evidence that they result in long-term behavior modification and they currently have insufficient follow-up. — Prosecutor (*National Assessment Program: 1994 Survey Results,* National Institute of Justice, Washington, DC, 1995)

Shock incarceration, a term often used for boot camps, is one of the most controversial alternatives to prison. The idea is not new. For example, Elmira Reformatory had a military regimen in the 1800s. After World War II, the British set up quasi-military detention centers for adolescents in England and Wales. These centers, which emphasized tough discipline, were intended to give teenagers the "short, sharp shock that would end their criminal careers." The programs continued into the 1960s and 1970s despite research that showed their recidivism (rearrest) outcomes were no better than other institutional programs.

FIRST CAMPS

In the United States, the first modern correctional boot camp opened in Georgia in 1983. Faced with unprecedented overcrowding in its prisons and jails, Georgia was looking for alternatives to incarceration for adult offenders. Oklahoma began its program in 1984, and by the end of 1988, 15 programs were operating in nine states. The majority of programs have been started since 1990. (See Table 10.1 for boot camp characteristics.)

As of January 1, 1998, according to the Criminal Justice Institute (*The Corrections Yearbook — 1998*), 33 correctional agencies (state and federal) operated 49 camps for adult inmates. This is the fewest number of adult boot camps in operation in the United States since 1993, when there were 46 camps. In 1995, 75 adult boot camps were in operation. The 49 camps housed 6,857 inmates: 6,349 males and 508 females. The average length of stay for the inmates was five months at an average daily cost per inmate of $59.76. Costs ranged from $32.00 per inmate per day in South Carolina to $113.98 in Minnesota.

Nine jail systems operated a total of 15 boot camps for 1,015 prisoners. The length of the programs averaged three months, and the average cost was $69.54.

In addition, 7 probation agencies operated 10 boot camps, and three parole agencies operated 3 boot camp programs. The average stay at a probation boot camp was six months and at a parole boot camp, five months. The average daily cost was $59.65 per probationer and $49.00 per parolee. (Of the three states that ran probation and parole boot camps — Maryland, New York, and Ohio — only Ohio reported a cost per day figure.)

According to "Prisons: Policy Options for Congress" (*Congressional Issue Brief*, JoAnne O'Bryant, September 1998), the Federal Bureau of Prisons operated one Intensive Confinement Center (prison boot camp) for males (209 inmates) and one for females (112 inmates). In 1996, 500 male and female inmates completed this program.

PUBLIC, POLITICIANS, AND CRIMINAL JUSTICE ADMINISTRATION

Boot camps are generally popular with politicians and the public and usually get positive media attention. They are intended to be both punitive in their rigid discipline and rehabilitative in the self-esteem they claim to confer upon successful completion of the program. Shock incarceration is intended to motivate prisoners, teach respect for oneself and others, and break the destructive cycles of behavior. Virtually all work on the assumption that a military regimen is beneficial.

The major selling points for boot camps have been saving money and reducing prison crowding. However, the major factor contributing to reduced costs and less overcrowding is that the boot camp programs are shorter in duration than traditional sentences, and thus participants are released earlier.

Despite positive publicity, the few studies of boot camps have found that the camps have not had a major effect on recidivism (see below). In *National Assessment Program: 1994 Survey Results* (Washington, DC, 1995), the National Institute of Justice reported the responses of over 2,500 directors of criminal justice agencies. About 42 percent of the directors of probation

and parole agencies indicated that they did not have boot camp programs and did not want or need them. Judges and trial court administrators expressed stronger support for boot camps. Eighty-two percent of the judges and 63 percent of trial court administrators indicated that boot camps were an available option in their states or jurisdictions, with about half of each group indicating a need for improvement in the boot camps. Less than 10 percent of the judges and trial court administrators stated they did not want boot camps as an option. (See Table 10.2.)

Directors of probation and parole agencies expressed concern about the effectiveness of boot camps and about the staff time required to monitor them. One director stated,

I personally feel that boot camps are a silly idea and a throwback to the '50s and '60s with no demonstrated value in positively impacting our population of offenders. Day treatment programs with prescriptive interventions, e.g., structured learning, offer the greatest promise of success.

TABLE 10.1			
Characteristics of Boot Camp Programs			
	Federal and State[1] (n=35)	**Local** (n=8)	**Juvenile** (n=9)
Year Opened			
Prior to 1988	7	0	0
1988–1990	13	2	0
1991–1993	14	6	6
1994	1	0	3
Capacity[2]			
Male	8,678	806	455
Female	626	102	0
Total Capacity	9,304	908	455
Minimum length of residential boot camp			
< 3 months	2	4	1
3 months	15	2	2
4 months	9	0	5
6 months	9	2	1

[1] There were 32 States known to operate boot camps at the time of the study. Since both Georgia and Oklahoma operate two different types of boot camps, they are treated separately in the table.

[2] When a program did not break out male and female capacity, it was counted as being male. Therefore, the female capacities may be undercounted.

Source: *A National Survey of Aftercare Provisions for Boot Camp Graduates*, National Institute of Justice, Washington, DC, 1996

Another director wrote that "boot camp aftercare [community supervision] has taken up half of the intensive probation slots and is not very effective." Other comments illustrated that workload concerns prevailed over the value of boot camp aftercare. According to one director, "The programs cause significant workload problems when agents assigned to them must be granted reduced caseload allowances, placing a burden on the other agents."

Many judges also commented on boot camps. One judge expressed his unhappiness: "Boot camp has proved a disappointment because a lack of follow-up skill training and supervision has resulted in graduates committing additional crimes." Another judge wrote, "I think boot camps are a good idea, but our present emphasis tends to be on offenders who have already been through probation and jail. A better plan might be to use boot camp on first-time offenders who are 'just drifting.'"

Several respondents believed that boot camps might be beneficial but that more follow-up was needed for participants in terms of aftercare services. One prosecutor noted, "Our concern with 'boot camp' programs is that there is little evidence that they result in long-term behavior modification and they currently have insufficient follow-up." A public defender stated, "Shock incarceration has had poor success because of the lack of options and structure upon release."

BOOT CAMP GOALS AND AIMS

The Center for the Study of Crime, Delinquency and Corrections (Southern Illinois University at Carbondale) studied federal, state, and boot camp programs and reported its findings in *"Boot Camp" Drug Treatment and Aftercare Interventions: An Evalu-*

ation Review (National Institute of Justice, Washington, DC, 1995). Although shock incarceration's acceptance by the public is based mostly on the appeal generated by "tough" media images of drill instructors, most adult boot camps surveyed were positively oriented towards developing programs aimed at offender rehabilitation. Table 10.3 lists the goals and aims as reported by the states.

Typically, the boot camp programs include physical training and regular drill-type exercise, housekeeping and maintenance of the facility, and often hard labor. Some states include vocational, educational, or treatment programs. Drug and alcohol counseling, reality therapy, relaxation therapy, individual counseling, and recreation therapy are often incorporated into shock incarceration programs. Many offenders in boot camps have drug problems — 95 percent of the participants in Mississippi, for example.

Virtually all programs give at least several hours of drug treatment weekly. All the programs closely regulate dress, talking, movement, eating, hygiene, etc. Obedience to rules reinforces submission to authority and forces the prisoners to handle a challenge that is both tedious and demanding.

TABLE 10.2

Boot Camps

Respondent Group	Currently Have Boot Camps	Current Boot Camps Need Improvement	Boot Camps Need to be Developed	Do Not Want/Need
Prosecutor	188 71.2 %	70.2 %	70 26.5 %	6 2.3 %
Public Defenders	129 71.7 %	71.3 %	29 16.1 %	22 12.2 %
Judges	129 81.7 %	55.8 %	25 15.8 %	4 2.5 %
Trial Court Administrators	82 62.6 %	50.0 %	37 28.2 %	12 9.2 %
Probation and Parole Agency Directors	149 42.9 %	45.0 %	51 14.7 %	147 42.4 %

Source: *National Assessment Program: 1994 Survey Results*, National Institute of Justice, Washington, DC, 1995

TABLE 10.3

The Importance of Shock Incarceration Aims, Goals, and Program Elements[a] as Reported by System Level Officials (n=31)

	Importance						
	1 **Primary**	**2**	**3**	**4** **Least**	**Not** **Applicable**	**Mean**	**S.D.**
CORRECTIONAL AIMS:							
Retribution	0	6.5	25.8	58.1	9.7	3.57	.63
Incapacitation	12.9	9.7	45.2	25.8	6.5	2.90	.98
Rehabilitation	51.6	35.5	6.5	0	6.5	1.52	.63
Deterrence	32.3	41.9	16.1	6.5	3.2	1.97	.89

GOALS[b]	Mean	S.D.	ELEMENTS[c]	Mean	S.D.
SYSTEM LEVEL:	**2.78**				
Reduce Crowding	2.87	1.71	Physical Training	1.55	.93
Improve Image of Corrections	3.58	1.48	Alcohol Treatment	2.42	1.15
Public Safety	1.58	1.03	Drug Treatment	2.39	1.20
Alternative to Longer-Term Incarceration	1.55	1.03	Substance Abuse Education	2.03	.98
Less Cost	2.32	1.28	Physical Labor	2.10	1.48
Politically Acceptable Alternative	2.42	0.92	Drill/Ceremony	1.74	1.03
Model for County Programs	5.16	2.24	Basic Education	2.53	1.31
			Vocational Education	3.36	1.45
INDIVIDUAL LEVEL:	**1.87**		Pre-Release Programming	2.79	1.40
Instill Respect for Authority	1.71	1.10	Post-Release Service Delivery	2.13	1.19
Promoting Discipline	1.55	0.89			
Less Criminal Activity	1.77	0.76			
Improve Confidence	1.94	1.18			
Reduce Drug Use	2.39	1.23			
Positive Social Behaviors	1.84	1.00			
PRISON CONTROL/MANAGEMENT:	**2.02**				
Clean, Healthy Environment	2.19	1.01			
Offender Accountability	1.84	1.24			
Positive Offender/Staff Contact	2.16	1.07			
Environment Promoting Rehabilitation	1.90	0.91			

[a]Elements identified by respondents as not being a program element were excluded from calculations of mean scores.
[b]Means of goals are based on a scale of 1 (very important) to 7 (not important at all).
[c]Means of elements are based on a scale of 1 (primary program element) to 6 (minor program element).
    Caution is urged in interpreting mean scores due to the use of rating scales.

Source: *"Boot Camp" Drug Treatment and Aftercare Intervention: An Evaluation Review*, National Institute of Justice, Washington, DC, 1995

BOOT CAMP PARTICIPANTS

Eligibility criteria are a way to ensure that a boot camp program meets its broader goals, whatever they may be, as well as screening out offenders who cannot tolerate the program regimen. Thus, criteria generally involve a balancing act and some fine-tuning.

Programs wanting to reduce prison crowding, for instance, do not have criteria that are too restrictive, or too few offenders will qualify. On the other hand, most programs do not accept dangerous offenders who require a high level of security or offenders whose placement in boot camp would provoke a public outcry. Typically, boot camps choose healthy, young, nonviolent offenders without prior prison experience who are willing to volunteer for a strenuous and demanding boot camp.

The age limits typically range between 25 and 35 years of age. (See Table 10.4.) Despite the voluntary nature of the program, some offenders might not have felt they had a real choice between a short-term boot camp and a long prison term.

TYPICAL DAY

In "Boot Camp Prisons in 1991" (*National Institute of Justice Journal*, November 1993), Doris Layton MacKenzie described a typical boot camp. Upon arrival at the boot camp, male inmates have their heads shaved (females may be permitted short haircuts) and are informed of the strict program rules. At all times they are required to address staff as "Sir" or "Ma'am," must request permission to speak, and must refer to themselves as "this inmate." Punishments for even minor rule violations are prompt, certain, and without a judicial hearing. The punishment frequently involves physical exercise such as push-ups or running in place. A major rule violation can result in dismissal from the program.

In a typical boot camp program for adult offenders, the 10- to 16-hour day begins with predawn reveille. Inmates dress quickly and march to an exercise yard where they participate in an hour or two of physical training and drill. Following this, they march to breakfast in a dining hall where they must stand at attention while waiting in line and move in a military manner when the line advances. Inmates are required to stand behind their chairs until commanded to sit and must eat without conversation.

After breakfast, they march to work sites, where they participate in hard physical labor that frequently involves community service, such as picking up litter in state parks or along highways. When the 6- to 8-hour workday is over, offenders return to the compound, where they participate in more exercise and drill. Evening programs that include counseling, life skills, academic education, or drug education and treatment follow dinner.

Figure 10.1 shows a daily schedule for offenders in New York shock incarceration facilities. Participants perform six hours of hard work per day. Over 40 percent of the inmates' time is spent in treatment and education. The program is divided as follows.

- Physical training, drill, and ceremony: 26 percent.

- Treatment and education sessions to treat addictions: 28 percent.

TABLE 10.4			
Eligibility Criteria for Boot Camps			
Eligibility Requirements	**Federal and State** (n=35)	**Local** (n=8)	**Juvenile** (n=9)
Maximum age			NA[1]
25 or under	7	3	
26–30	8	1	
31–35	7	0	
36–40	3	0	
No limit	10[2]	4	
Maximum sentence			NA[1]
Between 1 and 4 years	9	1	
Between 5 and 10 years	15	1	
Other[3]	11	6	
Requirement that enrollment be voluntary[4]	27	6	3
Exclude those with			
Prior incarceration	23	1	0
Violent crimes	33	6	3

[1] For juvenile programs the maximum age is the age of juvenile court jurisdiction, typically age 17. Minimum ages for these programs are 14 for six programs, 12 for one, 13 for one, and 16 for one. Sentence requirements do not apply.

[2] Includes the Federal program, which does not exclude older offenders but does give priority to offenders under age 36, and the Michigan program, which only accepts *probationers* under age 26 but accepts *inmates* of any age.

[3] Includes programs with sentences greater than 10 years and those with no maximums.

[4] Does not include two programs (Arizona and Hidalgo County, Texas) that do not have voluntary requirements but most of the participants do volunteer.

Source: *A National Survey of Aftercare Provisions for Boot Camp Graduates*, National Institute of Justice, Washington, DC, 1996

- Academic education: 13 percent.

- Hard labor on facility and community projects: 33 percent.

As their performance and time in the program warrant, inmates gradually earn more privileges and responsibility. A special hat or uniform may be the outward display of their new status. Those who successfully finish the program usually attend an elaborate graduation ceremony with visitors and family invited to attend. Awards are often presented to acknowledge progress made during the program.

In 1997, according to the Criminal Justice Institute (*The Corrections Yearbook — 1998*) 11,711 offenders, from 26 adult correctional agencies, completed boot camp programs. Of those successfully completing the programs, 1,193 were female and 10,518 were male. During 1997, 1,011 persons in four probation agencies successfully completed a boot camp program; 504 people, 95 of whom were female, successfully completed parole boot camps; and 2,193 people, including 28 females, successfully completed combined probation/parole agency boot camps.

Camps Are Not All Alike

Media accounts of boot camps all sound alike because they tend to highlight drill and discipline. However, observers of the boot camp movement emphasize how much the programs differ. More than half of the states devoted at least 50 percent of their program to military discipline, and few devoted less than 20 percent. Physical fitness or exercise programs took up less of the program day, typically falling in the 10 to 19 percent range and rarely exceeding one-third.

Time devoted to educational and counseling activities was the most variable percentage. For example, Pennsylvania allocated 70 percent of its program day to education and counseling, with 20 percent devoted to fitness and 10 percent to drill, discipline, and physical labor.

In contrast, South Carolina's program spent just 10 percent of the day on education and counseling and 10 percent on fitness; the remaining 80 percent of the day was devoted to military activities and work. In the Texas program, all participants received approximately five weeks of drug education.

In New York State, a military regimen is combined with substance abuse counseling, high school equivalency classes, and community service. Men and women speed up their release from custody by successfully completing the program. Upon completion, offenders are required to participate in an intensive six-month aftercare program that provides them with jobs, helps them stay employed, and improves their chances of success after release.

SUBSTANCE ABUSE PROGRAMS

Education was prominently featured in substance abuse programming in boot camp facilities, whether as the sole program component or as part of a broader treatment. When treatment and education programs merged, the dilution of the former often resulted (at least in the opinion of substance abuse programming providers). For example, those facilities that offered programs in both substance abuse education and treatment provided nearly 30 more hours for education

---

FIGURE 10.1

Daily Schedule for Offenders in New York Shock Incarceration Facilities

A.M.

5:30	Wake up and standing count
5:45–6:30	Calisthenics and drill
6:30–7:00	Run
7:00–8:00	Mandatory breakfast/cleanup
8:15	Standing count and company formation
8:30–11:55	Work/school schedules

P.M.

12:00–12:30	Mandatory lunch and standing count
12:30–3:30	Afternoon work/school schedule
3:30–4:00	Shower
4:00–4:45	Network community meeting
4:45–5:45	Mandatory dinner, prepare for evening
6:00–9:00	School, group counseling, drug counseling, prerelease counseling, decisionmaking classes
8:00	Count while in programs
9:15–9:30	Squad bay, prepare for bed
9:30	Standing count, lights out

Source: *Shock Incarceration in New York: Focus on Treatment*, National Institute of Justice, Washington, DC, 1994

instruction (70 hours versus 42 hours) than facilities that offered an education program only.

See Table 10.5 for a list of the various elements offered at the responding sites. While all the system-level administrators indicated that alcohol and drug treatment services were being provided in their shock incarceration facilities, only 75 percent of the site-level administrators and heads of the substance abuse treatment/education providers indicated that such services were provided. Thus, confusion apparently existed as to whether a drug/alcohol treatment actually existed.

Examination of the most and least often used treatment interventions offered at boot camp facilities suggests that most programs were oriented toward pragmatic skill-building as a means of helping offenders cope with problems and stresses they would face on returning to society. They focused on the following:

- Development of motivation and commitment to overcome dependence.

- Development of life skills (fiscal management, communication skills, constructive use of time).

- AIDS education and prevention.

- Relapse prevention strategies.

- Development of an aftercare plan to access community resources after release.

Traditional psychotherapeutic approaches, designed to uncover and deal with the offenders' underlying psychological and emotional problems, were used infrequently. The absence of programs addressing the unique psychosocial characteristics of the offenders, either through individual or small group therapies, raised questions about the effectiveness of shock incarceration treatment programming.

For many of the boot camps, drug abuse treatment was introduced as an afterthought after the boot camp was established, and so the programming was

TABLE 10.5

The Percentage of Facilities in Which Various Elements Exist as Reported by Systems-Level Officials, Site-Level Administrators, and Site-Level Substance Treatment Providers [b]

	System-Level Officials (n=27)	Site-Level Administrators (n=28)	Site-Level Substance Abuse Treatment/ Education Providers (n=28)
ELEMENTS	%	%	%
Physical Training	100	96	96
Alcohol Treatment	100	75	75
Drug Treatment	100	75	75
Substance Abuse Education	100	100	100
Physical Labor	100	96	96
Drill/Ceremony	100	100	100
Basic Education	96	93	100
Vocational Education	46	32	43
Pre-Release Programming	93	96	96
Post-Release Services Delivery	74	75	71

[a]Percentages have been rounded to nearest whole percent.
[b]In this table, percentages are presented only for those jurisdictions with system-level respondents (27 of 31), administrative survey respondents (28 of 32), and substance abuse survey respondents (28 of 29).

Source: *"Boot Camp" Drug Treatment and Aftercare Intervention: An Evaluation Review,* National Institute of Justice, Washington, DC, 1995

confined to "off hours" (during the evening or on the weekend). Moreover, most boot camp programs are of relatively brief duration (three to six months), which is inconsistent with what is known about the length of effective drug treatment programs. These aspects of the programming may undermine the purpose and success of the programs.

Most often, all offenders were placed in the treatment programs mandated by law or policy, and all received the same treatment. This finding was particularly troublesome to the researchers because the only study to examine the effect of the boot camp experience on substance abusers indicated that mandated treatment interventions in the community, based on legal instead of clinical factors, were not associated with reduced levels of offender recidivism. Moreover, additional study indicated that forcing people to receive treatment who did not believe they needed it may have also negatively affected offender adjustments and attitudes in other components of the shock incarceration program.

ARE BOOT CAMPS SUCCESSFUL?

Multisite Evaluation

To examine the success of shock incarceration programs, the National Institute of Justice sponsored an evaluation of eight state programs — Florida, Georgia, Illinois, Louisiana, New York, Oklahoma, South Carolina, and Texas (*Multisite Evaluation of Shock Incarceration: Evaluation Report*, Washington, DC, 1994). In 1999, this study was still considered to be the most comprehensive to date.

Attitude Change

The attitudes of offenders serving time in the shock incarceration programs were compared to the attitudes of demographically similar offenders serving time in "traditional" prisons. Attitudes toward the shock incarceration program (or prison) and antisocial attitudes were assessed once after offenders arrived at boot camp (or prison) and again three to six months later, depending on the length of the shock incarceration program.

Boot camp entrants became more positive about the boot camp experience over the course of the program. In contrast, prison inmates either did not change or developed more negative attitudes toward their prison experience. When antisocial attitudes were measured, there were no differences between boot camp inmates and prison inmates; both became less antisocial during their time in prison or camp.

Neither time devoted to rehabilitation nor the ability of the inmates to leave the program voluntarily was significantly related to program attitude difference scores. However, time devoted to rehabilitation, program rigor, and the voluntary aspect of the program appeared to lead to greater reductions in antisocial attitudes. The findings that both boot camp inmates and prison inmates become less antisocial during incarceration supports some current research indicating that prison may have some positive influence on some inmates. However, the characteristics of these offenders in the control group were different from those of the general prison population. These offenders were young nonviolent offenders who had less serious criminal histories.

Impact on Recidivism

Recidivism rates of those who successfully completed the shock incarceration program were generally similar to those of comparable offenders who spent a longer time in prison. The lower recidivism rates of some boot camps appeared to result from the process of selecting offenders for the program or from the intensive supervision given after graduation.

In five states (Oklahoma, Texas, Georgia, Florida, and South Carolina), the boot camp experience did not reduce recidivism. In the other three states (New York, Illinois, and Louisiana), there was some evidence, though inconclusive, that boot camp graduates may have had lower rates of recidivism.

Given that all shock incarceration programs are modeled after military boot camps with strict rules and discipline, physical training and hard labor, the different results suggest that the boot camp experience in itself does not successfully reduce recidivism. Programs in the states that experienced lower recidivism had six-month intensive supervision probation phases in the community following the boot camp. Each program had a strong focus on rehabilitation, voluntary participation, selection from prison-bound entrants, and longer program duration. Each had a high dropout rate. Any or all of these aspects of the programs could have had an impact on offenders with or without the boot camp atmosphere.

Impact on Prison Crowding

The major factor influencing prison bed savings was whether the boot camp program targeted prison-bound offenders. To reduce prison crowding, a sufficient number of prison-bound offenders must successfully complete the program, serving less time than they would otherwise have served in a conventional prison.

For example, an offender who receives a six-year sentence might be eligible for parole after serving one-half of the sentence. With additional "time-off" for good behavior, he or she might be paroled from prison after serving two years. In contrast, an offender sent to the boot camp with the same six-year sentence would become eligible for parole after completing the three-month boot camp program — a savings of 21 months.

Programs that empowered the Department of Corrections to select boot camp participants were most likely to alleviate prison crowding because they maximized the probability of selecting offenders who would otherwise have been sentenced to prison. When the sentencing judge has control over placement decisions, it is more likely the program will be used as an alternative to probation rather than to prison because judges often search for a sanction that falls somewhere between probation and prison in severity. While this may not be an unreasonable use of the program, it can have the undesirable side effect of "widening the net" of potential participants rather than shrinking it.

Other factors that affected the ability of boot camp programs to reduce prison crowding included

- How restrictive the eligibility and suitability criteria were (stricter criteria allow fewer prison-bound offenders to participate).

- Length of the program (programs that keep participants in boot camp longer are less likely to reduce prison crowding).

- Size of the program and graduation rates (smaller programs and those that graduate fewer offenders obviously keep fewer offenders out of prison).

Impact on Graduates During Community Supervision

Boot camp graduates did as well in adjusting to community supervision as parolees who had been released from traditional prisons. Only in Florida did boot camp graduates participate in more positive activities (employment, education, residential and financial stability, and treatment) than parolees.

The relatively high termination rate characteristic of Florida's program may explain the superior performance of the shock incarceration graduate sample. Over the course of three years, for example, approximately 50 percent of its participants were dismissed for disciplinary, medical, or emotional difficulties. Thus, those participants who succeeded in the boot camp phase of the program may have adjusted more positively to the community supervision for the same reasons that they successfully graduated from the program.

The performance of both parolees and boot camp graduates declined over time during the first year of community supervision. However, the more intensely offenders were supervised in the community (the more contacts they had with correctional officials), the better they adjusted. Therefore, supervision intensity may be a key factor in making offenders participate in positive activities (see above) during community supervision.

New York Evaluation

Costs

In New York, the Department of Corrections (DOCS) evaluates the boot camp program, and the Division of Parole (DOP) evaluates its aftercare program (community supervision). DOCS saves money in two ways: first, by reducing expenditures for care and custody and second, by avoiding capital costs for new prison construction. Graduation from boot camp is the only systematic way New York inmates can be released from prison before their minimum parole eligibility date. A shock incarceration program costs more per day per inmate than either medium or camp facilities because it offers more programming and has more staff. Nonetheless, it saves care and custody costs by shortening the terms of confinement for those who complete the program. The DOCS estimates it saves approximately $2 million in care and custody for every 100 shock incarceration graduates (about $20,000 per inmate).

Additionally, the DOCS estimates that the program freed up enough space to accommodate an additional 1,954 inmates. This saved $129.1 million in capital construction costs that would have been needed if the boot camp program did not exist (based on a per-bed capital cost of $52,000 for a camp bed and $86,000 for a medium security bed). The DOCS estimates a total saving of $305.3 million, although the figures do not include the added costs of intensive parole supervision.

Educational Improvements

During the six-month confinement, the average boot camp graduate increased both reading and math scores by about one grade level. Almost half (45 percent) increased their reading scores, with half of these improving two or more grade levels and 6 percent going up four or more grade levels. Three of five (61 percent) increased their math scores, with half of these improving two or more grade levels and 14 percent going up four or more grade levels.

Recidivism

After 12 months, 10 percent of the shock incarceration graduates returned to prison. This proportion was lower than the 16 percent of offenders who were eligible before shock incarceration was established, 15 percent of those screened but rejected by the DOCS (considered inmates), and 17 percent of those who withdrew or were removed from the program before completion.

After 24 months, 30 percent of the boot camp graduates returned to prison, compared to 36 percent of the pre-shock incarceration inmates, 36 percent for the considered inmates, and 41 percent of participants who failed to complete the program. At 36 months, boot camp graduates still returned to prison at lower rates, but the differences were only significant between the program graduates and the considered inmates.

It is possible that the differences in the return-to-prison rates were really due to differences that existed among the groups prior to the beginning of the program because the selection process chose those who would be better risks in the community. Furthermore, the research did not untangle the effects of the military atmosphere, the rehabilitation aspects, and the intensive supervision. Any or all of these components could affect the return-to-prison rates.

Arizona Program

In fall 1996, after seven years of boot camp programs, Arizona canceled its efforts. State officials believe that shock incarceration did not work as a way to save money and reduce crowded prisons. Dennis Palumbo, a professor of justice studies at Arizona State University, commented that "getting in their faces and calling them scum" does not correct problems. He continued that "marching and making them eat bad food isn't going to help a kid with a drug problem. They need treatment."

The director of the Department of Corrections admitted that the program was not cost-effective and the beds and staff were needed for the overcrowded prison conditions. One study indicated that only 22.6 percent of those admitted to the boot camps successfully completed the program. On the other hand, several teachers in the programs claimed that "it works" and that "there are so many people who could have had a chance in life [who] now won't."

AFTERCARE PROGRAMS

From May through December 1994, the American Institute for Research surveyed 52 boot camps and their aftercare programs, also called community supervision, for the National Institute of Justice. In *A*

National Survey of Aftercare Provisions for Boot Camp Graduates (Washington, DC, 1997), the institute found that boot camps do not necessarily lower rates of recidivism, but that this situation may be the result of shortcomings in aftercare programs for boot camp graduates.

Although recidivism rates appear lower for boot camps offering specialized programs, such as treatment, definitive studies have yet to be performed. Nonetheless, this survey found a number of models, such as transitional residential programs, or those having a liaison between boot camp and aftercare, that appear to hold promise for retaining the benefits of the boot camp experience when the graduate reenters the community.

Most programs release boot camp graduates to traditional probation and parole supervision. Of the 52 boot camp programs surveyed, only 13 programs (seven state, three local, and three juvenile) had developed aftercare programs specifically targeted to the boot camp population. All but two of these programs were limited to boot camp graduates who resided in the major metropolitan areas. This means that for most boot camp graduates, boot camp ends upon graduation. Graduates are, in essence, starting over when they reach the community, using techniques of behavior control and change that may be quite different from, and may possibly contradict, the strategies employed at boot camp. They no longer have the structured supervision available at boot camp.

The majority of those released from boot camp are placed on intensive probation/parole in their communities, but these programs stress the surveillance aspects of intensive supervision rather than services. Thus, aftercare may fall short of the goal of identifying problem areas that could be addressed through a system of increasingly severe punishments and arrangements for specific services.

Many statewide programs, however, have set requirements in addition to intensive supervision. For instance, the Massachusetts Boot Camp requires that graduates attend five Alcoholic Anonymous or Narcotics Anonymous meetings per week, adhere to a curfew, and submit to urine tests. Graduates of Louisiana's program must perform 100 hours of unpaid community service, honor a curfew, and meet with a parole officer at least four times weekly.

Another survey, *"Boot Camp" Drug Treatment*, (see above), also found a need for strong boot camp aftercare. Research found that criminally active drug users treated in noncorrectional settings reported increased criminal activities during the initial three-month post-treatment period, after which criminal activity steadily declined. Thus, support and monitoring have been considered critical steps toward community reintegration of the offender.

Nonetheless, approximately 25 percent of the survey respondents reported that post-release services were not a program component associated with their boot camp facilities. When aftercare services were provided, it appears that legal rather than clinical (need determined by professionals) factors dominated the decision process.

CRITICISM OF THE PROGRAMS

Critics contend that the basic rationale for correctional boot camps is flawed. Military boot camps serve a fundamentally different purpose — they train fighting units — and, furthermore, military boot camps are just the initial step in a much longer training process. The critics claim that correction boot camp aftercare programs are either nonexistent or insufficient.

Proponents respond that the purposes are not so dissimilar: military boot camps supply the basics of "discipline, responsibility, and self-esteem" that later training enhances. Correctional boot camps are designed to do the same. In addition, many of the programs not only provide military-type training, but also drug counseling and educational programs. Table 10.6 shows the military characteristics of state boot camp programs, while Table 10.7 shows that most states also offer non-militaristic programs.

Cruel and Unusual Punishment?

As Faith E. Lutze and David C. Brody claim in "Mental Abuse as Cruel and Unusual Punishment: Do Boot Camp Prisons Violate the Eighth Amendment?"

133

(*Crime & Delinquency*, Sage Publications, Inc., vol. 45, no. 2, April 1999), the harsh treatment in boot camps may be considered cruel and unusual.

The two most frequently used means of maintaining discipline are verbal confrontation and physical discipline, usually in the form of exercise. Inmates are often referred to as "maggot," "scumbag," or "nobody." Humiliating physical treatment may force inmates to carry logs on their backs or participate in excessive exercise in foul weather.

Supporters of correctional boot camps believe that offenders must be disciplined immediately for infractions so they learn to think before speaking or acting. Lutze and Brody suggest, however, that the aggressive confrontational military style, which might be considered verbally abusive, used in most correctional boot camps may lead to the physical and emotional abuse of inmates. Those with low self-esteem or a tendency to use aggression, especially, could be affected. These types of abusive treatment, they warn, may also lead to costly inmate litigation.

CONCLUSIONS

Doris Layton MacKenzie, in a report to Congress prepared for the National Institute of Justice (Chapter 9, "Criminal Justice and Crime Prevention," Lawrence W. Sherman et al., *Preventing Crime: What Works, What Doesn't, What's Promising*, University of Maryland, 1997), summarized the recent literature on adult boot camps, concluding that

- The military atmosphere, structure, and discipline of correctional boot camps does not significantly reduce the recidivism of releasees in comparison to serving time on parole or probation.

TABLE 10.6

Military Characteristics of State Boot Camp Programs for Adult Offenders		
Characteristic	Programs with this feature (N=29)	
	Number	Percent
Barracks-style housing	26[8]	90
Military titles (captain, sergeant, etc.)	29	100
Military-style protocol	29	100
Drill instructors	25[9]	86
Military-style uniforms for staff	22	79
Military-style uniforms for offenders	14	48
Grouping in platoons (members enter together)	25[10]	86
Summary punishment	25[11]	86
Group rewards and punishments	17	59
"Brig" or punishment cell	6	21
Public graduation ceremony	24	83

[8] Four of the States included here do not use barracks for all their boot camp programs. One State included here reported that they use quonset huts, rather than barracks.

[9] This feature is present only in Georgia's inmate and probation boot camps, not in the probation detention centers.

[10] This feature is present only in Georgia's inmate and probation boot camps, not in the probation detention centers. It is present in only one of Illinois' two boot camps.

[11] This feature is present only in Georgia's inmate and probation boot camps, not in the probation detention centers.

Source: *Boot Camps for Adult and Juvenile Offenders, Overview and Update*, National Institute of Justice, Washington, DC, 1994

- In programs where a substantial number of offenders are dismissed from the boot camp, the recidivism rates for those who complete the boot camp are significantly lower than the rates for those who were dismissed.

- Exploratory analyses suggest that programs incorporating components such as therapeutic activities during the boot camp and follow-up in the community may be successful in reducing recidivism, but this conclusion remains tentative until more research is complete.

Saving Costs and Space, or Not?

The National Institute of Justice, in "Key Legislative Issues in Criminal Justice: Intermediate Sanctions" (January 1997), reported that the few cost-benefit analyses of intermediate sanctions conducted have found that the financial payoff was smaller than expected. The studies did find, however, that when boot

TABLE 10.7

Programming in State Boot Camp Programs for Adult Offenders		
Characteristic	Programs with this feature (N=29)	
	Number	Percent
Military drill and discipline	29	100
Physical labor	28	97
Physical fitness or exercise programs	28[13]	97
Challenge or adventure programming	9[14]	31
Drug/alcohol counseling or education	29	100
Other counseling/therapy	24	83
Education	26	90
Vocational training or job preparation	15	52

[13] This feature is present only in Georgia's inmate and probation boot camps, not in the probation detention centers.

[14] This feature is present only in Georgia's inmate and probation boot camps, not in the probation detention centers.

Source: *Boot Camps for Adult and Juvenile Offenders, Overview and Update*, National Institute of Justice, Washington, DC, 1994

camps were designed expressly to maximize savings in prison beds, their impact on prison crowding and costs were significant.

For example, New York made several key decisions to maximize bed-space savings. The Department of Corrections (DOCS) established a high number of boot camps and chose "tougher" inmates than most other boot camps. By taking these steps, the DOCS saved a significant number of confinement months and beds. New York officials claimed that they saved substantial costs, and since boot camp graduates recidivate at about the same rate as regular inmates, public safety had not suffered.

However, a multi-jurisdictional study, *Multisite Evaluation of Shock Incarceration: Final Summary Report to the National Institute of Justice* (Washington, DC, 1994) found that only two-fifths of boot camps saved jurisdictions a significant number of prison beds. The report pointed out that while boot camps may reduce the need for bed space in prison, their use still requires future capital costs, and the substantial costs of aftercare programs must also be included.

CHAPTER XI

SENTENCING GUIDELINES, MANDATORY SENTENCING, AND THREE STRIKES LAWS

[Mandatory minimum sentences] have destroyed the discretion of judges. They are grossly unfair as they apply to youthful offenders in drug cases. For the most part, the sentences are excessive, particularly for first time offenders. — Judge J. Lawrence Irving, California, 1990

Congress decided to hit the problem of drugs, as they saw it, with a sledgehammer, making no allowance for the circumstances of any particular case.... Under the statutory minimum, it can make no difference whether he is a lifetime criminal or a first-time offender. Indeed, under this sledgehammer approach, it could make no difference if the day before making this one slip in an otherwise unblemished life, defendant had rescued fifteen children from a burning building, or had won the Congressional Medal of Honor while defending his country. — U.S. District Judge J. Spencer Letts, on having to impose a ten-year sentence on a situational offender

I firmly believe that any reasonable person who exposes himself or herself to this [mandatory minimum] system of sentencing, whether judge or politician, would come to the conclusion that such sentencing must be abandoned in favor of a system based on principles of fairness and proportionality. In our view, the Sentencing Commission is the appropriate institution to carry out this important task. — U.S. District Senior Judge Vincent L. Broderick, speaking for the Judicial Conference committee on Criminal Law in testimony before the Subcommittee on Crime and Criminal Justice of the House Committee on the Judiciary, July 28, 1993

SENTENCING GUIDELINES

Legislatively created commissions develop presumptive sentencing guidelines. These guidelines lay out the sentence structure within which a judge must operate. They contain enforcement mechanisms. If judges want to depart from the sentences recommended in the guidelines for a particular offender, they must hold a hearing to determine whether the facts warrant such a decision.

The main goal of presumptive sentencing guidelines is to impose just punishment on convicted offenders. For punishment to be just, it has to be proportionate, uniform, and neutral. To be proportionate, serious crimes should be punished more severely than minor crimes, and repeat offenders should be punished more severely than first-time offenders. To be uniform, punishment for similar offenders must be similar, and variations should be allowed only for very relevant reasons. To be neutral, punishments should not vary because of such factors as race, gender, and/or ethnicity.

IMPACT OF GUIDELINES ON SENTENCING PRACTICES

According to *The Impact of Sentencing Guidelines* (Dale Parent et al., National Institute of Justice, 1996), most evaluations of presumptive guidelines (see above) have had a mixed, but generally positive, record in the following areas:

- Achieving adherence to the guidelines by judges and other justice system officials — Studies show that judges, even those who publicly criticize the guidelines, adhere to them at a high rate.

- Improving sentencing neutrality — Virtually all studies of presumptive guidelines report sentencing uniformity and proportionality. However, it is difficult to compare sentencing patterns before and after guidelines took effect because general sentencing practices have become harsher. In addition, to avoid having impose the sentencing guidelines in some cases, many officials reduced the charges to lesser offenses.

- Improving sentencing neutrality — In Minnesota, the first state to implement presumptive guidelines, racial, ethnic, and gender differences declined, even though minority defendants were more likely to be imprisoned due to departures from the guidelines and men were still more likely to receive longer sentences than similarly situated women. An analysis of the U.S. Sentencing Commission guidelines found no compelling evidence of racial or ethnic bias in sentencing at the federal level. However, Blacks received longer sentences because of the differences in the mandatory minimums imposed for crack cocaine and powder cocaine (see below).

- Altering sentencing patterns in intended ways — Commissions in Minnesota, Oregon, and Washington intended to reduce imprisonment sentences for property offenders and increase them for violent offenders. In all three states, these outcomes were achieved. At the federal level, the sentencing commission sought to increase use of imprisonment and decrease the use of probation and succeeded in meeting these goals. However, Minnesota's experience suggests that when judicial departures from the guidelines are allowed, reversions to previous practices occur.

State legislators want to respond to voters' fear of crime and demands for tougher punishments while recognizing the need to limit spiraling correctional costs. Given these concerns, elected officials are interested in sentencing guidelines. Properly developed, presumptive sentencing guidelines can link the severity of punishment more rationally to the seriousness of crimes. They can modify the use of punishment so that available prison capacity is used for more serious and habitual offenders. They can ensure that punishments are applied more uniformly and more equitably.

TRUTH-IN-SENTENCING LAWS

Truth in sentencing supposedly lets offenders and the public know exactly how many years an inmate will be serving. For example, in states such as Connecticut, Florida, Illinois, Louisiana, Mississippi, New York, North Dakota, South Carolina, and Tennessee, laws require 85 percent of a sentence to be served. These laws usually apply to serious violent criminals, while all prison inmates in Florida, Mississippi, and Ohio fall under mandatory sentencing requirements. In Arkansas, offenders serve 70 percent of the sentence given. South Carolina has "no parole offenses" for which the offenders must serve 95 percent of their sentences and at least 80 percent before qualifying for work-release programs.

Four states — Indiana, Maryland, Nebraska, and Texas — have a 50 percent requirement, and three states — Idaho, Nevada, and New Hampshire — have a 100 percent requirement on the minimum sentence. (See Chapter IV, Table 4.21 for truth-in-sentencing requirements by state.)

MANDATORY SENTENCING

By 1994, all 50 states had at least one mandatory sentencing law. These most often required prison terms for certain offenses and a minimum number of years the offenders must serve. Judges could not offer parole or other alternative sentencing for these crimes despite any mitigating (moderating) circumstance. In Alabama, a person convicted of selling a small amount of drugs was sentenced to two years with an additional five years if the sale was made within three miles of a school or housing project and another five years if the sale was within three miles of both.

Federal mandatory minimum drug sentences for first-time offenders included five years with no parole for one gram of LSD, 100 plants or 100 kilos of mari-

137

juana, 5 grams of crack cocaine, and 100 grams of heroin. Five years were added to a drug sentence if the offender carried a gun during a drug offense. Michigan gave a life sentence to offenders convicted of delivering more than 650 grams of cocaine or heroin. Although aimed at kingpins (heads of narcotics rings), the law often hit youthful first-time offenders. Kingpins were often prosecuted under laws with lesser penalties as they plea bargained by turning in other dealers. Low-level dealers or addicts caught with them usually had very few names to "deal" (exchange names of other offenders for a reduction in charges).

Judge Stanley Sporkin, U.S. District Judge, upon sentencing a single homeless mother whose sole remuneration was to be leftover drugs, remarked,

> I do not know what efforts, if any, the government has made to bring to justice James, or any of the drug kingpins who are ultimately responsible for Ms. Jackson's possession of drugs. Too often ... this Court and other district courts find themselves sentencing underlings to substantial sentences while the drug overlords remain at large. In this case, and unfortunately too many others, the government seeks to justify a severe and disproportionate sentence by pointing to the need to fight the drug war. I will not treat the Renee Jacksons of the nation as stand-ins for drug kingpins simply because those genuinely deserving of harsh sentences are not before me. The drug war simply cannot be won on the backs of Renee Jackson and others like her.

IMPACT OF MANDATORY SENTENCING

Opponents of mandatory sentencing argue that judges can no longer take into account mitigating circumstances, reduce sentences, use alternative sentences, or assign the offender to parole. They argue that mandatory sentencing does not have a deterrent effect. A 1992 Delaware study showed that despite mandatory drug-sentencing laws, there was no reduction in drug arrests, sales, or use, but there was an increase in the prison population. States sometimes may not realize that mandatory sentencing laws add significant costs to the corrections system. In Louisi-

ana, an impact statement had to accompany any mandatory sentencing bills on how the law would affect trials, budgets, and prisons.

Federal Findings on Mandatory Sentencing

Mandatory sentencing exists side by side with sentencing guidelines. The Sentencing Reform Act of 1984 (PL 98-473) created the United States Sentencing Commission, an independent, expert commission designed to set criminal penalties (sentencing guidelines). Because Congress enacted mandatory minimums to show it was tough on crime before the first set of sentencing guidelines was issued, the commission automatically incorporated many of the mandatory minimum sentences into its guidelines. Chief Justice William Rehnquist (National Symposium on Drugs and Violence in America, 1993) commented,

> Mandatory minimums ... are frequently the result of floor amendments to demonstrate that legislators want to "get tough on crime." Just as frequently they do not involve any careful consideration of the effect they might have on the Sentencing Guidelines, as a whole. Indeed, it seems to me that one of the best arguments against any more mandatory minimums, and perhaps against some of those that we already have, is that they frustrate the careful calibration of sentences, from one end of the spectrum to the other, which the Sentencing Guidelines were intended to accomplish.

Not Effective

According to the Federal Judicial Center (Barbara S. Vincent and Paul J. Hofer, *The Consequences of Mandatory Minimum Prison Terms: a Summary of Recent Findings*, Washington, DC, 1994), federal mandatory minimum-sentence statutes have not helped reduce crime or drug availability, but have helped to incapacitate the most dangerous offenders. In New York, the mandatory minimum drug laws increased both the probability of incarceration upon conviction and the severity of the sentences imposed.

Not wanting to send small-time offenders away for long prison terms, many police, prosecutors, and judges have not always arrested, indicted, or convicted as many as they might have if the sentences were not so strict. The result has been that the overall probability of imprisonment after the law's enactment is lower than before the law. Nonetheless, the number arrested, indicted, and convicted is still rising.

In addition, conventional assumptions of deterrence theory may not apply to high-level drug traffickers. To be deterred, offenders must stop to weigh the costs and benefits, be aware of the penalties, find those penalties intolerable, and have other more attractive options. Very few of the offenders convicted under the federal mandatory minimum-standards statutes are organizers or leaders of an extensive drug operation.

Most drug offenders do not manage or supervise trafficking activity. In the profitable drug business, there are always replacements for the low-level drug dealers when they are arrested. These low-level offenders are the types who are easily replaced in a drug ring and whose removal by arrest does not disrupt drug distribution. The arrests do not act as a deterrent for those who control the drug trade.

Chief Justice William Rehnquist stated (June 18, 1993) that these laws were "perhaps a good example of the law of unintended consequences." Researchers maintain that every year there is evidence that mandatory minimums result in the lengthy incarceration of thousands of low-level offenders. These offenders could be effectively sentenced to shorter periods of time at an annual savings of several hundred million dollars.

In addition, researchers argue that the mandatory minimums do not narrowly target violent criminals or major drug traffickers. Proponents of mandatory sentences believe that the negative side effects are exaggerated and that mandatory minimums serve an im-

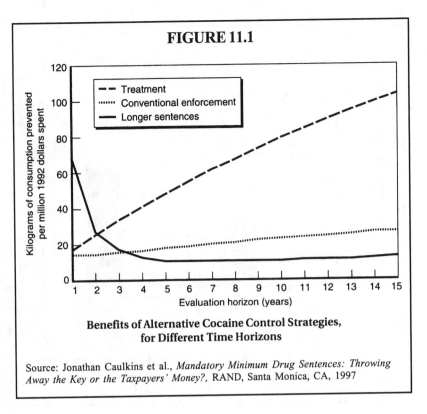

FIGURE 11.1

Benefits of Alternative Cocaine Control Strategies, for Different Time Horizons

Source: Jonathan Caulkins et al., *Mandatory Minimum Drug Sentences: Throwing Away the Key or the Taxpayers' Money?*, RAND, Santa Monica, CA, 1997

portant symbolic function and have a broad deterrent effect.

Mandatory Minimum Sentences for Drug Offenses

RAND Corporation is a nonprofit institute in Santa Monica, California, that "helps improve public policy through research and analysis." In its 1997 publication *Mandatory Minimum Drug Sentences — Throwing Away the Key or the Taxpayers' Money?*, Jonathan Caulkins, C. Peter Rydell, William Schwabe, and James Chiesa evaluated the "cost-effectiveness of mandatory minimum sentences" in relationship to crimes connected to cocaine distribution.

The analysis concluded that "mandatory minimum sentences are not justifiable on the basis of cost-effectiveness at reducing cocaine consumption, cocaine expenditure, or drug-related crime." Figure 11.1 shows how many kilograms of consumption would be prevented per million dollars spent on treatment for heavy users, conventional enforcement for typical drug dealers, and longer sentences over a period of time for typical drug dealers.

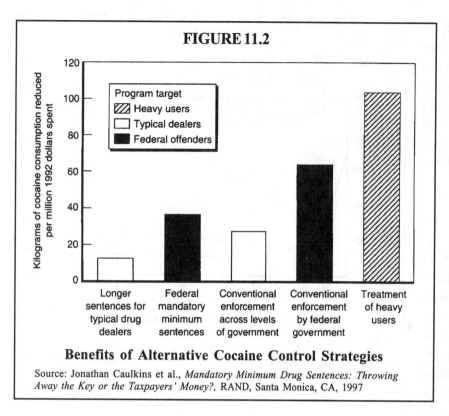

FIGURE 11.2

Kilograms of cocaine consumption reduced per million 1992 dollars spent

Program target
- ░ Heavy users
- □ Typical dealers
- ■ Federal offenders

Longer sentences for typical drug dealers / Federal mandatory minimum sentences / Conventional enforcement across levels of government / Conventional enforcement by federal government / Treatment of heavy users

Benefits of Alternative Cocaine Control Strategies

Source: Jonathan Caulkins et al., *Mandatory Minimum Drug Sentences: Throwing Away the Key or the Taxpayers' Money?*, RAND, Santa Monica, CA, 1997

sentences for higher-level dealers (federal mandatory sentences) lessened consumption more than longer sentences for all drug dealers. However, longer mandatory sentences at all levels of government were less cost-effective than conventional methods. (See Figure 11.2.)

The researchers found that mandatory minimums were cost-effective only if arrest costs were more than $30,000, and the dealer valued his time at more than $250,000 annually. For dealers making less and costing less to arrest, taxpayers' money would be better spent on conventional methods of corrections, and for dealers at the lower end, the money would be better spent on treatment.

At first, prices of cocaine would go up as drug dealers would want to be compensated for their increased risk because of potential longer sentencing. As prices went up, consumption immediately would go down. Benefits from reduced consumption would be immediate, while the costs for more prison cells would be in the future. If more users were treated, the immediate price of treatment would be higher, and the savings from reduced consumption would be in the future.

At two years out, treatment and longer mandatory sentences would reduce consumption at equal levels for the same amount of money; at three years out, conventional sentencing and longer sentences would reduce consumption at the same level. At 15 years, per million dollars spent, treatment would reduce consumption by over 100 kilograms, longer sentences would reduce consumption by almost 13 kilograms, and conventional enforcement would reduce consumption by more than 27 kilograms. (See Figure 11.1.)

When the same analysis was applied to higher-level dealers, those who run the drug distribution system, there were similar results. Mandatory minimum

Mandatory Minimums Are Not Applied Uniformly

Mandatory minimum penalties, combined with a power to grant exceptions, create a prospect of inverted sentencing. The more serious the defendant's crimes, the lower the sentence — because the greater his wrongs, the more information and assistance he has to offer to a prosecutor. Discounts for the top dogs have the virtue of necessity, because what makes the post-discount sentencing structure topsy-turvy is the mandatory minimum, binding only for the hangers on. What is to be said for such terms, which can visit draconian penalties on the small fry without increasing prosecutors' ability to wring information from their bosses? Our case illustrates a sentencing inversion. Such an outcome is neither illegal nor unconstitutional, because offenders have no right to be sentenced in proportion to their wrongs.... Still, meting out the harshest penalties to those least culpable is troubling because it accords with no one's theory of appropriate punishments. — Judge Frank J. Easterbook, U.S. Court of Appeals for the Seventh Circuit

A major goal of federal sentencing reform was to reduce disparity in sentencing; however, the federal mandatory minimums have been applied inconsistently. Charges carrying mandatory minimum sentences are often not pursued. Charges may be dropped after indictment, usually through a process of plea bargaining in which a defendant agrees to plead guilty to a lesser charge or to cooperate with the government and assist in prosecuting another offender.

The sentences applied may be fair sentences; however, the discretion is no longer in the hands of the judge but in those of the prosecutor, who may use mandatory sentencing as a tool to intimidate the accused or force plea bargaining. (See *Federal Judicial Center's Survey* below.)

Disparate Impact on Non-White Offenders

Studies by both the Sentencing Commission and the Federal Judicial Center have found that, among offenders who engaged in conduct warranting a mandatory minimum, White offenders were less likely than Blacks or Hispanics to receive the mandatory minimum term. Statutes having a disparate impact on Blacks include those that make offenses involving five or more grams of crack cocaine (a weekend's supply to a serious abuser) subject to the same mandatory minimum term of 56 years in prison as offenses involving 100 times that amount of powder cocaine.

Because Blacks are more likely to be prosecuted for crack offenses and Whites for powder cocaine offenses, the longer sentence lengths for smaller amounts of crack lead to longer prison terms for Blacks. Two other factors have the unintended consequence of reducing sentences for Whites more than those for Blacks: the discount afforded defendants who plead guilty and the discount for defendants who cooperate and provide substantial assistance. Whites tend to plead guilty and receive motions for reduction for cooperation more frequently than do Blacks.

TABLE 11.1

Attitudes toward mandatory prison sentences

By demographic characteristics, United States, 1995

Question: "In recent years, some legislatures have made imprisonment mandatory for convictions for some types of crimes. Do you think these mandatory sentences are a good idea, or should judges be able to decide who goes to prison and who doesn't?"

	Mandatory sentences are a good idea	Judges should decide	Both	Neither
National	52.9%	36.4%	6.0%	1.3%
Sex				
Male	52.2	38.3	5.8	1.0
Female	53.6	34.5	6.1	1.5
Race				
White	55.0	33.9	6.3	1.1
Black	45.7	48.6	3.8	1.9
Hispanic	43.2	44.6	2.7	2.7
Age				
18 to 29 years	47.7	44.6	5.4	0.5
30 to 39 years	53.4	35.4	9.0	0.4
40 to 59 years	55.3	35.5	2.8	1.9
60 years and older	55.2	28.7	6.9	2.9
Education				
College graduate	52.7	39.8	5.4	1.1
Some college	56.6	31.5	6.6	0.3
High school graduate	53.5	36.0	6.5	1.5
Less than high school graduate	39.6	44.6	5.0	4.0
Income				
Over $60,000	57.0	37.1	5.9	0.0
Between $30,000 and $60,000	53.7	35.7	6.1	1.4
Between $15,000 and $29,999	56.1	33.1	5.9	2.1
Less than $15,000	45.4	43.7	2.5	2.5
Community				
Urban	43.9	43.3	5.1	1.9
Suburban	57.8	33.1	5.3	0.0
Small city	46.3	41.5	6.9	2.1
Rural/small town	56.4	33.1	6.6	1.3
Region				
Northeast	47.5	39.0	8.5	1.7
Midwest	50.0	38.7	6.7	1.3
South	59.7	28.9	5.7	1.1
West	49.6	43.0	3.7	1.2
Politics				
Republican	59.7	31.4	6.1	0.7
Democrat	49.3	39.6	5.7	2.1
Independent/other	51.6	37.6	5.3	1.3

Note: The "don't know" category has been omitted; therefore percents may not sum to 100.

Source: Table constructed by SOURCEBOOK staff from data provided by Survey Research Program, College of Criminal Justice, Sam Houston State University.

Source: Kathleen Maguire and Ann L. Pastore, eds., *Sourcebook of Criminal Justice Statistics 1995*, Bureau of Justice Statistics, Washington, DC, 1996

The Department of Justice, however, found no significant differences in sentence lengths for Black defendants and White defendants who plead guilty and cooperate with authorities. Questions that need to be asked are

- Is crack cocaine sufficiently more dangerous than powder cocaine to justify harsher treatment? (See *Illegal Drugs — America's Anguish*, Information Plus, Wylie, Texas, 1999.)

- Should defendants who exercise their right to trial get longer sentences than those who plead guilty?

- Could ways be found to minimize the adverse impact of current policies on cooperation, for example, by taking into account the willingness of small-time drug defendants to cooperate and tell all they know, even though they are too low-level to have any useful information? All too often, king-pins who possess a lot of information are willing to talk to get reduced sentences, while low-level pushers get long mandatory terms because they have no information with which to bargain.

Weight of Drugs

An offender who sells 10 grams of heroin mixed with 89 grams of sugar has no required mandatory minimum term; the minimum for an offender who sells 10 grams of heroin mixed with 90 grams of sugar is five years. The courts struggle with cases in which the weight of suitcases in which drugs are hidden, wash water used to clean drug laboratory equipment, or paper wrapping that weighs hundreds of times as much as the drugs are added to the weight of the drugs in order to increase the sentence. Using the weight of mixtures penalizes persons lower in the distribution chain who typically dilute the drug. Atmospheric humidity and the type of paper used to carry the drug can dramatically affect the sentences.

Recommendations

In an April 1997 report to Congress, the United States Sentencing Commission concluded that the five-gram trigger should be increased to better target serious dealers. For powder cocaine, the commission sug-

gested that the trigger for the five-year mandatory sentence should be less than 500 grams. The commission stated,

Because nearly all cocaine is initially distributed in powder form until some later time in the distribution chain when some is then converted to crack, the Commission believes that it is appropriate to increase penalty levels for trafficking in powder cocaine to partially reflect the greater harms associated with crack and to reduce unwarranted sentencing disparity between powder and crack cocaine traffickers. In addition, the ease with which powder cocaine is converted to crack cocaine also suggests that some increase in powder cocaine penalties may be appropriate....

The Commission reiterated its 1995 conclusion that, when applicable, guideline enhancements should be used to account for harms related to crack and powder cocaine offenses with less reliance put on drug quantity. For example, any cocaine trafficker who possesses or uses a firearm or other dangerous weapon during a drug crime ought to receive a substantially enhanced sentence. Other factors, such as the use of juveniles in a drug trafficking offense, a defendant's prior drug-trafficking convictions, or a defendant's role in the offense, all are important in determining an appropriate drug sentence.

Vice Chairman Michael S. Gelacak, in a concurring opinion of the Commission's report, said that while he supported "severe sentences for serious criminal conduct," he opposed "a penalty structure that results in unfair sentences." He continued,

During the year 1993, of those sentenced for crack cocaine, 88.3 percent were Black and 95.4 percent were non-White. Even though the Commission has conceded that there was no intent by the Legislature that penalties fall disproportionately on one segment of the population, the impact of these penalties nonetheless remains. It is a little like punishing vehicular homicide while under the influence of alcohol more severely if the defendant had become intoxicated by ingesting cheap wine

TABLE 11.2

Rankings of guidelines areas requiring substantive change

Guideline Area	Respondent Group		
	District Judges	Circuit Judges	Chief Probation Officers
Departures	1	4	2
Use of Quantity in Drug Cases*	2	1	8
Relevant Conduct	3	3	5
Alternatives to Incarceration	4	8	4
Plea Bargaining	5	6	1
Role in the Offense	6	7	2
Use of Quantity in Fraud Cases	7	—	9
Multiple Counts	8	5	12
Standards of Appellate Review	9	12	14
Use of Quantity in Theft Cases	10	—	10
Retroactivity of Amendments	11	9	15
Lack of Clarity in Relevant Circuit Law	12	—	7
Acceptance of Responsibility	13	11	10
Supervised Release and Probation	14	13	13
Criminal History	15	10	6
Standard of Proof at Sentencing	—	1	—

*Circuit judges were asked to rank "Use of Quantity as a Sentencing Factor," rather than giving separate rankings for use of quantity in each specific area.

Note: Responses are listed in descending order according to district judge rankings. The circuit judge survey presented a list of issues for ranking slightly different from the district judge and chief probation officer survey; issues not presented to a particular respondent group are identified with lines through the corresponding cell in the table.

Source: *The U.S. Sentencing Guidelines: Results of the Federal Judicial Center's 1996 Survey, Report to the Committee on Criminal Law of the Judicial Conference of the United States*, Federal Judicial Center, Washington, DC, 1997

cide the sentences. Blacks, younger people, those with less than a high school education, and those earning less than $15,000 were more likely to want a judge to decide the case. (See Table 11.1.)

Federal Judicial Center's Survey

In 1996, the Federal Judicial Center surveyed federal district and circuit judges and chief probation officers for their opinions on the federal sentencing guidelines. The judges ranked being able to depart from the guidelines and use some discretion in sentencing as their main concerns. (See Table 11.2.)

They disliked that the prosecutors had so much discretion in determining charges. Narrative responses to open-ended questions reflected frustration with the power and discretion held by prosecutors under the guidelines in determining the charges. The second guideline in which the district judges wanted substantive change was the use of quantity in drug cases.

Some respondents commented,

The excessive power granted prosecutors by the guidelines scheme has resulted in a situation where the Court is viewed as a rubber stamp for the prosecutors' determination.... As a practical matter, prosecutors, by charging or not charging, by bargaining or not bargaining, and by making facts known — or failing to make facts known, control the ultimate sentence. Any system that permits such a result is wrong.

The respondents preferred advisory guidelines (52 percent of circuit judges, 67 percent of district judges,

rather than Scotch whiskey. That suggestion is absurd on its face and ought be no less so when the abused substance is cocaine....

The current policy focuses law enforcement efforts on the lowest level of the distribution line — the street dealer. Unless we ignore all evidence to the contrary, the current policy has little or <u>no</u> impact upon the drug abuse problem. The jails are full....

OPINIONS ON MANDATORY SENTENCING AND SENTENCING GUIDELINES

According to a 1995 survey (Survey Research Program, College of Criminal Justice, Sam Houston University), more than one-half of the respondents thought that mandatory sentences were a good idea, while just over one-third believed judges should de-

and 68 percent of probation officers) to mandatory penalties (0.2 percent of district judges and none of the others). Other choices (7 percent to 27 percent of the respondents) were "discretion-based sentencing with or without parole" and "other."

Responding to the question "to what classes of offenders do you think alternatives to incarceration should be made available" (the respondents could check more than one answer), most district judges (63.5 percent) and chief probation officers (56.1 percent) thought first-time offenders should be eligible. They were not in favor of fines being used instead of prison terms, but were agreeable to community confinement, boot camps, and home detention.

"THREE STRIKES AND YOU'RE OUT"

Public concern with violent crime in recent years has led state and federal lawmakers to pass legislation increasing penalties for criminal offenses, particularly violent crimes. Many states have adopted policies to lock up three-time felons for life without parole. These policies are referred to as the "three strikes and you're out" laws. (The baseball term "three strikes and you're out" was used during the campaign in Washington State in 1993, in which voters approved a Persistent Offender Act requiring life sentences with no parole for three-time serious felony offenders.) The purpose of these laws is to remove from society offenders convicted repeatedly of serious offenses for long periods of time, and in many cases, for life. Washington State and California were the first states to implement the "three strikes" laws in 1993 and 1994, respectively. In Wash-

---

TABLE 11.3
Comparison of Washington and California Strikes Laws

Type of Offense	Washington	California
Homicide	Murder 1 or 2 Controlled Substance Homicide Homicide by Abuse Manslaughter 1 or 2	Murder
Sexual Offenses	Rape 1 or 2 Child Molestation Incest of Child Sexual Exploitation	Rape Lewd Act on Child Continual Sexual Abuse of Child Penetration by Foreign Object Sexual Penetration by Force Sodomy by Force Oral Copulation by Force
Robbery	Robbery 1 or 2	Robbery
Felony Assault	Attempt Murder Assault 1 or 2	Attempt Murder Assault with a Deadly Weapon on a Peace Officer Assault with a Deadly Weapon by an Inmate Assault with Intent to Rape or Rob
Other Crimes Against Persons	Explosion with Threats to Humans Extortion Kidnaping 1 or 2 Vehicular Assault	Any Felony Resulting in Bodily Harm Arson Causing Bodily Injury Carjacking Exploding Device with Intent to Injure Exploding Device with Intent to Murder Kidnaping Mayhem
Property Crimes	Arson 1 Attempt Arson 1 Burglary	Arson Burglary of Occupied Dwelling Grand Theft with Firearm
Drug Offenses		Drug Sales to Minors
Weapons Offenses	Any Felony with Deadly Weapon Possession of Incendiary Device Possession of Prohibited Explosive Device	Any Felony with Deadly Weapon Any Felony Where Firearm Used
Other	Treason Promoting Prostitution Leading Organized Crime	

Source: John Clark, James Austin, and D. Alan Henry, " 'Three Strikes and You're Out': A Review of State Legislation," *Research in Brief*, National Institute of Justice, Washington, DC, 1997

---

ington, all three strikes must be for felonies specifically listed in the legislation. Under the California law, only the first two convictions need to be from the state's list of "strikeable" offenses. Any subsequent felony can count as the third strike. (See Table 11.3 for list of strikeable offenses for Washington and California.

TABLE 11.4

Variations in State Strikes Laws

State	Strike Zone Defined	Strikes Needed To Be "Out"	Meaning of "Out"
Arkansas	Murder, kidnaping, robbery rape, terrorist act	Two	Not less than 40 years in prison; no parole
	First-degree battery; firing gun from vehicle; use of prohibited weapon; conspiracy to commit murder, kidnaping, robbery, rape, first-degree battery, or first-degree sexual abuse	Three	Range of no parole sentences, depending on the offense
California	Any felony if one prior felony conviction from list of strikeable offenses (see Table 11.3)	Two	Mandatory sentence of twice the term for the offense involved
	Any felony if two prior felony convictions from list of strikeable offenses	Three	Mandatory indeterminate life sentence, with no parole eligibility for 25 years
Colorado	Any Class 1 or 2 felony or any Class 3 felony that is violent	Three	Mandatory life in prison with no parole eligibility for 40 years
Connecticut	Murder, attempt murder, assault with intent to kill, manslaughter, arson, kidnaping, aggravated sexual assault, robbery, first-degree assault	Two	Up to 40 years in prison
		Three	Up to life in prison
Florida	Any forcible felony, aggravated stalking, aggravated child abuse, lewd or indecent conduct, escape	Three	Life if third strike involves first-degree felony, 30–40 years if second-degree felony, 10–15 years if third-degree felony
Georgia	Murder, armed robbery, kidnaping, rape, aggravated child molestation, aggravated sodomy, aggravated sexual battery	Two	Mandatory life without parole
	Any felony	Four	Mandatory maximum sentence for the charge
Indiana	Murder, rape, sexual battery with weapon, child molestation, arson, robbery, burglary with weapon or resulting in serious injury, drug dealing	Three	Mandatory life without possibility of parole
Kansas	Any felony against a person	Two	Court may double term specified in sentencing guidelines
	Any felony against a person	Three	Court may triple term specified in sentencing guidelines
Louisiana	Murder, attempt murder, manslaughter, rape, armed robbery, kidnaping, any drug offense punishable by more than 5 years, any felony punishable by more than 12 years	Three	Mandatory life in prison with no parole eligibility

(continued)

In 1997, John Clark, James Austin, and D. Alan Henry, in " 'Three Strikes and You're Out': A Review of State Legislation" (National Institute of Justice, September 1997), studied variations in the "three strikes" laws in the 24 states that have legalized this type of legislation. They found that, although statutes may have

145

TABLE 11.4 (Continued)

State	Strike Zone Defined	Strikes Needed To Be "Out"	Meaning of "Out"
Louisiana (continued)	Any four felony convictions if at least one was on the above list	Four	Mandatory life in prison with no parole eligibility
Maryland	Murder; rape; robbery; first- or second-degree sexual offense; arson; burglary; kidnaping; carjacking; manslaughter; use of firearm in felony; assault with intent to murder, rape, rob, or commit sexual offense	Four, with separate prison terms served for first three strikes	Mandatory life in prison with no parole eligibility
Montana	Deliberate homicide, aggravated kidnaping, sexual intercourse without consent, ritual abuse of a minor	Two	Mandatory life in prison with no parole eligibility
	Mitigated deliberate homicide, aggravated assault, kidnaping, robbery	Three	Mandatory life in prison with no parole eligibility
Nevada	Murder, robbery, kidnaping, battery, abuse of child, arson, home invasion	Three	Court has option to sentence offender to one of the following: life without parole; life with parole possible after 10 years, or 25 years with parole possible after 10 years
New Jersey	Murder, robbery, carjacking	Three	Mandatory life in prison with no parole eligibility
New Mexico	Murder, shooting at or from vehicle and causing harm, kidnaping, criminal sexual penetration, armed robbery resulting in harm	Three	Mandatory life in prison with parole eligibility after 30 years
North Carolina	47 violent felonies; separate indictment is required with finding that offender is "violent habitual offender"	Three	Mandatory life in prison with no parole eligibility
North Dakota	Any Class A, B, or C felony	Two	If second strike is for Class A felony, court may impose extended sentence of up to life; if Class B felony, up to 20 years; if Class C felony, up to 10 years
Pennsylvania	Murder, voluntary manslaughter, rape, involuntary deviate sexual intercourse, arson, kidnaping, robbery, aggravated assault	Two	Enhanced sentence of up to 10 years
	Same offenses	Three	Enhanced sentence of up to 25 years
South Carolina	Murder, voluntary manslaughter, homicide by child abuse, rape, kidnaping, armed robbery, drug trafficking, embezzlement, bribery, certain accessory and attempt offenses	Two	Mandatory life in prison with no parole eligibility

(continued)

the same title, "three strikes and you're out" can have very different meanings in different states. For example, Georgia (and a number of other states) has a "two strikes" law, and California's "three strikes" law has a twist: it provides for doubling of sentences on a second felony conviction. Table 11.4 shows the differ-

TABLE 11.4 (Continued)

State	Strike Zone Defined	Strikes Needed To Be "Out"	Meaning of "Out"
Tennessee	Murder, especially aggravated kidnaping, especially aggravated robbery, aggravated rape, rape of a child, aggravated arson	Two, if prison term served for first strike	Mandatory life in prison with no parole eligibility
	Same as above, plus rape, aggravated sexual battery, aggravated robbery, especially aggravated burglary, especially aggravated child abuse, aggravated sexual exploitation of child	Three, if separate prison terms served for first two strikes	Mandatory life in prison with no parole eligibility
Utah	Any first- or second-degree felony	Three	Court may sentence from 5 years up to life
Vermont	Murder, manslaughter, arson causing death, assault and robbery with weapon or causing bodily injury, aggravated assault, kidnaping, maiming, aggravated sexual assault, aggravated domestic assault, lewd conduct with child	Three	Court may sentence up to life in prison
Virginia	Murder, kidnaping, robbery, carjacking, sexual assault, conspiracy to commit any of above	Three	Mandatory life in prison with no parole eligibility
Washington	Charges listed in Table 11.3	Three	Mandatory life in prison with no parole eligibility
Wisconsin	Murder, manslaughter, vehicular homicide, aggravated battery, abuse of child, robbery, sexual assault, taking hostages, kidnaping, arson, burglary	Three	Mandatory life in prison with no parole eligibility

Source: John Clark, James Austin, and D. Alan Henry, " 'Three Strikes and You're Out': A Review of State Legislation," *Research in Brief*, National Institute of Justice, Washington, DC, 1997

ences, from state to state, in how a "strike zone" is defined, how many strikes are required to be "out," and what it means to be "out."

Strike Zone

A strike zone refers to the crimes that constitute a strike and under what conditions those crimes become a strike. A strike generally is a serious offense, such as a violent felony, including murder, rape, robbery, arson, aggravated assault, and carjacking. Offenders convicted repeatedly of such crimes, usually violent and career criminals, may be incarcerated for many years or, in some cases, for life. These crimes apply in all 24 states that have enacted strikes laws. (See Table

11.4.) However, some states have included other offenses, such as the sale of drugs in Indiana, the sale of drugs to minors in California, any drug offense punishable by imprisonment for more than five years in Louisiana, treason in Washington State, and embezzlement and bribery in South Carolina.

Number of Strikes Needed to Be "Out"

There are variations in the number of strikes required to be "out." In South Carolina, a person convicted a second time for any of a list of "most serious offenses" is sentenced to life without parole. In North Dakota, two convictions of a felony can bring about an extended sentence. There is no third strike. Three strikes are required to be "out" in 20 states. However, seven states — Arkansas, California, Connecticut, Kansas, Montana, Pennsylvania, and Tennessee — also have increased sentences for two strikes, depending on the offense (Table 11.4).

What It Means to Be "Out"

States also vary in the punishments meted out when enough strikes have accumulated. Twelve states — Georgia, Indiana, Louisiana, Maryland, Montana, New Jersey, North Carolina, South Carolina, Tennessee, Virginia, Washington, and Wisconsin — impose mandatory life sentences with no possibility of parole (Table 11.4). (Virginia law provides for the release of prisoners 65 years of age and older who have served a specified length of time. In North Carolina, a law separate from the three-strikes statute allows those sentenced to life without parole to a review of their sentences after serving 25 years.)

In three states — California, Colorado, and New Mexico — parole is possible after an offender has struck out, but only after an offender has been incarcerated for a long period of time. In California, a minimum of 25 years must be served; in Colorado, 40 years must be served; and in New Mexico, 30 years must be served (Table 11.4).

Some States Have Increased Penalties

While most three-strikes laws demand mandatory minimum sentences, Arkansas, Connecticut, Kansas, and Nevada have recently passed laws increasing the possible penalties for multiple convictions for particular serious felonies, but leave the actual sentence to the discretion of the court (Table 11.4).

A judge in Connecticut can sentence an offender to 40 years in prison for a second conviction for certain serious felonies and to life imprisonment for a third such conviction. In Arkansas, judges may select either a mandatory sentence short of life imprisonment or a life sentence for a second or third strikeable offense.

The Kansas legislature passed sentencing guidelines that provide judges with a sentencing range based on the offense and the offender's prior record. A recent amendment permits judges to double guideline sentences for offenders convicted of certain listed violent felonies for a second time and triple them for a third conviction. Nevada law allows judges the option on a third-strike conviction of imposing a life sentence with parole possible after 10 years, or a 25-year sentence with parole possible after 10 years. Five states — Florida, North Dakota, Pennsylvania, Utah, and Vermont — permit sentences ranging up to life, depending on the state, when certain violent offenses are committed by repeat offenders. (See Table 11.4.)

Opinions of the "Three Strikes" Laws

The "three-strikes" law is popular with politicians because it makes them appear tough on crime. The public seems to favor the laws, too. People in California and Washington voted for the laws at the polls. However, Brandon Applegate et al., in "Assessing Public Support for Three Strikes and You're Out Laws: Global versus Specific Attitudes" (*Crime and Delinquency*, vol. 42, no. 4, October 1996), found that, when questioned more closely, people supported the broad idea of the "three-strikes" concept, but when presented with individual cases, they often did not think sentencing the offender to life in prison was necessary.

Given individual scenarios, only 7 percent thought life imprisonment was the appropriate punishment. Most supported 5 to 15 years in prison (24 percent for five years; 18 percent for 10 years, and 12 percent for 15 years). One scenario was a man who had been convicted of attempted aggravated burglary. While carrying a gun, he had attempted to burglarize $400 worth of property from an occupied home. His previous crimes had been a similar burglary and rape. The respondents took into account various circumstances, such as the nature of the offenses, length of time between crimes, characteristics of offender (mentally retarded, an older person), and the effect on the institutions (overcrowding of prisons).

Supporters of a "three-strikes law" think that it will protect the public by imprisoning habitual dangerous offenders and at the same time deter repeat offenders. They believe such legislation will save money because it will decrease the number of times certain offenders go through the system. In addition, proponents of the laws believe that justice is served when habitual offenders are locked up for life.

Opponents of the law argue that increasing the time served has not affected the violent crime rates. The penalty for the "third strike" is too harsh for criminals convicted of certain felonies, such as nonviolent crimes like drug possession. In addition, murderers are often set free to make room for more prisoners, while the "three-strikes" laws lock up for life those who have perhaps committed three robberies in their life, netting only hundreds of dollars. Critics believe the costs to the criminal justice system would be better spent on other alternatives and that the present habitual offender laws should incarcerate the truly dangerous offenders.

Also, older offenders who are beyond the peak ages of criminal activity would take up prison space. The Sentencing Project, a group that supports alternatives to prison sentences, holds that the new laws will not have much effect on violent crime because most violent crime is committed by young first-offenders. As they become older, criminals usually do not commit acts of violence.

Marc Mauer of the Sentencing Project claims that prosecutors often do not plea bargain for lesser charges with two-time felons who have minor roles in drug operations because they have no useful information. These low-level offenders get mandatory life sentences, while the high-level dealers who bargain for a lesser charge with their information get a reduced charge and avoid the sentencing impact of the "three-strike" laws.

IMPACT OF "THREE STRIKES AND YOU'RE OUT"

According to Walter Dickey and Pam Stiebs Hollenhorst, in "Three-Strikes Laws: Massive Impact in California and Georgia, Little Elsewhere" (*Overcrowded Times,* vol. 9, no. 6, December 1998), three-strikes laws are used most often in California and Georgia. (California has made more use of the law than other states, either due to the broad nature of the law or because other states already have harsh penalties in place with habitual offender laws.) In California

and Georgia, three-strikes laws have had important effects on prison populations, racial disparities, system crowding, plea bargaining, and other aspects of the justice system.

Besides these two states, 15 states reported six or fewer convictions under their three-strikes laws, and three (Montana, Utah, and Virginia) reported no convictions in 1998. Alaska, Connecticut, New Mexico, and South Carolina had implemented it only once. Only Florida, Nevada, and Washington reported more than 100 convictions. (See Table 11.5.)

The federal three-strikes law resulted in only 35 convictions by 1996. According to a spokesperson for the Office of Public Affairs, U.S. Department of Justice, by October 1997, there were 59 federal three-strikes provision requests, resulting in 35 convictions, 14 cases pending trial or sentencing, one acquittal, and nine cases withdrawn.

California

The most dramatic impact of the "three strikes and you're out" program has been in California, where by July 1998, there were 36,043 "second-strike" and 4,468 "third-strike" convictions (Table 11.5). While some states stipulate specific felonies that may cause the third felony, in California, any third felony may lead to a term of 25 years to life in prison. Since California treats any felony as a third-strike crime, the law is applied to many nonviolent, repeat felons. As an example, one resident of Redondo Beach, California, was convicted of a third strike for stealing a slice of pizza. Because the 27-year-old man had two prior robbery convictions, he was sentenced to 25 years to life under the three-strikes law.

As of March 1996, twice as many people had been sentenced for second- and third-strike marijuana possession (192) than the total combined number (89) of those sentenced for murder (40), rape (25), and kidnapping (24). In all, 85 percent of those sentenced under the law were convicted of nonviolent offenses as their final strike. As of June 1998, the offenses that trigger the third strike continued to be mostly property and drug crimes. Among second-strike cases, 37 percent were property crimes, 31 percent were drug

TABLE 11.5

Data on Use of "Three Strikes" Type Laws				

Jurisdiction	Year Law Enacted	Data Current as of:	Number of convictions	Comments
Alaska	1996	8/98	1	Although adopted following the wave of get-tough-on-crime legislation, Alaska faces prison overcrowding issues, and the law was narrowly tailored—all strikes must be for serious felonies, and a third strike earns a 40 to 99 year sentence.
Arkansas	1995	8/98	12	Two-strike provision allows 40 year sentence without parole; three strikes allows life sentence without parole. More frequently used is a habitual offender law that permits both graduated increases in length of sentences and reductions in parole eligibility.
California	1994	7/30/98	40,511	Second-strike convictions: 36,043 Third-strike convictions: 4,468
Colorado	1994	8/98	2	Used more often are Colorado's "big" and "little" habitual offender laws, under which 36 persons were sentenced in 1997.
Connecticut	1994	8/98	1	Connecticut does not have a mandatory-life type of law; instead its law permits enhanced sentences for persistent offenders by upgrading the felony one higher grade, e.g., a class B felony (10–20 years) becomes a class A (life sentence). There is one known person sentenced but may be others; an exact number is not extractable from the DOC database.
Florida	1995	6/98	116	In contrast, under Florida's 1988 habitual offender law, 23,000 persons have been sentenced (about 20 percent of the state prison population). The 1988 law allows for an imposition of a sentence double the statutory minimum for crimes committed.
Georgia	1994 One Strike and Two Strikes	3/31/98	57 serving life without parole for 2nd strike; 885 serving 20 years or more for a first strike.	Georgia's law covers "seven deadly sins" for which a first strike earns a minimum of 10 years without parole, and a second strike earns life without parole. Of the 1,833 persons serving various terms for a first strike, 617 were sentenced to life (with parole eligibility after 14 years), 7 were sentenced to 50 years or more, and 261 were sentenced to 20 years or more.
Indiana	1994 Life without parole	7/1/98	38	Indiana's habitual offender law is used more often: estimated at least 1,000 times over 20 years. It allows a sentencing enhancement for a person with two prior felonies, increasing the sentence up to three times the presumptive sentence for the underlying offense, not to exceed 30 years.
Louisiana	1994			DOC officials did not respond to request for information.
Maryland	1994 Four Strikes	12/97	1995: 3 1996: 1 1997: 1	Before 1994, about 250 people were sentenced under Maryland's 1975 law which provided for 25 years without parole for a third felony conviction. Amended in 1994, the law now provides for life without parole for a fourth strike when prison terms have been served for the first three strikes.
Montana	1995	8/98	0	Montana has a persistent offender statute that allows a sentence enhancement of 5–100 years to be served consecutively for certain repeat felons.
Nevada	1995	8/98	164 greater, 140 lesser, with parole options— see comment	Nevada has several life-sentence options under its "greater" and "lesser" habitual offender statutes which, depending on the nature of the crime, include life with no parole, life with parole possible after 10 years served, and 25 years with parole possible after serving 10.

(continued)

150

TABLE 11.5 (Continued)

				Continued: Data on Use of "Three Strikes" Type Laws
Jurisdiction	Year Law Enacted	Data Current as of:	Number of convictions	Comments
New Jersey	1995	8/17/98	6	Another statute provides for a life sentence with parole eligibility after serving 30 years; as of 1/1/98, 1,029 persons were serving such sentences (this number may also include some persons sentenced before 1980 who may have been eligible for parole after 14 years under a prior version of the law).
New Mexico	1994	8/98	1	The offense and conditions that qualify for life with parole eligibility after 30 years are very restrictive. Pre-existing law provided for sentencing enhancements of 1, 4, and 8 years on second, third, and fourth convictions.
North Carolina	1994	12/97	5 in fiscal year 96–97	During this time, although only 5 persons were sentenced to life without parole as violent habitual felons under Three Strikes and You're In, 15 death sentences and 47 life without parole sentences were imposed. In addition, 248 were sentenced as habitual felons on a fourth felony conviction. Of these, the most frequently occurring serious crimes are Felony Breaking and/or Entering (48), Possession of Stolen Goods (18), and Felony Possession of Cocaine (19). It is believed that the law is used as a bargaining chip to elicit guilty pleas, and that there may be others who qualify for a three-strikes conviction.
Pennsylvania	1995	8/98	3 through 1996	Data set is currently being compiled; numbers not yet available for 1997 or 1998.
South Carolina	1995	10/97	2 Strikes: 13 3 Strikes: 1 "No Parole" offenses: 811	South Carolina's 1995 Crime Bill contained three provisions relevant to "Non-Parolable" Inmates: Life without parole for repeat violent offenders under the two/three strikes provisions, and a new category of "no parole" offense for crimes committed after 1/1/96 which includes felonies punishable by 20 years or more, irrespective of criminal history, a group that includes proportionally more younger offenders (205 or 15 percent of the 1,349 currently serving nonparolable offenses are 21 or younger; 396 or 30 percent of this group show no prior criminal history).
Tennessee	1994	7/13/98	5	Tennessee has both a second- and third-strike provision, both of which can mandate life without parole depending on the offense. The state also has a 1989 habitual offender statute under which 156 persons have been sentenced.
Utah	1995	8/98	0	Utah's flexible sentencing structure allows for three possible sentences: 1–5 years, 1–15 years, and 5 years to life, and most serious crimes earn a lengthy indeterminate sentence. The Board of Pardons and Parole determines the release date and virtually never grants pardons. Because of this scheme, there has also been little use of a sentencing enhancement law for repeat offenders which ratchets a second degree felony (1–15) up to a first degree felony (5–life), under which just 16 persons have been sentenced since 1990. Prosecutors know that they can bargain away a three-strike enhancement in exchange for a guilty plea because a dangerous person is unlikely to be released yearly.
Vermont	1995	8/98	4	Considered a "habitual offender law," it provides for up to life for certain third strikes and for any fourth felony conviction.
Virginia	1994	8/98	0	Shortly after the law was passed, Virginia eliminated parole for all sentences, effectively negating the need for a three-strikes law.
Washington	1993	8/21/98	121	Washington has also sentenced 3 persons under its Two Strike Sex Offender law.
Wisconsin	1994	8/98	3	Reported by DOC analyst though could not be confirmed by DOC databases. In contrast, Wisconsin's habitual offender statute which permits increased penalties for persistent repeaters was applied to over 300 offenders per year in the past 3 years.
Federal Law	1994	10/97	35	By September 30, 1996 (the end of FY 1996), there were a total of 35 convictions under three strikes. Figures for FY 1997 are not yet available.

Source: Walter Dickey and Pam Stiebs Hollenhorst, "Three-Strikes Laws: Massive Impact in California and Georgia, Little Elsewhere," *Overcrowded Times*, vol. 9, no. 6, December 1998

crimes, and 19 percent were crimes against persons. Among third-strike cases, 39 percent were crimes against persons, 32 percent were property crimes, and 19 percent were drug crimes.

Prison Population and System Crowding

The crime rate in California has been declining in recent years, as it has for the nation. California's governor, secretary of state, and attorney general claim that three strikes is responsible for the decline. However, a 1997 statistical analysis by Lisa Stolzenberg and Steward J. D'Alessio, in "Three Strikes and You're Out": The Impact of California's New Mandatory Sentencing Law on Serious Crime Rates" (*Crime and Delinquency*, vol. 43, no. 4, October 1997), found no indication in nine of the state's 10 largest cities that three strikes had reduced either serious crime or petty theft rates below levels that would be expected based on the downward trends.

Because of the downward trends, prison projections have been revised downward, but much more prison space will be needed even to meet the revised estimates. Based on 1997 projections, the prison system will use up all available space by late 2000; by 2006, there will be a shortage of more than 70,000 beds. To keep capacity at its current level, California will have to build 15 new prisons, at a cost of $4.5 billion, by 2002, when, according to the Department of Corrections, 1 of 4 prisoners will be a second- or third-striker.

Going to Trial and Plea Bargaining

The "Three Strikes and You're Out" law seems to have encouraged felony offenders to go to trial rather than plead guilty. In June 1997, the State Judicial Council reported that jury trials were up by 13 percent in the first fiscal year following passage of three strikes, and another 4 percent in the second full year. Because there is much less plea bargaining, more county jails are overcrowded as three-strike defendants awaiting trial are occupying limited jail space. Other consequences of fewer plea bargains are that court resources, such as judges, intended for civil cases must now be transferred to criminal cases, and space needed for trials of three-strikes cases overflow to civil court space. Some counties temporarily have been forced to stop hearing civil lawsuits because their civil-case courtrooms are not available.

More trials mean increased costs and more backlogs. In March 1997, Fresno County (Fresno) attempted to deal with its three-strikes backlog by transferring some cases to a mock courtroom at the San Joaquin College of Law in Clovis, California. Ventura County (Ventura) experienced a 50 percent increase in felony trials due to three-strikes legislation, resulting in nearly $1 million in budget overruns for the offices of the district attorney and the public defender. In 1998, Los Angeles County officials estimated the added costs for the first full year after the three-strikes law at over $64 million. By 1998, one official estimated the cumulative cost to be $200 million.

Georgia

Georgia, while nowhere near California in terms of the number of people convicted under three-strikes legislation, has significantly increased its use of "one-strike" and "two-strikes" laws. The 1994 law covers "seven deadly sins" (murder or felony murder, armed robbery, kidnapping, rape, aggravated child molestation, aggravated sodomy, and aggravated sexual battery). For these crimes, a first strike results in a minimum of 10 years without parole, and a second strike brings life without parole. As of April 1998, 1,833 persons had been sentenced under the law and accounted for 4.4 percent of Georgia's 42,000 state prisoners. There has been no significant change in the Georgia prison population, as these inmates would be serving prison sentences anyway.

Most of the prisoners were serving time on a first strike for which they received sentences ranging from 10 years without parole to life with parole eligibility after 14 years. The average time to be served by first strikers is 16 years, and 21 percent will serve 20 years or more. The 57 persons who have been convicted a second time (and not convicted of capital murder) will serve life without parole.

Compared to Other Programs

The RAND Corporation (Peter Greenwood et al., *Diverting Children from a Life of Crime: What Are the Costs and Benefits?*, 1996) compared the cost-effectiveness of "three strikes and you're out" with long-term prevention programs designed to deter at-risk children from criminal activities. The study concluded that spending $1 million on constructing and operating prisons for repeat offenders would prevent 60 crimes annually.

Spending the same amount of money on parent-training programs could deter 157 crimes per year (parent-training programs cost an average of $3,000 per child), and investing $1 million in graduation-incentive programs could prevent 258 crimes annually (incentive programs typically cost about $12,500 per student). In addition, spending $1 million on programs to monitor the behavior of 12- and 13-year-old delinquents could avert 72 crimes annually.

Most researchers admit that the impact of the laws will not be known for many years. There are not enough statistics to prove the deterrence effect. The costs of incarcerating more prisoners will increase. For many proponents, the deterrent effects will balance the costs. If there is no significant deterrent effect, the building and operating of more prisons might not be worth the cost; however, if there is a significant deterrent effect, they might be.

A CONSEQUENCE: ELDER CARE

In 1996, 24,641 prisoners were over 55 years of age, a 7 percent increase from 1992. While only 915 prisoners were more than 75 years of age, that number represented a 56 percent increase from 1992. (See Table 11.6.) As of 1996, about 2.5 percent of those in federal prisons were at least 60 years old. By 1997, in Florida, the oldest prisoner was 89 years of age, and more than 300 prisoners were in wheelchairs.

Prison officials fear that, with more mandatory determinate sentencing, more crimes requiring life terms, and the "three strikes and you're out" rule, prisons will be housing an ever increasing number of elderly inmates. Jenni Gainsborough of the National Prison Project of the American Civil Liberties Union believes "it's all very foolish. Violent crime is a young man's game. We pay all this money to keep people in prison who could easily be safely living on the outside."

Prisons currently do not have the health-care facilities to provide the long-term care that the elderly

TABLE 11.6

Prisoner population over age 55
as of June 30, 1992, 1994, and 1996

Jurisdiction	Total over age 55			Total over age 75		
	1992	1994	1996	1992	1994	1996
Total	23,025	27,674	24,641	586	701	915

Source: Kathleen Maguire and Ann L. Pastore, eds., *Sourcebook of Criminal Justice Statistics 1996*, Bureau of Justice Statistics, Washington, DC, 1997

often require. One study found that 80 percent of those 63 to 80 years old claimed to have at least one medical problem and 60 percent asserted that they had at least three. As in the general population, prison administrators will have to face more patients with cancer, heart disease, mental incompetence, and Alzheimer's disease. Prisoners are not eligible for Medicare or Medicaid, so the states will have to pay for the costs of health care for elderly prisoners, which are estimated to be three times the costs for younger prisoners.

Administrators wonder where the money and staff will come from to handle inmates with these special needs. Facilities will have to be modified or new sections built to house the elderly population. Access ramps, dormitories or special cellblocks will have to be constructed not only to care for elderly inmates, but also to protect them from younger, more violent prisoners. More programs for those who cannot work or who have physical limitations will have to be implemented. Staff will also have to care for elderly inmates who are not ill, but who require care for their basic needs. Janet Thompson, attorney for Faye Copeland, the oldest woman on death row in 1996, commented that "the state's going to end up running a nursing home."

The question also arises as to what to do when elderly patients have served their sentences. After decades in prison, where do they go? Who will take care of them? Does the state have a right or responsibility to keep them in prison, or do the prisoners have a right to their freedom no matter what their physical or mental condition?

CHAPTER XII

PRISONERS, DRUGS, ALCOHOL, AND TREATMENT

What we're doing is simply a holding action. We've arrested more people than the prosecutors can prosecute, than the judges can convict, than the jails can hold. Until there's a demand reduction — and that means education and treatment — you're not going to see any change. — Captain Harvey Ferguson, former chief of narcotics enforcement, Seattle, Washington

Loading our prisons with nonviolent drug criminals means that, today, we are committing more nonviolent offenders to hard time than we are violent criminals, and there's little room left for the violent offenders who should be put away to make our streets safer. — Senator Paul Simon (D-CO), 1994

INCREASING NUMBER OF PRISON INMATES FOR DRUG OFFENSES

In 1997, drug offenders accounted for over 277,000 prisoners — 21 percent of state and over 60 percent of federal inmates. Figure 12.1 shows the growth in the number of prisoners serving a sentence for drug offenses from 1980 to 1997.

State Prisons

In 1997, 70.1 percent of drug offenders in state prisons were found guilty of trafficking in drugs and another 27.1 percent of possession of drugs. Many drug offenders had extensive criminal histories. More than half (53.8 percent) were on probation, parole, or had escaped at the time of their current arrest. More than 8 of 10 (82.6 percent) had been sentenced to prison or probation before (priors), and nearly half (45 percent) had three or more prior sentences. One-fourth (23.6 percent) had a prior violent offense. Nearly three-fourths (72.1 percent) of state offenders in 1997 had been involved

with cocaine or crack during their current offenses. Approximately 1 of 8 drug offenders had been involved with marijuana (12.9 percent) and heroin or other opiates (12.8 percent). One of 10 (9.9 percent) had been involved with stimulants. (See Table 12.1.)

More Drug Offenders in Prison . . .

The number of state prison inmates in custody for drug offenses increased elevenfold from 19,000 in 1980

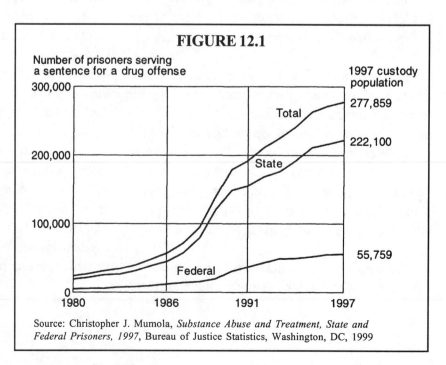

FIGURE 12.1

Number of prisoners serving a sentence for a drug offense

1997 custody population

Source: Christopher J. Mumola, *Substance Abuse and Treatment, State and Federal Prisoners, 1997*, Bureau of Justice Statistics, Washington, DC, 1999

TABLE 12.1

Drug Offenders Accounted for over 250,000 Prisoners; 21% of State, over 60% of Federal Prisoners in 1997

	Percent of drug offenders	
	State	Federal
Type of drug offense		
Possession	27.1%	5.3%
Trafficking[a]	70.1	85.8
Other	2.8	8.9
Status at arrest		
None	46.2%	75.9%
Status	53.8	24.1
On parole[b]	27.4	10.2
On probation	25.9	13.8
Escaped from custody	0.5	0.2
Criminal history		
None	17.4%	40.6%
Priors	82.6	59.4
Violent recidivists	23.6	12.1
Drug recidivists only	14.1	15.9
Other recidivists[c]	44.9	31.4
Number of prior probation/ incarceration sentences		
0	17.4%	40.6%
1	20.2	19.5
2	17.5	15.5
3-5	27.2	18.2
6-10	11.5	5.0
11 or more	6.3	1.2
Type of drug involved in current offense[d]		
Marijuana/hashish	12.9%	18.9%
Cocaine/crack	72.1	65.5
Heroin/other opiates	12.8	9.9
Depressants	1.2	0.6
Stimulants	9.9	11.0
Hallucinogens	1.1	1.7

[a]Includes those reporting an intent to distribute.
[b]Includes supervised release.
[c]Includes recidivists with unknown offense types.
[d]More than one type of drug may have been involved in the current offense.

Source: Christopher J. Mumola, *Substance Abuse and Treatment, State and Federal Prisoners, 1997*, Bureau of Justice Statistics, Washington, DC, 1999

... And More Being Sent

In 1985, about 1 in 7 inmates (13 percent) admitted to state prisons were admitted for drug crimes; throughout the 1990s, almost 1 in 3 (about 30 percent) were. Violent crimes accounted for 35 percent of state prison admissions in 1985 and 29.5 percent in 1996. (See Table 12.4 and Figure 12.3.)

Federal Prisons

Almost all of the increase in the population of federal prisons is attributable to a growth in the number of drug convictions. Prisoners sentenced for drug offenses made up the single largest group of federal inmates (60.2 percent) in 1996, up from 53.5 percent in 1990. (See Chapter V, Table 5.5.)

In 1997, almost 9 of 10 drug offenders (85.8 percent) in federal prisons were there because they had been found guilty of drug trafficking. Almost all those on drugs deal to support their habit. Another 5.3 percent had been convicted of drug possession. Drug offenders in federal prisons had less severe criminal histories than those in state prisons. One-fourth (24.2 percent) were on probation, parole, or had escaped at the time of their current arrest. Three out of 5 (59.4 percent) had a prior sentence. One-fourth (24.4 percent) had three or more prior sentences. About 1 of 8 drug offenders had had a prior violent offense. As with state prisoners, the largest proportion (65.5 percent) were involved with cocaine or crack at the time of their current offense. Nearly one-fifth (18.9 percent) of federal drug offenders were involved with marijuana or hashish, 11 percent with stimulants, and 9.9 percent with heroin or other opiates at the time of their current offense. (See Table 12.1.)

DRUG USE HISTORY

State Prisoners

In 1997, more than 4 of 5 (83 percent) state prisoners reported that they had used drugs at some time during the past, up slightly from 1991, when 79.4 declared they had used drugs in the past. In 1997, marijuana or hashish (77 percent) and cocaine or crack (49.2 percent) were the most commonly used drugs,

to 234,100 in 1996. In 1980, 173,300 inmates were in prison for violent offenses; by 1996, 487,900 were. In 1980, drug offenders accounted for 6 percent of the prisoners in custody of state correctional authorities; in 1985, for 9 percent; and in 1996, for 22.7 percent. Violent offenders made up 58.5 percent of those in custody in 1980, 54.5 percent in 1985, and 47.3 percent in 1996. (See Figure 12.2 and Tables 12.2 and 12.3. The statistics for 1980 and 1985 are not included on the tables.)

followed by hallucinogens and stimulants (over 28 percent each), heroin or opiates (24.5 percent), depressants (23.7 percent), and inhalants (14.4 percent). (See Table 12.5.)

In 1997, 56.5 percent of state prisoners reported that they had used drugs in the month prior to committing their current offense, up from 49.9 percent in 1991. Marijuana or hashish use rose from 32.2 percent in 1991 to 39.2 percent in 1997, while use of most other drugs remained about the same (Table 12.5).

Federal Prisoners

In 1997, nearly three-fourths (72.9 percent) of federal prisoners claimed to have used drugs in the past, up from 60.1 percent in 1991. As with state prisoners, marijuana or hashish (65.2 percent) and cocaine or crack (44.8

percent), were the most common choices. One of 5 federal prisoners reported past use of stimulants (20.9

FIGURE 12.2

Number of prisoners in custody of State correctional authorities, by offense type, 1980-96

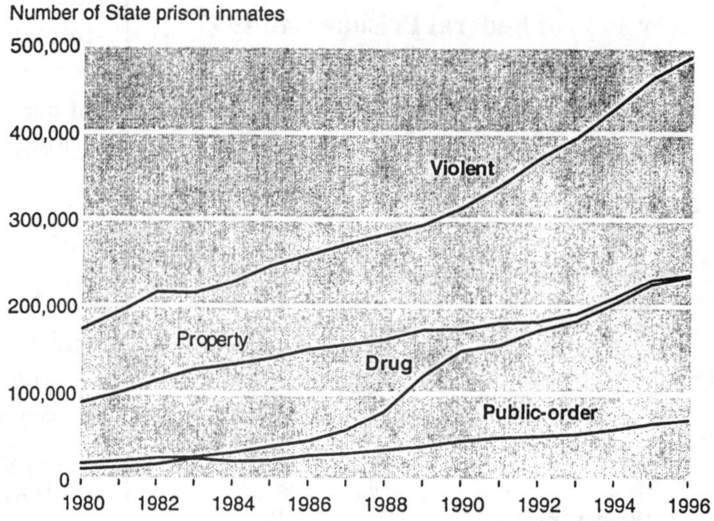

Source: *Correctional Populations in the United States, 1996*, Bureau of Justice Statistics, Washington, DC, 1999

TABLE 12.2

Estimated number of prisoners in custody of State correctional authorities, by the most serious offense, 1990-96

Most serious offense	Number of inmates in State prison						
	1990	1991	1992	1993	1994	1995	1996
Total	684,544	728,605	778,495	828,566	904,647	989,004	1,032,440
Violent offenses	313,600	339,500	370,300	395,700	429,100	464,200	487,900
Murder[a]	72,000	77,200	85,000	90,300	97,100	105,800	111,000
Manslaughter	13,200	13,100	14,100	14,800	15,400	16,500	16,700
Rape	24,500	25,500	29,500	31,300	34,000	37,100	38,600
Other sexual assault	39,100	43,000	46,400	49,800	54,400	58,500	62,300
Robbery	99,200	107,800	113,400	119,800	128,200	134,800	139,800
Assault	53,300	59,000	67,900	73,000	81,200	90,500	97,100
Other violent[b]	12,400	13,100	15,200	16,600	18,700	21,000	22,400
Property offenses	173,700	180,700	182,400	191,600	209,800	230,300	236,500
Burglary	87,200	90,300	90,400	93,600	100,700	107,500	109,500
Larceny	34,800	35,700	33,900	36,900	42,000	47,600	49,100
Motor vehicle theft	14,400	16,000	18,100	19,100	20,100	21,800	21,300
Fraud	20,200	20,400	20,100	21,300	23,600	26,200	27,400
Other property[c]	17,100	18,200	19,900	20,700	23,500	27,300	29,200
Drug offenses	148,600	155,200	172,300	183,200	202,600	225,200	234,100
Public-order offenses[d]	45,500	49,500	51,100	53,800	59,000	65,600	70,300
Other/unspecified[e]	3,100	2,900	3,100	4,400	4,100	3,700	3,600

Note: The offense distribution for yearend 1991 is based on data from the Survey of Inmates of State Correctional Facilities, conducted in August 1991. The offense distributions for other years are estimated using forward and backward stock-flow methods.
All estimates are based on the total number of prisoners in physical custody, including those with sentences of 1 year or less and those who were unsentenced. See definitions for the distinction between custody and jurisdiction counts. Due to rounding, detail may not sum to total.
[a]Includes nonnegligent manslaughter.
[b]Includes extortion, intimidation, criminal endangerment, and other violent offenses.
[c]Includes possession and selling of stolen property, destruction of property, trespassing, vandalism, criminal tampering, and other property offenses.
[d]Includes weapons, drunk driving, escape, court offenses, obstruction, commercialized vice, morals and decency charges, liquor law violations, and other public-order offenses.
[e]Includes juvenile offenses and unspecified felonies.

Source: *Correctional Populations in the United States, 1996*, Bureau of Justice Statistics, Washington, DC, 1999

percent) and hallucinogens (19 percent), while about 16.1 percent used heroin or opiates, 16.5 percent used depressants, and 7.7 percent used inhalants. (See Table 12.6.)

In 1997, the percentage (44.8 percent) of federal inmates reporting drug use in the month prior to committing their current offense was considerably higher than it had been in 1991 (31.8 percent). The use of marijuana or hashish (30.4 percent) during the month before the offense in 1997 increased significantly from 19.2 percent in 1991. The month-prior use of cocaine or crack also increased, rising from 15.4 percent in 1991 to 20 percent in 1997. Similarly, the use of

TABLE 12.3

Percent of prisoners in custody of State correctional authorities, by the most serious offense, 1990-96

Most serious offense	Percent of inmates in State prison						
	1990	1991	1992	1993	1994	1995	1996
Total	100%	100%	100%	100%	100%	100%	100%
Violent offenses	45.8%	46.6%	47.6%	47.8%	47.4%	46.9%	47.3%
Murder[a]	10.5	10.6	10.9	10.9	10.7	10.7	10.8
Manslaughter	1.9	1.8	1.8	1.8	1.7	1.7	1.6
Rape	3.6	3.5	3.8	3.8	3.8	3.8	3.7
Other sexual assault	5.7	5.9	6.0	6.0	6.0	5.9	6.0
Robbery	14.5	14.8	14.6	14.5	14.2	13.6	13.5
Assault	7.8	8.1	8.7	8.8	9.0	9.2	9.4
Other violent[b]	1.8	1.8	2.0	2.0	2.1	2.1	2.2
Property offenses	25.4%	24.8%	23.4%	23.1%	23.2%	23.3%	22.9%
Burglary	12.7	12.4	11.6	11.3	11.1	10.9	10.6
Larceny	5.1	4.9	4.4	4.5	4.6	4.8	4.8
Motor vehicle theft	2.1	2.2	2.3	2.3	2.2	2.2	2.1
Fraud	3.0	2.8	2.6	2.6	2.6	2.6	2.7
Other property[c]	2.5	2.5	2.6	2.5	2.6	2.8	2.8
Drug offenses	21.7%	21.3%	22.1%	22.1%	22.4%	22.8%	22.7%
Public-order offenses[d]	6.6%	6.8%	6.6%	6.5%	6.5%	6.6%	6.8%
Other/unspecified[e]	0.5%	0.4%	0.4%	0.5%	0.5%	0.4%	0.3%

Note: Offense distributions for yearend 1991 are based on data from the Survey of Inmates of State Correctional Facilities, conducted in August 1991. The offense distributions for other years are estimated using forward and backward stock-flow methods.
All estimates are based on the total number of prisoners in physical custody, including those with sentences of 1 year or less and those who were unsentenced. See definitions between custody and jurisdiction counts. Due to rounding, detail may not sum to total.
[a]Includes nonnegligent manslaughter.
[b]Includes extortion, intimidation, criminal endangerment, and other violent offenses.
[c]Includes possession and selling of stolen property, destruction of property, destruction of property, trespassing, vandalism, criminal tampering, and other property offenses.
[d]Includes weapons, drunk driving, escape, court offenses, obstruction, commercialized vice, morals and decency charges, liquor law violations, and other public-order offenses.
[e]Includes juvenile offenses and unspecified felonies.

Source: *Correctional Populations in the United States, 1996*, Bureau of Justice Statistics, Washington, DC, 1999

TABLE 12.4

Percent of sentenced prisoners admitted to State prisons, by the most serious offense, 1990-96

Most serious offense	Percent of new court commitments to State prisons[a]						
	1990	1991	1992	1993	1994	1995	1996
Total	100%	100%	100%	100%	100%	100%	100%
Violent offenses	26.8%	28.9%	28.6%	29.2%	29.3%	28.8%	29.5%
Murder[b]	2.7	3.0	2.9	3.0	3.1	2.9	2.8
Negligent manslaughter	1.2	1.3	1.2	1.3	1.2	1.2	1.1
Sexual assault[c]	5.5	5.6	5.7	6.0	6.1	5.9	6.0
Robbery	9.2	10.1	9.9	9.8	9.5	9.0	9.1
Aggravated assault	7.0	7.6	7.5	7.7	8.0	8.2	8.7
Other violent	1.3	1.4	1.3	1.4	1.6	1.6	1.8
Property offenses	32.3%	31.1%	31.2%	30.5%	29.6%	29.5%	29.0%
Burglary	14.5	13.5	13.3	12.9	12.4	11.9	12.0
Larceny/theft	8.1	8.0	8.1	8.0	7.7	7.8	7.5
Motor vehicle theft	2.6	2.4	2.5	2.4	2.4	2.4	2.1
Fraud	3.9	3.8	3.8	3.8	3.9	4.1	4.1
Other property	3.2	3.4	3.6	3.4	3.2	3.3	3.3
Drug offenses	31.7%	30.0%	30.4%	29.9%	30.2%	30.8%	30.2%
Public-order offenses	8.0%	8.9%	8.8%	9.3%	10.0%	10.2%	10.6%
Other	1.1%	1.1%	1.1%	1.1%	0.9%	0.7%	0.7%

Note: Data are from the National Corrections Reporting Program and are based on the most serious offense as reported by participating States. Data may not sum to total due to rounding.
[a]Includes only those with sentences of more than 1 year.
[b]Includes nonnegligent manslaughter.
[c]Includes rape and other sexual assault.

Source: *Correctional Populations in the United States, 1996*, Bureau of Justice Statistics, Washington, DC, 1999

157

depressants and stimulants in the month before committing the crime also rose between 1991 and 1997 (Table 12.6).

DRUG USE AT THE TIME OF THE MOST RECENT OFFENSE

One-third (32.6 percent) of state prisoners reported that they were under the influence of drugs when they committed their current offense. Prisoners incarcerated for drug offenses (41.9 percent) and property offenses (36.6 percent) reported the highest incidence of drug use at the time of the crime. Nearly 1 of 3 (29 percent) of violent offenders and 23.1 percent of public-order offenders were under the influence of drugs at the time of their current offense. The crimes most closely tied to drug influence were drug possession (42.6 percent), drug trafficking (41 percent), and robbery (39.9 percent). Prisoners who had committed manslaughter (17.4 percent) or sexual assault (21.5 percent) were least likely to be under the influence of drugs during the offense. (See Table 12.7.)

More than one-fifth (22.4 percent) of federal prisoners committed offenses while under the influence of drugs in 1997. One-fourth of drug offenders (25 percent) and violent offenders (24.5 percent) used drugs when committing the offense, as did 10.8 percent of property offenders. Those federal inmates imprisoned for murder (29.4 percent) and robbery (27.8 percent) were most likely to be under the influence of drug when committing their current offense (Table 12.7).

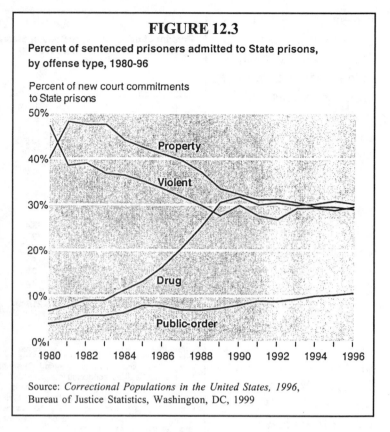

FIGURE 12.3

Percent of sentenced prisoners admitted to State prisons, by offense type, 1980-96

Percent of new court commitments to State prisons

Source: *Correctional Populations in the United States, 1996,* Bureau of Justice Statistics, Washington, DC, 1999

TABLE 12.5

Drug use of State prisoners, 1991 and 1997

Type of drug	Ever using drugs 1997	Ever using drugs 1991	Ever using drugs regularly[a] 1997	Ever using drugs regularly[a] 1991	Using drugs in the month before offense 1997	Using drugs in the month before offense 1991	Using drugs at the time of offense 1997	Using drugs at the time of offense 1991
Any drug[b]	83.0%	79.4%	69.6%	62.2%	56.5%	49.9%	32.6%	31.0%
Marijuana/hashish	77.0	73.8	58.3	51.9	39.2	32.2	15.1	11.4
Cocaine/crack	49.2	49.4	33.6	31.9	25.0	25.2	14.8	14.5
Heroin/opiates	24.5	25.2	15.0	15.3	9.2	9.6	5.6	5.8
Depressants[c]	23.7	24.0	11.3	10.8	5.1	3.8	1.8	1.0
Stimulants[d]	28.3	29.7	16.3	16.6	9.0	7.4	4.2	2.9
Hallucinogens[e]	28.7	26.9	11.3	11.5	4.0	3.7	1.8	1.6
Inhalants	14.4	--	5.4	--	1.0	--	--	--

Note: Detail adds to more than total because prisoners may have used more than one type of drug.
--Not reported.
[a]Used drugs at least once a week for at least a month.
[b]Other unspecified drugs are included in the totals.
[c]Includes barbiturates, tranquilizers, and Quaalude.
[d]Includes amphetamine and methamphetamine.
[e]Includes LSD and PCP.

Source: Christopher J. Mumola, *Substance Abuse and Treatment, State and Federal Prisoners, 1997,* Bureau of Justice Statistics, Washington, DC, 1999

TABLE 12.6

Drug use of Federal prisoners, 1991 and 1997

	Percent of Federal prisoners who reported —							
	Ever using drugs		Ever using drugs regularly[a]		Using drugs in the month before offense		Using drugs at the time of offense	
Type of drug	1997	1991	1997	1991	1997	1991	1997	1991
Any drug[b]	72.9%	60.1%	57.3%	42.1%	44.8%	31.8%	22.4%	16.8%
Marijuana/hashish	65.2	52.8	46.6	32.2	30.4	19.2	10.8	5.9
Cocaine/crack	44.8	37.3	28.2	20.6	20.0	15.4	9.3	7.7
Heroin/opiates	16.1	14.1	8.9	9.3	5.4	5.5	3.0	3.7
Depressants[c]	16.5	13.1	8.0	5.3	3.2	1.4	1.0	0.3
Stimulants[d]	20.9	16.8	12.9	8.3	7.6	3.9	4.1	1.8
Hallucinogens[e]	19.0	14.8	6.4	4.8	1.7	1.2	0.8	0.5
Inhalants	7.7	--	2.6	--	0.5	--	--	--

Note: Detail adds to more than total because prisoners may have used more than one type of drug.
--Not reported.
[a]Used drugs at least once a week for at least a month.

[b]Other unspecified drugs are included in the totals.
[c]Includes barbiturates, tranquilizers, and Quaalude.
[d]Includes amphetamine and methamphetamine.
[e]Includes LSD and PCP.

TABLE 12.7

Alcohol or drug use at time of offense of State and Federal prisoners, by type of offense, 1997

	Estimated number of prisoners[a]		Percent of prisoners who reported being under the influence at time of offense					
			Alcohol		Drugs		Alcohol or drugs	
Type of offense	State	Federal	State	Federal	State	Federal	State	Federal
Total	1,046,705	88,018	37.2%	20.4%	32.6%	22.4%	52.5%	34.0%
Violent offenses	494,349	13,021	41.7%	24.5%	29.0%	24.5%	51.9%	39.8%
Murder	122,435	1,288	44.6	38.7	26.8	29.4	52.4	52.4
Negligent manslaughter	16,592	53	52.0	. . .	17.4	. . .	56.0	. . .
Sexual assault[b]	89,328	713	40.0	32.3	21.5	7.9	45.2	32.3
Robbery	148,001	8,770	37.4	18.0	39.9	27.8	55.6	37.6
Assault	97,897	1,151	45.1	46.0	24.2	13.8	51.8	50.5
Other violent	20,096	1,046	39.6	32.2	29.0	15.9	48.2	37.2
Property offenses	230,177	5,964	34.5%	15.6%	36.6%	10.8%	53.2%	22.6%
Burglary	111,884	294	37.2	. . .	38.4	. . .	55.7	. . .
Larceny/theft	43,936	414	33.7	. . .	38.4	. . .	54.2	. . .
Motor vehicle theft	19,279	216	32.2	. . .	39.0	. . .	51.2	. . .
Fraud	28,102	4,283	25.2	10.4	30.5	6.5	42.8	14.5
Other property	26,976	757	36.0	22.8	30.6	16.4	53.2	34.6
Drug offenses	216,254	55,069	27.4%	19.8%	41.9%	25.0%	52.4%	34.6%
Possession	92,373	10,094	29.6	21.3	42.6	25.1	53.9	36.0
Trafficking	117,926	40,053	25.5	19.4	41.0	25.9	50.9	35.0
Other drug	5,955	4,922	29.9	19.7	47.1	17.1	59.2	29.0
Public-order offenses	103,344	13,026	43.2%	20.6%	23.1%	15.6%	56.2%	30.2%
Weapons	25,642	6,025	28.3	23.0	22.4	24.4	41.8	37.1
Other public-order	77,702	7,001	48.1	18.5	23.3	8.1	60.9	24.1

. . .Too few cases in the sample to permit calculation.
[a]Based on cases with valid offense data.
[b]Includes rape and other sexual assault.

Source of both tables: Christopher J. Mumola, *Substance Abuse and Treatment, State and Federal Prisoners, 1997*, Bureau of Justice Statistics, Washington, DC, 1999

Committing Crimes to Get Drug Money

In 1997, 19 percent of all state prison inmates and 16 percent of all federal prisoners claimed that they committed their current offense to get money for drugs. In 1991, 17 percent of state prisoners and 10 percent of federal prisoners cited drug money as the reason they committed their current offense.

CHARACTERISTICS OF DRUG USERS IN PRISON

Gender

In 1997, more than 8 of 10 (83 percent) of the nearly 1.15 million prisoners in state and federal prisons reported having ever used drugs. Nearly equal

159

percentages of men (82.9 percent) and women (84 percent) in state prisons had ever used drugs. Women in state prisons were somewhat more likely to have been regular drug users than men (73.6 and 69.3 percent, respectively). Women (62.4 percent) were also more likely than men (56.1 percent) to have used drugs in the month prior to the most recent offense. A higher proportion of women (40.4 percent) than men (32.1 percent) claimed to have been under the influence of drugs while committing the offense. (See Table 12.8.)

On the other hand, among federal prisoners, higher percentages of men reported drug use. More men (73.7 percent) than women (62.8 percent) ever used drugs in the past, and more men (58.1 percent) than women (47.2 percent) said they used drugs regularly. About 45.4 percent of the men and 36.7 percent of the women used drugs in the month prior to the offense. A higher percentage of men (22.7 percent) than women (19.3 percent) were under the influence of drugs when they committed their current offense. (See Table 12.8.)

Race/Ethnicity

Among state prisoners, there was little variance in drug use patterns across racial or ethnic groups. Similar percentages of non-Hispanic Whites (83.6 percent) and non-Hispanic Blacks (83.7 percent) reported past drug use, while 80.7 percent of Hispanics reported using drugs in the past. Slightly more Blacks (58.3 percent) than Whites (55.2 percent) and His-

TABLE 12.8

Levels of prior drug abuse, by selected characteristics
of State and Federal prisoners, 1997

| Characteristic | Estimated number of prisoners[a] | Percent of prisoners reporting use of drugs — | | | |
		Ever in the past	Used regularly[b]	In the month prior to offense	At the time of offense
All State prisoners	1,059,607	83.0%	69.6%	56.5%	32.6%
Sex					
Male	993,365	82.9%	69.3%	56.1%	32.1%
Female	66,242	84.0	73.6	62.4	40.4
Race/Hispanic origin					
White non-Hispanic	352,864	83.6%	70.5%	55.2%	33.9%
Black non-Hispanic	492,676	83.7	70.5	58.3	31.9
Hispanic	179,998	80.7	65.6	55.0	33.0
Other	34,069	79.0	66.7	52.7	27.8
Age					
24 or younger	209,343	84.1%	71.1%	63.2%	33.3%
25-34	404,034	86.4	72.9	60.0	35.0
35-44	311,999	86.3	73.4	56.5	34.5
45-54	103,470	70.5	55.2	40.4	22.7
55 or older	30,761	39.0	24.3	18.4	9.7
All Federal prisoners	89,072	72.9%	57.3%	44.8%	22.4%
Sex					
Male	82,646	73.7%	58.1%	45.4%	22.7%
Female	6,426	62.8	47.2	36.7	19.3
Race/Hispanic origin					
White non-Hispanic	26,616	77.2%	63.5%	49.4%	28.6%
Black non-Hispanic	33,697	77.5	61.9	47.2	22.2
Hispanic	24,349	63.5	45.5	37.5	16.9
Other	4,411	64.2	50.0	38.5	18.1
Age					
24 or younger	7,933	80.4%	65.4%	57.2%	28.1%
25-34	32,634	76.0	60.6	48.5	23.0
35-44	27,259	77.2	60.6	46.8	24.7
45-54	14,501	67.6	52.5	35.2	18.8
55 or older	6,746	43.6	28.6	24.3	11.8

[a]Based on probability of selection in the sample and adjusted to June 30, 1997, custody counts.
[b]Regular use is defined as once a week or more for at least a month.

Source: Christopher J. Mumola, *Substance Abuse and Treatment, State and Federal Prisoners, 1997*, Bureau of Justice Statistics, Washington, DC, 1999

panics (55 percent) used drugs in the month prior to the offense. About one-third of each group claimed to have been under the influence of drugs at the time the offense was committed. (See Table 12.8.)

In federal prisons, higher proportions of non-Hispanic Whites (77.2 percent) and non-Hispanic Blacks (77.5 percent) reported ever using drugs in the past than did Hispanics (63.5 percent). Similarly, more non-Hispanic Whites (63.5 percent) and non-Hispanic Blacks (61.9 percent) used drugs regularly than did

Hispanics (45.5 percent). A higher percentage of non-Hispanic Whites (28.6 percent) were under the influence of drugs when committing their current offense than were non-Hispanic Blacks (22.2 percent) and Hispanics (16.9 percent). (See Table 12.8.)

Age

Inmates who were less than 45 years of age in state (87 percent) and federal (76 percent) prisons reported similar levels of drug use, and their incidence of drug use was higher than that of older prisoners. Over 80 percent of state prisoners under the age of 45 reported some prior drug use, compared to about 55 percent of those ages 45 and older. About one-third of state prisoners under age 45 claimed they committed their offense while on drugs, compared to one-fifth of those 45 and older. In federal prisons, about half of inmates under age 45 had used drugs in the month prior to their offense, compared to about one-third of older prisoners. (See Table 12.8.)

ALCOHOL

The Bureau of Justice Statistics (BJS), in *Substance Abuse and Treatment, State and Federal Prisoners, 1997* (Washington, DC, 1999), found that assault, murder, and sexual

TABLE 12.9
Number of positive CAGE responses for State and Federal prisoners, by type of offense, 1997

| Type of offense | Estimated number of prisoners | Percent of prisoners, by the number of positive CAGE responses | | | |
		1 or more	2 or more	3 or more	4
All State prisoners	1,046,705	46.3%	35.1%	24.4%	12.2%
Violent	494,349	46.5%	35.4%	24.2%	11.7%
Property	230,177	47.9	37.6	27.3	14.7
Drug	216,254	40.9	28.1	19.1	9.0
Public-order	103,344	55.6	43.4	31.0	16.1
All Federal prisoners	88,018	34.9%	24.8%	16.3%	7.3%
Violent	13,021	40.5%	27.8%	18.8%	9.4%
Property	5,964	30.4	21.2	15.0	6.6
Drug	55,069	33.5	23.8	15.6	6.5
Public-order	13,026	36.9	26.7	17.1	8.7

TABLE 12.10
Levels of prior alcohol abuse, by selected characteristics of State and Federal prisoners, 1997

| Characteristic | Estimated number of prisoners* | Percent of prisoners reporting prior alcohol abuse | | |
		Ever had a "binge drinking" experience	Under the influence of alcohol at the time of offense	3 or more positive CAGE responses
All State prisoners	1,059,607	41.0%	37.2%	24.4%
Sex				
Male	993,365	41.8%	37.7%	24.5%
Female	66,242	29.9	29.1	23.4
Race/Hispanic origin				
White non-Hispanic	352,864	53.5%	42.7%	33.5%
Black non-Hispanic	492,676	31.9	33.0	18.6
Hispanic	179,998	39.9	36.7	22.0
Other	34,069	49.6	41.7	27.7
Age				
24 or younger	209,343	40.2%	30.7%	15.8%
25-34	404,034	42.3	37.7	24.8
35-44	311,999	42.3	41.3	28.6
45-54	103,470	37.4	37.7	28.5
55 or older	30,761	29.3	30.2	22.5
All Federal prisoners	89,072	30.3%	20.4%	16.2%
Sex				
Male	82,646	31.2%	20.9%	16.6%
Female	6,426	18.8	15.1	11.6
Race/Hispanic origin				
White non-Hispanic	26,616	38.3%	22.1%	19.3%
Black non-Hispanic	33,697	25.0	21.1	12.5
Hispanic	24,349	28.2	16.8	17.8
Other	4,411	34.9	26.0	17.6
Age				
24 or younger	7,933	31.8%	18.4%	12.0%
25-34	32,634	32.1	22.5	15.3
35-44	27,259	30.8	20.5	17.2
45-54	14,501	29.1	20.2	19.7
55 or older	6,746	20.8	13.4	14.5

*Based on probability of selection in the sample and adjusted to June 30, 1997, custody counts.

Source of both tables: Christopher J. Mumola, *Substance Abuse and Treatment, State and Federal Prisoners, 1997*, Bureau of Justice Statistics, Washington, DC, 1999

TABLE 12.11

Substance abuse treatment history of State and Federal prisoners, by reported prior substance abuse, 1997

| | Percent of prisoners | | | | | |
| | Total | | Alcohol- or drug-involved prisoners | | Under the influence of alcohol or drugs at the time of offense | |
Type of treatment	State	Federal	State	Federal	State	Federal
Ever in any treatment or programs	56.4%	46.4%	64.8%	51.4%	69.3%	66.1%
Any treatment	34.5	24.6	41.5	27.7	46.3	40.6%
Other alcohol/drug programs	43.1	35.4	49.4	39.2	52.5	50.8
Participated while under correctional supervision	47.8%	39.2%	55.2%	43.5%	59.2%	55.8%
Any treatment	26.2	18.9	31.7	21.3	35.5	30.4
In prison/jail	19.7	15.0	23.9	16.9	27.0	24.6
On probation/parole	15.0	8.4	18.3	9.6	20.6	14.6
Other alcohol/drug programs	37.5	30.9	43.2	34.4	46.2	44.9
In prison/jail	33.3	27.4	38.3	30.5	41.0	40.6
On probation/parole	17.2	10.1	20.5	11.4	22.6	16.1
Participated since admission	32.5%	28.2%	37.7%	31.6%	41.1%	42.7%
Any treatment	12.0	10.4	14.6	11.7	16.7	17.4
Residential facility or unit	6.9	7.3	8.5	8.2	10.1	12.4
Counseling by a professional	5.1	3.8	6.2	4.3	6.9	6.3
Detoxification unit	0.8	0.2	1.0	0.2	1.3	0.3
Maintenance drug	0.2	0.2	0.3	0.2	0.3	0.2
Other alcohol/drug programs	27.5	23.1	31.9	26.0	34.6	35.2
Self-help group/peer counseling	22.7	11.2	26.7	12.8	29.3	20.5
Education program	12.6	16.8	14.8	18.8	16.2	24.2
Estimated number of prisoners	1,047,933	87,839	806,758	73,103	543,869	29,468

Note: Detail adds to more than total because prisoners may have participated in more than one type of treatment program.

Source: Christopher J. Mumola, *Substance Abuse and Treatment, State and Federal Prisoners, 1997*, Bureau of Justice Statistics, Washington, DC, 1999

---

assault were the offenses most closely tied to alcohol use at the time of the offense. In 1997, one-third (37.2 percent) of state and one-fifth (20.4 percent) of federal inmates claimed to have been under the influence of alcohol at the time they committed their current offense. Among state inmates, 43.2 percent of public-order offenders and 41.7 percent of violent offenders were drinking at the time of the offense, followed by 34.5 percent of property offenders and 27.4 percent of drug offenders. More than half (52 percent) of negligent manslaughter crimes were committed while under the influence of alcohol (generally driving while

---

TABLE 12.12

Drug treatment of State and Federal prisoners since admission, by levels of prior drug use, 1991 and 1997

	Estimated number of prisoners, 1997		Percent of prisoners reporting participation							
			Drug treatment since admission				Other drug abuse program since admission			
			State		Federal		State		Federal	
Level of prior drug use	State	Federal	1997	1991	1997	1991	1997	1991	1997	1991
All prisoners	1,048,752	87,720	9.7%	24.5%	9.2%	15.7%	20.3%	15.5%	20.0%	10.1%
Prisoners who used drugs										
Ever	870,558	63,979	11.5%	31.1%	12.4%	26.3%	24.0%	19.6%	26.0%	16.9%
Regularly*	729,578	50,244	13.1	33.9	14.5	30.9	26.4	22.2	29.6	20.1
In the month before offense	592,611	39,275	14.6	36.5	15.4	33.7	28.3	23.7	31.7	22.0
At the time of offense	338,481	19,507	18.0	41.0	18.9	39.4	32.2	27.2	38.0	25.4

*Regular use is defined as once a week for at least a month.

Source: Christopher J. Mumola, *Substance Abuse and Treatment, State and Federal Prisoners, 1997*, Bureau of Justice Statistics, Washington, DC, 1999

intoxicated that resulted in a death), as were 48.1 percent of "other public-order" offenses. Fewer fraud (25.2 percent) and drug trafficking (25.5 percent) offenses were committed while the offender was inebriated. (See Table 12.7.)

Among federal prisoners, 24.5 percent of violent offenses were committed while under the influence of alcohol, as were 20.6 percent of public-order offenses, 19.8 percent of drug offenses, and 15.6 percent of property offenses. Nearly half (46 percent) of assault offenses were committed while the perpetrator was drinking, as were 38.7 percent of murders. However, only 10.4 percent of fraud offenses and 18 percent of robbery offenses were committed while the perpetrator was drinking. (See Table 12.7.)

According to the CAGE* diagnostic questionnaire, 24.4 percent of state prisoners reported experiences consistent with a history of alcohol abuse or dependence (at least three positive responses). The incidence of alcohol abuse among state prisoners varied somewhat by offense type. A larger proportion of public-order offenders (31 percent) responded positively to the CAGE questionnaire, followed by property offenders (27.3 percent), and violent offenders (24.2 percent). Drug offenders (19.1 percent) were the least likely to have a positive response to the CAGE questionnaire. (See Table 12.9.) It is important to remember when reading these statistics that alcoholics and drug abusers tend to lie about (underestimate) their drinking and drug use.

CHARACTERISTICS OF ALCOHOL USE AMONG PRISONERS

Gender

Previous alcohol abuse was most common among White male prisoners. Among state prisoners, males (41.8 percent) were more likely than females (29.9 percent) to report binge drinking. In addition, males (37.7 percent) were more likely than females (29.1 percent) to claim to have been under the influence of alcohol at the time of their current offense. However, similar proportions of males (24.5 percent) and females (23.4 percent) fit the CAGE profile of alcohol dependence. (See Table 12.10.)

Similarly, among federal prisoners, a higher percentage of men (31.2 percent) than women (18.8 percent) said they had experienced binge drinking, and a higher percentage of men (20.9 percent) than women (15.1 percent) admitted being under the influence of alcohol when committing their current offense. However, men (16.6 percent) in federal prison were more likely than women (11.6 percent) to have met the CAGE criteria for alcohol dependence. (See Table 12.10.)

Race/Ethnicity

Non-Hispanic Whites reported the highest levels of alcohol abuse among state prisoners. More non-Hispanic Whites (53.5 percent) than non-Hispanic Blacks (31.9 percent) or Hispanics (39.9 percent) reported ever having had a binge drinking experience. A higher percentage of non-Hispanic Whites (42.7 percent) than non-Hispanic Blacks (33 percent) or Hispanics (36.7 percent) claimed to have been under the influence of alcohol when they committed their current offense. One-third (33.5 percent) of non-Hispanic Whites reported positive responses on the CAGE questionnaire, compared to 18.6 percent of non-Hispanic Blacks and 22 percent of Hispanics. (See Table 12.10.)

Non-Hispanic White federal inmates reported the highest percentage of binge drinking (38.3 percent), followed by Hispanics (28.2 percent) and non-Hispanic Blacks (25 percent). However, there was little variance by race or ethnicity among federal prisoners

---

*A CAGE questionnaire is a diagnostic device used to detect a person's history of alcohol abuse or dependence. CAGE is an acronym for the four questions asked on the questionnaire — attempts to (C)ut back on drinking, (A)nnoyance at others' criticism of one's drinking, feelings of (G)uilt about drinking, and needing a drink first thing in the morning as an (E)ye opener to steady the nerves. The set of questions determines a person's likelihood of alcohol abuse by the number of positive responses to these four questions.

who reported being intoxicated when committing their offense. (See Table 12.10.)

Age

Age differences played a very small role in prior alcohol abuse or dependence for either state or federal inmates. Among state prisoners, similar percentages of those between the ages of 25 and 54 reported comparable incidences of binge drinking, being under the influence of alcohol when committing the current crime, and fitting the CAGE profile. The same held true for federal prisoners. (See Table 12.10.)

DRUG AND ALCOHOL TREATMENT

State Prisoners

Only one-third (34.5 percent) of state inmates reported that they had participated in any alcohol or drug abuse treatment (including time spent in a residential facility, professional counseling, detoxification, or use of a maintenance drug) in the past. Since being admitted to prison, 12 percent of state prisoners had participated in the same types of drug or alcohol treatment. Two-fifths (43.1 percent) of state detainees reported past participation in other alcohol or drug abuse programs, including self-help groups, peer counseling, and education/awareness programs. Of these, one-fourth (27.5 percent) of state inmates participated in these programs since their most recent admittance to prison. A little more than half (56.4 percent) of state inmates had taken part in either substance abuse treatment or other alcohol and drug programs in the past. One-third (32.5 percent) of state prisoners began treatment after admission to prison. (See Table 12.11.)

Federal Prisoners

Among federal prisoners, one-fourth (24.6 percent) reported that they had participated in any alcohol or drug abuse treatment (including time spent in a residential facility, professional counseling, detoxification, or use of a maintenance drug) in the past. Since being admitted to prison, 10.4 percent of federal prisoners had participated in the same types of drug or alcohol treatment. One-third (35.4 percent) of federal inmates reported past participation in other alcohol or drug abuse programs, including self-help groups, peer counseling, and education/awareness programs. Of these, one-fourth (23.1 percent) of federal inmates participated in such programs since their most recent admittance to prison. Slightly less than half (46.4 percent) of federal prisoners had taken part in either substance abuse treatment or other alcohol and drug programs in the past. More than one-fourth (28.2 percent) of federal detainees began treatment after admission to prison. (See Table 12.11.)

Less Participation in Drug Treatment Since 1991

Between 1991 and 1997, the percentage of both state and federal inmates who reported being treated for drug abuse after admission to prison dropped. In

TABLE 12.13

Types of alcohol treatment received by State prisoners since admission, by prior alcohol use, 1997

| | Percent of State prisoners |
| | Prisoners' reported prior alcohol abuse |
Type of alcohol treatment or program since admission	Committed offense under the influence of alcohol
Any treatment or program	38.8%
Treatment	14.4%
Residential facility or unit	8.7
Professional counseling	6.3
Detoxification unit	1.0
Maintenance drug	0.1
Other programs	33.7%
Self-help group/peer counseling	28.8
Education	15.6
Estimated number of State prisoners	387,137

*Binge drinking is defined as having consumed in a day as much as a fifth of liquor, equivalent to 20 drinks, 3 bottles of wine, or 3 six-packs of beer.

Source: Christopher J. Mumola, *Substance Abuse and Treatment, State and Federal Prisoners, 1997*, Bureau of Justice Statistics, Washington, DC, 1999

164

1991, 24.5 percent of state prisoners received drug treatment after being admitted to prison; in 1997, only 9.7 percent reported receiving drug treatment. Of federal prisoners, in 1991, 15.7 reported treatment since being admitted to prison; in 1997, 9.2 reported receiving treatment. (See Table 12.12.)

Since 1991, fewer prisoners using drugs in the past reported treatment after admission to prison. In 1991, of those prisoners using drugs in the month before the current offense, 36.5 percent of state prisoners and 33.7 percent of federal prisoners reported receiving treatment. By 1997, only 14.6 percent of state prisoners and 15.4 percent of federal prisoners reported receiving help. In 1991, 41 percent of state prisoners and 39.4 percent of federal prisoners using drugs at the time they committed their current offense reported receiving drug treatment while in prison. By 1997, only 18 percent of state and 18.9 percent of federal prisoners who had used drugs when they committed their current offense were receiving treatment. (See Table 12.12.)

Increased Participation in Other Programs Since 1991

On the other hand, enrollment in other drug abuse programs, such as self-help or peer groups and drug education classes, rose between 1991 and 1997. These are cheaper programs for the authorities because they do not require professionals to run them. In 1997, 20.3 percent of state inmates and 20 percent of federal inmates reported taking part in drug abuse programs during their current prison term, up from 1991, when 15.5 percent of state prisoners and 10.1 percent of federal prisoners had participated in such programs (Table 12.12).

In 1997, of those using drugs in the month prior to committing their current offense, 28.3 percent of state and 31.7 percent of federal prisoners were enrolled in substance abuse programs, compared to the 1991 figures of 23.7 percent of state prisoners and 22 percent of federal prisoners. In 1997, 32.2 percent of state prisoners and 38 percent of federal prisoners who were using drugs at the time of their current offense were taking part in drug abuse programs. The proportions of prisoners enrolled in those programs in 1991 were lower, with 27.2 percent of state and 25.4 percent of federal prisoners participating. (See Table 12.12.)

Participation in Alcohol Abuse Programs

State prisoners who had abused alcohol were less apt to report participation in alcohol treatment than in other abuse programs. More state prisoners who committed their offense while under the influence of alcohol enrolled in self-help or peer groups (28.8 percent) and education classes (15.6 percent) after admission to prison. Fewer state prisoners participated in residential treatment (8.7 percent) or professional counseling programs (6.3 percent). (See Table 12.13.)

Federal prisoners who had histories of alcohol abuse also reported greater enrollment in alcohol abuse programs than in treatment. About one-fifth (19.3 percent) of federal prisoners who had committed their

TABLE 12.14

Types of alcohol treatment received by Federal prisoners since admission, by prior alcohol use, 1997

Type of alcohol treatment or program since admission	Percent of Federal prisoners — Prisoners' reported prior alcohol abuse — Committed offense under the influence of alcohol
Any treatment or program	36.0%
Treatment	13.8%
Residential facility or unit	9.6
Professional counseling	4.9
Detoxification unit	0.4
Maintenance drug	0.1
Other programs	30.5%
Self-help group/peer counseling	17.8
Education	19.3
Estimated number of Federal prisoners	17,829

*Binge drinking is defined as having consumed in a day as much as a fifth of liquor, equivalent to 20 drinks, 3 bottles of wine, or 3 six-packs of beer.

Source: Christopher J. Mumola, *Substance Abuse and Treatment, State and Federal Prisoners, 1997*, Bureau of Justice Statistics, Washington, DC, 1999

current offense while drinking enrolled in alcohol education classes and self-help or peer groups (17.8 percent) after incarceration, while 9.6 percent participated in residential treatment and 4.9 percent sought professional counseling. (See Table 12.14.)

Both types of programs are available to prisoners. The data do not specify whether the prisoners choose the type of help they get or whether they take whatever is available to them at the time they enroll.

CHARACTERISTICS OF PRISONERS RECEIVING TREATMENT

Gender

Among state prisoners involved with drugs or alcohol, women (55.6 percent) were more likely than men (40.5 percent) to have ever been treated for substance abuse. In addition, women (19.6 percent) were more likely than men (14.2 percent) to have been treated since being admitted to prison. However, equal proportions of men (49.4 percent) and women (49.3 percent) reported ever participating in a substance abuse program in the past, and 31.9 percent of each reported participation since being admitted to prison. (See Table 12.15.)

Percentages were much closer for federal prisoners involved with drugs or alcohol. Better than 1 of 4 women (28.8 percent) and men (27.6 percent) reported ever being treated for substance abuse, and approximately 1 of 8 women (13.3 percent) and men (11.6 percent) reported being treated since being admitted to prison. One-fourth of women (25.2 percent) and men (26.1 percent) participated in other substance abuse pro-

grams since their admission to prison, but women (34.2 percent) were less likely than men (39.6 percent) to have ever participated in a substance abuse program in the past. (See Table 12.16.)

Race/Ethnicity

In state prisons, non-Hispanic White inmates (51.8 percent) were more likely than non-Hispanic Black (36.6 percent) or Hispanic (33.8 percent) inmates to have ever received treatment for substance abuse. Non-Hispanic White detainees (17 percent) were somewhat more likely than non-Hispanic Black (13.5 percent) or Hispanic (12.5 percent) prisoners to have been treated for substance abuse since being incarcerated. Similarly, non-Hispanic White inmates (58 percent) were more likely than non-Hispanic Black (46.7 percent) or Hispanic (39.2 percent) inmates in state prisons to have ever participated in other substance abuse programs. In addition, non-Hispanic White prisoners (36.3 percent) were more likely than non-Hispanic Black (31.6 percent) or Hispanic (23.9 percent) prisoners to have taken part in other substance abuse programs since admission to prison (Table 12.15).

TABLE 12.15

Alcohol- or drug-involved State prisoners treated for substance abuse, by selected characteristics, 1997

| Characteristic | Estimated number of State prisoners | Percent of alcohol- or drug-involved State prisoners reporting — | | | |
| | | Treatment for substance abuse | | Participation in other substance abuse programs | |
		Ever	Since admission	Ever	Since admission
Total	806,758	41.5%	14.6%	49.4%	31.9%
Sex					
Male	754,418	40.5%	14.2%	49.4%	31.9%
Female	52,340	55.6	19.6	49.3	31.9
Race/Hispanic origin					
White non-Hispanic	271,345	51.8%	17.0%	58.0%	36.3%
Black non-Hispanic	367,331	36.6	13.5	46.7	31.6
Hispanic	142,610	33.8	12.5	39.2	23.9
Other	25,472	46.2	16.2	54.2	34.8
Age					
24 or younger	158,705	29.3%	10.2%	37.9%	22.6%
25-34	316,744	43.1	15.2	50.2	33.1
35-44	242,579	47.4	16.8	54.4	35.5
45-54	71,936	42.4	14.9	53.9	35.5
55 or older	16,794	36.7	10.1	52.4	31.8

Source: Christopher J. Mumola, *Substance Abuse and Treatment, State and Federal Prisoners, 1997*, Bureau of Justice Statistics, Washington, DC, 1999

As with state prisoners, non-Hispanic White inmates (39.5 percent) in federal prison were more likely to have received treatment for substance abuse than non-Hispanic Blacks (25.7 percent) or Hispanic (19 percent) inmates. A larger proportion of non-Hispanic Whites (16 percent) also reported receiving treatment since being admitted to federal prison than non-Hispanic Blacks (11.9 percent) or Hispanics (8.2 percent). Similarly, non-Hispanic Whites (51.6 percent) were more likely than non-Hispanic Blacks (39 percent) or Hispanics (28.1 percent) to have ever taken part in other substance abuse programs. In addition, non-Hispanic Whites (34.9 percent) were more likely than non-Hispanic Blacks (25 percent) or Hispanics (18.5 percent) to have participated in other substance abuse programs after being admitted to prison. (See Table 12.16.)

Age

Age did not seem to matter. About 2 of 5 state prisoners between the ages of 25 and 54 reported ever receiving treatment for substance abuse. Approximately 1 of 6 had received treatment since admittance. About one-half of state prisoners between the ages of 25 and 54 reported ever taking part in other substance

abuse programs, and one-third said they had participated in other substance abuse programs since entering prison. (State inmates older than 54 and younger than 25 reported lower incidences of participation in substance abuse treatment or other programs.) (See Table 12.15.)

As with state prisoners, the rate of treatment for federal inmates varied little by age. About 3 of 10 of prisoners between the ages of 25 and 54 reported ever receiving treatment for substance abuse, and approximately 1 of 8 in each age group had received treatment since being admitted to prison. About two-fifths of federal prisoners between the ages of 25 and 54 said they had taken part in other substance abuse programs, and one-fourth reported participating in other substance abuse programs since being admitted to prison. (As with state inmates, federal prisoners older than 54 or younger than 25 reported lower rates of participation in substance abuse treatment or other substance abuse programs.) (See Table 12.16.)

TREATMENT PROGRAMS

Drug treatment programs in prisons began in the 1930s at federal institutions in Lexington, Kentucky, and Fort Worth, Texas. Many have been ineffective and poorly run. In 1997, according to the Criminal Justice Institute, only about 14 percent of inmates participated in drug programs. The *New York Times* reported that, although 1 of 6 inmates receives some kind of treatment, only about 2 percent have the kind of serious rehabilitation that changes the inmates' behavior for a lifetime. Most are "just say no" types of treatment programs that last for several weeks. Most of the

TABLE 12.16

Alcohol- or drug-involved Federal prisoners treated for substance abuse, by selected characteristics, 1997

Characteristic	Estimated number of Federal prisoners	Percent of alcohol- or drug-involved Federal prisoners reporting —			
		Treatment for substance abuse		Participation in other substance abuse programs	
		Ever	Since admission	Ever	Since admission
Total	73,103	27.7%	11.7%	39.2%	26.0%
Sex					
Male	67,856	27.6%	11.6%	39.6%	26.1%
Female	5,247	28.8	13.3	34.2	25.2
Race/Hispanic origin					
White non-Hispanic	20,178	39.5%	16.0%	51.6%	34.9%
Black non-Hispanic	28,514	25.7	11.9	39.0	25.0
Hispanic	21,185	19.0	8.2	28.1	18.5
Other	3,225	29.1	7.3	38.5	29.1
Age					
24 or younger	6,736	21.8%	8.1%	35.2%	24.0%
25-34	27,500	27.3	12.5	39.2	26.4
35-44	22,634	30.2	12.6	41.9	27.6
45-54	11,074	32.8	13.7	40.8	26.8
55 or older	5,159	15.0	4.5	29.5	17.7

Source: Christopher J. Mumola, *Substance Abuse and Treatment, State and Federal Prisoners, 1997*, Bureau of Justice Statistics, Washington, DC, 1999

participants are rearrested after release.

The most effective programs take many months but reduce the rearrest rate considerably. A study in California (*Controlling Cocaine: Supply Versus Demand Programs*, Peter Rydell and Susan Everingham, RAND Corporation, Santa Monica, California, 1994) showed that for every $1.00 spent on effective drug treatment, the state saved $7.00 in costs of crime and imprisonment. States that had established serious drug treatment programs, such as New York and Texas, have been cutting back due to budget constraints.

Drug treatment advocates say that drug treatment programs have fallen victim to prison expansion. According to Richard Rosenfeld, a professor of criminology at the University of Missouri at St. Louis, "What is particularly tragic is that drug treatment in prison has proven to be effective as an anti-crime program.... This is an unintended consequence of prison expansion. Each time we spend a dollar on building a new prison or expanding an existing one, it is one less dollar for drug treatment." In January 1999, President Bill Clinton announced that he would propose $215 million in his next budget for testing and treating prisoners for drug use. Approximately $115 million is currently budgeted for fighting drug use by prisoners, parolees, and probationers.

In 1995, Joseph Califano, head of the National Center on Addiction and Substance Abuse (CASA) at Columbia University, commented that "The average American thinks we've got guys in jail like the ones Jimmy Cagney and Humphrey Bogart played in the 1930s. In reality, the prisons are wall to wall with alcohol and drug abusers and the mentally ill. They're not hardened criminals; they're people who can change. But they can't change without help."

Not all inmates participate in the programs offered. Inmates may refuse to participate or may have already completed the program. Inmates may not qualify —

TABLE 12.17

Arrest rates of Stay'n Out TC participants are lower

Arrest Rate

	Stay'n Out TC	Milieu Therapy	Counseling	No Treatment
Males	26.9%	34.6%	39.8%	40.9%
Females	17.8%	(this type of treatment not offered)	29.2%	23.7%

Source: "Prison-Based Therapeutic Communities: Their Success with Drug-Abusing Offenders," *NIJ Journal*, National Institute of Justice, February 1996

they may be too new to the institution or not close enough to the end of their sentence or they may be rule breakers, under administrative segregation, or in the wrong custody level. Facilities may also keep some slots open to gain flexibility to deal with unexpected situations.

Therapeutic Community

The most effective treatment for inmates is provided in a therapeutic community (TC). TCs typically house clients in residential settings that offer opportunities for intensive intervention and support that may not be available in out-patient care. As applied to corrections, clients live isolated from the rest of the prison population and receive treatment to change negative patterns of behavior, thinking, and feeling that predispose them to drug use. Participation generally lasts for an extended period. The time and the isolation are primary resources; the isolation shields clients from competing demands of street, work, friends, and family.

TCs offer other features, including the use of ex-offenders and ex-addicts as staff, use of confrontations and support groups, and a set of rules and sanctions to govern behavior. In prisons, TCs also focus on criminal behavior, sex abuse, and other issues. It may be this multiple focus that explains why TCs are more likely to be successful in the long run than programs aimed mainly at drug abuse. Treatment for drug abusers in jails is more limited than in prisons, in part because inmates stay there for less time.

168

Evaluations of TC Programs

The Stay'n Out prison-based TC program was begun in New York in 1977 by recovered addicts who were also ex-offenders. The program successfully reduced recidivism for both men and women. Program participants had a significantly lower rearrest rate than those receiving no treatment and those receiving all other types of treatment. (See Table 12.17.)

The main conclusion of the evaluation was that hard-core drug abusers who remain in the prison-based TC longer were much more likely to succeed than those who left earlier. As time participating in TC treatment increased, recidivism declined. Male and female clients did significantly better on parole if they remained in the program 9 to 12 months rather than terminating earlier or later. (See Table 12.18.)

Two evaluation studies produced similar results. A three-year follow up evaluation of an Oregon program (Cornerstone) found that 71 percent of the graduates stayed out of prison, while only 26 percent of the dropouts of the program did. A second evaluation also showed that a much higher percentage of graduates (75 percent) stayed out of prison than did dropouts (37 percent). The longer the time in treatment, the less likely the inmate was to be rearrested.

The Amity Prison TC program (California), established in 1989, lasts 12 months and provides an aftercare (any community program aimed at helping those released from prisons or residential care) in a community-based TC. A study of the California program found that while 63 percent of a control group was reincarcerated within a year after parole, only 26 percent of those who completed the program plus the aftercare were reincarcerated.

Key-Crest (Delaware) also showed success in keeping participants drug-free and arrest-free. The program has a primary stage of 12-month intensive residential treatment (Key). The second phase consists of inmates nearing release working outside the institution while spending nonwork time in the setting of the TC (Crest). Inmates who participated in both phases tended to be more successful than others in staying drug- and arrest-free. (See Table 12.19.)

A Sound Investment

According to the National Institute of Justice (NIJ), the programs are cost-effective. Programs such as Stay'n Out cost about $3,000 to $4,000 more than the standard correctional cost per inmate per year, and programs such as Cornerstone cost a little over twice as much because they have a higher number of professional staff members and lighter caseloads. However, the savings in crime-related and drug-use associated costs pay for the treatment in about two to three years. NIJ concludes that treatment lowers crime and health costs, as well as related social and criminal justice costs.

TABLE 12.18

Favorable outcomes for parolees increase as amount of time in Stay'n Out program increases

Time in Stay'n Out

Successfully Discharged From Parole	Less than 3 months	3–6 months	6–9 months	9–12 months	More than 12 months
Males	49.2%	58.0%	62.0%	77.3%	57.0%
Females	79.0%	NA	NA	92.0%	77.0%

Source: "Prison-Based Therapeutic Communities: Their Success with Drug-Abusing Offenders," *NIJ Journal*, National Institute of Justice, February 1996

The greater the investment in rehabilitating the most severe offender-addicts, the greater the probable impact. These studies have shown that chronic heroin and cocaine users (about 3 to 10 percent of all offenders) who commit a large percentage of crimes are responsive to TC treatment if it continues long enough. The studies also showed TCs are effective with diverse locales and populations.

TABLE 12.19

Participants in Key-Crest tended to remain drug-free and arrest-free longer

After 6 Months	Key-Crest	Crest Only	Key Only	HIV Education
Drug-free	94%	84%	54%	38%
Arrest-free	92%	85%	82%	62%
After 18 Months	Key-Crest	Crest Only	Key Only	HIV Education
Drug-free	75%	46%	34%	17%
Arrest-free	72%	60%	46%	36%

Source: "Prison-Based Therapeutic Communities: Their Success with Drug-Abusing Offenders," *NIJ Journal*, National Institute of Justice, February 1996

AMOUNT OF DRUG TRAFFICKING IN PRISON

Many inmates claim that drugs are easily attainable in prison, while prison administrators maintain that the inmates are exaggerating. James Flateau, a spokesperson for the New York State Department of Correctional Services, in a *New York Times* interview, denied the "widespread availability" of drugs. However, he continued, "unless you searched everyone going in and out, kept all packages out, and locked all inmates in their cells for 24 hours a day, you're going to have contraband."

Indeed, the price of drugs in the barter economy of prisons is the equivalent of 3 to 10 times the street price, indicating a smaller supply. Bobby Lewis, a senior security specialist with the Federal Bureau of Prisons, declared in a *New York Times* interview, that denial of the drug trade in prison is a "public relations gimmick. If a warden acknowledges he has a drug problem, he's going to pay a terrible price," so most present their prisons as places where drugs are kept out.

Probably the only prison without heavy drug trafficking is the federal maximum security prison at Marion, Illinois, where inmates are locked in their cells most of the day and visitors are separated by a glass window. A normal visitation day in a Washington, DC, prison has 80 prisoners sitting in the room with two or three visitors each. Prolonged hugging and kissing can cover up exchanges of drugs. Even with searches of both the inmates and the visitors, the presence of drugs can go undetected.

According to some prisoners, with mandatory sentencing sending more nonviolent people to prison for longer periods of time, many inmates take up drugs because they wish to deaden themselves to the boredom and discouragement they face and to the often hostile, violent environment. In addition, with more and more inmates in prison for possessing and trading in drugs, there is a ready market.

Drug Sweeps

According to the National Criminal Justice Association (*Justice Bulletin*, vol. 16, no. 4, April 1996), more states are staging surprise lock-downs and raids to stem the amount of drugs in their prisons. For example, on October 24, 1995, more than 600 corrections officers conducted a cell-by-cell raid and strip search at the prison in Graterford, Pennsylvania, the nation's fifth largest state prison. The search turned up more than 200 weapons and several hundred dollars in cash, but only a very small amount of drugs. Officials assumed that once the raid began, the inmates either flushed drugs down the toilets or swallowed them.

170

A similar raid at the Muskegon Correctional Facility in Michigan was conducted after the inmates at the facility tested at a rate of 6 percent for positive use of drugs, compared to the statewide average of 3.8 percent. The search found two alcohol stills, two to three ounces of cocaine and heroin, and about one ounce of marijuana, as well as basic prison-made weapons.

SMOKING

More and more correctional institutions have banned smoking within the facilities. For example, more than 13 of 62 New York counties have prohibited or announced their intention to prohibit smoking in their jails. In neighboring Connecticut, 14 of the state's 27 prisons ban smoking; the rest operate at least one nonsmoking housing unit. In New Jersey's 12 adult prisons, inmates cannot smoke if their cellmates are nonsmokers.

Death row inmates in California and Texas are not allowed to smoke, even before their executions. Larry Todd, a spokesperson for the Department of Criminal Justice in Texas, in a *New York Times* interview, maintained that nicotine was just another drug. "We wouldn't give them a shot of whisky or cocaine so I doubt we'd give them a cigarette," he declared.

Many inmates and guards oppose the smoking bans, asserting that cigarettes soothe their nerves in a highly stressful atmosphere. Meanwhile, the black-market price of cigarettes has soared, with individual cigarettes selling for as much as $3.00 and a single puff for $1.00. Some inmates have requested smoking and nonsmoking facilities.

While corrections departments know that it is difficult to curtail the smoking habit among inmates, many have enacted no-smoking policies because of a growing number of complaints and fears of lawsuits from nonsmoking prisoners and guards who worry about the health risks of secondhand smoke. In 1993, in *Helling v. McKinney* (509 U.S. 25), the Supreme Court held that inmates have a constitutional right under the Eighth Amendment's protection against cruel and unusual punishment not to be exposed to cellmates' tobacco smoke if the exposure creates an extreme health hazard.

At the end of 1996, the Third Court of Appeals in Texas rejected a prisoner's arguments that prisoners' rights were violated when Texas banned smoking in prisons in 1995. According to the opinion, in order to assert a claim under either constitution (federal or state), the complainant was required to establish that the alleged wrongful action interfered with a protected right. "Neither the state nor the federal constitution protects a citizen's interest in smoking."

In a similar case in 1994, a federal judge issued an injunction to limit smoking in the District of Columbia's Lorton Correctional Complex in Lorton, Virginia, as the staff had failed to enforce the policy of only allowing smoking in certain areas. The judge ruled that "the effect of this lack of enforcement is particularly harsh on those prisoners with pre-existing medical conditions," and that "deliberate indifference exists where a prison official 'knows of and disregards an excessive risk to inmate health and safety' " (*Farmer v. Brennan*, 1511 U.S. 825, 1994).

Jails and prisons also come under many new ordinances prohibiting smoking in public buildings. In Westchester County, New York, for example, the county jail bans smoking to comply with a county order prohibiting smoking in county buildings.

CHAPTER XIII

PRISONERS' RIGHTS — COURT DECISIONS AND RELATED LAWS

He is for the time being the slave of the state. — Ruffin v. Commonwealth, 1871

Simply because prison inmates retain certain constitutional rights does not mean that these rights are not subject to restrictions and limitations. — Bell v. Wolfish, 1979

Prisoners do not shed all constitutional rights at the prison gate. — Sandin v. Conner, 1995

NO RIGHTS

Until the 1960s, the courts took little notice of prisoners' rights. Prisoners fell under the jurisdiction of the executive departments of federal, state, and local governments. In 1871, a Virginia court, in *Ruffin v. Commonwealth* (62, Va. 790, 1871), commented that a prisoner "has, as a consequence of his crime, not only forfeited his liberty, but all his personal rights except those which the law in its humanity accords to him. He is for the time being the slave of the state."

Eighty years later, in *Stroud v. Swope* (187 F. 2d. 850, 9th Circuit, 1951), a federal circuit judge asserted that "we think it well settled that it is not the function of the courts to superintend the treatment and discipline of persons in penitentiaries, but only to deliver from imprisonment those who are illegally confined." Correctional administrators considered that prisoners lost all constitutional rights after conviction, that the prison staff knew what should be done for the prisoner, and that prisoners had privileges, not rights, that could be taken away arbitrarily (William C. Collins, *Legal Responsibility and Authority of Correctional Officers*, American Correctional Association, Laurel, Maryland, 1982).

PRISONERS HAVE RIGHTS

In the 1960s, not only did women and minorities demand civil rights and protesters march against the

Vietnam War, but prisoners insisted that they, too, needed the protection of the courts. Indeed, in 1964, the Supreme Court changed its position of noninterference in the prison system to one of involvement. In *Cooper v. Pate* (378 U.S. 546), the Supreme Court ruled that the Civil Rights Act of 1871 (42 United States Code 1983) granted protection to prisoners. The law states that

> Every person who, under color of any statute, ordinance, regulation, custom, or usage, of any State or Territory or the District of Columbia, subjects, or causes to be subjected, any citizen of the United States or other person within the jurisdiction thereof to the deprivation of any rights, privileges, or immunities secured by the Constitution and laws, shall be liable to the party injured in an action at law, suit in equity, or other proper proceeding for redress.

With the *Cooper* decision, the Supreme Court announced that prisoners had rights guaranteed by the Constitution and could ask the judicial system for help in challenging the conditions of their imprisonment. (Cases brought under this law are called Section 1983 lawsuits. One in every 10 civil lawsuits in U.S. District Courts is a Section 1983 lawsuit.) Between 1966 and 1992, prisoners' suits in federal courts skyrocketed from 218 to 26,824 (Figure 13.1). Since then, laws have been passed making it harder for prisoners to sue.

Observers differ about the nature of the lawsuits, how the federal courts process them, and the manner in which they are resolved. Many consider some of the lawsuits frivolous and not warranting the scarce resources of federal courts. Others think that some lawsuits have merit, but that the federal courts tend to treat all Section 1983 lawsuits in an assembly line fashion with little or no individual attention.

Nonetheless, despite different opinions about this substantial body of litigation, there is very little systematic data on which to draw conclusions and to inform Congress of policy recommendations (*Challenging the Conditions of Prisons and Jails: A Report on Section 1983 Litigation*, Bureau of Justice Statistics, Washington, DC, 1995).

FIGURE 13.1
National trends in the number of state prisoners and Section 1983 lawsuits

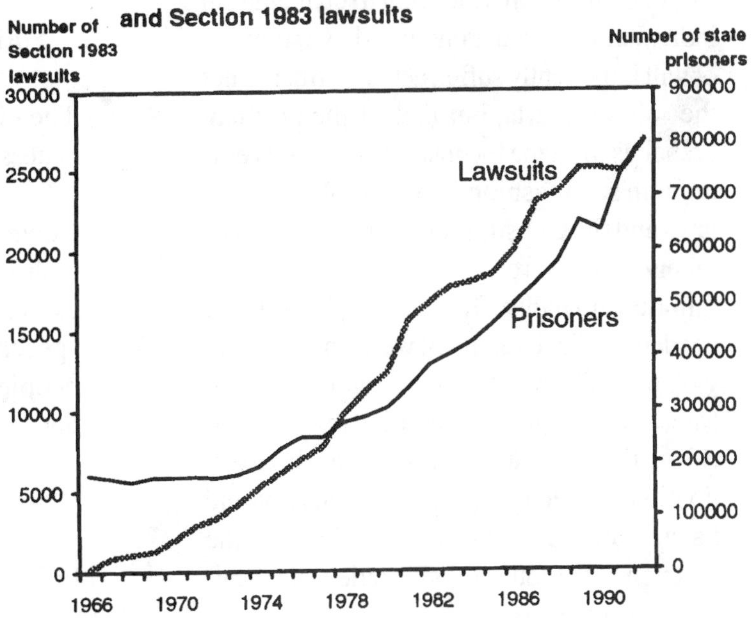

Source: *Challenging the Conditions of Prisons and Jails: A Report on Section 1983 Litigation*, Bureau of Justice Statistics, Washington, DC, 1995

ACCESS TO THE COURTS

In *Johnson v. Avery* (393 U.S. 483, 1969), the Supreme Court emphasized the basic purpose of the writ of *habeas corpus* (petitions) in enabling those unlawfully imprisoned to obtain their freedom. The justices asserted that "it is fundamental that access of prisoners to the courts for the purpose of presenting their complaints may not be denied or obstructed." In this case, the High Court ruled that, until the state provides some reasonable alternative to assist inmates in the preparation of petitions for post-conviction relief, it "may not validly enforce a regulation which absolutely bars inmates from furnishing such assistance to other prisoners."

The state interest in preserving discipline did not outweigh the rights of the prisoners to be able to file petitions. The High Court had already ruled that states could not deny a writ of *habeas corpus* to prisoners who could not pay a filing fee (*Smith v. Bennett*, 365 U.S. 708, 1961). Furthermore, a state must furnish prisoners not otherwise able to obtain one with a transcript of prior hearings (*Long v. District Court*, 385 U.S. 192, 1966). In *Bounds v. Smith* (430 U.S. 817,

1977), the Court further asserted that prison authorities must "assist inmates in the preparation and filing of meaningful legal papers by providing prisoners with adequate law libraries or adequate assistance from persons trained in the law."

Inmates of various prisons operated by the Arizona Department of Corrections (ADOC) alleged that ADOC officials were furnishing them with inadequate legal research facilities and thereby depriving them of their right of access to the courts, in violation of *Bounds v. Smith*. In *Samuel A. Lewis, Director, Arizona Department of Corrections, et al., Petitioners v. Fletcher Casey, Jr., et al* (64 LW 4587, 1996), the court held in favor of the correctional department as the inmates failed to show widespread actual injury.

Bounds did not create an abstract, free-standing right to a law library or legal assistance; rather it acknowledged the right of access to the courts. Inmates have to prove that the alleged shortcomings in the prison library or legal assistance program hindered their efforts to pursue a non-frivolous legal claim. In addition, the Court relied on a constitutional principle that prevents courts of law from undertaking tasks assigned to the political branches.... It is the role of courts to provide relief to claimants, in individual or class actions, who have suffered, or will imminently suffer, actual harm; it is not the role of courts, but that of the political branches to shape the institutions of government in such fashion as to comply with the laws and the Constitution.... If — to take another example from prison life — a healthy inmate who had suffered no deprivation of needed medical treatment were able to claim violation of his constitutional right to medical care,... simply on the ground that prison medical facilities were inadequate, the essential distinction between judge and executive would have disappeared: it would have become the function of the courts to assure adequate medical care in prisons.

Bounds did not guarantee prison law libraries and legal assistance programs. They are only "one constitutionally acceptable method to assure meaningful access to the courts." There can be "alternative means to achieve that goal." The inmate has to show that his access to the courts was so "stymied by inadequacies of the law library that he was unable even to file a complaint."

FOURTEENTH AMENDMENT

Prisoners bring their cases to the federal courts by accusing the prison systems of violating the First, Fourth, and Eighth Amendments (see below for definitions) and the due process clauses of the Fifth and Fourteenth Amendments of the U.S. Constitution. The Fifth Amendment provides that "no person" should "be deprived of life, liberty, or property" by the federal government "without due process of the law [legal proceedings]."

The Fourteenth Amendment states that no state should "deprive any person of life, liberty, or property without due process of law." Through a series of court cases, the Supreme Court has ruled that the Fourteenth Amendment insures that the rights guaranteed to the people by the Bill of Rights, which applied originally only to the federal government, cannot be taken away by state governments. The following sections describe some prisoner rights cases.

FIRST AMENDMENT CASES

The First Amendment of the U.S. Constitution guarantees that

Congress shall make no law respecting an establishment of religion, or prohibiting the free exercise thereof; or abridging the freedom of speech, or of the press; or the right of the people peaceably to assemble; and to petition the government for a redress of grievances.

Censorship

In *Procunier v. Martinez* (416 U.S. 396, 1973), the Supreme Court ruled that prison officials cannot censor inmate correspondence unless they

show that a regulation authorizing mail censorship furthers one or more of the substantial governmental interests of security, order, and rehabilitation. Second, the limitation of First Amendment freedom must be no greater than is necessary or essential to the protection of the particular governmental interest involved.

Prison officials can refuse to send letters that detail escape plans or encoded messages but cannot censor inmate correspondence simply to "eliminate unflattering or unwelcome opinions or factually inaccurate statements." Because prisoners retain rights, when "a prison regulation or practice offends a fundamental constitutional guarantee, federal courts will discharge their duty to protect constitutional rights."

However, the Court recognized that it was "ill-equipped to deal with the increasingly urgent problems of prison administration." Running a prison takes expertise and planning, all of which, said the Court, is part of the responsibility of the legislative and executive branches. The task of the judiciary, on the other hand, is to establish a standard of review for prisoners' constitutional claims that is responsive to both the need to protect inmates' rights and the policy of judicial restraint.

174

In 1974 (*Pell v. Procunier*, 417 U.S. 817), the High Court held that federal prison officials could prohibit inmates having face-to-face media interviews. The Court reasoned that judgments regarding prison security "are peculiarly within the province and professional expertise of corrections officials, and in the absence of substantial evidence in the record to indicate that the officials have exaggerated their response to these considerations, courts should ordinarily defer to their expert judgement in such matters." Prisoners had other means in which to communicate with the media.

In 1985, in *Nolan v. Fitzpatrick* (451 F. 2d 545), the First Circuit Court ruled that inmates had the right to correspond with newspapers. The prisoners were limited only in that they could not write about escape plans or include contraband material in their letters.

The Missouri Division of Corrections permitted correspondence between immediate family members who were inmates at different institutions and between inmates writing about legal matters, but allowed other inmate correspondence only if each prisoner's "classification/treatment team" thought it was in the best interests of the parties.

Another Missouri regulation permitted an inmate to marry only with the superintendent's permission, which can be given only when there were "compelling reasons" to do so, such as a pregnancy. In *Turner v. Safley* (482 U.S. 78, 1987), the Supreme Court found the first regulation constitutional and the second one unconstitutional.

The court held that the "constitutional right of prisoners to marry is impermissibly burdened by the Missouri marriage regulation." The Supreme Court had ruled earlier that prisoners had a constitutionally protected right to marry (*Zablocki v. Redhail*, 434 U.S. 374, 1977), subject to restrictions due to incarceration, such as time and place and prior approval of a warden. However, the Missouri regulation practically banned all marriages.

The findings in *Turner v. Safley* have become a guide for prison regulations in America. The High Court observed that

When a prison regulation impinges on inmates' constitutional rights, the regulation is valid if it is reasonably related to legitimate penological interests.... First, there must be a "valid, rational connection" between the prison regulation and the legitimate government interest put forward to justify it.... Moreover, the government objective must be a legitimate and neutral one.... A second factor relevant in determining the reasonableness of a prison restriction ... is whether there are alternative means of exercising the right (sic) that remain open to prison inmates. A third consideration is the impact accommodation of the asserted constitutional right will have on guards and other inmates, and on the allocation of prison resources generally.

Religious Beliefs

While inmates retain their First Amendment freedom to practice their religions, the courts have upheld restrictions on religious freedom when the corrections department needs to maintain security, when economic considerations are involved, and when the regulation is reasonable.

The legal definition of religion is not limited to mainstream faiths. The judiciary ruled that witchcraft qualifies as a religion, although the courts did not recognize an inmate-created sect called Church of the New Song, whose faith required them to be "served steak and wine from time to time." While prisoners have not brought any suits against correctional institutions for violating their freedom of beliefs, several have challenged prison authorities for prohibiting religious practices.

Religious Services

In general, the courts have ruled that inmates have the right to practice their beliefs, subject to restrictions that correctional officials deem necessary for the safe running of the prison. The correctional administrators cannot arbitrarily prohibit practices of an established religion unless it can prove the customs create "a clear and present danger" to the operation of the facility.

175

The District of Columbia jail allowed, at public expense, interdenominational services, as well as services by Catholics, Jews, Protestants, Unitarians, the Salvation Army, and other religious groups. Public funds paid for Protestant and Catholic chaplains and for religious medals. An honorarium was paid to a rabbi when needed.

Several times in 1959, a group of Muslims requested permission to hold religious services. The Director of Corrections of the District of Columbia, Donald Clemmer, refused the requests because of his belief that "Muslims teach racial hatred." The director also confiscated a religious medal from the petitioner William Fulwood because Clemmer thought the medal was symbolic of a doctrine of hate and wearing it would promote racial tension in the prison. The jail administration also did not allow Fulwood to correspond with Elijah Muhammad, the leader of the Black Muslims, or subscribe to the Los Angeles *Herald Dispatch* because it carried a column by Elijah Muhammad.

In 1962, the U.S. District Court of the District of Columbia (*Fulwood v. Clemmer*, 206 F. Supp 370) ruled that by allowing some religious groups to hold religious services and by conducting such services at public expense while denying that right to Muslims, the jail officials had discriminated against the Muslim inmates. These acts violated "the Order of the Commissioners of the District of Columbia No. 6514-B, dated Nov. 25, 1953, which requires prison officials to make facilities available without regard to race or religion."

The court held the same opinion on the distribution and wearing of religious medals. However, on the issue of correspondence and the newspaper subscription, the court stated that the judiciary "lacked general supervisory powers over prisons, and in absence of ... abuse of discretion by prison officials, courts should not interfere."

In 1972, in *Cruz v. Beto* (405 U.S. 319), Fred A. Cruz, a Buddhist serving in a Texas prison, claimed that, while other prisoners were allowed use of the prison chapel, prison officials refused Buddhists the right to hold religious services. For sharing religious materials with other prisoners, Cruz was placed in solitary confinement on a diet of bread and water for two weeks.

The court stated that prison officials are "accorded latitude in the administration of prison affairs, and prisoners necessarily are subject to appropriate rules and regulations." However, prisoners have the right to petition the government for "redress of grievances," and the federal courts, while they do not "sit" to supervise prisons, must "enforce constitutional rights of all 'persons,' including prisoners." The court concluded that "reasonable opportunities must be afforded to all prisoners to exercise the religious freedom guaranteed by the First and Fourteenth Amendments without fear of penalty."

A 5 to 4 split Supreme Court, in *O'Lone v. Shabazz* (482 U.S. 340, 1987), declared that "state prison officials acted in a reasonable manner" and were not violating First Amendment freedoms when they did not allow inmates who were members of the Islamic faith to attend religious services held on Friday afternoons. "Prison policies were related to legitimate security and rehabilitative concerns, alternative means of exercising religious faith with respect to other practices were available, and placing Islamic prisoners into work groups so as to permit them to exercise religious rights would have adverse impact" on the running of the prison.

In the opinion of the four dissenters, however, when

exercise of the asserted right is not presumptively dangerous ... and where the prison has completely deprived an inmate of that right, then prison officials must show that "a particular restriction is necessary to further an important governmental interest...." The prison in this case has completely prevented respondent inmates from attending the central religious service of their Moslem faith....

The State has neither demonstrated that the restriction is necessary to further an important objective nor proved that less extreme measures may not serve its purpose.... If a Catholic prisoner were prevented from attending Mass on Sunday, few would regard that deprivation as anything but absolute even if the prisoner were afforded other opportunities to pray, to discuss the Catholic faith with others, and even to avoid eating meat on Friday if there were a preference.

Food

Courts have ordered pork-free diets for groups whose religion forbids their eating pork, although they must make up a significant portion of the inmate population. However, pork does not have to be eliminated from the menu if a sufficient variety of other foods are offered.

In addition, there are limits to what a prison administration can be expected to do. In *Benjamin v. Coughlin* (708 F. Suppl. 570, 1989), a federal court in New York upheld the refusal of the New York Department of Correctional Services to meet the dietary conditions requested by the Rastafarians, a religion with origins in Jamaica.

Depending on the sect of the religion, the group wanted no meats, no canned foods or dairy products, no food that had been grown with non-organic pesticides or fertilizers, and food cooked in natural materials, such as clay pots. The court ruled that meeting the demands would overburden the prison system both administratively and financially.

Religious Jewelry

In 1996, the U.S. 7th Circuit Court of Appeals, in *Sasnett v. Sullivan* (91 F.3d 1018), held that, under the Religious Freedom Restoration Act, the Wisconsin prison system could not prevent inmates from wearing religious jewelry. Prison officials had banned such items, arguing that they could be used as weapons. However, while the prison administrators had banned jewelry, they had not prevented inmates from having rosary beads, which could be used to strangle someone. The court concluded that "the burden of justification is on the state and it has not been carried."

Hair and Dress

Michael G. Gallahan, a Cherokee Indian, practiced his religious beliefs, including having worn long hair since age five. Tenets of his religion recognized hair as a "sense organ" and taught that loss of hair was equated to losing part of the body. Prison officials had established hair-length regulations because of the belief that long hair was a convenient place for hiding weapons, could obscure facial identification, and could cause sanitary problems.

In *Gallahan v. Hollyfield* (516 F. 2d 1004, 1981), a U.S. District Court in Virginia ruled "a prisoner is not stripped of all rights on incarceration; specifically, he retains those First Amendment rights that are not inconsistent with his status as a prisoner or with the legitimate penological objectives of the corrections system." The judges found that Gallahan "established a sincere belief in his religion" and that the state's reasons were "insufficient" to enforce the hair-length regulation, especially since Gallahan had agreed to wear his hair tied back in a ponytail.

On the other hand, a 1992 appellate court decision, in *Scott v. Mississippi Department of Corrections* (961 F.2d 77), upheld haircut rules in a case involving a Rastafarian hairstyle. The court maintained that

it is not for us to impose our own ideas about prison management upon those who attempt the reasonable regulation of that nearly impossible task... [T]he loss of absolute freedom of religious expression is but one sacrifice required by ... incarceration.

The Sixth Circuit Court of Appeals, in *Abdullah v. Kinnison,* (769 F. 2d 345, 1985), ruled that a prison directive requiring practicing Muslims to keep white prayer robes in the institutional chapel, rather than in cells, was justified by security reasons and did not violate the First Amendment.

12-Step Programs

As a precondition to his continued participation in a family reunion program, David Griffin had been re-

177

quired to participate in a substance abuse program modeled after Alcoholics Anonymous (A.A.), which makes references to "God" and a "Higher Power." He claimed that the requirement to participate in such a program violated his right to practice atheism under the First Amendment.

In 1996, the New York Court of Appeals, the state's highest court, in *Griffin v. Coughlin* (NY CtApp, No 73), concluded that

> use of A.A. by the state correctional system as an essential component of an exclusive compulsory attendance ... program violates the Establishment clause.... Here, the state has exercised coercive power to advance religion by denying benefits of eligibility for the family reunion program to atheist and agnostic inmates who object and refuse to participate in religious activity.... No secular drug and alcohol addiction treatment program devoid of A.A.'s practices and doctrines is offered as a substitute.

The dissenters thought that although the 12-step program may be perceived as

> somewhat religious, [it] remains overwhelmingly secular in philosophy, objective, and operation.... The inmate was not compelled to participate in the ... program. He voluntarily chose the course of action that placed his agnosticism and non-beliefs at risk because he wished to receive something he is not unqualifiably entitled to from the state.

FOURTH AMENDMENT

The Fourth Amendment guarantees the "right of the people to be secure ... against unreasonable searches and seizures ... and no warrants shall issue, but upon probable cause...." The courts have not been as active in protecting prisoners under the Fourth Amendment as under the First and Eighth Amendments. In *Bell v. Wolfish* (441 U.S. 520, 1979, see below), the Supreme Court asserted that

> simply because prison inmates retain certain constitutional rights does not mean that these rights are not subject to restrictions and limitations.... Maintaining institutional security and preserving internal order and discipline are essential goals that may require limiting or retraction of the retained constitutional rights of both convicted prisoners and pretrial detainees. Since problems that arise in the day-to-day operation of a corrections facility are not susceptible to easy solutions, prison administrators should be accorded wide-ranging deference in the adoption and execution of policies and practices that in their judgment are needed to preserve internal order and discipline and to maintain institutional security.

Based on this reasoning, the High Court ruled that body searches did not violate the Fourth Amendment. "Balancing the significant and legitimate security interest of the institution against the inmates' privacy interest, such searches can be conducted on less than probable cause and are not unreasonable."

In another Fourth Amendment case (*Hudson v. Palmer*, 46 U.S. 517, 1984), the Supreme Court upheld the right of prison officials to search a prisoner's cell and seize property.

> The recognition of privacy rights for prisoners in their individual cells simply cannot be reconciled with the concept of incarceration and the needs and objectives of penal institutions.... [However, the fact that a prisoner does not have a reasonable expectation of privacy] does not mean he is without a remedy for calculated harassment unrelated to prison needs. Nor does it mean that prison attendants can ride roughshod over inmates' property rights with impunity. The Eighth Amendment always stands as a protection against "cruel and unusual punishments."

Prisoners can sue for loss of their personal property. Also, to protect privacy, a federal court, in *Lee v. Downs* (641 F. 2d 1117, 1981), ruled that the prison staff must be of the same sex to supervise inmates during bathing or strip searches.

EIGHTH AMENDMENT

The Eighth Amendment guarantees that "cruel and unusual punishment [not be] inflicted." The Eighth Amendment has been used in cases involving overcrowding of prisons and the failure of prison officials to provide minimal conditions for health and protection from assault by other prisoners. The Supreme Court has established several tests to determine whether conditions or actions violated the Eighth Amendment:

- Did the actions or conditions offend concepts of "decency and human dignity and precepts of civilization which Americans profess to possess"?

- Was it "disproportionate to the offense"?

- Did it violate "fundamental standards of good conscience and fairness"?

- Was the punishment unnecessarily cruel?

- Did the punishment go beyond legitimate penal purposes?

Isolation Cells

In *Holt v. Sarver* (300 F. Supp 82, 1969), a U.S. district court in Arkansas found "solitary confinement or close confinement in isolation units of prisons not unconstitutional per se, but, depending on circumstances, it may violate the Eighth and Fourteenth Amendments." Isolation cells in an Arkansas prison were used for prisoners who broke rules, those who needed protective custody to protect them from other inmates, and those who were

general escape or security risks or who were awaiting trial on additional charges.... Confinement in isolation cells was not "solitary confinement" in the conventional sense of the term. On the contrary, the cells are substantially overcrowded.... The average number of

men confined in a single cell seems to be four, but at times the number has been much higher (up to ten and eleven).

While the judges agreed that "if confinement of that type is to serve any useful purpose, it must be rigorous, uncomfortable, and unpleasant. However, there are limits to the rigor and discomfort of close confinement which a State may not Constitutionally exceed."

The court found that the confinement of inmates in these isolation cells, which were "overcrowded, dirty, unsanitary, and pervaded by bad odors from toilets, constituted cruel and unusual punishment." The court also asserted that "prolonged confinement" of numbers of men in the same cell under unsanitary, dangerous conditions was "mentally and emotionally traumatic as well as physically uncomfortable. It is hazardous to health. It is degrading and debasing; it offends modern sensibilities, and, in the Court's estimation, amounts to cruel and unusual punishment."

In addition, those inmates who were not in isolation slept together in barracks where many of the inmates had weapons and attacked each other. While the court recognized that assaults, fights, and killings occurred in all penal institutions, the Arkansas Farm had not taken reasonable precautions. Prisoners should at least be "able to fall asleep at night without fear of having their throats cut before morning, and the State has failed to discharge a constitutional duty in failing to take steps to enable them to do so."

Punitive Isolation

In the 1970s, Arkansas sentenced inmates to punitive isolation in extremely small cells for an indeterminate period of time, with their status being reviewed at the end of each fourteen-day period. While most were released within fourteen days, many remained in that status for weeks or months, depending upon their attitudes, as appraised by prison personnel. Usually the inmates shared a cell with one other inmate, and at times three or four were together, causing them to sleep on the floor. Considering that these were violent men, filled with "frustration and hostility," and that some were

179

"dangerous and psychopaths," confining them together caused threatening situations that produced "a forcible response from prison personnel."

The lower courts found that the force used by the guards was excessive and declared that "confinement of prisoners in punitive isolation for more than 30 days constituted cruel and unusual punishment and was impermissible." In *Finney v. Hutto* (548 F. 2d. 740, 1977), the United States Court of Appeals agreed.

Medical Care

Deliberate Indifference

On November 9, 1973, J. W. Gamble, an inmate of the Texas Department of Corrections, was injured while performing a prison work assignment. Although he complained numerous times about his back injury and was given pills, the guards accused him of malingering. In January, the disciplinary committee placed Gamble in solitary confinement for refusing to work. On February 4, he asked to see a doctor for chest pains and blackouts. Almost twelve hours later, a medical assistant saw him and had him hospitalized.

The next morning, after an electrocardiogram, he was placed on Quinidine for treatment of irregular cardiac rhythm and moved to administrative segregation. On February 7, after experiencing pain in his chest, left arm, and back, Gamble asked to see a doctor and was refused. The next day he was refused again. After finally seeing the doctor again on February 9 and given Quinidine, Gamble swore out a complaint that the staff had "subjected him to cruel and unusual punishment in violation of the Eighth Amendment, made applicable to the States by the Fourteenth."

In past decisions, the Court had concluded that "deliberate indifference to serious medical needs of prisoners constitutes the 'unnecessary and wanton infliction of pain' " (*Gregg v. Georgia,* 428 U.S. 153, 1976). This is true whether the indifference is displayed by prison doctors in their response to the prisoner's need or by prison guards who deny or delay access to treatment or interfere with the treatment. However, in *Estelle v. Gamble* (429 U.S. 97, 1976), the Supreme Court ruled that "every claim by a prisoner that he has not received adequate medical treatment" does not mean a violation of the Eighth Amendment.

An "inadvertent failure to provide adequate medical care" is not "an unnecessary and wanton infliction of pain" or "repugnant to the conscience of mankind.... Medical malpractice does not become a constitutional violation merely because the victim is a prisoner." Only deliberate indifference "can offend 'evolving standards of decency' in violation of the Eighth Amendment." Because Gamble saw medical personnel 17 times over three months, the court did not find this a violation of the Eighth Amendment. "A medical decision not to order an X-ray or like measures does not represent cruel and unusual punishment."

Future Consequences

In *Helling v. McKinney* (509 U.S. 25, 1993), the Court ruled that a Nevada inmate had the right to bring a court action because he had been assigned to a cell with another prisoner who smoked five packs of cigarettes daily, and he had not been informed of the health hazards that he could incur by bunking with a heavy smoker. Quoting its earlier decision in *DeShaney v. Winnebago County Dept. of Social Services* (489 U.S. 189, 1989), the Court declared

[W]hen the State takes a person into its custody and holds him there against his will, the Constitution imposes upon it a corresponding duty to assume some responsibility for his safety and general well being.... The rationale for this principle is simple enough: when the State by the affirmative exercise of its power so restrains an individual's liberty that it renders him unable to care for himself, and, at the same time fails to provide for his basic human needs — e.g., food, clothing, shelter, medical care, and reasonable safety — it transgresses the substantive limits on state action set by the Eighth Amendment.

The justices asserted that prison administrators could not

ignore a condition of confinement that is sure or very likely to cause serious illness and needless suffering the next week or month or year. In *Hutto v. Finney* (437 U.S. 678, 1978), we noted that inmates in punitive isolation were crowded into cells and that some of them had infectious maladies such as hepatitis and venereal disease. This was one of the prison conditions for which the Eighth Amendment required a remedy, even though it was not alleged that the likely harm would occur immediately and even though the possible infection might not affect all of those exposed.... Nor can we hold that prison officials may be deliberately indifferent to the exposure of inmates to a serious, communicable disease on the ground that the complaining inmate shows no serious current symptoms.

The Supreme Court sent the case back to the district court for retrial, where McKinney had to prove his allegations to show that the Eighth Amendment was violated and that "society considers the risk that the prisoner complains of to be so grave that it violates contemporary standards of decency to expose anyone unwillingly to such a risk." However, in 1992, the director of the Nevada State Prisons had adopted a smoking policy restricting smoking to specified areas, which made McKinney's case virtually moot (a hypothetical case — only cases involving real injury can be considered by the courts).

Indifference Must Be Deliberate

In *Wilson v. Seiter* (501 U.S. 294, 1991), the Supreme Court upheld the judgment that prisoners "claiming that conditions of confinement constituted cruel and unusual punishment were required to show deliberate indifference on the part of prison officials." In *Estelle v. Gamble*, the court had established that the Eighth Amendment could be applied to some "deprivations that were not specifically part of the sentence but were suffered during imprisonment."

However, the High Court emphasized that the prison staff had to "possess a sufficiently culpable state of mind." The court explained that "if the pain inflicted is not formally meted out as punishment by the statute or the sentencing judge, some mental element must be attributed to the inflicting officer before it can qualify" as a violation of the Eighth Amendment.

Guards Assaulting Prisoners

In 1983, Keith Hudson, an inmate at the state penitentiary in Angola, Louisiana, argued with Jack McMillian, a guard, who placed the inmate in handcuffs and shackles to take him to the administrative lockdown area. On the way there, Hudson testified that McMillian punched him in the mouth, eyes, chest, and stomach. Another guard held him, and the supervisor on duty watched. Hudson sued, accusing the guards of cruel and unusual punishment.

A magistrate found that the guards used "force when there was no need to do so" and the supervisor allowed their conduct, thus violating the Eighth Amendment. The Court of Appeals for the Fifth Circuit, however, reversed the decision, ruling that

inmates alleging use of excessive force in violation of the Eighth Amendment must prove: (1) significant injury; (2) resulting 'directly and only from the use of force that was clearly excessive to the need'; (3) the excessiveness of which was objectively unreasonable; and (4) that the action constituted an unnecessary and wanton infliction of pain.

The court agreed that the use of force was unreasonable and was a clearly excessive and unnecessary infliction of pain. However, the Court of Appeals found against Hudson because his injuries were "minor" and "required no medical attention."

The Supreme Court, in *Hudson v. McMillian* (503 U.S. 1, 1992), disagreed that the inmate had to suffer serious injury. In *Whitney v. Albers* (475 U.S. 372, 1986), the court had earlier ruled that guards, during prison disturbances or riots, must balance the need "to maintain or restore discipline" through force against the risk of injury to inmates. Those situations require prison officials "to act quickly and decisively" and allow guards and administrators leeway in their actions.

Under the *Whitney* decision, the "extent of injury suffered by an inmate is one factor" considered to determine whether the use of force was unnecessary. However, the absence of serious injury, while "relevant ... does not end" the Eighth Amendment inquiry. The question must be asked whether the force applied was a "good faith effort to maintain or restore discipline, or maliciously and sadistically to cause harm." Although the circuit court termed the blows "minor," the Supreme Court viewed the extent of Hudson's injuries as no basis to dismiss his claims.

Private Officer Liability

Ronnie McKnight was a prisoner at the South Central Correctional Center (SCCC) in Tennessee. The Corrections Corporation of America (CCA) had a contract with Tennessee to operate some of its correctional facilities, including the SCCC. Under 42 U.S.C. Section 1983, McKnight sued two of CCA's correctional officers, Daryll Richardson and John Walker, for allegedly violating his Eighth Amendment constitutional right to be free from cruel and unusual punishment by holding him in restraints while transporting him to another prison. McKnight claimed that the restraints caused him serious medical injury requiring hospitalization, that Richardson and Walker ignored his protests, and that they ridiculed him after he complained about the restraints.

The two correctional officers filed a motion to dismiss the complaint on the grounds that they were entitled to qualified immunity as correctional officers (*McKnight v. Rees*, 88 F. 3d 417, 425, [CA 1996]). The district court denied the motion to dismiss. The U.S. Court of Appeals for the Sixth Circuit affirmed the lower court's decision, agreeing that Richardson and Walker were not entitled to qualified immunity as employees of a private, for-profit corporation.

As a rule, private parties are not granted qualified immunity because they do not serve the public interest. According to the court, privately employed correctional officers, while serving the public interest in operating a correctional facility, are not "principally motivated by a desire to further the interest of the public

at large." Likewise, private corporations are not "principally concerned with enhancing the public good."

The court held that the private company and its employees have a greater motive to maximize profits by overstepping the bounds of constitutional rights. Therefore, the "increased threat of injury by violation of constitutional guarantees counsels against granting qualified immunity" to private correctional officers.

The court conducted a cost-benefit analysis and determined that private companies can include the increased threat of liability in their proposal when negotiating for state contracts, so "the state may pay more to obtain private correctional services, but less to monitor them on an ongoing basis." Moreover, the court found that qualified immunity is used as an incentive to encourage talented candidates to enter public service. The court concluded that this reasoning did not apply to this case, as private correctional officers are not public servants and are not motivated by the same intentions as a candidate for public office. The court held that "prison guards employed by a private firm are not entitled to a qualified immunity from suit by prisoners charging a Section 1983 violation."

Safety

Dee Farmer, a preoperative transsexual with feminine characteristics, had sometimes been in with the general prison population, but sometimes had been segregated. He claimed to have been assaulted after being transferred from a lower level correctional facility to a higher security institution with more violent prisoners, where he was placed in the general population. Farmer brought suit alleging that the prison officials had acted with "deliberate indifference" to his safety.

The lower courts ruled in favor of the prison officials on grounds that they lacked "actual knowledge of a potential danger" and were not "reckless in a criminal sense." The Supreme Court, in *Farmer v. Brennan* (511 U.S. 825, 1994), returned the case to the district court for retrial because the lower court may have erred in placing "decisive weight" on Farmer's failure to notify the prison administrators of a danger.

The Supreme Court held that

a prison official may be held liable under the Eighth Amendment for acting with "deliberate indifference" to inmate health or safety only if he knows that inmates face a substantial risk of serious harm and disregards that risk by failing to take reasonable measures to abate it.

The Court further asserted that prison officials have a duty to

protect prisoners from violence at the hands of other prisoners. However, a constitutional violation occurs only where the deprivation alleged is, objectively, "sufficiently serious,"... and the official has acted with "deliberate indifference" to inmate health or safety.

Deliberate indifference entails something more than negligence, but is satisfied by something less than acts or omissions for the very purpose of causing harm or with knowledge that harm will result.... It is the equivalent of acting recklessly.

The Amendment outlaws cruel and unusual "punishments," not "conditions," and the failure to alleviate a significant risk that an official should have perceived but did not, while no cause for commendation, cannot be condemned as the infliction of punishment under the Court's cases....

However, this does not mean that prison officials will be free to ignore obvious dangers to inmates. Whether an official had the requisite knowledge is a question of fact subject to demonstration in the usual ways, and a fact finder may conclude that the official knew of a substantial risk from the very fact that it was obvious. Nor may an official escape liability by showing that he knew of the risk but did not think the complainant was especially likely to be assaulted by the prisoner who committed the act.

It does not matter whether the risk came from a particular source or whether a prisoner faced the risk for reasons personal to him or because all prisoners in his situation faced the risk. But prison officials may not be held liable if they prove that they were unaware of even an obvious risk or if they responded reasonably to a known risk, even if the harm ultimately was not averted.

On December 9, 1996, the U.S. Court of Appeals for the Seventh Circuit, in *Babcock v. White* (CA 7, No 94-3806), held that a prisoner cannot claim damages on the issue that prison officials failed to prevent exposure to a risk of harm. According to principles of law, the inmate has standing in a court only if the officials failed to prevent harm. However, this ruling does not exclude suits arising from a continuous disregard for a prisoner's safety or ones based on claims of psychological injury.

Court Orders to Improve Conditions

In 1971, four inmates, without the help of attorneys, brought a suit before the federal District Court in Louisiana challenging the conditions in the state penitentiary at Angola. After hearing an investigator's report on the conditions of the facility, the judge issued an order for reforms. Finally, in 1999, after dramatic improvements at the maximum-security prison, a federal judge closed the case saying, "It is ordered that all court supervision over Louisiana State Penitentiary is terminated." The warden of the prison does not plan to change anything put in place by the court order, and the governor's office is committed to running the prison in a manner that the court would approve of.

Some states, such as Wisconsin, have had only one or two facilities under court orders, while others, such as South Carolina, have had their entire state prison system under court order. Some states have only one or two conditions to reform, while others have to correct "total conditions." (See Chapter VI for more on overcrowded conditions.) The National Prison Project of the American Civil Liberties Union annually publishes *Status Report: State Prisons and the Courts,* listing the states and territories under court orders.

183

In 1981, the Supreme Court, in *Rhodes v. Chapman* (45 U.S. 337), held that "even if no single condition of confinement would be unconstitutional in itself, exposure to the cumulative effect of prison conditions may subject inmates to cruel and unusual punishment."

An Alabama Case

In *Pugh v. Locke* (406 F. Suppl 318, 1976), a U.S. district court in Alabama declared the

conditions of confinement in the Alabama penal system constituted cruel and unusual punishment where they bore no reasonable relationship to legitimate institutional goals and, as a whole, created an atmosphere in which inmates were compelled to live in constant fear of violence, in imminent danger to their physical well-being, and without opportunity to seek a more promising future.

The court also enjoined (stopped) the state from

maintaining a prison system that was not otherwise in compliance with constitutional requirements in respect to overcrowding, segregation and isolation, classification, mental health care, protection from violence, living conditions, food service, correspondence and visitation, educational, vocational work and recreational opportunities, physical facilities, and staff....

and ordered it corrected. The four main Alabama facilities housed anywhere from 200 to more than 400 inmates over capacity. The effects of overcrowding were "heightened by the dormitory style of arrangements." Bunks were packed so tightly that inmates could not walk between them. Sanitation and security were impossible to maintain. Overcrowding also caused inmates to sleep on mattresses in hallways and next to the urinals. Old and filthy mattresses helped spread contagious diseases and body lice. The buildings possessed inadequate heating and ventilation systems. The facilities were "overrun with roaches, flies, mosquitoes, and other vermin."

Plumbing was inadequate. In one facility, one toilet served 200 men. Toilets either did not flush or overflowed. Personal hygiene was impossible. The state supplied soap and razor blades. Only those who could afford to buy toothpaste, toothbrushes, shampoo, shaving cream, razors, or combs could obtain them. Household cleaning supplies were not available for the inmates to keep their living spaces clean.

Food service conditions were also unsanitary. Food was improperly stored in dirty storage areas and was often infested with insects. Dishwashers did not reach the minimum temperature for sanitation. Eating and drinking utensils were unsuitable; some inmates used tin cans for drinking containers. Inmates who worked in food services were not trained properly in sanitation methods. A U.S. public health officer testified at the trial that he "found these facilities wholly unfit for human habitation according to virtually every criterion used for evaluation by public health inspectors."

Prisoners were assigned to various Alabama institutions on the availability of space and not on which facility was most appropriate for their crime or condition. Offenders suffering from mental disorders went unidentified and were housed throughout the prison population.

Violent inmates are not isolated from those who are young, passive, or weak. Consequently, the latter inmates are repeatedly victimized.... Emotional and physical disabilities which require special attention pass unnoticed.

Understaffing of the facilities allowed inmates to

assume positions of authority and control over other inmates, creating opportunities for blackmail, bribery, and extortion.... [M]ost prisoners carry some form of homemade or contraband weapon, which they consider to be necessary for self-protection.... An inmate required to live in these circumstances stands no chance of leaving the institution with a more positive and constructive attitude than the one he or she brought in.... Further, this Court finds that these conditions create an environment that not only makes it impossible for inmates to rehabilitate themselves, but also makes dehabilitation [worsening of inmates attitudes and abilities to cope with the outside world] inevitable.

The court also found fault with the lack of recreational programs to occupy free time and any "meaningful opportunities to participate in vocational, educational or work activities." Prisoners received 25 cents per week from the state without a way to earn extra money to purchase necessities for personal hygiene or to supplement the inadequate prison diet. However, the prison did little to control the flow of money, and those with money could also buy "drugs, alcohol, sex, changes in institutional records, and special privileges."

The court declared that the use of isolation and segregation cells was unconstitutional as they were overcrowded, had no beds, no lights, and no running water, and had a hole in the floor for a toilet, which could only be flushed from the outside. The inmates in punitive isolation got only one meal daily, were not permitted any exercise or reading material, and could shower only once every 11 days. Offenses for being placed in these cells ranged from swearing at the guards to murder.

Because of these conditions, the court set up minimum constitutional standards for the entire penal system and appointed an independent committee to help the board of corrections make the changes. In 1984, the court stopped actively supervising the orders after "substantial compliance" had been achieved. In 1988, the court finally dismissed the case.

A Texas Case

Texas provided another major Eighth Amendment case. In 1980, a district court declared the entire state prison system unconstitutional on overcrowding and conditions and appointed a special master to correct the problems. In *Ruiz v. Estelle* (679 F.2d 115, 1982), the Fifth Circuit Court of Appeals upheld the ruling. The court asserted that for the judiciary to find the totality of conditions of confinement unconstitutional, they must be cruel and unusual and "not merely harsh or restrictive."

The circuit court agreed with the district court that the correctional board had to reduce the overall inmate population and that each inmate should be provided with 40 square feet of space. The district judge thought the overcrowded conditions were a threat to the inmates' safety, fostered the lack of privacy, increased stress and tension, and furthered the possible spread of disease.

The Texas Department of Corrections argued that the inmates were not in the overcrowded cells or dormitories most of the day. However, the court found that many were idle in their living quarters because of a shortage of guards in the work fields. The threat to inmates in dormitories was great because potentially "assaultive inmates are present in great numbers in every dormitory" and the dormitories were "practically unsupervised." This resulted in a "constant threat to the inmates' personal safety." The circuit court also upheld the district court's appointment of special masters and monitors to supervise the implementation and compliance of its ruling, but declared the order "too sweeping" in that it permitted the master to give the district court reports based on his own observations without a formal hearing.

In May 1998, then-Texas Attorney General Dan Morales filed a motion requesting that a federal court release Texas from a final judgment from the lawsuit. The state made the request under the 1996 federal Prison Litigation Reform Act (PL 104-134). The act says that, if there are no ongoing constitution violations, states whose prison systems were subject to a final court judgment may seek to end that judgment two years after passage of the act. According to Morales, "Texas has run a constitutional prison system for more than a decade, with the past six years totally free of court supervision or oversight."

Following a 1999 ruling from the U.S. District judge not to dismiss the case, the Fifth U.S. Circuit Court of Appeals upheld the Prison Litigation Reform Act, limiting federal control of prison systems and lessening judicial involvement in inmates' complaints. This ruling paves the way for Texas to be released from federal supervision.

185

Restrictive and Harsh Punishment Is Constitutional; Wanton and Unnecessary Infliction of Pain Is Unconstitutional

In *Rhodes v. Chapman* (452 U.S. 337, 1981), the Supreme Court ruled that housing prisoners in double cells was not cruel and unusual punishment. The justices maintained that

> conditions of confinement, as constituting the punishment at issue, must not involve the wanton and unnecessary infliction of pain, nor may they be grossly disproportionate to the severity of the crime warranting imprisonment. But conditions that cannot be said to be cruel and unusual under contemporary standards are not unconstitutional. To the extent such conditions are restrictive and even harsh, they are part of the penalty that criminals pay for their offenses against society.

The Court concluded that the Constitution "does not mandate comfortable prisons," and only those "deprivations denying the 'minimal civilized measure of life's necessities'" violate the Eighth Amendment.

DUE PROCESS COMPLAINTS

Due process (procedural fairness, fair hearings) in the prison setting usually concerns disciplinary procedures. Most of the time, disciplinary action is taken on the word of the guard or the administrator, and the inmate has little opportunity to challenge the charges. Rules are often vague or not formally written out. Disrespect toward a guard is defined most of the time by the guards themselves.

The Supreme Court, however, has affirmed that procedural fairness should be used in some institutional decisions. In 1974, in *Wolff v. McDonnell* (418 U.S. 539), the Supreme Court declared that a Nebraska law providing for sentences to be shortened for good behavior created a "liberty interest." Thus, if an inmate met the requirements, prison officials could not deprive him of the shortened sentence without due process, according to the Fourteenth Amendment. (The Fourteenth Amendment states that "no state shall ... deprive any person of life, liberty, or property, without due process of law....") The High Court asserted that due process required that prisoners in procedure resulting in loss of good-time or in imposition of solitary confinement be afforded advance written notice of claimed violation, written statement of fact findings, and the right to call witnesses and present documentary evidence where such would not be unduly hazardous to institutional safety or correctional goals....

> A prisoner is not wholly stripped of constitutional protections and though prison disciplinary proceedings do not imply the full panoply of rights due a defendant, such proceedings must be governed by a mutual accommodation between institutional needs and generally applicable constitutional requirements.

However, the inmate at a procedural hearing does not have a right to have counsel (lawyer, advisor) in the proceedings. Silence at a hearing can be used against the inmate because it is a disciplinary hearing, not a criminal proceeding. If incriminating testimony by an inmate could be used in later criminal proceedings, then he must be offered immunity if forced to testify (*Baxter v. Palmigiano,* 425 U.S. 208, 1975).

While the Supreme Court found dormitory bunking unconstitutional in certain cases (see above), in *Bell v. Wolfish* (441 U.S. 520, 1979), it ruled that putting two persons in a room intended for one did not necessarily violate the Constitution. At the Metropolitan Correctional Center (MCC), a federally operated short-term custodial facility in New York City designed mainly for pretrial detainees, inmates challenged the constitutionality of the facility's conditions. As this was a pretrial detention center, the challenge was brought under the due process clause of the Fifth Amendment (see above). The District Court and the Court of Appeals found for the inmates, but the Supreme Court disagreed. Chief Justice William Rehnquist argued that

While confining a given number of people in a given amount of space in such a manner as to cause them to endure genuine deprivations and hardship over an extended period of time might raise serious questions under the Due Process Clause as to whether those conditions amounted to punishment, nothing even approaching such hardship is shown by this record.

Detainees are required to spend only seven or eight hours in their room, during most or all of which they presumably are sleeping. The rooms provide more than adequate space for sleeping.... While "double bunking" may have taxed some of the equipment or particular facilities in certain of the common areas, ... this does not mean that the conditions at the MCC failed to meet the standards required by the Constitution. Our conclusion in this regard is further buttressed by the detainees' length of stay (most are released in 60 days).

The High Court also ruled in *Bell* that the administrator could constitutionally prohibit inmates from receiving books that were not mailed directly from publishers, book clubs, or bookstores, and stop the delivery of packages of food and personal items from outside the institution. The administrator could also have body-cavity searches of inmates following contact visits with persons from the outside and require the detainees to remain outside their rooms during inspection. (See above for observation on limitations of prisoner rights in *Bell v. Wolfish*.)

EARLY RELEASE

Two cases decided in 1997 pertained to prisons releasing inmates early to relieve overcrowding and then later revoking their release status. Beginning in 1983, the Florida legislature enacted a series of laws authorizing the awarding of early release credits to prison inmates when the state prison population exceeded predetermined levels. In 1986, Kenneth Lynce received a 22-year prison sentence on a charge of attempted murder. In 1992, he was released based on the determination that he had accumulated five different types of early release credits totaling 5,668 days, including 1,860 days of "provisional credits" awarded as a result of prison overcrowding.

Shortly thereafter, the state attorney general issued an opinion interpreting a 1992 statute as having retroactively canceled all provisional credits awarded to inmates convicted of murder and attempted murder. Lynce was arrested and returned to custody. He filed a *habeas corpus* petition alleging that the retroactive cancellation of provisional credits violated the *ex post facto* clause of the Constitution.

The Supreme Court agreed with Lynce. In *Lynce v. Mathis* (65 LW 4131, 1997), the Court ruled that to fall within the *ex post facto* prohibition, a law must be "retrospective" and "disadvantage the offender affected by it" (*Weaver v. Graham*, 450 U.S. 24, 29), 1981). The 1992 statute was clearly retrospective and disadvantaged Lynce by increasing his punishment.

Oklahoma's Preparole Conditional Supervision Program took effect whenever the state prisons became overcrowded and authorized the conditional release of prisoners before their sentences expired. The Pardon and Parole Board determined who could participate in the program. An inmate was eligible for preparole after serving only 15 percent of his sentence, while he was eligible for parole after one-third of his sentence had elapsed.

Ernest Harper was released under the preparole program. After he spent five apparently uneventful months outside prison, the governor denied him preparole. He was returned to prison without a hearing and on less than five hours' notice.

Despite his claim that his reincarceration deprived him of liberty without due process in violation of the Fourteenth Amendment, the Oklahoma Court of Criminal Appeals, and the Federal District Court denied him *habeas corpus* relief. The corrections department argued that the Court had ruled that a hearing was not necessary to transfer a prisoner from a low-security prison to a higher-security one and that was what they were doing in this case.

The Tenth Circuit Court of Appeals, however, held that the preparole program was sufficiently like parole and a program participant was entitled to procedural protections. In *Leroy L. Young v. Ernest Eugene Harper* (65 LW 4197, 1997), the Supreme Court upheld the decision of the Tenth Circuit Court. It ruled that Oklahoma had violated Harper's due process rights by sending him back to prison without giving him a hearing to show that he had not met the conditions of the program.

HARDER TO BRING SUIT

In 1995, the Supreme Court, in *Sandin v. Conner* (115 S.Ct. 2293), made it harder for prisoners to bring constitutional suits to challenge due process rights. In a 5-4 decision, the majority made it clear it was frustrated with the number of due process cases, some of which they felt clogged the judiciary system with unwarranted complaints, such as claiming a "liberty interest" (see above) in not being transferred to a cell with an electrical outlet for a television.

Sandin v. Conner concerned an inmate in Hawaii who was not allowed to call witnesses at a disciplinary hearing for misconduct that had placed him in solitary confinement for 30 days. The Court of Appeals of the Ninth Circuit had held in 1993 that the inmate, Demont Conner, had a "liberty interest," allowing him a range of procedural protections in remaining free from solitary confinement. The Supreme Court overruled the Court of Appeals, affirming that the inmate had no "liberty interest." Due process protections play a role only if the state's action has infringed on some separate, substantive right that the inmate possesses. For example, Wolff's loss of good time credit was a substantive right that he possessed (see above). The punishment Conner had received "was within the range of confinement to be normally expected" since he was serving 30 years to life for a number of crimes, including murder.

"States may create liberty interests which are protected by the due process clause," but these will be limited to actions that "impose atypical and significant hardship on the inmate in relation to the ordinary incidents of prison life." Being put in solitary confinement in a prison where most inmates are limited to their cells most of the day anyway is not a liberty-interest issue. Because there was no liberty interest involved, how the hearing was handled was irrelevant. The decision did not overturn any prior court decisions and did not discuss cases brought to the Court under the Eighth Amendment.

Based on this ruling, only when prison staff imposes "atypical and significant hardship on the inmate" should a federal court consider the complaint a potential violation of a prisoner's constitutional right to due process of law. Any other actions, such as mismanaged disciplinary hearings or temporary placement in solitary, are just complaints about the "ordinary incidents of prison and life and should not be considered violations of the Constitution."

Chief Justice Rehnquist asserted that past Supreme Court decisions have "led to the involvement of Federal courts in the day-to-day management of prisons, often squandering judicial resources with little offsetting benefit to anyone." Judges should allow prison administrators the "flexibility" to "fine tune" the ordinary incidents of prison life.

This decision continues the more conservative trend of the Supreme Court. Prior to the 1960s, prisoners had few rights, but the climate of reform and protest in the 1960s brought about a rash of inmate cases, giving prisoners new legal power. The more conservative social milieu of the 1980s led to more judicial restraint as the courts sought to balance the constitutional rights of the prisoners with the security interests of the correctional administrators.

RECENT LEGISLATION

In 1994, Congress, in the Violent Crime Control Act (PL 103-322), made it harder for the federal judiciary to "hold prison or jail crowding unconstitutional under the Eighth Amendment." The law made it illegal for federal courts to find, in general terms, that overcrowding is unconstitutional. The inmate must prove that the crowding caused the infliction of "cruel and unusual punishment" on that particular inmate.

In 1996, the passage of the Prison Litigation Reform Act of 1995 (PL 104-134) made it harder for prisoners to bring individual suits and class actions and for the courts to take over the running of prisons if they found problems. For example, before an inmate can bring a suit, all administrative remedies must be "exhausted."

The law also prohibits a prisoner from bringing another suit if the "prisoner has had three or more actions in federal courts" that were "dismissed as frivolous." In addition, a prisoner's suit is also prohibited if it failed to "state a claim on which relief could be granted, or sought monetary relief from a defendant immune from such relief, unless the prisoner is under imminent danger of serious physical injury."

Is the 1996 Reform Law Constitutional?

This section may be challenged in the courts since it would appear to prevent any relief for actions when a prisoner no longer faces the threat of serious harm or property damages. In addition, the law requires the courts to review prisoner complaints before putting them on the court docket or soon thereafter and to dismiss the complaints if they seem frivolous or malicious or fail to state a claim on which relief can be granted.

Not only will the law limit the cases coming before the courts, but it will also limit the type of relief the courts may order. Courts cannot give any relief to an inmate "unless the court finds that such relief is narrowly drawn, extends no further than necessary to correct the violation of the Federal right, and is the least intrusive means necessary to correct the violation of the Federal rights."

The law limited the court's "authority to release or prohibit admission of prisoners, or required that three-judge courts issue such orders." It limits the "court's authority to appoint special masters to conduct hearings and prepare findings of fact." The law also limits legal fees that can be paid. (*Resource Guide for Managing Civil Rights Litigation*, Federal Judicial Center, Washington, DC, 1996.)

Cases contesting the constitutionality of the law are being filed across the country. For example, a district court judge in Iowa held that the "three strikes" limit on filings was unconstitutional. Also under discussion in the courts is the retroactivity of various features of the law and whether the law violates separation of powers.

Making it more difficult for prisoners to get help in suits, the 1996 federal appropriations act [sec 504(a)(15)] also prohibited recipients of funds from participating in any litigation on behalf of prisoners. As a result, the Legal Services Corporation (LSC), which provides lawyers for impoverished litigants, adopted an interim rule effective as of August 29, 1996, prohibiting participation of LSC recipients in any litigation on behalf of a person incarcerated in federal, state, or local prisons.

In July, 1996, a federal judge eliminated decrees governing New York City jails that had stemmed from earlier lawsuits complaining of overcrowded, unsafe, and unsanitary conditions. Mayor Rudolph Giuliani had requested the court to do so after the Prison Litigation Reform Act had been signed. The mayor said that it would save the city millions of dollars once the court-supervised decrees were removed. In an interview in the *New York Times*, Robert Gangi, executive director of the Correctional Association of New York, an advocacy group, commented that while inmates occasionally filed frivolous lawsuits, these decrees protected the rights of prisoners and corrected many problems that could return without the courts watching.

IMPORTANT NAMES AND ADDRESSES

American Bar Association
740 15th St. NW
Washington, DC 20005
(202) 662-1010
FAX (202) 662-1032
www.abanet.org

American Civil Liberties Union
Foundation (ACLU)
National Prison Project
1875 Connecticut Ave. NW, Suite 410
Washington, DC 20009-5728
(202) 234-4830
FAX (202) 234-4890

American Correctional Association
4380 Forbes Blvd.
Lanham, MD 20706
(301) 918-1800
FAX (301) 918-1900
(800) 222-5646
www.corrections.com/aca

American Jail Association
2053 Day Road, Suite 100
Hagerstown, MD 21740
(301) 790-3930
FAX (301) 790-2941
www.corrections.com/aja
aja@corrections.com

Amnesty International, USA
600 Pennsylvania Ave. SE, 5th floor
Washington, DC 20003
(202) 544-0200
FAX (202) 546-7142
www.amnesty.org

Bureau of Justice Statistics
810 7th St. NW
Washington, DC 20531
(202) 307-0765
(800) 732-3277
FAX (202) 307-5846
www.ojp.usboj.gov/bjs
askbjs@ojp.usboj.gov

Campaign for an Effective Crime Policy
918 F St. NW, Suite 505
Washington, DC 20004
(202) 628-1903
FAX (202) 628-1091
www.crimepolicy.org
staff@crimepolicy.org

Criminal Justice Institute
213 Court St. 6th Floor
Middletown, CT 06457
(860) 704-6400
FAX (860) 704-6420
www.cji-inc.com
cji@netcom.com

Families Against Mandatory Minimums
1612 K St. NW, Suite 1400
Washington, DC 20006

(202) 822-6700
FAX (202) 822-6704
www.famm.org
famm@famm.org

Federal Bureau of Investigation (FBI)
935 Pennsylvania Ave. NW
Washington, DC 20535
(202) 324-3691
FAX (202) 324-4705
www.fbi.gov

Federal Bureau of Prisons
320 1st St. NW
Washington, DC 20534
(202) 307-3198
FAX (202) 514-6620
www.bop.gov

Federal Judicial Center
1 Columbus Circle NE
Washington, DC 20002-8003
(202) 273-4160
FAX (202) 273-4019
www.fjc.gov

Justice Research and Statistics
Association
444 North Capitol St. NW
Washington, DC 20001
(202) 842-9330
FAX (202) 842-9329
www.jrsa.org

Juvenile Justice and Delinquency
Prevention
810 7th St. NW
Washington, DC 20531
(202) 307-5911
FAX (202) 307-2093
www.ojjdp.ncjrs.org

NAACP Legal Defense and
Educational Fund
1444 I St. NW, 10th Floor
Washington, DC 20005
(202) 682-1300
FAX (202) 682-1312
NY Office: (212) 219-1900

National Center on Institutions and
Alternatives
3125 Mt. Vernon Ave.
Alexandria, VA 22305
(703) 684-0373
FAX (703) 684-6037
www.ncianet.org/ncia
ncia@igc-apc.org

National Conference of State Legislatures
1560 Broadway, Suite 700
Denver, CO 80202
(303) 830-2200
FAX (303) 863-8003
www.ncsl.org

National Council on Crime and
Delinquency
685 Market St., Suite 620
San Francisco, CA 94105
(415) 896-6223
FAX (415) 896-5109
www.nccd.crc.org

National Criminal Justice Association
444 Capitol St. NW, Suite 618
Washington, DC 20001
(202) 624-1440
FAX (202) 508-3859
www.sso.org/cja

National Criminal Justice Reference
Service
P.O. Box 6000
Rockville, MD 20849-6000
(800) 732-3277
(800) 851-3420
www.ncjrs.org

National Institute of Justice
810 7th St. NW
Washington, DC 20531
(202) 307-2942
FAX (202) 307-6394
www.ojp.usdoj.gov/nij
askncjrs@ncjrs.org

National Legal Aid and Defender
Association
1625 K St. NW, #800
Washington, DC 20006
(202) 452-0620
FAX (202) 872-1031
www.nlada.org
info@nlada.org

The Sentencing Project
1516 P St. NW
Washington, DC 20005
(202) 628-0871
FAX (202) 628-1091
www.sentencingproject.org
staff@sentencingproject.org

U.S. Parole Commission
5550 Friendship Blvd.
Suite 420
Chevy Chase, MD 20815
(301) 492-5990
FAX (301) 492-6694

U.S. Sentencing Commission
1 Columbus Circle NE
Suite #2-500, South Lobby
Washington, DC 20002
(202) 728-6800
FAX (202) 273-4529
www.ussc.gov

RESOURCES

The Bureau of Justice Statistics (BJS) of the U.S. Department of Justice is a major source of data and information concerning crime, sentencing, and inmates. *Correctional Populations in the United States, 1996* (1999) summarizes information on inmates in the nation's jails and prisons. Other valuable BJS publications include *Truth in Sentencing in State Prisons* (1999), *Substance Abuse and Treatment, State and Federal Prisoners, 1997* (1999), *Prison and Jail Inmates at Midyear 1998* (1999), *Capital Punishment, 1997* (1998), *Prisoners in 1997* (1998), *Census of State and Federal Correctional Facilities* (1997), *Felony Sentences in State Courts, 1996* (1999), *Prison Sentences and Time Served for Violence* (1995), *Justice Expenditure and Employment Extracts, 1992* (1997), *Lifetime Likelihood of Going to State or Federal Prison* (1997), and *Characteristics of Adults on Probation, 1995* (1997). The BJS also produced the *Sourcebook of Criminal Justice Statistics 1997* (1998), with the Hindelang Criminal Justice Research Center, State University of New York, Albany.

The National Institute of Justice (NIJ) researches criminal issues. Some of the NIJ publications used in this publication are *Research in Brief*, "Three Strikes and You're Out: A Review of State Legislation" (1997), *Boot Camps for Adult and Juvenile Offenders (1994), National Assessment Program: 1994 Results* (1995), *Boot Camps for Juvenile Offenders: An Implementation Evaluation of Three Demonstration Programs* (1996), *Key Legislative Issues in Criminal Justice: Mandatory Sentencing* (1997), *A National Survey of Aftercare Provisions for Boot Camp Graduates* (1996), *"Boot Camp" Drug Treatment and Aftercare Interventions: An Evaluation Review* (1995), *Multisite Evaluation of Shock Incarceration* (1994), and *Shock Incarceration, New York* (1994).

The Federal Bureau of Investigation's *Crime in the United States — 1997* (1998) provides the latest arrest statistics and crime rates. The National Institute of Corrections (Longmont, Colorado) provided information on prisons and jails in its *Fees Paid by Jail Inmates: Findings from the Nation's Largest Jails* (1997). The Centers for Disease Control and Prevention (CDC) publishes studies in its *Morbidity and Mortality Weekly Report*, including "Prevention and Control of Tuberculosis in Correctional Facilities" (June 7, 1996) and "HIV/AIDS Education and Prevention Programs for Adults in Prisons and Jails and Juveniles in Confinement Facilities — United States, 1994" (April 5, 1996).

The Office of Juvenile Justice and Delinquency Prevention (OJJDP), an excellent resource on juvenile justice, produced *Juveniles Taken into Custody: 1993 Report* (1995), *Boot Camps for Juvenile Offenders* (1996), *Juveniles in Residential Placement* (1997), *Transferring Serious Juvenile Offenders to Adult Courts* (1997), *Juvenile Delinquents in the Federal Criminal Justice System* (1997), and *Juvenile Offenders and Victims: 1997 Update on Violence* (1999).

The United States General Accounting Office (GAO), an investigative agency of the U.S. government, publishes many valuable reports, including *Federal and State Prison Inmate Populations, Costs, and Projection Models* (1996) and *Private and Public Prisons: Studies Comparing Operation Costs and/or Quality of Service* (1996).

Information Plus thanks the Sentencing Project (Washington, DC) for permission to use information from its reports *Americans Behind Bars: The International Use of Incarceration, 1995* (Marc Mauer, 1997), and *Intended and Unintended Consequences: State Racial Disparities in Imprisonment* (1997). Information Plus also thanks The Edna McConnell Clark Foundation for providing *Seeking Justice: Crime and Punishment in America*. We thank The National Association of State Budget Officers for information from its publication *1997 State Expenditure Report* (1998).

The Criminal Justice Institute annually publishes *The Corrections Yearbook* (Camille Camp and George Camp, Middletown, CT, 1998). The American Jail Association provides a bimonthly magazine *American Jails*, which furnishes current information on issues concerning jail systems.

The National Center on Institutions and Alternatives granted permission to use information from *The Real War on Crime — The Report of the National Criminal Justice Commission* (Steven R. Doniger, ed., 1996). *Crime and Delinquency* (Sage Publications) contained three helpful articles: "Mental Abuse as Cruel and Unusual Punishment: Do Boot Camp Prisons Violate the Eighth Amendment?" (Faith E. Lutze and David C. Brody, vol. 45, no. 2, April 1999), "Getting Tough on Prisoners: Results from the National Corrections Executive Survey, 1995" (W. Wesley Johnson et al., vol. 43, no. 1, January 1997), and "Assessing Public Support for Three Strikes and You're Out Laws: Global versus Specific Attitudes" (Brandon K. Applegate et al., vol. 42, no. 4, October 1996). Information Plus thanks Sage Publications for permission to use some of its material.

Other sources include *The Impact of "Three Strikes and You're Out" Laws: What We Have Learned* (1996) and *Evaluating Boot Camp Prisons* (1994) from the Campaign for an Effective Crime Policy (Washington, DC) and *The Case for Shorter Prison Terms: The Illinois Experience* (1994) from the National Council on Crime and Delinquency (San Francisco). Information Plus is grateful to both organizations for permission to use their tables.

The RAND Corporation, a "nonprofit institution that helps improve public policy through research and analysis," produced *Three Strikes and You're Out: Estimated Benefits and Costs of California's New Mandatory Sentencing Law* (Peter Greenwood et al., 1994) and *Mandatory Minimum Drug Sentences: Throwing Away the Key or the Taxpayers' Money?* (Jonathan P. Calkins et al., 1997). Information Plus thanks RAND for permission to use its material. Information Plus also appreciates the use of material from the Survey Research Program, College of Criminal Justice, Sam Houston State University. We are grateful to Castine Research for permitting us to use material from *Overcrowded Times*, a bimonthly publication that reports on crime and punishment worldwide.

191

INDEX